1984.

Cindy —
It's been so
good to know you.
Thank you for your faithful
support of our ministry.
God bless you.
In C[...]
Jim & [...]

D0593999

· BILL BRIGHT ·

PROMISES

A Daily Guide to Supernatural Living

A Campus Crusade for Christ book from
HERE'S LIFE PUBLISHERS, INC.

Bill Bright is the founder and president of Campus Crusade for Christ International. Serving in more than 150 countries, he and his staff are dedicated to helping fulfill the Great Commission in this generation. Dr. Bright did graduate study at Princeton and Fuller Theological Seminary and has been the recipient of many honors and awards, including the honorary degrees of Doctor of Laws, Doctor of Divinity and Doctor of Letters.

·BILL BRIGHT·

PROMISES

A Daily Guide to Supernatural Living

A Campus Crusade for Christ book from
HERE'S LIFE PUBLISHERS, INC.

Promises
A Daily Guide to Supernatural Living
by
Bill Bright

A Campus Crusade for Christ Book

Published by
HERE'S LIFE PUBLISHERS, INC.
P.O. Box 1576
San Bernardino, CA 92402

ISBN 0-86605-086-X
HLP Product No. 400499
Library of Congress Catalog Card 82-072302
© 1983 by Campus Crusade for Christ, Inc.
All rights reserved.

Manufactured in the United States of America

Unless otherwise indicated, Scripture quotations are from *The Living Bible,* © 1971 by Tyndale House Publishers, Wheaton, Illinois, and used by permission. Other Scripture quotations are from the King James Version (KJV), the New American Standard Bible (NAS), the Phillips translation, the Revised Standard Version (RSV) and the Modern Language Bible.

Dedication

To Erma Griswold, a gracious lady whose loving, tireless, self-giving spirit has helped to lighten my personal load and enhance my ministry in a very special way for 20 years.

Vonette and I are deeply grateful to her for the way she has been used of God to enrich our lives and serve with us the entire ministry of Campus Crusade for Christ/Here's Life around the world.

Acknowledgments

It has been my desire for several years to assemble some of God's thousands of promises in a book that would be helpful on a daily basis for anyone who is seeking the supernatural, Spirit-filled life. The people listed below have been of particular assistance in bringing this book to fruition and I wish to thank them and acknowledge their service and support.

Dave Orris and Les Stobbe for their patience and encouragement when my busy schedule made it impossible to meet several deadlines.

John Boone for assistance in my many travels and in checking references.

Dave Enlow for transcribing and editing tapes for nearly 400 daily promises.

Erma Griswold for careful final editing and polishing.

Jean Bryant for helping to bring the daily promises together into book form.

Introduction

The Christian life, according to the claims and promises of God's holy, inspired Word, is meant to be an exciting adventure, an abundant, fruitful life, characterized by the supernatural.

It all began years ago on the night of our Lord's human birth outside that little village of Bethlehem. The angel announced it to the shepherds guarding their flocks when he said, "I bring you the most joyful news ever announced, and it is for everyone! The Savior — yes, the Messiah, the Lord — has been born tonight in Bethlehem."

Almost two thousand years have passed and it is still the most joyful news ever announced.

Consider if you will the miracle of that event. Our omnipotent Creator God, who spoke the whole universe into being, came to earth as a little baby, and was laid in a humble manger, fulfilling everything the prophets of the old Testament had foretold hundreds of years before about His birth. He grew to manhood — both perfect God and perfect man — and at the age of thirty he began the public ministry for which He came to this world. He taught as no man had ever taught. He performed miracles such as no man had ever performed. He lived the most holy life ever lived. In further fulfillment of prophecy, He died on the cross for our sins, and three days later was raised from the dead. He is alive! The tomb in which His body was placed following His crucifixion is empty.

The chairman of the Garden Tomb Association in Jerusalem asked me to deliver the message there one Easter, on the resurrection of our Lord. It was an electrifying experience to stand only a few feet away from that empty tomb and proclaim the power and glory of His resurrection to more than 2,500 believers and nonbelievers from scores of countries around the world. Jesus of Nazareth was the most revolutionary person who ever lived. He changed the course of history. He divided time—into B.C. (before Christ) and A.D. (anno Domini, the year of our Lord).

Dr. Charles Habib Malik, former president of the United Nations General Assembly, world-famous philosopher who received fifty honorary degrees from the most prestigious universities in the world, said,

> There are revolutions and there are counter revolutions; the greatest revolution ever was Jesus Christ Himself; not His miracles, not His ideas, not His teachings, not His moral principles, great and novel and revolutionary as all these things are, but He Himself. For nothing is greater, more revolutionary and unbelievable than, nothing is as great as, the Gospel of the crucified, resurrected and glorified God who is to come again to judge the

living and the dead (Charles Habib Malik, *A Christian Critique of the University*, Downers Grove, IL: University Press, 1982, pp. 30, 31.

Blaise Pascal was a famous French physicist and philosopher, a mathematician and spiritual thinker whose Christian philosophy echoed that of Augustine. Pascal said,

Not only do we only know God through Jesus Christ, but we only know ourselves through Jesus Christ; we only know life and death through Jesus Christ. Apart from Jesus Christ we cannot know the meaning of our life or our death, of God or of ourselves.

Thus without Scripture, whose only object is Christ, we know nothing, and can see nothing but obscurity and confusion in the nature of God and in nature itself. (Blaise Pascal, *Pascal's Pensèes* (417), A.J. Krailsheimer, trans., NY: Penguin Books, 1966, p. 158).

Jesus claims that God the Father has given Him all authority in heaven and earth (Matthew 28:18). The Scriptures proclaim that He is God incarnate, the visible expression of the invisible God (Colossians 1:15).

In Him dwells all the fullness of the godhead bodily (Colossians 2:9).

We are complete in Him (Colossians 2:10).

He invites all men, "Come to Me all who are weary and heavy-laden, and I will give you rest" (Matthew 11:28, NAS).

Peace I leave with you, My peace I give unto you; not as the world giveth, give I unto you. Let not your heart be troubled, neither let it be afraid (John 14: 27, KJV).

Follow me, and I will make you fishers of men (Matthew 4:19, KJV).

You shall receive power when the Holy Spirit has come upon you; and you shall be My witnesses both in Jerusalem, and in all Judaea and Samaria, and even to the remotest part of the earth (Acts 1:8, NAS).

Paul reminds us in Ephesians, "God has allowed us to know the secret of His plan, and it is this: He purposed long ago in His sovereign will that all human history shall be consummated in Christ, that everything that exists in Heaven or earth should find perfection and its fulfillment in Him" (Ephesians 1:9, 10, Phillips translation).

But here is a staggering thing, that in all which will one day belong to Christ, we have been promised to share (Ephesians 1:11). Think of it. This wonderful Savior, the omnipotent Son of God, has come to live in the lives of all who receive Him (John 1:12).

Our bodies become temples of the living God (1 Corinthians 3:19).

At the very moment He comes to take up residence in our lives, we become children of God (John 1:12).

Our sins are forgiven (Colossians 2:13).

We have eternal life (1 John 5:11, 12).

And His many promises become a call to a supernatural life. Consider, for example, this promise from Jesus, "The works that I do, shall [you] do also; and greater works than these shall [you] do; because I go to the Father. . . . If you ask Me anything in My name, I will do it" (John 14:12, 14, NAS).

Some time ago an editorial in a national publication raised some very significant questions: Where are all of the so-called born-again, evangelical Christians? It is estimated that over sixty million adults in America claim to be born again, yet crime continues to accelerate at an alarming rate. There are epidemics of drug addiction, alcoholism, venereal diseases, divorces, and teen-age pregnancies and abortions, as well as many other similarly serious problems. Are not Christians supposed to be the salt of the earth and the light of the world? If there are so many Christians, why is there such little evidence of their influence in our society?

These questions continue to sober me and prompt me to remind Christian believers that we are, indeed, light and salt, men and women of destiny, world-changers. We are called of God to be holy as He is holy and whatever God commands us to do, He always enables us to do by His Holy Spirit.

That is what this devotional book is all about, a daily reminder that we are called to live supernatural lives for the glory of God.

In 1979 I wrote the first book of a triolgy, *Believing God for the Impossible — A Call to Supernatural Living. The Holy Spirit — The Key to Supernatural Living* followed in 1980. Now, after several years of preparation and prayer, I am happy to share my joy and excitement over the truths contained in this book, *Promises — Daily Guide to Supernatural Living*. It is my earnest prayer that the rights and authority of every reader, as a child of God, will be claimed as that person considers these daily reminders of our spiritual heritage, and that every promise from the inspired Word of God will become a joyful reality for supernatural living.

Bill Bright
Arrowhead Springs

The Bible's No. 1 Promise

"For God so loved the world, that He gave His only begotten Son, that whosoever believeth in Him should not perish, but have everlasting life" (John 3:16, KJV).

As I travel from country to country, I find that millions of people in many countries and cultures are receiving Christ into their lives after hearing about Him for the first time. Millions of others would respond joyfully if they fully understood the truth of John 3:16, the most wonderful promise ever given to man.

Only through His indwelling presence can they live supernaturally. The first prerequisite to supernatural living, of course, is life — eternal life, supernatural life from God. I encourage you to meditate often on the content of this God-inspired promise:

God: The omnipotent Creator — loving, sovereign, holy, all-wise, ever-present, compassionate God who flung a hundred billion or more galaxies into space merely by speaking.

So loved: His love is unconditional and inexhaustible.

He gave: a gift that can never be earned by our good works, but can be received only by faith.

His only begotten Son: the most precious, priceless gift ever given — Jesus.

That whosoever: you and I and every person who inhabits the world.

Believeth in Him: believes that He is the Son of God and the Savior of the world, the one who died on the cross for the sins of all people everywhere and who was raised from the dead.

Should not perish: should not be eternally separated from God. "The Lord...is not willing that any should perish" (2 Peter 3:9, KJV).

But have everlasting life: not only in heaven, but also on earth, experiencing the supernatural, everlasting life of the indwelling, risen Savior.

Bible Reading: Romans 5:6-11

ACTION POINT: If I am not already a believer in Christ, I will receive Him into my life as Savior and Lord today. If I am a believer and have not already done so, I will acknowledge His lordship in my life and begin to draw upon His resurrection power as a way of life. As I continue to claim His promise, I am confident that the result will be a full, abundant and supernatural life.

You Can Know the Spirit's Fullness

"Be filled...with the Holy Spirit, and controlled by Him"
(Ephesians 5:18).

An enthusiastic, attractive couple traveled from their home in Chicago to Arrowhead Springs to share with me an idea about which they were very excited.

"We heard one of your filmed lectures on 'How to Be Filled With the Holy Spirit.' Our lives have been dramatically changed as a result of what you shared," they said. "We have come all this way to encourage you to go on nationwide television and tell Christians how they can know the fullness and power of the Holy Spirit and experience His revolutionary impact in and through their lives."

I am humbly grateful to God for the privilege of sharing these great truths concerning the Holy Spirit with tens of millions of people throughout the world, often with the same dramatic results experienced by this remarkable couple.

The disciples were with Jesus for more than three years. They heard Him teach as no man had ever taught. They saw Him perform miracles such as no man had ever performed — raising the dead, restoring sight to the blind and cleansing lepers. Though they were exposed to the most godly life ever lived on earth, during Jesus' time of crisis, Judas betrayed Him, Peter denied Him and all the others deserted Him.

Jesus knew His disciples were fruitless, quarreling, ambitious, self-centered men, so — on the eve of His crucifixion — He told them, "It is to your advantage that I go away; for if I do not go away, the Helper (Holy Spirit) shall not come to you; but if I go, I will send Him to you...He will guide you into all the truth...He shall glorify Me; for He shall take of Mine, and shall disclose it to you" (John 16:7,13,14 NAS).

Bible Reading:
Galatians 5:5,16-18,22,23,25

ACTION POINT: Today I will receive by faith the power of the Holy Spirit in order to live a supernatural life and be a supernatural witness. I will continue to study the scriptural references and various books concerning the Holy Spirit, so that I will better understand His role in my life.

Abundant Life for the Asking

"The thief's purpose is to steal, kill and destroy. My purpose is to give life in all its fullness" (John 10:10).

For me, the Christian life is an exciting, joy-filled adventure. It has been that way through more than 30 years of walking with the Lord. If you are not already experiencing such a life, it can be the same for you today, tomorrow and the rest of your days, no matter what the circumstances.

Jesus promised the full and abundant life for all those who walk in faith and obedience. His "exceeding great and precious promises" include every kind of provision for you — spiritual, emotional, material.

You start by getting to know God — who He is, what He is like and the benefits we enjoy when we belong to Him. Your view of God influences all the rest of your relationships. Scripture says the righteous shall live by faith. Faith must focus on an object, and the object in which we have our faith is God and His inspired Word.

But how do we acquire that kind of faith? "Faith comes by hearing, and hearing by the Word of Christ" (Romans 10:17, NAS). It is as simple as that. You are building up your storehouse of faith every time you read the Word of God, every time you hear the Word of God and every time you memorize the Word of God.

Our view of God determines the quality and degree of our faith. A small view of God results in a small faith. Great faith is the result of a correct biblical view of God — recognizing Him as great, mighty, all-wise and worthy of our trust.

Our view of God as sovereign, holy, loving, righteous, just and compassionate produces these same qualities in our lives. If we view Him as a God of love and forgiveness, we are prompted to love and forgive others also.

Bible Reading: John 7:36-39

ACTION POINT: Through the enabling of the Holy Spirit, I determine to begin practicing the presence of God in my life — every moment of the day. I will begin by meditating on His attributes through storing portions of His Word in my heart and mind. As a result, by faith I expect to experience and share with my family and friends the full and abundant life which Jesus promised to all who are His.

Anything at All

"Yes, ask anything, using my name, and I will do it!" (John 14:14).

"What is the most important thought your mind has ever entertained?" someone once asked Daniel Webster, one of the greatest intellects in American history.

"My accountability to God," he replied.

In John 14:14 we find a marvelous promise, one that surely gives ample reason for our accountability to God!

Yet, in the face of those overwhelming words, most Christians do not live joyful and fruitful lives. Why? Because they have a limited view of God. Most of us sit at God's banquet table of blessing and come away with crumbs — simply because of our lack of knowledge of God and faith to trust and obey Him.

Nothing is so important in the Christian life as understanding the attributes of God. No one can ever begin to live supernaturally and have the faith to believe God for "great and mighty" things if he does not know what God is like, or if he harbors misunderstandings about God and His character.

Would you like to live a joyful, abundant and fruitful life — every day filled with adventure? You can!

What is God like to you? Is He a divine Santa Claus, a cosmic policeman, a dictator or a big bully? Many people have distorted views of God and as a result are afraid of Him because they do not know what He is really like.

Our heavenly Father yearns for us to respond to His love. It is only as we respond to a scriptural view of God that we are able to come joyfully into His presence and experience the love and adventure and abundant life for which He created us and which He promised us.

Bible Reading: Mark 11:22-26

ACTION POINT: I will meditate upon John 14:14 throughout the day, and I will claim His provision for a need I have or know that someone else has.

An Infusion of Power

"Even the youths shall be exhausted, and the young men will all give up. But they that wait upon the Lord shall renew their strength. They shall mount up with wings like eagles; they shall run and not be weary; they shall walk and not faint" (Isaiah 40:30,31).

I flew all night from Los Angeles to New York for a very important meeting with the president of one of the major television networks, and after only three hours in New York flew back across the continent to Portland, Oregon, to speak that night at a conference of several hundred pastors.

Every fiber of my being ached with fatigue as I waited for my luggage in the Portland airport. In only 30 minutes I would be speaking to the pastors, yet I felt about as spiritual as a head of cabbage. Suddenly I felt impressed to pray, "Lord, do You have something You would like to share with me?"

Immediately I felt a leading to turn to the 40th chapter of Isaiah. As I read those familiar words, which at that instant had new, inspiring meaning for me, I sensed a surge of strength, energy, and power flow into and through my body. I suddenly felt that I could have thrown my luggage over the building and run to the meeting several miles away.

I could hardly wait to stand before those servants of God and proclaim to them the wonder and majesty, the glory and power, the faithfulness and love of our God. Within a half hour or so, I did have that privilege and God empowered and anointed me for the occasion in a most unusual and marvelous way.

Bible Reading: Isaiah 40:25-29

ACTION POINT: As I discover a need for renewed strength today, I will say with the psalmist, "I will go in the strength of the Lord God" (Psalm 71:16a, KJV). I will repeat that solemn declaration throughout the day, and by faith will claim His supernatural strength for my every physical and spiritual need.

Strong Love Is the Proof

"And so I am giving a new commandment to you now — love each other just as much as I love you. Your strong love for each other will prove to the world that you are My disciples" (John 13:34,35).

A Navajo Indian woman who had been healed of a serious ailment by a missionary doctor was greatly impressed by the love he manifested.

"If Jesus is anything like the doctor," she said, "I can trust Him forever."

The doctor was a living example of the above promise. When Jesus spoke these words, the entire known world was filled with hate, war and fear. The Jews and the Gentiles hated each other. The Greeks and the Romans hated each other.

But with the resurrection of the Lord Jesus and the day of Pentecost came a breath of heavenly love. Those who received Jesus, the incarnation of love, into their lives and who chose to obey His command began to love one another. The pagan world looked on in amazement and said of the believers, "How they love one another!"

Within a few years following this command to love one another, the gospel had spread like a prairie fire throughout the known world. The miracle of God's love, His supernatural *agape*, had captivated multitudes throughout the decadent, wicked Roman Empire.

Tragically, today one seldom hears "How they love one another!" about Christians. Instead there is far too much suspicion, jealousy, criticism and conflict between Christians, churches and denominations. The unbelieving world often laughs at our publicized conflicts.

But those individuals who do demonstrate this supernatural love are usually warmly received by nonbelievers as well as believers. The churches that obey our Lord's command to "love one another" usually are filled to overflowing and are making a great impact for good and for the glory of God. They represent a highly desirable alternative to secular society.

How does one love supernaturally? By faith. God's Word *commands* us to love (John 13:34,35). God's Word *promises* that He will enable us to do what He commands us to do (1 John 5:14,15).

Bible Reading: 1 John 3:14-19

ACTION POINT: Through the enabling of the Holy Spirit, I will by faith love others and thus prove that I am a true disciple of the Lord Jesus.

An Open Line to God

"And we are sure of this, that He will listen to us whenever we ask Him for anything in line with His will. And if we really know He is listening when we talk to Him and make our requests, then we can be sure that He will answer us" (1 John 5:14,15).

John, chairman of the board of deacons in a large, successful church, refused to respond — though hundreds of others did — to my invitation to be filled with the Holy Spirit by faith.

Following the meeting, he came to me in tears.

"I have dedicated and rededicated my life to Christ many, many times, always to no avail," he said. "I didn't dare respond to your invitation, because I knew I would fail again."

I explained that my invitation was different. "God's power to live a holy life and be a fruitful witness is released by faith, based on His faithfulness and the authority of God's Word."

When John understood this, he responded enthusiastically and prayed, asking God to fill him with His Spirit. His life was changed, as have been thousands of others as they have come to understand how to be filled and empowered by the Holy Spirit by faith moment by moment, day by day.

On the basis of His *command* to be filled (Ephesians 5:18) and His *promise* that if we ask for anything in accordance with God's will, He will hear and answer us (1 John 5:14,15), we know that we can be filled with the Holy Spirit — as a way of life.

Bible Reading: Matthew 7:7-11

ACTION POINT: I will humble myself before the Lord and tell Him that I want to live a holy life, that I want to be a man/woman of God. I will surrender the control of my life to Christ, turn from all known sin, and by faith on the basis of His command and His promise, receive the fullness of the Holy Spirit. By faith, I expect to live the supernatural, Spirit-empowered life in a moment-by-moment, day-by-day dependence on the Holy Spirit.

All Your Plans and Paths

"Oh, the joys of those who do not follow evil men's advice, who do not hang around with sinners, scoffing at the things of God: But They delight in doing everything God wants them to, and day and night are always meditating on His laws and thinking about ways to follow Him more closely. They are like trees along a river bank bearing luscious fruit each season without fail. Their leaves shall never wither, and all they do shall prosper" (Psalm 1:1-3).

Of all the great promises from God's Word, I claim none more frequently than these. As I focus on the attributes of God, I truly "delight myself in the Lord" and experience the full, adventuresome life which our Lord promised.

The psalmist expands on what it means to delight ourselves in the Lord. Note these three things: First, we should delight in doing everything God wants us to do; second, day and night we should meditate on His laws; and third, we should always be thinking about ways to follow Him more closely.

Sam had been a loser all of his life, a failure in everything that he attempted. As a result he had developed a very poor self-image and a defeatist attitude.

"Can you help me?" he pleaded. "I really don't know what to do — I am about ready to give up."

Together we read and discussed Psalm 1. He agreed to delight himself in the Lord and to follow the three-fold formula for spiritual success found in this psalm. Immediately his life began to change and within six months the results were dramatic.

"I begin every day delighting myself in the Lord," he said. "I spend special time studying and memorizing God's Word, telling Him that I want to do everything He wants me to, and I am always thinking about ways to follow Him more closely.

"I am no longer discouraged and defeated. My self-respect and confidence have been restored and I am truly experiencing the fulfillment of God's promise: '*All* you do shall prosper.' "

The successful, fruitful, joyful Christian who lives a supernatural life is one whose thoughts are focused on our wonderful God and His attributes, who knows and obeys His Word and who delights himself in Him.

Bible Reading: Proverbs 3:1-6

ACTION POINT: I determine with the help of the Holy Spirit to delight myself daily in the Lord and experience the reality of His promise, "All you do shall prosper."

Seeking God's Face

"If My people, which are called by My name, shall humble themselves, and pray, and seek My face, and turn from their wicked ways: then will I hear from heaven, and will forgive their sin, and will heal their land" (2 Chronicles 7:14, KJV).

"Humility is perfect quietness of heart," Andrew Murray once wrote. "It is to expect nothing, to wonder at nothing that is done to me, to feel nothing done against me. It is to be at rest when nobody praises me, and when I am blamed or despised. It is to have a blessed home in the Lord, where I can go in and shut the door, and kneel to my Father in secret, and am at peace as in a deep sea of calmness, when all around and above is trouble."

For years, I have claimed God's promise recorded in 2 Chronicles 7:14. My emphasis has been on the humbling of ourselves and turning from sin. But recently a minister friend made a passing reference to the phrase, "seeking God's face," and it triggered in my mind some new thoughts about this great promise from God.

In a sense, the humbling of ourselves and turning from sin are the by-products, or end results, of coming to know God as He is, by meditating upon His character and attributes. To "seek God's face" is to meditate upon His sovereignty, His holiness, His power, His wisdom, His love — getting to know *Him* as He is.

The disciples of the first-century church were mightily used of God because of their exalted view of Him. There was nothing too great for Him. God could do anything. The church today can once again experience that same dynamic that characterized those first believers if we, too, become totally absorbed in the character and attributes of our great God.

It is then that we will truly begin to believe God for supernatural, impossible things and make a great impact for good on the world.

Bible Reading: Psalm 145:5-12

ACTION POINT: I will deliberately choose to seek God's face today by meditating on His attributes, found in Psalm 145, and by looking for Him in every circumstance of my life this day.

Nothing You Cannot Do

"I can do all things through Christ, which strengtheneth me" (Philippians 4:13, KJV).

What would you give for the power to live a truly holy, fruitful life? Strangely enough, it is yours for the asking. If your problem is timidity in witnessing, God promises to help you share your faith with others: "For the Holy Spirit, God's gift, does not want you to be afraid of people, but to be wise and strong, and to love them and enjoy being with them" (2 Timothy 1:7).

If it is victory over temptation, He reminds us that temptation is not a sin; it is only in the yielding that it becomes sin.

If you need victory in your thought-life, He promises to allow no tempting or testing above that you are able to bear — and that certainly includes your thought-life (1 Corinthians 10:13). You are invited to "cast all your anxiety upon the Lord, because He cares for you" (1 Peter 5:7).

If it is forgiveness you seek, He offers it freely. "If we confess our sins, He is faithful and just to forgive us our sins, and to cleanse us from all unrighteousness" (1 John 1:9, KJV).

In short, you have no burden, no problem, no need that is too big for our Lord to handle. "Ye receive not, because ye ask not," He reminds us.

If your need is for physical healing, know that He is able to heal you if it is His will. If His answer to your prayer is no, thank Him for the sure knowledge that His grace is sufficient in the midst of pain and suffering. Acknowledge His sovereign right to be God in your life, whatever the cost may be. "Commit everything you do to the Lord. Trust Him to help you do it and He will" (Psalm 37:5).

Bible Reading: Philippians 4:6-12

ACTION POINT: I will begin this day — and every day — by committing everything I do to the Lord and expecting Him to help me. I will remember that I can do everything God asks me to do with the help of Christ, who gives me the strength and power (Philippians 4:13).

Love Without Limit

"I have given them the glory You gave Me — the glorious unity of being one, as We are — I in them and You in Me, all being perfected into one — so that the world will know You sent Me and will understand that You love them as much as You love Me" (John 17:22,23).

One day, as I was reading this prayer of Jesus to God the Father, I leaped from my chair in excitement when I realized that God loves me as much as He loves His only begotten Son!

What is more, He loves us unconditionally. That means He loves us not because we are good, or worthy of His love, but simply because of who He is.

Of course, the miracle of it all is that when Jesus, who is the incarnation of God's love, comes to live within us, that same supernatural love becomes operative within us, enabling us to love others supernaturally as well.

Agape (sacrificial, supernatural and unconditional love) is best described in the well-known and oft-quoted 13th chapter of 1 Corinthians:

"Love is very patient and kind, never jealous or envious, never boastful or proud, never haughty or selfish or rude. Love does not demand its own way. It is not irritable or touchy. It does not hold grudges and will hardly even notice when others do it wrong. It is never glad about injustice, but rejoices whenever truth wins out. If you love someone you will be loyal to him no matter what the cost. You will always believe in him, always expect the best of him, and always stand your ground in defending him."

Bible Reading: John 17:15-21

ACTION POINT: When things go wrong today — or any day — I will choose to remember that God loves me just as much as He loves His only begotten Son! And I will tell everyone who will listen about God's supernatural love for them.

Be Strong in Character

"Dear brothers, is your life full of difficulties and temptations? Then be happy, for when the way is rough, your patience has a chance to grow. So let it grow, and don't try to squirm out of your problems. For when your patience is finally in full bloom, then you will be ready for anything, strong in character, full and complete" (James 1:2-4).

A friend of mine had been very successful in business, but after he became a Christian everything seemed to go wrong. Problem after problem seemed to plague him. Yet he never seemed to be discouraged or defeated.

As we counseled together, he assured me that there was no unconfessed sin in his life. So I rejoiced with him that God was preparing him for a very important responsibility in His kingdom. That is exactly what happened. He is now the director of a very fruitful ministry for our Lord. The problems and testing served to help equip him to be a better ambassador for Christ.

If you are experiencing difficulties in your life — physical illness, loss of loved ones, financial adversity — remember the above admonition from God's Word. Be happy, knowing that God will work in your life to accomplish His holy purpose.

You can decide how you will respond to problems and temptations — you can either become critical and cynical, or as an act of the will, by faith, you can choose to believe that our sovereign, loving God is allowing this to happen in your life for your own good and for His glory.

Even the hairs of your head are numbered. "His eyes run to and fro throughout the whole earth, to shew Himself strong in the behalf of them whose heart is perfect toward Him" (2 Chronicles 16:9, KJV). He is tender, loving and compassionate, concerned about your every need.

Bible Reading: James 1:5-12

ACTION POINT: When difficulties and temptations enter into my life I will — as an act of the will, by faith in God's faithfulness to His promises — rejoice and be glad, knowing that He is always with me and will never forsake me. As I trust Him and obey Him, He will supernaturally turn tragedy to triumph, and He will change heartache and sorrow to joy and rejoicing. I will trust Him in the darkest night of circumstances.

Perfect in His Sight

"But Christ gave Himself to God for our sins as one sacrifice for all time, and then sat down at the place of highest honor at God's right hand, waiting for His enemies to be laid under His feet. For by that one offering He made forever perfect in the sight of God all those whom He is making holy" (Hebrews 10:12-14).

All the sins you and I have ever committed or ever shall commit — past, present and future — are forgiven the moment we receive Christ, according to God's Word. Think of it and rejoice!

Then you may rightly ask, "If all of my sins — past, present and future — are forgiven, why do I need to confess my sins?"

According to God's Word, confession is an act of obedience and an expression or demonstration of faith that makes real in our experience what is already true concerning us from God's point of view.

Through the sacrifice of Christ, He sees us as righteous and perfect. The rest of our lives on earth are spent maturing and becoming in our experience what we already are in God's sight.

This maturing process is accelerated through the faithful study of God's Word, prayer, witnessing for Christ, and spiritual breathing — exhaling through confessing our sins and inhaling by appropriating the fullness of God's Holy Spirit by faith.

If you retake the throne, the control center, of your life through sin (a deliberate act of disobedience) breathe spiritually. First, *exhale by confession.* "If we confess our sins, He is faithful and just to forgive us our sins, and to cleanse us from all unrighteousness" (1 John 1:9, KJV).

Next, *inhale by appropriating the fullness of God's Spirit by faith.* Trust Him now to control and empower you by faith according to His command to "be filled with the Spirit" (Ephesians 5:18).

Bible Reading: Hebrews 10:19-25

ACTION POINT: Today I will study God's Word, pray and invite the Holy Spirit to lead me to someone whose heart He has prepared to receive Christ. Also, I will practice spiritual breathing whenever any attitude, action, motive or desire that is contrary to God's will short-circuits God's power in my life. I will confess it and by faith inhale by appropriating the fullness and power of God's Holy Spirit.

A Blessing So Great

"Bring all the tithes into the storehouse so that there will be food enough in my Temple; if you do, I will open up the windows of heaven for you and pour out a blessing so great you won't have room enough to take it in" (Malachi 3:10).

Tom and Marti were newlyweds. They were just getting started in business and had all the expense of setting up housekeeping. So they found their budget severely strained. In fact, the bills were piling up. Then they were challenged to tithe their gross income. Their first response was, "Impossible! We can't even pay our present bills, let alone take 10 percent off the top."

As they prayed together, however, they felt definitely led that this was God's will. Since they wanted to please Him by obeying His command, they began systematically and faithfully to give priority to their tithe. At first, it was nip and tuck, and some of the other obligations had to wait. But after a few months they were amazed to see how they were able to accomplish more with the nine-tenths than they had previously been able to accomplish with the total amount.

Now they are enthusiastic over the privilege of laying up treasures in heaven, seeking first the kingdom of God. Tithing was only the beginning. Now they are giving 40 percent off the top because God has prospered them so abundantly.

I began to tithe as a new Christian when I was made aware of the scriptural principle that everything belongs to God and we are only stewards during our brief time here on earth. Actually a tithe is the Old Testament concept, and according to the New Testament concept every believer has the privilege of laying up treasures in heaven far beyond the amount of the tithe. There is a law of sowing and reaping: The more you sow, the more you reap.

To the Christian, it is not how much we give to God; it is how much we have left after we have given to Him — and to His kingdom.

Bible Reading: Malachi 3:5-9

ACTION POINT: Today I will take inventory of my giving to the Lord. I will begin at least to tithe, expecting that God, as He promised Malachi, "will open the windows of heaven and pour out a blessing so great that I won't have room enough to take it in."

Your Paths Made Plain

"Trust in the Lord with all thine heart; and lean not unto thine own understanding. In all thy ways acknowledge Him, and He shall direct thy paths" (Proverbs 3:5,6, KJV).

A young seminary graduate came to see me while he was investigating various possibilities of Christian service. In particular, he had come to discuss the ministry of Campus Crusade.

"In what way do you expect God to reveal His place of service for you?" I asked him.

"I'm following the 'closed-door policy,' " he replied. "A few months ago I began to investigate several opportunities for Christian service. The Lord has now closed the door on all but two, one of which is Campus Crusade. If the door to accept a call to a particular church closes, I'll know that God wants me in Campus Crusade."

Many sincere Christians follow this method — often with most unsatisfactory and frustrating results. God does sometimes use closed doors in the life of a Spirit-controlled Christian, as the apostle Paul experienced on different occasions, but generally one does not discover God's perfect will through a careless "hit-or-miss" attitude that ignores a careful evaluation of all the issues.

Such an approach is illogical because it allows elements of chance to influence a decision rather than a careful, intelligent, prayerful evaluation of all the factors involved. It is unscriptural in that it fails to employ the God-given faculties of reason that are controlled by the Holy Spirit.

Why not follow the "open-door policy" of Proverbs 3:5,6, trusting God for His clear direction? This is God's provision for supernatural living.

Bible Reading: Psalm 37:3-7

ACTION POINT: In every decision today, whether small or large matters, joyfully and with anticipation I will trust in the Lord with all my heart, knowing that He will direct my path to supernatural living. I will encourage others also to trust in the Lord.

The Supernatural Power of Praise

"With Jesus' help we will continually offer our sacrifice of praise to God by telling others of the glory of His name. Don't forget to do good and to share what you have with those in need, for such sacrifices are very pleasing to Him" (Hebrews 13:15,16).

S ometimes, in my busy schedule which takes me from country to country and continent to continent, my body is weary, my mind is fatigued, and if I am not careful, my heart will grow cold. I have learned to meditate on the many blessings of God and to praise Him as an act of the will. As I do so, my heart begins to warm and I sense the presence of God.

The psalmist often catalogued the blessings of God and found new reason to praise Him. I would like to share with you several reasons why I believe praise of God is so important in the life of the believer.

First, God is truly worthy of praise. Second, praise draws us closer to God. Third, all who praise God are blessed. Fourth, praise is contagious. Fifth, Satan's power is broken when we praise God. Sixth, praise is a witness to carnal Christians and non-Christians. Seventh, praise opens our hearts and minds to receive God's message. Eighth, praise is a form of sacrifice. Ninth, praise makes for a more joyful life. Tenth, praise enhances human relationships. Eleventh, praise is a supernatural expression of faith.

A further elaboration of the benefits and power of praise is found in my book *Believing God for the Impossible*. An entire chapter is devoted to this exciting subject.

With the promise of His blessings, so clearly delineated by the psalmist, comes the privilege and responsibility of offering up sacrifices of praise, and this leads to a supernatural life made possible by the indwelling Holy Spirit.

Bible Reading: Jeremiah 33:9-14

ACTION POINT: I will look deliberately today for reasons to praise my heavenly Father, knowing that I will find many. Whether I feel like it or not, I will praise Him throughout the day, seek to do good and to share His love with others, knowing that such sacrifices are pleasing to Him.

How to Skip Judgment

"Now I say that each believer should confess his sins to God when he is aware of them, while there is time to be forgiven. Judgment will not touch him if he does" (Psalm 32:6).

Mary had rebelled against the preaching of her Nazarene father, a godly pastor. She lived with her boy friend in open defiance of her biblical teaching. Now, God was disciplining her because of disobedience. She was miserable, filled with hate and resentment, when a mutual friend brought her to my office for counsel.

I shared with Mary that just as a loving father disciplines a disobedient child, so God in His love for us disciplines us when we are disobedient. Actually, "child training" would be a more accurate way of describing what God does for us when we are disobedient.

Like Mary, many Christians unnecessarily go through all kinds of adversity: financial, emotional, marital and family problems, and even physical illness. More often than not, God is trying to get their attention. But because they refuse to listen and obey Him, they are disciplined and their misery continues.

Beware, of course, that you do not assume that every time friends or loved ones have difficult experiences, they are being disciplined by God because of disobedience. It may well be that God is working in their lives as He did in Job's, not because of disobedience but to help them mature and become more fruitful and effective witnesses or models of His grace to others.

When you personally, like Mary, are going through adversity, however, and problems continue to plague your life, you would do well to look into the mirror of God's Word. Ask the Holy Spirit to show you if there is any unconfessed sin in your life. If there is, be quick to turn to the Lord, confess your sins and receive His forgiveness and cleansing in order to avoid further chastening.

Bible Reading: Psalm 32:1-5

ACTION POINT: I will write down on paper, for my own personal information only, any known weakness, sin or sins that are plaguing me today. I will confess that sin, or those sins, and receive by faith God's forgiveness and cleansing. (If you are continuing to breathe spiritually, you will not allow sins to accumulate, for the moment you become aware of sin you confess it to the Lord and keep on walking in the light as He is in the light.)

To Keep You From Sin

"How can a young man stay pure? By reading Your Word and following its rules. I have tried my best to find You — don't let me wander off from Your instructions. I have thought much about Your words, and stored them in my heart so that they would hold me back from sin" (Psalm 119:9-11).

Carl, a Christian leader who had made a mess of his life, wept as he shared his defeat. "As a young Christian," he said, "I was warned that God's Word would keep me from sin, or sin would keep me from God's Word.

"For many years," he continued, "I studied and obeyed God's Word faithfully. A few years ago I became very busy and took less and less time for God's Word. So when temptation came, I had no strength to resist. Now my life and marriage have disintegrated and I am thinking of committing suicide."

If you do not already have a daily practice of spending time alone with God — studying, reading, memorizing and meditating on His Word, and spending time with Him in prayer — I encourage you to do so, beginning today. The spiritual food of God's Word is absolutely essential for victorious, supernatural living. Great benefit can be found in listening to recordings of the Old and New Testaments, sermons and Christian music on your cassette player, in your home and in your car as you travel.

Scientists and health nutritionists confirm that our physical well-being is largely determined by the food we eat. For example, many people cannot tolerate high quantities of refined foods, such as sugar, white flour and chocolate. When they eat such foods, they become seriously ill physically, mentally and emotionally. Some have even been known to develop criminal tendencies because of what is often diagnosed as hypoglycemia, caused by poor nutrition.

In like manner, our spiritual bodies are influenced by what we absorb from God's Word and other scripturally based writings. It is impossible to be happy, healthy, strong, virile and fruitful for God without a regular intake from the Word of God.

Bible Reading: Philippians 4:8,9

ACTION POINT: I will determine, with the help of the Holy Spirit, to set aside time each day to read the Bible and pray and wait upon God for His leading and maturing in my life.

A New Life to Enjoy

"The Ten Commandments were given so that all could see the extent of their failure to obey God's laws. But the more we see our sinfulness, the more we see God's abounding grace forgiving us. Before, sin ruled over all men and brought them to death, but now God's kindness rules instead, giving us right standing with God and resulting in eternal life through Jesus Christ our Lord.

"Well, then, shall we keep on sinning so that God can keep on showing us more and more kindness and forgiveness? Of course not! Should we keep on sinning when we don't have to? For sin's power over us was broken when we became Christians and were baptized to become a part of Jesus Christ; through His death the power of your sinful nature was shattered. Your old sin-loving nature was buried with Him by baptism when He died, and when God the Father, with glorious power, brought Him back to life again, you were given His wonderful new life to enjoy" (Romans 5:20-6:4).

"When I think upon God, my heart is so full of joy that the notes dance and leap, as it were, from my pen," replied the great musician Haydn when asked why his church music was so cheerful. "And since God has given me a cheerful heart it will be pardoned me that I serve Him with a cheerful spirit."

A careful reading of 1 John 2 helps us realize that we will not want to sin if we really are children of God, any more than a butterfly would want to crawl on the ground as it once did as a caterpillar. "Someone may say, 'I am a Christian; I am on my way to heaven; I belong to Christ.' But if he doesn't do what Christ tells him to, he is a liar" (1 John 2:4).

"The person who has been born into God's family does not make a practice of sinning, because now God's life is in him; so he can't keep on sinning, for this new life has been born into him and controls him — he has been *born again*" (1 John 3:9).

Bible Reading: Romans 5:15-19

ACTION POINT: I will thank God often throughout the day for the fact that I don't *have* sin. He has made a way of escape. "For sin's power over us was broken when we received Christ." So, I will "resist the devil" and he will flee from me. Today I will enjoy my new life in Christ by demonstrating a joyful spirit.

He Will Tell You

"I advise you to obey only the Holy Spirit's instructions. He will tell you where to go and what to do, and then you won't always be doing the wrong things your evil nature wants you to" (Galatians 5:16).

Major conflicts in life are resolved when, by an act of the will, one surrenders to the control of the Holy Spirit and faces temptation in His power.

It should be explained that there is a difference between temptation and sin.

Temptation is the initial impression to do something contrary to God's will. Such impressions come to all people, even as they did to the Lord, and they are not sin in themselves.

Temptation becomes sin when we meditate on the impression and develop a strong desire, which is often followed by the actual act of disobedience.

For practical daily living, we simply recognize our weakness whenever we are tempted and obey the Holy Spirit's instructions. When we do yield to temptation, we breathe spiritually and resume our walk with God.

"At what point does one who practices spiritual breathing become carnal again?" Whenever one ceases to believe God's promise that He will enable us to be victorious over all temptations. The fact is, one need never be carnal again. So long as a believer keeps breathing spiritually, there is no need to live a life of defeat.

The moment you realize that you have done that which grieves or quenches the Spirit, you simply exhale spiritually by confessing immediately, and then inhale as by faith you claim God's forgiveness and the fullness of the Holy Spirit, and you keep walking in the light as God is in the light.

Bible Reading: Galatians 5:17-26

ACTION POINT: I will consciously seek to obey the Holy Spirit's instructions revealed to me in His holy, inspired Word.

Sure Road to Faith

"So, then, faith cometh by hearing, and hearing by the Word of God"
(Romans 10:17, KJV).

Martin Luther said he studied his Bible in the same way he gathered apples. First, he shook the whole tree, that the ripest might fall; then he shook each limb, and when he had shaken each limb, he shook each branch, and after each branch, every twig; and then he looked under every leaf. He admonishes us:

"Search the Bible as a whole, shaking the whole tree. Read it rapidly, as you would any other book. Then shake every limb — study book after book.

"Then shake every branch, giving attention to the chapters when they do not break the sense. Then shake each twig, by a careful study of the paragraphs and sentences. And you will be rewarded if you will look under each leaf, by searching the meaning of the words."

Seek to know the Lord with all your heart. While you may have no difficulty in worshiping the omnipotent God, you cannot really know God unless you study His Word. The one who spoke and caused the worlds to be framed is waiting to reveal Himself to you personally.

Faith is not given to those who are either undisciplined or disobedient. Faith is a gift of God which is given to those who trust and obey Him. As we master His Word and obey His commands, our faith continues to grow.

It is my strong conviction that it is impossible to ask God for too much if our hearts and motives are pure and if we pray according to the Word and will of God.

Every time you and I open and read God's Word carefully, we are building up our storehouse of faith. When we memorize the Word, our faith is being increased. When we study or teach a Sunday school lesson, or hear a sermon faithfully expounding the Word, we are growing in faith.

Bible Reading: Hebrews 11:1-6

ACTION POINT: I will read, study, memorize and meditate upon God's Word daily, knowing that in the process my faith will grow, for "faith comes by hearing, and hearing by the Word of God."

He Sets Us Free

"I don't understand myself at all, for I really want to do what is right, but I can't. I do what I don't want to — what I hate...When I want to do good, I don't; and when I try not to do wrong, I do it anyway....It seems to be a fact of life that when I want to do what is right, I inevitably do what is wrong...So you see how it is: my new life tells me to do right, but the old nature that is still inside me loves to sin. Oh, what a terrible predicament I'm in! Who will free me from my slavery to this deadly lower nature? Thank God! It has been done by Jesus Christ our Lord. He has set me free" (Romans 7:15,19,21,24,25).

Harry gave every indication of being a happy, joyful, fruitful Christian. He was active in every major event of the church and many large citywide Christian efforts. He always had a high visibility, and because of his extrovertive, outgoing personality he seemed to be a model Christian.

Then one day I saw the real Harry. He just blurted it out.

"I'm a hypocrite — miserable, defeated, frustrated. I've lived a lie and worn a mask all my life, never wanting to reveal my true self. But I need help. I'm seriously thinking of committing suicide. I just can't live the Christian life, no matter how hard I try."

As I began reading Romans 7:15-25, he said, "That is my biography, the story of my life. I've done everything I know to find victory — to live the Christian life as I know I'm supposed to live it. But everything fails for me no matter how hard I try."

I encouraged him to read on. Paul asks the question in the 25th verse,

"Who will free me from my slavery to this deadly lower nature?" Then he answers that question by saying, "Thank God! It has been done by Jesus Christ our Lord. He has set me free."

If you are living a carnal life, as described in Romans 7, you can be liberated to experience a full and abundant, victorious and fruitful life, as you by faith claim the fullness and power of the Holy Spirit day by day, moment by moment.

Bible Reading: Romans 7:18-23

ACTION POINT: By faith, I will claim the power of the Holy Spirit to enable me to live the abundant, supernatural life that Jesus promised, so that I can bring glory to God by bearing much fruit.

When You Open the Door

"Look! I have been standing at the door and I am constantly knocking. If anyone hears Me calling him and opens the door, I will come in and fellowship with him and he with Me" (Revelation 3:20).

"One morning I wanted to feed the birds," a saint once said. "It was gray and cold, and the ground was covered with snow. I stepped out on the porch and flung them handfuls of crumbs and called to them. But there they sat, cold and hungry and afraid. They did not trust me.

"As I sat and watched and waited, it seemed to me I could get God's viewpoint more clearly than ever before. He offers, plans, waits, hopes, longs for all things for our good. But He has to watch and wait as I did for my timid friends."

What a simple thing it is to open a door!

That still, small voice of conscience that pricks you from time to time is probably Christ Himself knocking at the door of your heart. He is waiting for that very simple act by which you open that door — an act of your will acknowledging that Christ is making a claim upon your life. He has that right; He died for you.

If you are not absolutely sure that Christ is in your life, that you would go straight to heaven if you died today, you can be sure right now.

By faith, respond to the invitation of Jesus and open the door of your life to Him. Why not make this your prayer:

"Lord Jesus, I need You. I know You are the Son of God, the Savior of all men. Thank You for dying on the cross for my sins. I open the door of my life and receive You as my Savior and Lord.

"Thank You for forgiving my sins and giving me eternal life. Take control of my life. Make me the kind of person You want me to be. Enable me to live a supernatural life beginning today. Amen."

If you asked Christ to come into your life, by faith, trusting that He has answered your prayer even as He has promised, then you can know with absolute certainty that He has done so.

Bible Reading: John 14:23-27

ACTION POINT: If I am already absolutely sure of my salvation, I will invite someone else today to pray this prayer. If I am not sure of my own spiritual condition, I will pray it for myself.

Christ Our Attorney

"If anyone publicly acknowledges Me as his friend, I will openly acknowledge him as My friend before My Father in heaven. But if anyone publicly denies Me, I will openly deny him before My Father in heaven" (Matthew 10:32,33).

S ome time ago, I challenged a famous and successful statesman to share his Christian faith.

"I believe that religion is personal and private, not something to wear on your sleeve," he replied. "I am a Christian, but I don't want to talk about it."

I reminded him that Jesus loved him enough to die for him. His disciples were so convinced of the urgency of passing on to others the message of God's love and forgiveness through Christ that they, and many thousands like them — though they died as martyrs — did not give up their efforts to get the message to us.

Further, I reminded him of the words of Jesus, "He that is not with Me is against Me" (Matthew 12:30, KJV) and the passage above from Matthew 10.

He was very sobered by my remarks. After a few minutes, he said, "I agree with you. I realize how wrong I have been. I had never realized how far off course I had gotten. I need to rethink all of my priorities and give Christ His rightful place in my life."

"My challenge to laymen," R. G. Le Tourneau, one of America's leading industrialists and Christian statesmen, once said, "is that when Christ said, 'Go ye into all the world, and preach the gospel,' He did not mean only preachers but everyone who believed in Him as the Lord of glory. . . . . . .My challenge to you is for a return to this first-century conception of Christianity where every believer is a witness to the grace of the Lord Jesus Christ."

Bible Reading: Psalm 119:41-48

ACTION POINT: Today I will publicly acknowledge my love for Christ, and through the enabling of the Holy Spirit I will live today so that others will *want* what I have, and I will speak so that they will *know* what I have.

No More Fears

"There is no fear in love, but perfect love casteth out fear: because fear hath torment. He that feareth is not made perfect in love" (1 John 4:18, KJV).

"If I could hear Christ praying for me in the next room," declared Robert Murray McCheyne, "I would not fear a million enemies. Yet distance makes no difference. He is praying for me: 'He ever liveth to make intercession.'"

Is there some fear in your life over which you do not have victory? Whether it is great or small, you can gain victory over that fear through claiming, by faith, God's supernatural love for yourself and for others, for "perfect love casts out fear."

That promise makes it imperative that you and I claim God's *agape*, the supernatural love described in 1 Corinthians 13, love for God, for our neighbors, for ourselves and for our enemies — for all men. As we do this, we can begin to practice that perfect love, showing it to our families and to friends and neighbors.

No fear is too small for Christ to handle, and certainly none is too large. Remember, "God hath not given us the spirit of fear; but of power, and of love, and of a sound mind" (2 Timothy 1:7, KJV). If fear does not come from God, then we must reject that spirit of fear as coming from the enemy of men's souls.

Fear of the future is a large fear for many people, but sometimes the seemingly small fears — of crowds, of heights, whatever — can cause more distress than greater fears. It is in these instances that God demonstrates His faithfulness to fill our hearts with His love and to cast out fear.

Faith is the most effective foe of fear, and "faith comes by hearing, and hearing by the Word of God."

Bible Reading: 2 Timothy 1:6-12

ACTION POINT: Today I will recognize any kind of fear in my life for what it is: an attempt of the enemy to sabotage my effectiveness as a disciple of the Lord Jesus Christ. By faith I will claim God's supernatural love for myself and others, and thereby gain victory over fear. As I pray for myself, I shall pray for others also who experience the same devastating results of fear.

The Sound Mind Principle

"For God hath not given us the spirit of fear; but of power, and of love, and of a sound mind" (2 Timothy 1:7, KJV).

Some years ago, a young college graduate came to me for counsel concerning God's will for his life. "How can I know what God wants me to do?" he asked.

Briefly, I explained a helpful approach to knowing the will of God: following what I call the "sound mind principle" of Scripture.

In less than an hour, by following the suggestions contained in this principle, the young man discovered what he had been seeking for years. He discovered not only the work which God wanted him to do but also the organization and manner in which he was to serve our Lord. Today he is serving Christ as a missionary in Africa, where he and his wife are touching the lives of thousands throughout the entire continent.

What is this "sound mind principle"? This verse refers to a well-balanced mind — a mind that is under the control of the Holy Spirit. It involves the practice of determining God's wisdom and direction through use of your mind saturated with God's Word, instead of relying *only* on emotional impressions. Though God often leads us through impressions, He generally expects us to use our "sound minds."

For example, when you have an important decision to make, take a sheet of paper, list all the positive and negative factors. Then consider what God's Word has to say about the matter — directly or indirectly. Be sure you are controlled by the Holy Spirit, then make your decision on the basis of what seems obvious, unless God specifically leads you to the contrary.

"Be not conformed to this world: but be ye transformed by the renewing of your mind, that ye may prove what is that good, and acceptable, and perfect, will of God" (Romans 12:2, KJV).

Bible Reading: 2 Timothy 1:8-12

ACTION POINT: In every major decision I face today, I will apply the sound mind principle to determine God's will in the matter, unless God specifically and supernaturally leads me to do something else which is also consistent with Scripture.

He Orders Your Steps

"The steps of a good man are ordered by the Lord: and He delighteth in his way" (Psalm 37:23, KJV).

Miriam Booth — a beautiful, brilliant, cultured woman — daughter of the Salvation Army founder, began her Christian work with great promise. She had unusual success. Before long, however, disease struck her and brought her to the point of death. A friend visiting her one day said it seemed a pity that a woman so capable should be hindered by illness from doing the Lord's work. "It is great to do the Lord's work," she replied with gentle grace, "but it is greater to do the Lord's will."

Are you looking for direction, for purpose, for meaning to your life?

The psalmist wanted to make it very plain that the person who is "good," the one who is clothed with the righteousness, the goodness of Christ, can have the absolute assurance that His steps, one by one, moment by moment, hour by hour, day by day, are ordered by the Lord (planned and directed by Him).

That wonderful truth is made even more meaningful by the reminder that our "stops" as well are directed by the Lord. He knows when we need to slow down, to wait on Him. As a Christian leader once said, after several weeks of being bedridden: "I needed to be flat on my back so that the only way I could look was up."

Finding the will of God has been difficult for many people — for most of us at one time or another. But the truth remains that He promises to give wisdom to any who ask, and we have that privilege when we belong to Him by virtue of having received the Lord Jesus Christ as our personal Savior.

If you are facing a crossroad in your life, wait on Him and avoid the usual rush to a decision that might be disastrous. "He is faithful who promised." Depend upon Him to make the way clear as you lay the decision prayerfully before Him.

Bible Reading: Isaiah 58:9-14

ACTION POINT: When I need wisdom for a specific decision today, I will breathe an earnest prayer for direction. Then I will thank God for the clear leading which He promises and for enabling me to continue living the supernatural life, as He directs my steps.

You Can Be Sure This Is God's Will

"In everything give thanks; for this is the will of God in Christ Jesus concerning you" (1 Thessalonians 5:18, KJV).

"Always give thanks for everything?" my friend Jim remarked with impatience bordering on anger. "How can I give thanks to God when my wife is dying of cancer? I would be a fool, and besides I don't feel thankful. My heart is breaking. I can't stand to see her suffer any more."

Jim was a Christian, but he had not yet learned how to appropriate the supernatural resources of God by faith. He had not heard that the Holy Spirit produces the supernatural, spiritual fruit of love, joy, peace, patience, kindness, goodness, faithfulness, gentleness and self-control. He did not know that the Holy Spirit was ready and eager to lift his load, fill his heart with peace and enable him to demonstrate a thankful attitude, even in times of heartache, sorrow and disappointment.

About the same time, I had a call from a beloved friend and fellow staff member, Bob. "I'm calling to ask for your prayers," he said. "My wife has an inoperable brain tumor, but we are trusting the Lord for a miracle. We are both thanking God, for we know He makes no mistakes and we are ready for whatever happens."

Bob and Alice were controlled by the Holy Spirit, responding as Spirit-filled persons are equipped to respond. Though God did not heal Alice's ailing body, He performed a greater miracle by providing the supernatural resources which enabled Bob and Alice to praise and give thanks to God as a powerful testimony of His love and grace in their behalf.

Bible Reading: 1 Thessalonians 5:11-17

ACTION POINT: Knowing that "all things work together for good to those who love God" — and that includes me — I determine through the enabling of the Holy Spirit to obey God today as an expression of faith by thanking Him *in* everything and *for* everything.

Power to Become Rich

"Always remember that it is the Lord your God who gives you power to become rich, and He does it to fulfill His promise to your ancestors" (Deuteronomy 8:18).

A Christian woman whom I knew, worth many millions of dollars, panicked when the stock market dropped and she lost almost one million dollars. Even though she had tens of millions in reserve, she was filled with apprehension and fear that she would die a pauper. She had never discovered the adventure and freedom of "giving and receiving" in a trust relationship with God.

Conversely, a businessman called me long distance a short time later to tell me how excited he was over the way God was blessing his new business venture. He had decided to give all the profits — potentially millions — toward helping to reach the world for Christ.

"I am sending $50,000 for Here's Life in Asia," he said. "And there will be much more later. I don't want to invest in buildings. I want to invest this money where it will be used immediately to win and disciple people for Christ."

The principle is the same, whether you have $100 or $1 million. Ask God to tell you what to do toward helping to fulfill the Great Commission. Second, look for a worthy, proven project that you can support monthly, if only modestly, in addition to your commitment to your local church.

As your faith in God's love and trustworthiness grows, prayerfully make a faith promise pledge that is greater than you are capable of fulfilling with your present income.

Bible Reading: Malachi 3:7-12

ACTION POINT: I will ask God today to help me trust Him to give — by faith — more than I can possibly afford to give toward His work, with the certainty that He will supply all my needs and enable me to meet my faith promise pledge supernaturally.

He Knew His Future

"Jesus answered and said unto them, 'Destroy this temple, and in three days I will raise it up'" (John 2:19, KJV).

A missionary in Turkey sought to teach the truth of the resurrection of Christ to a group of people.

"I am traveling, and have reached a place where the road branches off in two ways," he said. "I look for a guide, and find two men — one dead, and the other alive. Which of the two must I ask for direction — the dead or the living?"

"Oh, the living!" cried the people.

"Then," said the missionary, "why send me to Mohammed, who is dead, instead of to Christ, who is alive?"

Jesus is the only person who has ever accurately predicted his own resurrection. He said He would be raised from the dead on the third day after dying on the cross for our sins, and He was!

Further, He was seen on many different occasions after His resurrection — once by as many as 500 people. He still lives today in the hearts of all who have placed their faith in Him, demonstrating His life of love and forgiveness through them.

Whenever men meet the living Christ, they are changed. The whole course of history has been changed because of Him.

"The gospel not only converts the in-dividual, but it also changes society," historian Philip Schaff wrote. "Everywhere the gospel has been preached, dramatic change has resulted. It has established standards of hygiene and purity, promoted industry, elevated womanhood, restrained antisocial customs, abolished human sacrifices, organized famine relief, checked tribal wars and changed the social structure of society.

"Born in a manger and crucified as a malefactor, He now controls the destinies of the civilized world and rules a spiritual empire which embraces one-third of the inhabitants of the globe."

Bible Reading: John 2:20-25

ACTION POINT: I will reflect often today on the fact that the risen Christ of history is the same loving Savior who now lives within me, offering me His love, His peace, His comfort, His wisdom, His strength. I will claim by faith His resurrection life to enable me to live supernaturally each moment of every day.

God's Secret Plan for You

"God has told us His secret reason for sending Christ, a plan He decided on in mercy long ago; and this was His purpose: that when the time is ripe He will gather us together from wherever we are — in heaven or on earth — to be with Him in Christ, forever" (Ephesians 1:9,10).

One day a distinguished scientist questioned Michael Faraday, chemist, electrician and philosopher.

"Have you conceived to yourself what will be your occupation in the next world?" he asked.

Hesitating a moment or two, Faraday replied, "Eye hath not seen, nor ear heard, neither have entered into the heart of man, the things that God hath prepared for them that love Him."

And then he added, in his own words, "I shall be with Christ, and that is enough."

Although nearly two thousand years have passed since He walked this earth, Jesus still stands as the ultimate expression of ethics and morality. Whatever one might think about Christians or the church, he will find no blemishes in the character of Jesus.

Perhaps the greatest testimony that can be given regarding the character of Jesus' teachings is that they are still changing men and nations throughout the world today. Now, as before, those who listen to Him inevitably say, "No man ever spoke like this man!" (John 7:46, RSV).

God's Word tells us that Jesus had the same temptations we do, though He never once gave way to them and sinned (Hebrews 4:15). Our Lord thus stands out as the supreme example of one who practiced the things that He taught to others and that He expects of His followers.

We still stand today in the shadow of God's sure promise: "For God has allowed us to know the secret of His plan, and it is this: He purposes in His sovereign will that all human history shall be consummated in Christ, that everything that exists in heaven or earth shall find its perfection and fulfillment in Him. And here is the staggering thing that in all which will belong to Christ we have been promised a share" (Ephesians 1:9-11, Phillips).

Bible Reading: Ephesians 1:11-14

ACTION POINT: Today I will meditate upon the fact that I am a child of God, an heir of God and joint-heir with Christ; and upon the startling, incredible fact that I am related to Him and share with Him in all of this indescribable privilege and blessing. As a result I will claim His supernatural love and power and will speak more freely to others of my relationship with Him.

How to Assure Success

"Early the next morning the army of Judah went out into the wilderness of Tekoa. On the way Jehoshaphat stopped and called them to attention. 'Listen to me, O people of Judah and Jerusalem,' he said. 'Believe in the Lord your God, and you shall have success! Believe His prophets, and everything will be all right!' " (2 Chronicles 20:20).

God does the same things for us in our time that He did so often in the Old and New Testament accounts of His power and grace.

I remember an eventful week at the University of California in Berkeley in 1966 when the president of the university was fired by the board of regents during the turbulent days of student revolution. Campuses throughout California erupted in anger and violence.

On the Berkeley campus, however, about 600 Campus Crusade staff members and students had gathered from across America to present the claims of Jesus Christ to more than 27,000 students. During the week, through some 80 meetings in dormitories, fraternity and sorority houses, international groups, at athletic banquets and faculty breakfasts and luncheons, in personal appointments and finally at a great meeting of some 8,000 gathered in the Greek theater, almost every student had an opportunity to hear the good news of God's love through Christ. Literally thousands responded.

When the camera crews from the local television stations rushed out to film the predicted violence, they were amazed to find that the Berkeley campus, fountainhead of the radical student revolution, was remarkably quiet. Music, singing and sharing the gospel of our Lord Jesus Christ prevailed. Many point to that week as a turning point in the direction of a world-famous university.

Light is more powerful than darkness. Believing God and obeying His commands assure eternal dividends.

Bible Reading: Joshua 1:5-9

ACTION POINT: Today I resolve to believe God and do those things He directs me to do, regardless of the consequences. Then I am assured of success as, by faith, I live the supernatural life in the power of the Holy Spirit.

Using Our Abilities

"Why is it that He gives us these special abilities to do certain things best? It is that God's people will be equipped to do better work for Him, building up the church, the body of Christ, to a position of strength and maturity; until finally we all believe alike about our salvation and about our Savior, God's Son, and all become full-grown in the Lord — yes, to the point of being filled full with Christ" (Ephesians 4:12,13).

We would be poor stewards if we ignored the special abilities the Holy Spirit has given to us.

We must use our abilities to glorify Christ, not to glorify ourselves, or some other person, or even to glorify the gift itself.

Peter says, "Are you called to preach? Then preach as though God Himself were speaking through you" (1 Peter 4:11). Do you possess musical ability? Share it with the rest of Christ's family. Peter goes on, "Are you called to help others? Do it with all the strength and energy that God supplies, so that God will be glorified through Jesus Christ — to Him be glory and praise forever and ever."

We have the obligation to use our God-given abilities in a scriptural manner to help equip others for Christian service. The apostle Paul writes that spiritual gifts are given "for the equipping of the saints for the work of service, to the building up of the body of Christ" (Ephesians 4:12, NAS).

In order to live supernaturally, it is important for us always to exercise our abilities in the power and control of the Holy Spirit — never through our own fleshly efforts.

Bible Reading: Ephesians 4:11-16

ACTION POINT: My motivation for using my spiritual gift(s) and abilities will be solely to glorify Christ through helping to equip other members of His body to be more effective and fruitful for Him.

Your Source of Strength

"......*the joy of the Lord is your strength*" (Nehemiah 8:10b, KJV).

At a London train station one day, a woman was stopped by an elderly man.

"Excuse me, ma'am," he said, "but I want to thank you for something."

"Thank *me!*" the woman exclaimed.

"Yes'm, I used to be the ticket collector, and whenever you went by you always gave me a cheerful smile and a 'good mornin'.' You don't know what a difference it made to me.

"Wet weather or dry, it was always the same, and I thought to myself, 'Wonder where she gets her smile from; one can't always be happy, yet she seems to.' I knew that smile must come from inside somehow.

"Then one morning you came by and you had a little Bible in your hand. I said to myself, 'Perhaps that's where she gets her smile from.' So on my way home that night I bought a Bible, and I've been reading it, and I've found Christ. Now I can smile, too, and I want to thank you."

As you and I seek to be God's witnesses today, in dependence on the supernatural power of the indwelling Holy Spirit, we should be mindful constantly of the fact that the joy of the Lord can indeed be our strength. That joy inevitably will shine on our faces, regardless of circumstances.

In the words of an anonymous poem:
"If you live close to God
And His infinite grace,
You don't have to tell;
It shows on your face."

Bible Reading: Psalm 16:6-11

ACTION POINT: I will make a conscious effort to reflect the joy of my indwelling Lord in such a way that it will glow on my very countenance. While it is true that joy is a fruit of the Spirit, it is also true that the reflection of that joy is my responsibility. But I will go a step further. I will tell everyone who will listen about the one who is the source of my joy.

PROMISES – DAY 35

Underneath: Everlasting Arms

"The eternal God is your Refuge, and underneath are the everlasting arms. He thrusts out your enemies before you . . ." (Deuteronomy 33:27, LB. *". . . with us is the Lord our God to help us, and to fight our battles"* (2 Chronicles 32:8, KJV).

Susan was broken-hearted. She had just lost her first child at birth. The trauma of that experience had affected her relationship with her husband and with everyone else around her. She had become cynical and moody. She blamed God for what had happened and said, "I hate Him. Why would this happen to me? Where was God when I was going through the birth pangs, the excruciating pain of giving birth to a stillborn child? Why didn't He give me a healthy baby?"

I was reminded of a statement that I had heard in response to a similar anguished plea: "Where was God when I lost my son?"

The answer: "Where He was when His own Son died on the cross for our sins."

We do not understand the mystery of why God allows tragedy, heartache and sorrow, but we do know that those who trust the eternal God as their refuge will experience the reality of His promise that "underneath are the everlasting arms."

Sometime later I talked with a godly Christian leader whose son had just taken his own life. Of course this man and his wife were devastated. Their hearts were broken. But what a difference in their reaction. Even through his tears this great Christian was saying, "I know I can trust God. He is a loving God. He is my refuge, and I feel His strength and compassion and care for me and my loved ones. My wife and I and all of our family are rededicating ourselves to Him as an expression of our love and confidence in His trustworthiness."

Bible Reading: Psalm 91:1-7

ACTION POINT: As an expression of my confidence in God and His love and faithfulness I will make a special effort to visualize those everlasting arms of love spread out beneath me, ready for any fall I may take like a giant net below a trapeze artist. That will give me courage in the face of every obstacle and assurance despite my weaknesses.

He Maintains the Seasons

"As long as the earth remains there will be springtime and harvest, cold and heat, winter and summer, day and night" (Genesis 8:22).

On his way to a country church one Sunday morning, a preacher was overtaken by one of his deacons.

"What a bitterly cold morning," the deacon remarked. "I am sorry the weather is so wintry."

Smiling, the minister replied, "I was just thanking God for keeping His Word."

"What do you mean?" the man asked with a puzzled look on his face.

"Well," the preacher said, "more than 3,000 years ago God promised that cold and heat should not cease, so I am strengthened by this weather which emphasizes the sureness of His promises."

It is most reassuring to realize that we serve a God who keeps His promises, for He is the same God who makes possible the supernatural life for the believer. Part of that supernatural life is the ability to accept our lot in life, to be able to say with the psalmist:

"This is the day the Lord hath made; we will rejoice and be glad in it" (Psalm 118:24, KJV).

"Springtime and harvest" reminds us that as we sow the seed of the Word of God, He is faithful to give the increase — in His own good time. He simply asks and expects that we be faithful in our part, which is to give out His Word — to plant — at every possible opportunity.

The Christian who lives the supernatural life is enabled by the Holy Spirit to rejoice under all circumstances and to interpret every problem, adversity, heartache and sorrow in a positive light.

Bible Reading: Genesis 8:15-21

ACTION POINT: I will give thanks to the Lord for His faithfulness, no matter what the circumstances. I will faithfully plant the Word of God today whenever and wherever possible, realizing that our faithful God will produce the promised harvest.

Children of God

"But to all who received Him, He gave the right to become children of God. All they needed to do was to trust Him to save them" (John 1:12).

My wife, Vonette, had been active in the church since she was a little girl, and I assumed that she was a Christian. However, after my proposal and during our engagement, I realized she had never received Christ, though she was a very moral, religious person.

Because of the emotional involvement, I hesitated to press her to receive Christ because I was afraid she would go through the motions of receiving Him to please me, which certainly would not be pleasing to our Lord. So I asked the Lord to send someone who could introduce her to Christ. He clearly led me to call upon a dear friend, the late Dr. Henrietta Mears, who had played such a vital role in my own spiritual growth.

One day at Forest Home, a Christian conference center in California, Dr. Mears took time to talk with Vonette. "Receiving Christ," she explained, "is simply a matter of turning your life — your will, your emotions, your intellect — completely over to Him." With that, the great transaction took place and Vonette became a new creature in Christ.

Similarly, in India, a convert from Hinduism could neither read nor write, so he asked others to read the Bible to him. His favorite verse was John 1:12.

"I have received Him," he said, "so I have become a son of God."

Radiantly happy, he returned to his village.

"I have become a son of God," he proclaimed. And his life was so transformed and his simple witness so effective that the other villagers all wanted to become "sons of God," too.

That radiant convert led the whole village to Christ — and hundreds of others besides. A poor, illiterate, former Hindu, he realized that he had indeed become a son of God and he longed for others to become sons as well.

Bible Reading: John 1:6-11

ACTION POINT: I will make certain first of all that I have truly received Jesus Christ as my Savior and Lord by faith — with the intellect, the emotions, the will. Then I will seek to be God's instrument in helping to introduce others to Him as well.

Refuge for the Oppressed

"All who are oppressed may come to Him. He is a refuge for them in their time of trouble" (Psalm 9:9).

The late evangelist Henry Moorehouse once faced a disturbing dilemma. His little paralyzed daughter greeted him as he entered the house bearing a package for his wife.

"Where is Mother?" he asked, after kissing and embracing his daughter.

"Mother is upstairs," the girl responded.

"Well," Moorehouse said, "I have a package for her."

"Oh," the girl pleaded, "let me carry the package to Mother."

"Why, Minnie dear," her father replied, "how can you carry the package? You can't carry yourself."

With a smile, the girl continued, "That is true, Papa. But you can give me the package, and I will carry the package — and you will carry me."

Taking her up in his arms, Moorhouse carried his daughter upstairs — little Minnie and the package, too. Then he saw his own position before the Lord: he had been carrying a heavy burden in recent days, but was not God carrying Him?

In similar fashion, you and I often feel the weight of heavy burdens — sometimes forgetting that even as we carry them we are being carried by our heavenly Father, who is a "refuge for them in their time of trouble."

Bible Reading: Psalm 9:10-14

ACTION POINT: As I carry my burdens today — large or small — I will recognize that my heavenly Father is carrying me, and I will pass this wonderful truth on to others who are weighted down with the loads and cares of daily living.

He Hears Our Cries

"Lord, You know the hopes of humble people. Surely You will hear their cries and comfort their hearts by helping them" (Psalm 10:17).

Some time ago Nancy DeMoss, who with her beloved husband, Art (one of my dearest friends), had launched a fruitful ministry to executives, called to share an exciting experience. It had been raining all day, and a downpour was predicted for that evening. More than 1300 guests were coming to their home for a lawn dinner to hear the gospel presented by the well-known Christian leader, Charles Colson.

They prayed that the rain would stop, and — miracle of miracles — except for only a few drops of moisture, the rain was held back, though around them, they later learned, there had been a downpour. The gospel had been presented and hundreds had responded to the invitation to receive Christ, and as the guests were on their way home, the rain came — but the harvest was over. The God of nature had heard their prayers and responded.

On another occasion, during EXPLO '74 in Seoul, Korea, as over a million people came each of five evenings to the famous Yoida Plaza, we prayed God would hold back the rain — but He chose to bless us in other ways, and the rain came. As it fell, God overruled and the people were drawn closer to each other and to the Lord.

Literally hundreds of thousands claimed to have received Christ during the week. In fact, more than a million — according to the officials — indicated that they had received Christ in just one evening. As a result, we gladly praised and thanked God for the rain.

God always knows what is best. He knows the hopes of humble people, and He will hear our cries and comfort our hearts. Sometimes He withholds the rain; other times He sends the rain and with it the outpouring of His blessings.

Bible Reading: Psalm 10:12-16

ACTION POINT: Knowing that God is worthy of my trust, that He controls not only the affairs of men and nations but also the laws of nature, I will submit my requests to Him today and be willing to abide by His decisions, knowing also that He makes no mistakes. I shall rejoice and give thanks to Him no matter what happens.

The Heavens Declare God's Glory

"The heavens are telling the glory of God; they are a marvelous display of His craftmanship" (Psalm 19:1).

When King David was a small lad, his father assigned him the care of the sheep. Day after day, night after night he cared for his sheep as a loving shepherd. No doubt on numerous occasions he would lie on his back and look up at the sun and the vastness of space, during the daytime. At night, the stars and the moon would seem so close that he could almost reach them, as he would talk to the God of his fathers.

The vast expanse of creation captivated him, and instinctively he knew that God, who created it all, was his God and he could trust Him with his life, so that just before he went against the giant Goliath he could say to King Saul, "When I am taking care of my father's sheep and a lion or a bear comes and grabs a lamb from the flock, I go after it with a club...I've done it to both lions and bears, and I'll do it to this heathen Philistine too, for he has defied the armies of the living God. The Lord who saved me from the claws and teeth of the lion and the bear will save me from this Philistine" (1 Samuel 17:34-37). When David went out against Goliath, he said to the giant, "You come to me with a sword and a spear, but I come to you in the name of the Lord of the armies of heaven and of Israel" (1 Samuel 17:45). Then, with a sling and a stone, he killed the Philistine.

I personally believe David triumphed because his confidence in God came not only from the teachings of the holy Scriptures, but also from the experience that he had had with God, who created all the heavens and the earth.

Bible Reading: Psalm 19:2-6

ACTION POINT: I will make a special point to study the vastness of God's creation through books about science and to take time — not only in Scripture, but also in books of science — to notice the handiwork of God's beautiful creation, conscious that it will help me to become more sensitive and alert to the needs of others.

God's Word Gives Joy and Light

"God's laws are perfect. They protect us, make us wise, and give us joy and light" (Psalm 19:7,8).

Professor William Lyon Phelps, one of Yale University's most famous scholars, said, "A knowledge of the Bible without a college education is more valuable than a college education without the Bible."

Why would he say this? Our verse gives us the answer. The Word of God (1) protects us, (2) makes us wise, (3) gives us joy, and (4) gives us light.

There are many other benefits that come from reading the Word of God. With dividends like these, we are indeed robbing ourselves of untold blessings when we neglect His holy, inspired Word for any reason whatever.

It is my privilege to counsel many thousands of people with just about every kind of problem conceivable — need for salvation, poor self-image, marital problems, financial problems, health problems, loss of loved ones, insecurity, fear, and on and on. One could think of every kind of personal need and problem that man faces, and inevitably there is an answer in the Word of God.

I do not know of any individual who has ever received Christ without some understanding of the Word of God. It is for this reason that I included in *The Four Spiritual Laws* booklet, which I wrote in the 1950's, the parenthetical statement on page 2: "References contained in this booklet should be read in context from the Bible wherever possible."

By 1983, it was estimated that more than a billion copies of *The Four Spiritual Laws*, which contains the distilled essence of the gospel, had been printed (including translations into every major language) and distributed throughout the world, resulting in many millions of people responding to Christ. Still, it cannot compare with God's Word, nor can any other piece of Christian or secular literature. There is something unique and powerful about holding the Bible in your hand and reading it with your own eyes, for it speaks with authority and power possessed by no other book ever written.

Bible Reading: 2 Timothy 3:14-17

ACTION POINT: God's Word is the most important book ever written, and the most important book that I could possibly read. Today I will read it for at least 15 minutes with renewed devotion, dedication and sensitivity to its mighty revolutionary power to transform lives and enable children of God to live supernaturally.

Wait and He Will Help

"Don't be impatient. Wait for the Lord, and He will come and save you! Be brave, stouthearted and courageous. Yes, wait and He will help you" (Psalm 27:14).

Our surveys of hundreds of thousands of Christians throughout the world indicate that most Christians do not witness because of their fear. Even Timothy seems to have had the same problem.

His father in the faith, the apostle Paul, reminded him, as recorded in 2 Timothy 1:7, "For God hath not given us the spirit of fear; but of power, and of love, and of a sound mind" (KJV). That is the reason our Lord promised, in Acts 1:8, "Ye shall receive power, after that the Holy Ghost has come upon you: and ye shall be witnesses" (KVJ).

The Holy Spirit is the only one who can enable us to overcome fear. So, as we claim the promises of God and appropriate the fullness and power of His Holy Spirit, we can know that courage.

A Japanese schoolboy once showed his courage in a way that puts many of us to shame.

"He belonged to a school in Nagasaki containing 150 boys, and he was the only Christian among them all. He brought his lunch to school, as he lived at a distance, and he dared to fold his hands and ask a blessing every day before he ate.

"He had some enemies among the boys who went to the master of the school and accused him of 'doing something in the way of magic.' The master thereupon called the lad before the school and asked him what he had been doing.

"The little fellow spoke up bravely, explaining that he was a Christian, and that he had been thanking God and asking Him to bless the food. At once the master burst into tears, putting his head down on the desk.

" 'My boy,' he said, 'I too am a Christian; but I was afraid to tell anyone. Now, with God's help I will try to live as a Christian ought to live.' "

Bible Reading: Isaiah 40:27-31

ACTION POINT: Today I shall, through the enabling of the Holy Spirit, be brave, stouthearted and courageous as I go forth to tell others about the Lord Jesus Christ.

Set Upon a Rock

"For in the time of trouble He shall hide me in His pavilion: in the secret of His tabernacle shall He hide me; He shall set me up upon a rock" (Psalm 27:5, KJV).

Doug and Judy stood at the graveside of their little Timothy — their only child — who had been run over by a drunken driver while riding his tricycle on the sidewalk. It was a senseless, one-in-a-million, freak kind of accident, but their little lad was gone forever from their loving embraces.

As they wept, I consoled them with the promises of God's Word: "In the time of trouble, He shall hide us in His pavilion, in the secret of His tabernacle shall He hide us. He shall set us upon a rock."

In the words of Jesus, I shared with them His promise, "Come unto me, all ye that labor and are heavy laden, and I will give you rest" (Matthew 11: 28, KJV). "Peace I leave with you; My peace I give unto you; not as the world giveth, give I unto you. Let not your heart be troubled, neither let it be afraid" (John 14:27, KJV).

Man's words are never adequate in a time like this. Only the holy, inspired Word of God, revealed through the indwelling Holy Spirit, can help us to comprehend and experience the reality of His promises.

What a joy to be able to tell people — burdened people, grieving people — that we serve God, who not only saves to the uttermost, but who also is the God of all comfort. As His Holy Spirit empowers us, let us share the good news of an all-loving, ever-wise Savior.

Bible Reading: Psalm 27:1-4

ACTION POINT: Today I will ask God to help me to be sensitive to the hurts and heartaches of others, so that I can comfort them with the Word of God through the enabling of the Holy Spirit. And when I face grievous troubles, I too will look to the rock, Christ Jesus, and claim His wonderful promises for comfort and strength.

He Bears and He Gives

"What a glorious Lord! He who daily bears our burdens also gives us our salvation" (Psalm 68:19).

Did it ever occur to you that you are disobeying God when you carry your own burdens, when you are worried, frustrated and confused over circumstances? That is exactly what God's Word says.

In 1 Peter 5:7, God gives a specific command to His children, "Cast...*all* your cares upon Him; for He careth for you" (KJV). Not to cast all of one's cares upon the Lord is to disobey Him and to deny oneself that supernatural walk with God among men.

Is it not logical to believe that He who loved us so much that He was willing to give His only begotten Son would also be faithful to keep His promise to bear our burdens daily?

As the psalmist so aptly states, the Lord bears our burdens on a daily basis. For the believer, the day will never come when God fails to carry our load, to strengthen us, to impart power to us through His indwelling Holy Spirit — if we but ask.

Marvel of marvels, the psalmist points out, our heavenly Father not only is our great burden-bearer; He is also the very one who gives us our salvation and the assurance of eternal life. How could anyone ask for more!

With the sure knowledge that our sins are forgiven (salvation) and the assurance that He knows all about every burden we face — more important, He bears them for us — our lives should reflect honor and glory to Him by the way in which we share His blessings and the message of His great love with others.

Provision for the supernatural life is promised in the Old Testament as well as the New, as evidenced by this glorious promise in the Psalms.

Bible Reading: Psalm 68:15-18

ACTION POINT: Today I will take careful inventory of my burdens and my worries and be sure that I am casting them all on the Lord with the certain knowledge that He cares for me. I will also encourage those around me to cast their cares upon the Lord.

Deliverance from Fears

"I sought the Lord, and He heard me, and delivered me from all my fears" (Psalm 34:4, KJV).

Susie seemed outwardly to be a well-poised, lovely young wife and mother with everything under control. She was active in her church and attended other Christian gatherings during the week. But secretly she was filled with fear from which psychologists and psychiatrists with whom she consulted were unable to set her free.

She became very discouraged and depressed. "What can I do?" she asked through her tears. "I have everything to live for and no real reason to be afraid, but my days are consumed with worry and dread and fear, as I anticipate all kinds of evil things happening to me, to my husband, to my children."

"Do you believe that God in heaven has the power to remove your fears, Susie?" I asked.

"Yes, of course," she replied.

"Do you believe He loves you?"

"Yes, I believe that."

"Do you believe He wants to remove that fear from you?" And I read her the above passage.

We turned together to 1 John 5:14,15: "If we ask anything according to God's will, He hears and answers." This is the promise that every believer can claim whenever there is a command or another promise. I asked her if she would like to join with me in a prayer of faith that God would deliver her according to this promise.

Together we prayed, and though there was no immediate, dramatic deliverance, with the passing of days God set her free. Day after day she claimed by faith this and other promises from God's holy, inspired Word.

Are you plagued with fears? Are your days consumed with worry? Saturate your mind with God's truth — God's supernatural promises — and begin to claim by faith this supernatural life which is your heritage in Christ.

Bible Reading: Psalm 34:1-7

ACTION POINT: At the first sign of a fear in my life, I will commit it to the Lord and trust Him for deliverance, and I will seek to help others whose hearts are filled with fear. I will seek to introduce them to the Prince of Peace — the God of all comfort.

Reap in Joy

"They that sow in tears shall reap in joy. He that goeth forth and weepeth, bearing precious seed, shall doubtless come again with rejoicing, bringing his sheaves with him" (Psalm 126:5,6, KJV).

How long has it been since you have shed tears of compassion over those who do not know our Savior as you pray for their salvation? Is God using you to introduce others to Christ? Is your church a center of spiritual harvest? If not, it is quite likely that you and other members of your church are shedding few tears over the lost.

It is a promise of God that when we go forth with a burdened heart sharing the precious seed of the Word of God, proclaiming the most joyful news ever announced, we can be absolutely assured — beyond a shadow of doubt — that we shall reap the harvest and, in the process, experience the supernatural joy that comes to those who are obedient to God.

It is a divine formula. But where does that burden and compassion for the souls of men originate? In the heart of God. And it is only as men are controlled and empowered by the Holy Spirit of God that there can be that compassion. It is not something that we can work up, not something that we can create in the energy of the flesh, but it is a result of walking in the fullness and power of the Holy Spirit, with minds and hearts saturated with the Word of God.

The Old Testament references to sowing are often accompanied by sorrow and anxiety, evidenced by the tears to which the psalmist refers. As a result, the time of reaping is one of inexpressible joy.

Bible Reading: Proverbs 11:27-31

ACTION POINT: Today I will ask the Holy Spirit of God who dwells within me to give me a greater burden for the souls of those around me, so that I may indeed weep genuine tears of compassion as I go forth sowing precious seed. I know that I shall reap abundantly and, in the process, experience the joy which comes to those who obey God by weeping, sowing and reaping.

Saved From Our Troubles

"This poor man cried to the Lord — and the Lord heard him and saved him out of his troubles" (Psalm 34:6).

It was a high-security penitentiary — filled with murderers, drug pushers, bank robbers and others who had committed major crimes and many who would never see the light of day again outside those bleak, gray prison walls. At an evangelistic service, however, one inmate after another stood to share how Christ had forgiven him of his sins and how, even though he had committed murder or some other serious crime, he knew with assurance that he was now a child of God.

Many of these men expressed in different words, as I sat there listening with tears streaming down my cheeks, "I am so glad I'm in prison, for it was here I found Jesus Christ, and I would rather be in prison with Christ in my heart than to be living in a palatial mansion without any knowledge of God's love and forgiveness through His Son."

Often I talk with people — on planes, on campuses, at public meetings — who are poor, not only materially but also physically and spiritually. What a joy to be able to share with them the good news that God cares.

A "poor man's" first cry must be one of repentance and confession, so that a divine relationship is established: Father and son. Conversion must come by the Spirit of God, before deliverance can come in the less important areas of one's life.

But after that Father-son relationship has been established, how wonderful to be able to assure such a one that God truly cares — enough to "save him out of his troubles." Oftentimes that entails enduring such troubles for a time, but never more than we are able to bear. The supernatural life promises victory — in the midst of adversity.

Bible Reading: 2 Corinthians 5:14-19

ACTION POINT: I will assure people whom I encounter today who are in trouble that God cares and promises deliverance. There is nothing more important that I could do for another person than to help him know Christ, so I will seek out those who are in need of a Savior so that they, too, can experience the liberating power of God's love through Jesus Christ.

A Singing Heart

"And whenever the tormenting spirit from God troubled Saul, David would play the harp and Saul would feel better, and the evil spirit would go away" (1 Samuel 16:23).

King Saul had disobeyed God and the spirit of the Lord had left him. Instead, the Lord had sent a tormenting spirit that filled him with depression and fear. As a result, some of Saul's aides sent for David, who was not only a talented harp player but was handsome, brave and strong and had good, solid judgment. What is more, the Lord was with him.

Every believer experiences warfare between flesh and spirit. As an act of the will we decide whether we are going to allow the flesh or the Spirit to control our lives. One of the best ways to cause an evil spirit to go away is to listen to music of praise and worship and thanksgiving to God. The language of heaven is praise. Listen to music that causes your heart to sing praises to God. Also, saturate your mind with the Word of God. The psalms especially exalt and honor God and express the praise of the psalmist.

I like to begin the day praising God on my knees. During the course of the day, I listen to cassette tapes of praise music as well as recorded portions of Scripture that are appropriate and sermons that are helpful.

Are you discouraged, depressed, frustrated? Have problems in your life caused you to feel that God has left you? If so, may I encourage you to begin to praise the Lord. Purchase cassettes that honor our Lord, that cause your heart to sing and make melody to the Lord, and play them over and over again.

Bible Reading: Psalm 92:1-5

ACTION POINT: Today I will make a special point of praising the Lord not only through the reading of psalms but also by listening to music of praise. I will remember that praise is one of the expressions of a life that is lived in the supernatural power of God.

Is Your Faith Worth Sharing?

"But the path of the just is as the shining light, that shineth more and more unto the perfect day" (Proverbs 4:18, KJV).

I had just finished giving a message, challenging students and young executives to commit their lives to helping to fulfill the Great Commission when Steve approached me with words that shocked me. I had known him for a long time and believed his life to be totally committed to Christ.

"If I were to respond to your challenge to take what I have to the rest of the world," he said, "I'm afraid not much would be accomplished, because my brand of Christianity — quite frankly — is not that attractive, exciting or fruitful."

He went on to share how he was not experiencing the joy of the resurrection in his life. The study of the Word of God had no appeal, his prayer life was nil and it had been a long time since he had introduced anyone to Christ. His outward evidence of being a man of God was just a facade, by his own admission.

What about you? Is your brand of Christianity truly the revolutionary, first-century kind that helped turn the world upside down and that changed the course of history? If not, it can be — and that is what this daily devotional guide is all about.

Every Christian needs to echo daily the sentiments of an unknown poet:

> My life shall touch a dozen lives
> Before this day is done,
> Leave countless marks of good or
>   ill,
> Ere sets the evening sun.
> This, the wish I always wish,
> The prayer I always pray;
> Lord, may my life help other
>   lives
> It touches by the way.

That goal should reign supreme during my waking hours — to touch lives for eternity. For if the all-powerful God, in the Person of His Holy Spirit, truly lives and reigns and triumphs, surely I can tap into that supernatural power and give evidence of it in my life.

Bible Reading: Proverbs 4:14-19

ACTION POINT: Knowing that this dark world desperately needs light, I will trust God to let His light shine through me today. I pray that my life will be so radiant, joyful, attractive and fruitful for Christ that it will demonstrate the kind of Christianity that can be exported to others, to members of my family, neighbors and friends, as well as to people in other countries.

Security for the Children

"Reverence for God gives a man deep strength; his children have a place of refuge and security" (Proverbs 14:26).

Mary, the daughter of African missionaries, recalled how her father — the leader of a large missionary thrust — would on occasion call the family together and share something in his life that he felt was not pleasing to God, which he would confess both to the Lord and to his family whenever they happened to be involved.

This he did for at least two reasons: (1) he had a reverential fear of God, a fear that he might grieve or quench the Spirit by acts of disobedience, and (2) he wanted to be an example to his wife and children, not parading as one who was perfect. Like them, he needed to breathe spiritually, exhaling and confessing his sins whenever he became aware of them, and inhaling and appropriating the fullness of God's Holy Spirit by faith so that he could keep walking in the light as God is in the light.

He would then ask other members of the family if they wanted to share anything in their lives that was grieving or quenching the Spirit, so that together they might pray for each other. This, Mary said, was such an encouragement to her and to other members of the family, helping her to have a greater sense of security and feel-ing of refuge, knowing that her father was a man of God who was honest with the Lord and with his family.

The example of her father and mother had played an important role in inspiring her to become a missionary as well, and now God is using her in a marvelous way for His glory.

In a day when children and young people lack a feeling of security, perhaps more than at any other time in history, it behooves Christian parents to cooperate with God in helping to provide for their families such a sense of security and refuge.

Bible Reading: Proverbs 14:15-21

ACTION POINT: I will begin to pray regularly that God will grant to me an understanding of His attributes as I study His Word so that I will learn to reverence God and thereby provide refuge and security to those who look to me for leadership.

Exalting a Nation

"Godliness exalts a nation, but sin is a reproach to any people" (Proverbs 14:34).

God's Word (1 Timothy 2:2) reminds us that we are to pray for those in authority over us, so that we can live in peace and quietness, spending our time in godly living and thinking much about the Lord.

We should pray daily for all those in authority over us, from the precinct to the White House, and we should seek through the writing of letters and personal appointments to communicate God's love to each one of them, so that they may contribute to those qualities of godliness that will cause the blessing of God to continue to be poured out upon this nation.

One day I walked into a senator's office in Washington, D.C. I had never met the man before, but a mutual friend had suggested that I drop by to see him.

Within a few minutes it seemed as if we had known each other for a lifetime. A natural opportunity arose for me to ask him if he were a Christian, and I was able to share the good news of the gospel with him through the Four Spiritual Laws. Before I left his office, the senator said he would like to receive Christ.

Another time, I spoke at a congressman's home, to which several other congressmen and their wives had been invited. After the meeting, several individuals requested personal appointments.

I went by the office of one of the congressmen the next day.

"Did what I said last night make sense to you?" I asked him.

"It surely did," he replied.

"Would you like to receive Christ?" I asked. He said that he would and knelt beside his couch to pray.

Down the hall, I shared Christ with still another congressman who had been present the night before. He too said he would like to receive Christ. All three of these men and many others continue to walk with God, seeking His wisdom to help them lead our nation wisely.

Because "godliness exalts a nation," we feel it is important for every Christian to pray for and witness to all of our nation's elected officials. Supernatural enablement of the Holy Spirit is available to assist us in our communication.

Bible Reading: Psalm 33:12-16

ACTION POINT: I will pray today for one or more of our nation's leaders, and I will seek opportunities to witness to them and other governmental leaders personally or through correspondence.

Hunger and Thirst

"Blessed are they which do hunger and thirst after righteousness: for they shall be filled" (Matthew 5:6, KJV).

Do you hunger and thirst after righteousness, for the fullness and power of the Holy Spirit in your life? If so, you can claim that fullness and power right now by faith.

"The great difference between present-day Christianity and that of which we read in these letters (New Testament epistles)," declared J. B. Phillips in his introduction to the *Letters to Young Churches,* "is that to us it is primarily a performance; to them it was a real experience.

"We are apt to reduce the Christian religion to a code, or, at best, a rule of heart and life. To these men it is quite plainly the invasion of their lives by a new quality of life altogether. They do not hesitate to describe this as Christ living in them."

The disciples were used of God to change the course of history. As Christian homemakers, students, businessmen and professionals, we have that same potential and privilege today.

The amazing fact that Jesus Christ lives in us and expresses His love through us is one of the most important truths in the Word of God. The standards of the Christian life are so high and so impossible to achieve, ac-cording to the Word of God, that only one person has been able to succeed. That person is Jesus Christ.

When we receive Christ into our lives, we experience a new birth and are also indwelt by the Holy Spirit. From that point on, everything we need — including wisdom, love, power — to be men and women of God and fruitful witnesses for Christ is available to us simply by faith, by claiming this power in accordance with God's promise.

Bible Reading: Romans 10:6-10

ACTION POINT: "Dear Lord, create within me a hunger and thirst after righteousness that is greater than my hunger and thirst for meat and drink for my physical body. By faith I claim the supernatural power of the Holy Spirit to enable me to live a victorious, fruitful life to the glory of God and to share this good news of the Spirit-filled life with everyone who will listen."

Inherit My Holy Mountain

"Let's see if the whole collection of your idols can help you when you cry to them to save you! They are so weak that the wind can carry them off! A breath can puff them away. But he who trusts in Me shall possess the land and inherit My Holy Mountain" (Isaiah 57:13).

It was the very last week prior to our deadline for raising two million dollars to purchase the property at Arrowhead Springs for our international Campus Crusade for Christ headquarters. A dear friend had offered a $300,000 matching fund as a gift if we could raise the balance of the $2 million by a certain date.

Because of a very heavy speaking schedule at both the student and faculty conferences held at Arrowhead, I was unable to make any significant contribution to the raising of funds. And yet somehow in my heart of hearts I knew that God was going to supply our need in a miraculous way.

The late Dr. V. Raymond Edman, then president of Wheaton College, was one of the featured speakers at the conferences. At breakfast, one day Dr. Edman shared with my wife, Vonette, and me this very meaningful verse in Isaiah — a verse that God had impressed upon him that morning to share with us as he prayed about our urgent financial needs.

Now we were all the more encouraged to believe God in an even greater way than before. We truly expected to see Him provide the remaining funds — miraculously. In the evening of the day of the deadline, I was informed that we still needed $33,000 and that every possible source of revenue had been exhausted. There was nothing more, humanly speaking, we could do. Yet, through a series of circumstances between 11:00 and midnight, those funds were pledged, and we met the deadline. Exactly at midnight, the last of God's miracles had been wrought and the goal had been reached. God had promised, "He who trusts in Me shall possess the land and inherit My Holy Mountain" — Arrowhead Springs.

Bible Reading: Isaiah 57:10-15

ACTION POINT: Whether the need be for funds, for health, for wisdom, or whatever, I will believe God to supply my every need as He has so wonderfully promised in His Word to those who trust in Him.

The Kingdom of Heaven

"Happy are those who are persecuted because they are good, for the Kingdom of Heaven is theirs" (Matthew 5:10)

Have you ever been persecuted because of your faith in Christ? If so, how did you respond?

While Francis Xavier was preaching one day in one of the cities of Japan, a man walked up to him as if he had something to say to him privately. As the missionary leaned closer to hear what he had to say, the man spat on his face.

Without a word or the least sign of annoyance, Xavier pulled out a handkerchief and wiped his face. Then he went on with his important message as if nothing had happened. The scorn of the audience was turned to admiration.

The most learned doctor of the city happened to be present.

"A law which teaches men such virtue, inspires them with such courage, and gives them such complete mastery over themselves," he said, "could not but be from God."

Supernatural power and enablement by God's Holy Spirit make that kind of behavior possible for every believer. Furthermore, that kind of behavior probably will do more to attract and influence an unbelieving world than words ever can.

With Christ as our example, love as our motive, and humility as our covering, let us depend on God's Holy Spirit for the wisdom and strength required to respond to mistreatment in a Christlike way. Then, and only then, are we in a position to reflect honor and glory to the Lord Jesus Christ.

Bible Reading: Matthew 5:7-12

ACTION POINT: Mindful that millions of Christians have died as martyrs getting the message of God's good news through to men, and remembering that "all who live godly lives in Christ Jesus shall suffer persecution," I will not shrink from whatever the Lord may have in store for me today as His witness. Drawing upon the supernatural resources of God, I will demonstrate by my words and witness that I belong to Christ.

Don't Worry

"So don't be anxious about tomorrow. God will take care of your tomorrow too. Live one day at a time" (Matthew 6:34).

The taxi driver who drove me from the airport to the hotel in Virginia Beach stated several times that he was having difficulty making ends meet for his wife and 2-year-old son.

He had two jobs and worked seven days a week. Even so, he could hardly get by. The rent was high; the utility bills were extravagant, and he was trying to save enough money so that he could move to another city where the hourly wages were considerably higher. There, he would be able to achieve a better way of life.

I asked him if he went to church.

"No," he said, "I don't have time. I'm too busy."

During the next 30 minutes we talked about the love of God, and God's purpose and plan for men which was revealed to us in the person of Jesus Christ.

"I once went to church as a young man," he said, "and my mother is very religious. In fact, she used to preach to me all the time. But somehow I have gotten away from God and from the church."

I shared with him the *Four Spiritual Laws,* and the prayer: "Lord Jesus, I need You. Thank You for dying on the cross for my sins. I open the door of my life and receive You as my Savior and Lord. Thank You for forgiving my sins and giving me eternal life. Take control of the throne of my life. Make me the kind of person You want me to be."

By the time we reached the hotel, he was ready to pray that prayer in all earnestness, from the depths of his heart. So he offered the prayer, and I prayed with him. And it seemed as though, before my very eyes, the load he had been carrying for so long was lifted and that God, who had made the promise, had already begun to fulfill that promise.

Bible Reading: Matthew 6:28-33

ACTION POINT: Today I will ask God to help me forget the conflicts and unfortunate memories of the past: to take no anxious thought for tomorrow, and to joyfully live in the reality of His supernatural presence and provision.

Anything You Ask

"You can get anything — anything you ask for in prayer — if you believe" (Matthew 21:22).

God's Word reminds us that we have not because we ask not (James 4:2). Jesus said, "If ye abide in Me, and My words abide in you, ye shall ask what ye will, and it shall be done unto you" (John 15:7, KJV).

A godly widow with six children was facing great stress. The family had eaten their last loaf of bread at the evening meal. The next morning, with no food in the house, the trusting mother set seven plates on the table.

"Now, children," she said, gathering them around her, "we must ask God to supply our need."

Just as she finished her prayer, one of the children shouted, "There's the baker at the door."

"I was stalled in the snow," the baker said, after entering the house, "and I just stopped by to get warm. Do you need any bread this morning?"

"Yes," said the mother, "but we have no money."

"Do you mean to say you have no bread for these children?" he asked.

"Not a bit," said the mother.

"Well," said the baker, "you will soon have some." Whereupon he returned to his wagon, picked up seven loaves and brought them into the house. Then he laid one on each plate.

"Mama!" one of the children cried out. "I prayed for bread, and God heard me and sent me bread."

"And me!" chorused each of the children, feeling that God had answered personally.

God does not require us to have great faith. We are simply to have faith in a great God.

Bible Reading: Mark 11:20-26

ACTION POINT: I will continue to abide in Christ and have His Word abide in my heart, so that when needs arise today — whether large or small; physical, material or spiritual — I will choose to place my simple faith in God, knowing that He is willing and able to hear and answer prayer. I will also encourage others to join me in the great adventure of prayer.

Great and Mighty Things

"Call unto Me, and I will answer thee, and shew thee great and mighty things, which thou knowest not" (Jeremiah 33:3, KJV).

How long has it been since you have prayed for great and mighty things — for the glory and praise of God?

I find in God's Word at least six excellent reasons you and I should pray for "great and mighty things": to glorify God; to communicate with God; for fellowship with God; because of Christ's example; to obtain results; and to provide spiritual nurture.

There is a sense in which I pray without ceasing, talking to God hundreds of times in the course of the day about everything. I pray for wisdom about the numerous decisions I must make, for the salvation of friends and strangers, the healing of the sick, and the spiritual and material needs of the Campus Crusade for Christ ministry — as well as for the needs of the various members of the staff and leaders of other Christian organizations and the needs of their ministries.

I pray for the leaders of our nation and for those in authority over us at all levels of government. I even pray about the clothes I wear, on the basis of the people I am to meet — that the way I dress, as well as my words and actions, will bring glory to God.

But there is another sense in which there is a set-apart time each day for prayer — I often kneel quietly before the open Bible and talk with God as I read His Word.

Before I begin to read the Bible, I ask the Holy Spirit, who inspired its writing, to make my reading meaningful. Throughout the reading I often pause to thank God for His loving salvation and provision, to confess the lack in my own life revealed by the Scriptures, to ask Him for the boldness and faith His apostles displayed and to thank Him for new insights into His divine strategy for reaching the world with the gospel.

Bible Reading: Jeremiah 33:4-8

ACTION POINT: Today I will call unto God, expecting Him to show me great and mighty things beyond anything I have ever experienced, for His glory and for the blessing of those about me, that they may know that God does supernatural things in response to the faith and obedience of His children.

The End Will Come

"And the Good News about the Kingdom will be preached throughout the whole world, so that all nations will hear it, and then, finally, the end will come" (Matthew 24:14).

I applaud every effort to warn Christians and nonbelievers to be ready for our Lord's return, as Scripture clearly teaches that He will come again and has delayed His return in order that more people might have a chance to hear the gospel. To this end, we must give priority to taking the gospel to all men everywhere throughout the world.

However, we dare not wrongly interpret the Scriptures, as so many in previous generations have done, resulting in a lack of concern for the souls of men and a failure to correct the evils of society.

God expects us as His children to be His representatives here on earth. We are to love with His love, sharing the message of salvation with all who will listen and helping to meet the needs of widows, orphans and prisoners in His name.

True believers in previous generations have always been at the forefront of moral and social reforms as well as being active in evangelism. Child labor laws, women's suffrage and abolition of slavery, for example, grew out of a mighty spiritual awakening that swept England through the ministry of John Wesley, George Whitefield and their colleagues.

We in our generation must be no less concerned about injustice wherever we find it. The most important way to solve our social ills, however, is to change the hearts of men by introducing them to our Lord Jesus Christ. Our priority commitment as Christians must be to disciple and evangelize in obedience to our Lord's command.

Then we should instruct new believers that "loving our neighbors as ourselves" includes helping them where they hurt. But remember, the Lord cares more about the soul than He does about the body. The body will soon perish but the soul will live forever.

Bible Reading: Matthew 24:7-13

ACTION POINT: I will keep my priorities straight — first sharing the good news of salvation to as many as possible, but at the same time demonstrating love and compassion to widows, orphans, prisoners and all who are in need, in obedience to our Lord's command.

I Am With You Always

"And then teach these new disciples to obey all the commands I have given you; and be sure of this — that I am with you always, even to the end of the world" (Matthew 28:20).

When David Livingstone sailed for Africa the first time, a group of his friends accompanied him to the pier to wish him *bon voyage.*

Concerned for the safety of the missionary, some of his well-wishers reminded him of the dangers which would confront him in the dark land to which he was journeying. One of the men tried to convince him he should remain in England.

Opening his Bible, Livingstone read the six decisive words that had sealed the matter for him long before: "Lo, I am with you always."

Then turning to the man who was especially concerned about his safety, Livingstone smiled before he gave a calm reply.

"That, my friend, is the word of a gentleman," he said. "So let us be going."

For many years, I have visited scores of countries on each continent, each year traveling tens of thousands of miles, as the director of the worldwide ministry of Campus Crusade for Christ. What a joy and comfort it is to know that I am never outside of His care! Whether at home or abroad, He is always with me, even to the end of the world. I can never travel so far away that He is not with me.

And so it is with you, if you have placed your trust and faith in Jesus Christ. You have His indwelling Holy Spirit as your constant companion — the one who makes possible the supernatural life that is the right and privilege of every believer. How important that we never lose sight of this truth: *He is with us always.*

Bible Reading: Matthew 28:16-20

ACTION POINT: Today I am reminded afresh that Jesus, to whom God has given all authority in heaven and earth, is with me; that He will never leave me nor forsake me; that His supernatural power is available to me moment by moment, enabling me to do all that God has called me to do — if only I will trust and obey Him.

We Hear His Voice

"My sheep recognize My voice, and I know them, and they follow Me. I give them eternal life and they shall never perish. No one shall snatch them away from Me, for My Father has given them to Me, and He is more powerful than anyone else, so no one can kidnap them from Me. I and the Father are one" (John 10:27-30).

Are you one of God's "sheep"? Do you know for sure that you are a child of God? Do you have any question about your salvation? How do you know that Christ is in your life and that you have eternal life and that no one can take you away from our Lord? What is the basis of your assurance?

Frequently, one hears a Christian share the dramatic testimony of how Christ changed his life from years of drug addiction, gross immorality or some other distressing problem. On the other hand, there are many, like myself, who have knelt quietly in the privacy of the home, at a mountain retreat, or in a church sanctuary, and there received Christ into their lives with no dramatic emotional experience at that time of decision. Both are valid, authentic ways to come to Christ.

The apostle Paul had a dramatic conversion experience. However, Timothy, his son in the faith, had learned of Christ from his mother and grandmother in his early youth. The important thing is not how you met Christ, but the assurance that you are a child of God, your sins have been forgiven and you have eternal life. It is not presumptuous or arrogant to say that you know these things to be true, because God's Word says so (1 John 5:11-13): "And what is it that God has said? That He has given us eternal life, and that this life is in His Son. So whoever has God's Son has life; whoever does not have His Son, does not have life. I have written this to you who believe in the Son of God so that you may *know* you have eternal life."

Bible Reading: John 10:22-26

ACTION POINT: As one of God's sheep, I will ask the Holy Spirit to help me be more sensitive and alert to the voice of my Savior, in order that I may follow Him more closely and always obey Him, and especially that I may be sensitive to what He would have me say to those around me who are in need of His love and forgiveness.

The Only Way

"Jesus told him, 'I am the Way — yes, and the Truth and the Life. No one can get to the Father except by means of Me' " (John 14:6).

Dr. Bob Pierce, founder of World Vision, was conducting a great city-wide campaign in Tokyo and asked me to be in charge of the student phase of the crusade. So day after day, for more than a month, I spoke to thousands of students on many campuses, presenting the claims of Christ and challenging the students to receive Him as their Savior and Lord.

Many thousands responded, but occasionally a student would object and say that Jesus had no relevance for the Japanese — that Christianity is for the Westerner, not for the Asian. They were surprised when I reminded them that Jesus was born and reared in and carried out His ministry in the Middle East and that He was in many ways closer to them culturally and geographically than He was to me.

I reminded them, and I want to remind you, that though the Lord Jesus Christ was born in Bethlehem and grew up in Nazareth, in what is now Israel, He came to this world to die for all people in all lands.

The Scripture reminds us, "Whosoever will may come." In addition to coming to Him for salvation, Christians have the privilege of coming to God the Father a thousand times, and more, each day in prayer in the name of Jesus. This is because He is our mediator, unlike anyone else who has ever lived — Mohammed, Buddha, Confucius. No other religious leader died for us and was raised from the dead.

Jesus alone can bridge the great chasm between the holiness of God and the sinfulness of man, because He personally has paid the penalty for our sins. God proved His love for us by sending Christ to die for us while we were still in our sins.

Bible Reading: John 14:1-5

ACTION POINT: Today I will ask the Holy Spirit to examine my heart to see if there be any wicked way in me, so that I can confess and turn from my sin. I will visualize our mediator — the Lord Jesus Christ — seated at the right hand of God making intercession for me. I will also ask the Lord to lead me today to someone who does not yet know our Savior, that I may share with him or her the most joyful news ever announced.

PROMISES – DAY 62

Strong and Steady

"And patience develops strength of character in us and helps us trust God more each time we use it until finally our hope and faith are strong and steady" (Romans 5:4).

God's Word communicates the same truth to us in James 1:2-4, "Dear brothers, is your life full of difficulties and temptations? Then be happy, for when the way is rough, your patience has a chance to grow. So let it grow, and don't try to squirm out of your problems. For when your patience is finally in full bloom, then you will be ready for anything, strong in character, full and complete."

Anyone who has ever been used of God in any significant way has learned to be patient. God's ways are not always our ways, and since the just are to live by faith, by faith we can say, "I can trust God. His timing is better than my timing and His ways are better than my own."

Learning the lesson of patience is a lifelong endeavor. But since it is a fruit of the Spirit, it is something we can claim by faith and cultivate at every possible opportunity. On many occasions God has impressed upon me that there were certain things He wanted me to do, but these projects sometimes were not completed for many years after the original impression was given. However, in the process God gave me the ability to be patient, to trust Him, and the reward has been well worth the waiting.

Since we know that God's timing is always perfect, we do well to wait upon Him for answers to our prayers — no matter how urgent they may seem to us at the moment, because our God is never late. He does all things perfectly.

Bible Reading: Romans 5:1-6

ACTION POINT: By faith, I will claim today the help of the Holy Spirit to enable me to be more patient as I live the supernatural life to which God has called me. As I face problems, testings and temptations, I will know that they are for my good, to develop strength of character so that I may serve God more effectively.

Love Means Obedience

"The one who obeys Me is the one who loves Me; and because he loves Me, My Father will love him; and I will too, and I will reveal myself to him" (John 14:21).

A Campus Crusade staff member handed me a copy of *Sports Illustrated* with a cover picture of the Heisman Trophy winner.

Proudly, he said, "I would like to introduce you to your great-grandson."

When I asked him what he meant, he explained. "You led Jim to Christ, Jim led me to Christ, and I led Steve [the Heisman Trophy winner] to Christ."

What a joy to see God's wonderworking power in this chain reaction of spiritual multiplication.

There is something exciting and wonderfully rewarding about seeing one whom you have discipled grow and mature, and lead others to Christ and disciple them, generation after generation. Such an experience often brings even more fulfillment than you derive from your own personal ministry of introducing others to the Lord Jesus.

For example, I have always taken special delight and pleasure whenever Vonette, our sons Zachary and Bradley, or many others whom I have discipled through the years, do something special for the Lord — much more than as though I were doing it personally.

By investing your life in helping others to receive Christ and grow in the Lord, you will in turn be helping still others to experience the abundant life which only true disciples of the Lord Jesus Christ experience. Today's verse equates love for Christ with obedience to His commands. Two of the most important commands our Lord has given to His followers, which will result in His revealing Himself to us, are "Follow Me, and I will make you fishers of men" (Matthew 4:19, NAS); and, "Make disciples of all the nations" (Matthew 28:19, NAS). He is saying to us, "Teach the things that I have taught you."

Bible Reading: John 14:22-26

ACTION POINT: Today I will seek to obey my Lord by telling others about Him and by seeking to disciple others who have already committed their lives to Christ. I have the assurance that my Lord will manifest Himself to me in special ways as I walk in faith and obedience.

How Dearly God Loves Us

"...we are able to hold our heads high no matter what happens and know that all is well, for we know how dearly God loves us, and we feel this warm love everywhere within us because God has given us the Holy Spirit to fill our hearts with His love" (Romans 5:5).

For years I had often spoken on the subject of love — the greatest privilege and power known to man. But, as in the case of most sermons on love, something was missing.

Then many years ago, in an early hour of the morning, I was awakened from a deep sleep. I knew that God had something to say to me. I felt impressed to get up, open my Bible and kneel to read and pray.

What I discovered during the next two hours has since enriched my life and the lives of tens of thousands of others. I learned *how* to love. With this discovery, God gave me the command to share this wonderful truth with Christians around the world.

There are five things every person needs to know about love.

First, God loves us with an unconditional love. The love that God has for us is without measure and will continue forever.

Second, we are commanded to love. " 'Love the Lord your God with all your heart, soul, and mind.' This is the first and greatest commandment," (Matthew 22:37,38). We are commanded to love our neighbors as ourselves and we are even to love our enemies.

Third, we cannot love in our own strength.

Fourth, we *can* love with God's love. It was God's love that brought us to Christ.

Fifth, we love by faith. Everything about the Christian life is based on faith. We love by faith just as we received Christ by faith, just as we are filled with the Holy Spirit by faith and just as we walk by faith.

In 1 John 5:14,15, we read: "And this is the confidence that we have in Him, that, if we ask anything according to His will, He heareth us: And if we know that He hear us, whatsoever we ask, we know that we have the petitions that we desired of Him" (KJV).

Bible Reading: Romans 8:14-17

ACTION POINT: I will make a list of everyone I do not like. Then, on the basis of God's command to love all men, I will claim the promise of 1 John 5:14,15 and begin to love others by faith as a way of life.

No Longer Under Law

"So there is now no condemnation awaiting those who belong to Christ Jesus" (Romans 8:1).

What an exciting fact! We are no longer under the law. We have been liberated from the bondage of trying to please God through our self-effort.

What is our motivation under grace? Under law our motivation was fear, and desire for reward and blessing; under grace, our basic motivation is an expression of gratitude — an inward appreciation and response to God's love and grace.

Why do we do what we do as Christians? We should respond because we, like the apostle Paul, are constrained by the love of Christ. We live for the glory of God. You will remember that the apostle Paul had been beaten, imprisoned, shipwrecked, starved, buffeted, criticized and condemned, yet he said, "The love of Christ constrains me."

Even if there were no rewards for those who live godly lives and obey our Savior, the reward of knowing Him as our God and Father, being forgiven of sin and cleansed from all guilt, is more than just enough; it is unfathomable. We can know Him, love Him, worship Him and serve Him by faith — here and now!

A young man I know is writing a book on how to become rich in the kingdom of God. He is basing his theme on the rewards that will be his by winning souls. "I want to be rich in heaven," he says.

That may be a worthwhile goal, but it is not mine. Mine is gratitude and love. I love Him because He first loved me — died for me, liberated me, set me free.

Bible Reading: Romans 8:2-6

ACTION POINT: I will sing praises and give thanks in my heart to the Lord upon every remembrance of the liberty and grace that is mine in Christ Jesus, and I will tell everyone who will listen that we are no longer in bondage to sin, for Christ has set us free.

Share His Treasures

"For His Holy Spirit speaks to us deep in our hearts, and tells us that we really are God's children. And since we are His children, we will share His treasures — for all God gives to His Son Jesus is now ours too. But if we are to share His glory, we must also share His suffering" (Romans 8:16,17).

You may cringe, as I do, at the thought of suffering for Jesus. As He reminds us in Mark 10, anything we ever give up for Him will be given to us a hundred times over, with persecution. Quite frankly, I have never relished the thought of being persecuted. Yet, again and again, in my own experience I have known the reality of that supernatural presence of God, that peace that passes all understanding, during times of suffering and persecution.

Our Lord Himself, knowing that He was on His way to the cross, spoke of peace, love and joy more than at any other time in His ministry. The apostle Paul knew all kinds of suffering. He was in prison frequently; he was beaten, and he finally died as a martyr for his faith. Yet, even while in prison, he wrote of joy and peace — "Count it all joy," he said. "Rejoice ever more."

Philippians 3:10 records the desire of his heart: "That I may know Him, and the power of His resurrection, and the fellowship of His sufferings, being made conformable unto His death" (KJV). Apart from the fellowship of His sufferings, Paul knew that he would never mature and become like the Lord Jesus Christ. "Adversity is the touchstone of character."

All men suffer; however, the disobedient Christians and the unbelievers suffer far more than the obedient, Spirit-filled Christians, because most of the problems of life are self-imposed and when they suffer, they suffer alone, for they are on their own. But the Spirit-filled, obedient, faithful servant of God always knows the reality of God's faithfulness.

Bible Reading: Romans 8:18-23

ACTION POINT: Since it is my desire to be conformed to the image of Christ, to share His glory and His treasure, I will gladly share His suffering, knowing that He will be with me, ministering to me, caring for me, enveloping me with His love and peace. And I will share this word of encouragement with others who may not understand the faithfulness of God.

You Can Bear It

"There hath no temptation taken you but such as is common to man: but God is faithful, who will not suffer you to be tempted above that ye are able: but will with the temptation also make a way to escape, that ye may be able to bear it" (1 Corinthians 10:13, KJV).

I find great comfort and encouragement in this promise from God, one of my favorite Scriptures. Believing in this promise has saved me from falling into sin more times than I could ever begin to count.

As Christians, we are on the offensive. We do not have to cringe, trembling in our boots, wondering when Satan is going to attack again and what form it will take. We are the ones on the move. We are to be the aggressors, for we have God's promise that the gates of hell shall not prevail against us (Matthew 16:18).

There is no stronghold of Satan that cannot be recaptured for our Lord, who promises to fight for us. God's Word reminds us that all authority in heaven and on earth is given to the Lord Jesus, and He promises always to be with us, never to leave us.

Satan would have you believe that there is no hope for you. You are discouraged, you have financial problems, physical problems, sorrow from losing loved ones. The whole world seems to be caving in on you, and Satan says, "God doesn't love or care for you. He can't help you. You're on your own. You might as well give up."

When that temptation comes, we cry out to God in believing prayer and we resist the enemy who is the author of depression. He is the author of negative thinking. He is the author of criticism, lies and all things that are contrary to the will of God.

If we are going to take a proper offense, we must live in the power of the Holy Spirit. That is the reason our Savior — after commanding the disciples to go and preach the gospel to all men everywhere — also commanded them to wait in Jerusalem until they were endued with power from on high. "Ye shall receive power, after that the Holy Ghost is come upon you: and ye shall be witnesses unto me both in Jerusalem, and in all Judea, and in Samaria, and unto the uttermost part of the earth" (Acts 1:8, KJV).

The key to escaping temptation and resisting sin is faith in the faithfulness of God to keep His promise that you will not be tempted more than you are able to bear.

Bible Reading: 1 Corinthians 10:9-12

ACTION POINT: I will not go into the spiritual battle unarmed, but will count on God's Holy Spirit to make a way of escape when temptation comes. I will tell others how they too can be victorious over temptation.

More and More Like Him

"The Lord is the Spirit who gives them life, and where He is there is freedom (from trying to be saved by keeping the laws of God). But we Christians have no veils over our faces; we can be mirrors that brightly reflect the glory of the Lord. And as the Spirit of the Lord works within us, we become more and more like Him" (2 Corinthians 3:17,18).

You and I can be mirrors that reflect the glory of the Lord, since we have no veils over our faces. As the Spirit of the Lord works within us and we mature, we become more and more like Him. What a tremendous truth!

Two tendencies to error occur as we consider the concept of law and grace. One is legalism; the other is license. Legalism is that means of seeking to live according to the law, trying to merit God's favor by keeping rules and regulations in the energy of the flesh.

The other problem is license. Some Christians become so excited about their freedom in Christ that they go overboard and bring reproach and disgrace to the name of Christ. "Relax," they say. "Do what comes naturally." But they forget God's warning in Romans 14. Anything we do that causes our brother to stumble is sin. Often these same Christians tell us, "Don't witness for Christ unless you feel like it."

Quite honestly, I would not witness very often if I waited until I felt like it.

Why do I witness? Because our Lord modeled it and He commands His followers to witness, and out of a deep sense of gratitude and thanksgiving to God for what He has done for me. I do not wait until I feel like it; I have already been given the command.

Jesus said, "Follow Me and I will make you fishers of men." The apostle Paul said, "Everywhere I go I tell everyone who will listen about Christ." We are not to wait for some emotional, mystical impression of the Spirit. Liberty is not legalism, nor is it license. It is the privilege of doing the will of God in the power of the Holy Spirit.

Bible Reading: 2 Corinthians 3:8-16

ACTION POINT: With all of my heart, I want to be more and more like Jesus Christ. To this end, I will avoid legalism and license and embrace the freedom I have in Him to live a holy life and to be a fruitful witness, and to reach out to the multitudes of unchurched men and women who are hungry to know the reality of the living God.

His Power to Change

"But our homeland is in heaven, where our Savior the Lord Jesus Christ is; and we are looking forward to His return from there. When He comes back He will take these dying bodies of ours and change them into glorious bodies like His own, using the same mighty power that He will use to conquer all else everywhere" (Philippians 3:20,21).

George Gallup, Jr., a deeply religious man and dear personal friend, has just completed a very important survey asking people, in face-to-face, in-depth interviews, key questions about heaven and hell and other aspects about life beyond death.

One result indicated that two-thirds of all American adults — or 100 million people — believe in an after-life. But what was surprising, said Gallup, was that about 15 percent of those surveyed in one poll indicated they had had an unusual near-death experience — seeing figures or objects that beckoned them to a world beyond life on earth.

Dwight L. Moody caught a glimpse of the glory awaiting him a few hours before leaving this earth for his heavenly mansion.

"Earth recedes, heaven opens before me," he said, awakening from a sleep. "If this is death, it is sweet. There is no valley here. God is calling me, and I must go."

A son stood by his bedside. "No, no, father," he said, "you are dreaming."

"No," said Moody, "I am not dreaming. I have been within the gates. I have seen the children's faces."

A short time passed, then followed what his family thought to be the death struggle. "This is my triumph," Moody said. "This is my coronation day. It is glorious!"

Nothing in that true story contradicts Scripture in any way. One of God's choice saints simply had a foretaste of his heavenly home, related for our joy and encouragement and edification.

Bible Reading: John 14:1-6

ACTION POINT: Realizing afresh that my homeland is in heaven with my Savior, the Lord Jesus Christ, and that the time of my departure from this earth is unknown but certain, I shall take advantage of every opportunity to encourage others to be ready for their time of departure, as I prepare for my own.

Thank Him for Answers

"Don't worry about anything; instead, pray about everything; tell God your needs and don't forget to thank Him for His answers. If you do this you will experience God's peace, which is far more wonderful than the human mind can understand. His peace will keep your thoughts and your hearts quiet and at rest as you trust in Christ Jesus" (Philippians 4:6,7).

Some years ago there was an occasion when my world was crumbling. All that my associates and I had worked and planned for in the ministry of Campus Crusade for Christ was hanging by a slender thread which was about to break.

Because of a series of unforeseen circumstances, we were facing a financial crisis which could bankrupt the movement and result in the loss of our beautiful facilities at Arrowhead Springs, California, acquired just a few years earlier.

Already thousands of students and laymen from all over the world were receiving training which would influence millions of of lives for Christ. Now we were in danger of losing it all.

When the word came to me that everything we had planned and prayed for was in jeopardy and almost certain to be lost, I fell to my knees and began to give thanks to the Lord. Why?

Because many years before I had discovered that thanksgiving demonstrates faith, and faith pleases God. When we demonstrate faith through thanksgiving, as an expression of obedience and gratitude to God, He releases His great power in our behalf so that we can serve Him better. Miraculously, God honored our faith and what could have been disaster and tragedy turned to victory and triumph. The end result was that we were stronger financially than we had ever been.

God fights the battles for those who trust and obey Him.

Bible Reading: I Timothy 2:1-6

ACTION POINT: With God's help, my life will be characterized by praise and thanksgiving to God as an expression of my faith in Him and obedience to His commands. Today I will share the goodness and trustworthiness of God with at least one other person.

Nothing Against You

"This includes you who were once so far away from God. You were his enemies and hated him and were separated from him by your evil thoughts and actions, yet now He has brought you back as His friends. He has done this through the death on the cross of His own human body, and now as a result Christ has brought you into the very presence of God, and you are standing there before Him with nothing left against you — nothing left that He could ever chide you for" (Colossians 1:21,22).

Have you ever claimed your right to holiness, not by virtue of anything you have done, but on the basis of what Christ has done and is doing for you?

This passage of Scripture explains how holiness is available to every believer. By acknowledging and receiving His gift of eternal life through Christ, we have been brought into the very presence of God. Now we are candidates for the supernatural filling of the Holy Spirit.

After we have claimed our right to holiness, we must confess all our known sins and appropriate, by faith, the fullness of the Holy Spirit, asking Him to give us spiritual insight into the true meaning of God's Word.

"And so, dear brothers, I plead with you to give your bodies to God. Let them be a living sacrifice, holy — the kind He can accept. When you think of what He has done for you, is this too much to ask? Don't copy the fashions and customs of this world, but be a new and different person with a fresh newness in all you do and think. Then you will see from your own experience how His ways will really satisfy you" (Romans 12:1,2).

Bible Reading: 2 Corinthians 5:17-21

ACTION POINT: By faith I will claim my right to holiness and, on the basis of Christ's finished work on the cross in our behalf, I will encourage others to do the same.

Truly Rich

"Do you want to be truly rich? You already are if you are happy and good. After all, we didn't bring any money with us when we came into the world, and we can't carry away a single penny when we die" (1 Timothy 6:6,7).

If you had the choice of choosing between great wealth and good health and a happy, joyful relationship with our Lord, which would you choose? Though many would choose wealth I am sure that if you are a Christian, you would gladly choose to live modestly the rest of your life if necessary in order to experience daily the joy of your salvation.

During all of my career, I, an agnostic, had worked hard to successfully develop my business interests. Then, in the providence of God, I was brought face to face with Christ and His Word. "What does it profit a man if he gain the whole world and lose his own soul?"

It was as though God touched my mind to enable me to understand that I could eat only one meal at a time, wear one suit of clothes at a time and take nothing with me when I die. I understood for the first time that being truly rich does not involve the accumulation of vast wealth, but it involves knowing and doing the will of God — in walking in intimate, vital, personal fellowship with Him daily as a way of life.

Fanny Crosby, the hymnwriter, gave us more than eight thousand gospel songs. Although blinded at the age of six weeks, she never held any bitterness in her heart because of it.

"I think it is a great pity that the Master did not give you sight when He showered so many other gifts upon you," a friend once said to her.

"Do you know," she responded quickly, "that if at birth I had been able to make one petition, it would have been that I should be born blind."

"Why?" asked the astounded clergyman.

"Because," she replied, "when I get to heaven, the first face that shall ever gladden my sight will be that of my Savior."

Bible Reading: Luke 12:25-31

ACTION POINT: As I figuratively sit at God's banquet table today, I will feast upon His spiritual bounties and not be satisfied with the crumbs of materialism.

Supernatural Wisdom — by Faith

"If you want to know what God wants you to do, ask Him, and He will gladly tell you, for He is always ready to give a bountiful supply of wisdom to all who ask Him; He will not resent it" (James 1:5).

Often — many times a day — I need divine wisdom, not only in the multitudes of decisions that I must make daily, but also in the witnessing situations the Lord brings across my path. No doubt you recognize a similar need in your life.

All I have to do to have His presence guide me, if my heart is right with Him, is to ask in faith, and He promises the wisdom I need for each day and for each moment of the day.

If we are going to live supernatural lives, and if we are going to demonstrate to others that they, too, can live such a life, then we must begin to think and act differently. And that is possible only as we go to the source of all divine wisdom.

This verse from Scripture assures us that God's ear is always open to this kind of prayer. And of course the wisdom to which James refers is more than factual knowledge. It is the light of life, in which we can walk without stumbling.

Why does one need to pray to gain this wisdom? Perhaps because prayer is humbling and involves an acknowledgment of our inadequacy. Prayer opens our hearts and lives to the transforming influence of the Spirit of God.

Bible Reading: James 1:6-12

ACTION POINT: Knowing that I need God's wisdom if I am to serve Him effectively and please Him today, I will obey Him — and claim His supernatural work in my life — by asking for His wisdom when I face a decision.

Praying for Me

"Wherefore He is able also to save them to the uttermost that come unto God by Him, seeing He ever liveth to make intercession for them" (Hebrews 7:25, KJV).

George had tried to live a Christian life for many years, but finally gave up.

"It's no use," he said. 'I have tried and tried and failed and failed. I have dedicated, rededicated, consecrated and reconsecrated my life to Christ, and nothing happens. I am a total failure."

Whereupon I read him this and several other key verses of Scripture, emphasizing the role that Christ plays in our behalf at the right hand of the Father.

"Did it ever occur to you," I asked, "that Jesus right now is aware of your every need and is interceding for you?"

That very thought overwhelmed him, and he fell to his knees with tears of gratitude.

"Oh," he said, "I knew that Jesus died for me and shed His blood for my sins. But somehow I had never made the connection between the cross and His present role of interceding for me."

"If I could hear Christ praying for me in the next room," declared the famous Christian statesman, Robert Murray McCheyne, "I would not fear a million enemies. Yet distance makes no difference. He is praying for me. 'He ever liveth to make intercession.' "

When Satan tempts me with discouragement and frustration, often I can visualize a scene that brings instant victory over the enemy. At the right hand of God is a room — a prayer room, if you please — and kneeling there is the Lord Jesus Christ Himself, praying specifically for me and my needs. *He is interceding for me!*

Bible Reading: Romans 8:31-34

ACTION POINT: I will allow no burden or problem or need or frustration or discouragement to defeat me any longer. Instead, I will visualize Christ Himself praying for me, and since all authority in heaven and earth belongs to Him, I will expect victory over Satan and all the unseen forces of evil in order that I may live a supernatural life according to my spiritual heritage. I will also seek to share this exciting truth with someone else today. Oh, what good news to share!

Tried in the Test Tube

"These trials are only to test your faith, to see whether or not it is strong and pure. It is being tested as fire tests gold and purifies it — and your faith is far more precious to God than mere gold; so if your faith remains strong after being tried in the test tube of fiery trials, it will bring you much praise and glory and honor on the day of His return" (1 Peter 1:7).

A friend of mine has experienced great tragedy in his life — at least ten major things that seem to have gone wrong.

"I see you as a man of God," I have said to him during several counseling sessions. "I see you as a man who loves the Lord Jesus with all of your heart. In light of all the things that are happening to you, however, I am prompted to ask, 'Is there any sin in your life? Are you doing anything to dishonor the Lord?' "

"Absolutely nothing," he said. "My life is transparent before God. He can do anything He wants with me. I have turned my back on business success [he was an outstanding businessman], and I have given everything I have to the Lord."

The beautiful thing about this whole experience is that this man is rejoicing in the Lord Jesus while enduring things that would break the average person. Every time he emerges from a crisis, his face seems to glow all the more. He is praising God all the more.

He blesses me every time I am with him. "Lord, thank You," I say. "Thank You for his example."

Those who are mightily used of God often experience, like Job, some degree of adversity. Such adversity may be God's discipline for disobedience and unconfessed sin, or it may be — as in the case of Job, and I believe in the case of my friend — God's way of preparing you for a greater testimony for our Lord. "Whom the Lord loveth He chasteneth."

Bible Reading: James 1:2-5

ACTION POINT: I will look upon my trials as part of God's way of strengthening my faith and my life to prepare me for a more powerful witness for His glory.

Do the Will of God

"And the world is fading away, and these evil, forbidden things will go with it, but whoever keeps doing the will of God will live forever" (1 John 2:17).

There are few questions more frequently asked of me than this, "How can I know God's will for my life?" or "How can I know what God wants me to do in this particular situation?"

"When I was crossing the Irish Channel one starless night," said F. B. Meyer, a saint of yesteryear, "I stood on the deck by the captain and asked him, 'How do you know Holyhead Harbor on so dark a night as this?'

"'You see those three lights?' he asked. 'All of them must line up together as one, and when we see them so united, we know the exact position of the harbor's mouth.'

"When we want to know God's will, there are three things which always concur: the inward impulse, the Word of God and the trend of circumstances — God in the heart and God in circumstances, indicating His will. Never start until these three things agree."

If we are to keep doing the will of God, as this verse in 1 John suggests, it is of course imperative that we know how to determine the will of God. F. B. Meyer's words of wisdom, based on years of experience, are a good starting point.

The average person lives his life, dies and vanishes from the world scene, soon to be forgotten. But the influence of all who do God's will lives on forever. Therefore, every individual should frequently and carefully evaluate how he invests his time, talents and treasure to be sure he truly is living not for worldly values but for the cause of Jesus Christ.

"Only one life, 'twill soon be past; only what's done for Christ will last."

Bible Reading: Romans 12:1-3

ACTION POINT: As clearly as I am able to discern God's will for my life, I will follow Him and do His will instead of following the ways of the anti-God world system which is fading away.

Father and Son

"For a person who doesn't believe in Christ, God's Son, can't have God the Father either. But he who has Christ, God's Son, has God the Father also" (1 John 2:23).

An angry young student leader of a leftist movement approached me after one of my lectures on campus.

"I resent your poisoning the minds of these students with your religious ideas," he said, obviously trying to start an argument.

Instead of responding in kind, I asked him to come to our home for dinner where we could talk quietly and more in depth. He accepted the invitation.

After dinner, we discussed our individual views concerning God and man and the way we felt our ideas could best help man to maximize his potential. He objected when I started to read from the Bible.

"I don't believe anything in the Bible," he said.

"Well," I said, "if you don't mind, I would like to read you a few portions of Scripture which will help you better understand why I became a Christian after many years of agnosticism. I didn't believe in God or the Bible either, but something wonderful happened to me which changed my thinking — in fact, my whole way of life. These are some of the Scriptures which made a great impression on my thinking, and I would like to share them with you."

Reluctantly he agreed to listen. So I read portions of John 1, Hebrews 1 and Colossians, finally coming to this key verse in 1 John. My new student friend asked questions along the way. Before leaving that night, the miracle occurred and he wrote in our guest book, "The night of decision."

Bible Reading: 1 John 4:14-17

ACTION POINT: Rather than try to defend the supernatural Word of God, I will simply present it in the power of the Holy Spirit and let the Word of God be its own defense.

Not Hard at All

"Loving God means doing what He tells us to do, and really that isn't hard at all; for every child of God can obey Him, defeating sin and evil pleasure by trusting Christ to help him" (1 John 5:3,4).

I believe that we are on the threshold of witnessing the greatest spiritual revival in the history of the church. I believe that the Great Commission will indeed be fulfilled before the return of our Lord Jesus Christ (Matthew 28:19,20; Mark 13:10).

Today, however, because of the subtle ways of the world system, there are more carnal Christians than at any other time in history. But the Bible tells us that the tide will turn and that the church will soon enter its finest hour.

We are beginning to see that turning of the tide. More and more Christians are discovering how to live supernaturally in the power and control of the Holy Spirit. The gospel is being spread throughout the world by many committed Christians who are determined, by faith, to help fulfill the Great Commission in this generation, whatever the cost.

I do not know anyone, however, who loves this world system who has ever been used of God in any significant way. There is nothing wrong with money and other material success. However, we are to wear the cloak of materialism loosely. We are to set our affection on Christ and His kingdom, not on the material things of this world.

The Lord left us with this wonderful promise: ". . .every child of God can obey Him, defeating sin and evil pleasure by trusting Christ to help him." Inviting Christ to help us is our decision to make. It is simply a matter of the will.

Bible Reading: 1 John 5:1-8

ACTION POINT: I will obey God and trust Christ to defeat sin and evil pleasure in my life, so that I can live a supernatural life and help take His gospel to all men throughout the world.

Praise Brings Blessings

"Go through His open gates with great thanksgiving; enter His courts with praise. Give thanks to Him and bless His name. For the Lord is always good. He is always loving and kind, and His faithfulness goes on and on to each succeeding generation" (Psalm 100:4,5).

I would like to suggest several reasons why I believe praising God is so important in the life of the believer.

First, God is truly worthy of praise. He is worthy of praise because of who He is and because of all He has done for us. The psalmist reminds us, "Praise the Lord! Yes, really praise Him! I will praise Him as long as I live, yes, even with my dying breath" (Psalm 146:1,2).

We praise God for who He is and for His attributes — His love, His sovereignty, His wisdom, His power, His greatness, goodness and compassion, His faithfulness, His holiness and His eternal, unchanging nature.

These and other characteristics of God are described in many passages. Three of my favorites are Isaiah 40, Psalm 139 and Psalms 145-150.

Second, we praise God for His benefits to us. Though too numerous to mention, some of them are expressed in Psalm 103.

No wonder the psalmist concluded this list of great benefits by calling upon all who read this passage, "Let everything everywhere bless [praise] the Lord. And how I bless [praise] Him too!"

Yes, we are to praise God first of all because of who He is, and then we are to praise Him for His blessings to us. We should never take for granted the benefits we enjoy as a result of belonging to Him.

Bible Reading: Psalm 103:1-8

ACTION POINT: Praise toward God throughout the day will be on my lips as I recall His many attributes and all His benefits to me.

God Answers While We Are Praying

"So don't worry at all about having enough food and clothing. Why be like the heathen? For they take pride in all these things and are deeply concerned about them. But your heavenly Father already knows perfectly well that you need them, and He will give them to you if you give Him first place in your life and live as He wants you to" (Matthew 6:31-33).

Whenever God impresses you with a need, you can always be assured that He will supply that need, often through others.

I remember the first time I asked God for a specific amount of money. We needed $485 for a particular ministry. While I was still on my knees in prayer, there came a knock at the door and the mailman handed me a registered letter containing a check for $500. Earlier, a young man from Zurich, Switzerland, had written his parents that he had received Christ through our ministry at UCLA, and he mentioned my name as one who had helped him. His parents and their daughter had then flown all the way from Zurich to California to learn how they also could become Christians. God honored their desire and after prayer and counsel they had gone home rejoicing in the assurance of their salvation. Now they were writing and sending this generous check to express their gratitude.

Later, we needed $10,000, and God impressed us to pray for that amount. An hour after we prayed, a man whom I did not know well called to say, "I am a new Christian, and I don't know how God speaks to man, but you have been on my mind all day, so I thought it might be that God was trying to tell me something. I thought I would just call to see if you have a need."

I told him we had just prayed for $10,000. He said, "That's a lot of money, but I'll call you back in an hour."

An hour later he called to say he would send a check the next day for $10,000 as a loan without interest. He added, "If God continues to bless me and my business, I will give you the money."

God greatly blessed his faith and obedience, and a year later the loan became a gift. God has graciously demonstrated His faithfulness on thousands of occasions and often in even greater ways.

For those who seek first God's kingdom, He promises, "I will answer them before they even call Me. While they are still talking to Me about their needs, I will go ahead and answer their prayers" (Isaiah 65:24). If our hearts and motives are pure and we seek always to please Him in what we do, we can never ask Him for too much. We can always be assured that our faithful God will answer us as we pray in accordance with His Word and will.

Bible Reading: Matthew 6:24-33

ACTION POINT: I will remember the faithfulness of God, that so long as my heart and my motives are pure and I pray according to His Word and will, He will hear me and answer me even before I pray.

How to Gain Understanding

"For ever, O Lord, Thy Word is settled in heaven. Thy faithfulness is unto all generations" (Psalm 119:89,90, KJV).

A story is told of a young woman who had been informed about a famous novel. She was interested in reading it, but as she began to read the novel, she found it dry and uninteresting. She would put it down to read something else, and then she would come back and try to read it again because her friends said it was an excellent book.

Even with the high recommendations of her friends, the book just did not captivate her. Then one day she met the author. He was very handsome and personable. They became interested in each other, and she fell in love with him.

Now she could hardly wait to read the novel. It was the most exciting book she had ever read, for she had fallen in love with the author.

This is what happens with the Scriptures when we love the Author, the Lord Jesus Christ.

During my years of skepticism and agnosticism, I found the Bible very dry and difficult to read and I believed it was filled with "all kinds of errors and inconsistencies." Then after becoming a Christian I began to read the Bible again. It was a completely different book, filled with exciting, life-changing truth. All the "errors and contradic-

tions" were gone.

Why the difference? The non-believer or disobedient Christian does not understand spiritual truth (1 Corinthians 2:14). The Spirit-filled believer is taught by the Holy Spirit, who illumines the truth which He revealed to the original authors as recorded in the Bible.

Bible Reading: Psalm 119:129-136

ACTION POINT: I will ask God to give me a love for His holy, inspired Word. Then things that happen in my life which I do not understand will be made clear as I go to the source of all true understanding, the Word of God.

Loving and Kind

"But His joy is in those who reverence Him, those who expect Him to be loving and kind" (Psalm 147:11).

C an you imagine an intelligent person saying no to Christ if he fully understood how much God loves him and if he realized that when he receives Christ his sins are all forgiven and he is given eternal life together with new meaning and purpose for his present life?

The non-believer who does not know all these things continues to live in disobedience, rejecting God's love and forgiveness. Why? Simply because he does not understand; he lacks information.

It is difficult to imagine a person saying no to such a wonderful life of challenge and adventure with the risen Christ if that person knows all the facts about who Christ is and why He came to this world.

It is the same with the Christian who is living in spiritual poverty. He often continues to live a frustrated, fruitless life, simply because he just does not understand who the Holy Spirit is and what the supernatural life is all about. But lack of knowledge is not the only obstacle to enjoying the supernatural life.

Pride: Pride, which is an exaltation of self instead of God, is the root cause of all sin. This defeating aspect of our human nature has kept many Chris-

tians from living supernaturally. Pride is not the same as a God-given healthy love and acceptance of oneself.

Fear of man: Peer pressure keeps many Christians from living the supernatural life. "The fear of man brings a snare" (Proverbs 29:25, NAS).

Many are afraid to be different, or are ashamed to witness for Jesus Christ who loved us and gave Himself for us. "But His joy is in those who reverence Him, those who expect Him to be loving and kind."

Bible Reading: Psalm 147:5-10

ACTION POINT: I will claim the enabling power of the Holy Spirit to overcome pride and fear of man, I will reverence the Lord and expect Him to be loving and kind as He promised.

According to Your Faith

"Then touched He their eyes, saying, According to your faith be it unto you" (Matthew 9:29, KJV).

A poor heathen woman, after receiving Christ as her Savior, was remarkable for her simple faith. She decided to take Him literally at His word.

A few months after her conversion her little child became ill, and recovery was doubtful. Ice was needed for the little one, but in that tropical country, away from the world's large cities, such a thing was not to be had.

"I'm going to ask God to send ice," the mother said to a missionary.

"Oh," came the quick reply, "but you can't expect that He will do that."

"Why not?" asked the simple-hearted believer. "He has all the power, and He loves us. You told us so. I'll ask Him, and I believe He'll send it."

She did ask Him, and strange things began to happen. Soon there came up a heavy thunderstorm, accompanied by hail. The woman was able to gather a large quantity of hailstones. The cold application was just what the child needed. Recovery of the sick child soon followed. In our sophistication and intellectualism we, like the missionary and most other Christians, would tend to question the audacity of such a prayer.

Faith as a little child always brings the desired answer. "According to your faith be it unto you." And where does such faith originate? "Faith comes by hearing, and hearing by the Word of God."

Bible Reading: Matthew 9:27-31

ACTION POINT: If my storehouse of faith proves insufficient to enable me to live supernaturally or to believe God for a specific need, I will spend time in His Word to build up that storehouse of faith.

Our Hearts' Desires

"Therefore I say unto you, What things soever ye desire, when ye pray, believe that ye receive them, and ye shall have them" (Mark 11:24, KJV).

Jesus, assuming that our lives are pure and we are Spirit-filled, declares that our heartfelt desires will be God-given. When God gives us those desires, He then gives us the power to fullfill them (Philippians 2:13). Sometimes when God gives you a desire that is based upon Scripture, one that springs from pure motives and a desire to glorify Him, that desire may continue over a period of time as you continue in the spirit of prayer and seek counsel of other godly people who also walk in the Spirit, but you can be assured that whatever God has placed in your heart, He will do.

For example, one of the great desires of my heart as a new Christian was to produce a film on the life of Jesus. I contacted and sought the counsel of the late Cecil B. De Mille who produced the magnificent "King of Kings," which, after more than fifty years is still being viewed by millions of people each year throughout the world. I continued to pray and many years later discussed with members of our Board of Directors whether or not we should produce such a film. They encouraged me to do whatever God led me to do, but made it clear that funds would have to be available before we could produce the film. The years passed — more than

thirty years, in fact. Then miracle of miracles, in a marvelous way at Arrowhead Springs God brought together John Heyman, a well-known film producer and director, and Bunker and Caroline Hunt to provide the finances, and the film, *Jesus*, became a dramatic reality.

Already, this film has been translated into more langues than any film in history and it is our goal to complete the translation into at least 271 langues which will represent every group in the world with a million or more population. We expect to have at least 2,000 teams showing the film each night to as many as four million people or even more when this massive project is in full swing. It is our prayerful objective that at least one billion people will be introduced to a personal relationship with Jesus Christ through the ministry of this film.

My point is, the desire was placed in my heart and, though that desire did not continue on a daily basis, from time to time God would remind me and I would pray for and claim again by faith the fulfillment of that dream. And now, years later, this desire is becoming a joyful reality.

Bible Reading: Psalm 21:1-7

ACTION POINT: Whenever a desire to do something special for God is impressed upon my mind and heart, I will check to see if it is scriptural, and if it will bring glory to God. When it meets all biblical standards and the counsel of godly people, I will believe God for its supernatural fulfillment.

Cheer Up; He Has Overcome

"I have told you all this so that you will have peace of heart and mind. Here on earth you will have many sorrows and trials; but cheer up, for I have overcome the world" (John 16:33).

I know of few promises in all the Word of God that offer more assurance and encouragement than this one.

The apostle Paul was an aggressive soldier of God who carried the gospel far and wide throughout the known world. He was greatly used of God to expand the territorial borders of Christendom. All that Paul did, he did in the name of Christ and through the power and control of the Holy Spirit.

But there was great opposition to Paul's ministry. Consequently, he always seemed to be in the center of spiritual warfare. He knew his enemies, Satan and the world system, and their subtle, deceiving devices.

Throughout his Christian life, he suffered various kinds of persecutions, including stonings, beatings and imprisonment. In spite of such harsh persecution, Paul could write, "Rejoice in the Lord always; again, I will say, rejoice" (Philippians 4:4, NAS).

It was during Paul's imprisonment in Rome, about 61 or 62 A.D., that he wrote to the church at Ephesus. The theme of his letter is supernatural living, and he talks about the Christian's spiritual warfare. He tells us that the battle we fight is against Satan and the spiritual forces of wickedness, not against other people.

The apostle Paul experienced the supernatural peace of heart and mind which Jesus promised, a promise which we too can claim, in times of difficulty, testing and even persecution.

Bible Reading: John 16:25-32

ACTION POINT: Today I will claim the peace of heart and mind which Jesus promised to all who trust and obey Him. Deliberately and faithfully I will seek to put on the whole armor of God so that I will be fully prepared to withstand the wiles of the enemy and thus live a supernatural life for the glory of God.

We Are Each a Part

"Each of us is a part of the one body of Christ. Some of us are Jews, some are Gentiles, some are slaves and some are free. But the Holy Spirit has fitted us all together into one body. We have been baptized into Christ's body by the one Spirit, and have all been given that same Holy Spirit" (1 Corinthians 12:13).

I find that most Christians agree that the Holy Spirit baptizes the believer into the Body of Christ, as this verse affirms. But the unity of the body is divided here on earth by many differences of interpretation concerning a "second baptism," speaking in tongues and "Spirit-filling."

Most believers agree, however, that we are commanded to live holy lives and the Holy Spirit supernaturally makes this human impossibility a reality. He does this when we totally submit ourselves to His indwelling love and power. Or, to use a metaphor of the apostle Paul, "For all of you who were baptized into Christ have clothed yourselves in Christ" (Galatians 3:27, NAS).

In His high-priestly prayer, our Lord prayed that we who are believers may be one with Him, even as He and the Father were one. We are commanded to love one another. "By this shall all men know that ye are my disciples, if ye have love one to another" (John 13:35, KJV). No one who criticizes his brother is Spirit-filled. No one who sows discord among his brethren is Spirit-filled. In fact, the test as to whether or not we are controlled by the Holy Spirit is how we love our brothers.

It is my joy and privilege to know most of the famous Christian leaders of our time, men and women whom God is using in a mighty way to help change our nation and some other nations of the world with the gospel. How I rejoice at every good report that comes to me of God's blessing upon their lives and ministries. In fact, it is one way of checking my own walk with Christ. If I were jealous and critical, fault-finding and sowing discord, I would know that I am not walking in the light as God is in the light.

Bible Reading: 1 Corinthians 12:14-20

ACTION POINT: I will not allow my interpretation of the Spirit-filled life to separate me from other members of the body of Christ, but will love them and seek to promote unity among believers.

The Holy Spirit Enlightens

"But the man who isn't a Christian can't understand and can't accept these thoughts from God, which the Holy Spirit teaches us. They sound foolish to him, because only those who have the Holy Spirit within them can understand what the Holy Spirit means. Others just can't take it in" (1 Corinthians 2:14).

Though I have been a Christian for more than 35 years, I still have much to learn. I am far from perfect. And I do not ever expect to be — in this lifetime. Only our Lord Jesus Christ was without sin.

However, I know from experience that the more time I spend with God through reading, studying, memorizing and meditating on His Word, with the help of the Holy Spirit to interpret God's truth to me, the more I become like our Lord Jesus Christ, God's Son.

When you spend time daily in Bible reading and study, your life will change. After reading God's Word consistently for several months, you will be amazed by the things God has done in your life.

How can we understand the Bible? How can we experience its life-changing influence in our lives?

The non-believer and the disobedient, carnal Christian have difficulty in understanding the Bible because they must rely on their human faculties in their attempt to understand things that are of a spiritual nature in God's Word.

As Paul writes to the church at Corinth, ". . .the natural man receiveth not the things of the Spirit of God: for they are foolishness unto him: neither can he know them, because they are spiritually discerned" (KJV).

Bible Reading: 1 Corinthians 2:9-13

ACTION POINT: Since the Holy Spirit inspired holy men of old to record God's Word, the Bible, I will ask Him to interpret God's message to my own life, and today I will encourage someone, or several others, to depend upon the Holy Spirit and to join me in living a supernatural life for the glory of God.

As a Man Thinketh

"For as he thinketh in his heart, so is he...." (Proverbs 23:7, KJV).

"**E**very day in every way I am becoming better and better," declared the French philosopher Emile Coué. But it is said that he committed suicide.

Positive thinking by a nonbeliever without a biblical basis is often an exercise in futility. Though I agree with the basic concept of positive thinking, so long as it is related to the Word of God, there is a difference between positive thinking and supernatural thinking. We do not think positively so that we can know Christ better; we come to know Christ better, which results in supernatural thinking. The basis of our thinking is God's Word; supernatural thinking is based upon the attributes of God.

When a man says, "I am going to be enthusiastic, by faith, as an act of the will," or "I am going to rejoice, by faith, as an act of the will," he is simply drawing upon his rights as a child of God, according to the promises of God.

In supernatural thinking, we apply the promises of God, knowing with certainty that if we ask anything according to His will, He will hear and answer us.

Some well-known Christian leaders emphasize "positive thinking" and "possibility thinking." They are men whom I admire and with whom I agree basically in this regard because the Christian life is a positive life. "As a man thinketh in his heart, so is he."

But I prefer to use what I believe to be the more scriptural definition of the Christian life — supernatural thinking, which includes — but goes far beyond — both positive thinking and possibility thinking.

Bible Reading: Proverbs 23:1-6

ACTION POINT: Today I will claim by faith a promise or promises from God's Word which will help me to live a supernatural life.

Rivers of Living Water

"For the Scriptures declare that rivers of living water shall flow from the inmost being of anyone who believes in me" (John 7:38).

I was explaining to a group of Christians the meaning of Proverbs 15:13-15, "A happy face means a glad heart, a sad face means a breaking heart. When a man is gloomy, everything seems to go wrong and when he is cheerful everything seems to go right."

God's Word reminds us that the source of joy is the Holy Spirit (1 Thessalonians 1:6). So if a man is filled with the Spirit, he will have a joyful heart. When we are filled with the Spirit, we will express love by singing and making melody in our hearts to the Lord. A happy heart will inevitably produce a joyful countenance (Ephesians 5:18-21).

If we do not have a joyful, peaceful countenance, there is reason to question whether we have a loving, joyful heart. And if we do not have a loving, joyful heart, it is not likely that we are filled with the Spirit.

One Christian leader, who had heard me speak, approached me later. He just happened to have a very somber, stern countenance. He explained to me that this was a new concept to him, and since he was reared in another culture, he felt that his somber countenance was a cultural thing.

"In our part of the world [the Middle East]," he said, "we don't smile and express ourselves like American Christians."

Together we analyzed the Scripture and concluded that culture has nothing to do with this truth, since Jesus, Paul and other writers of the New Testament were also born in the Middle East. If we truly understand the Spirit-filled life, whatever our cultural background, the joy of the Lord will flow from us — from our "innermost being shall flow rivers of living water" (John 7:38, NAS).

Bible Reading: John 7:33-37

ACTION POINT: Recognizing love, joy and peace as trademarks of the Spirit-filled life, I will consciously seek to be Spirit-controlled so that these expressions will be a natural overflow of my life. I will teach this spiritual truth to others today.

To Encourage Us

"These things that were written in the Scriptures so long ago are to teach us patience and to encourage us, so that we will look forward expectantly to the time when God will conquer sin and death" (Romans 15:4).

Tom had a "short fuse" and frequently exploded in anger when he was disappointed with himself or others. Then he received Christ and began to study the Word of God, obey its commands and walk in the fullness of the Holy Spirit.

His life began to change, gradually at first, until, as he told me recently, it has now been a long time since he has allowed his old nature to express his impatience.

The story is told of an impatient man who prayed and kept praying for God to grant him the virtue he so desperately needed.

"Lord," he prayed, "give me patience, and give it to me now!"

Patience, however, is a virtue that is developmental in nature, to a large degree. It is the result of walking in the fullness and power of the Holy Spirit (Galatians 5:22,23). It develops out of a good heart and a godly attitude (Luke 8:15). It is spawned sometimes during times of tribulation. Remember, it is a fruit of the Spirit.

Paul writes, "If we must keep trusting God for something that hasn't happened yet, it teaches us to wait patiently and confidently" (Romans 8:25).

So patience comes from hope and trust in God. And finally, we learn patience through the study and personal application of God's Word in our lives, as suggested in Romans 15:4, "These things that were written in the Scriptures so long ago are to teach us patience and to encourage us."

Bible Reading: Romans 15:1-6

ACTION POINT: When delays and seeming denials occur, I will exercise patience, with the help of the indwelling Holy Spirit.

His Mark of Ownership

"He has put His brand upon us — His mark of ownership — and given us His Holy Spirit in our hearts as guarantee that we belong to Him, and as the first installment of all that He is going to give us" (2 Corinthians 1:22).

S ome time ago, a young Christian came to share his problems. He was very frustrated and confused, and he spoke of the constant defeat and fruitlessness which he experienced in the Christian life.

"You don't have to live in defeat," I said to him.

The young man registered surprise.

"You can live a life of victory, a life of joy, a life of fruitfulness," I assured him. "In fact, by the grace of God — and to Him alone be the glory — for more than 25 years as a Christian I do not recall a single hour of broken fellowship with the Lord Jesus."

He was really shocked at that.

"Do you mean you haven't sinned in 25 years?" he asked.

"No, that's not what I mean," I replied. "I have sinned regrettably, I have grieved and quenched the Spirit at times with impatience, anger or some other expression of the flesh. But when I grieve the Spirit, I know exactly what to do. I breathe spiritually. I confess my sin to God and immediately receive His forgiveness and cleansing, and by faith I continue to walk in the fullness and power of the Holy Spirit."

Bible Reading: 1 Corinthians 12:3-11

ACTION POINT: Realizing that a believer can live a supernatural, holy life only as he yields to the control of the Holy Spirit, I will seek to practice holiness in my personal life and encourage other Christians to do the same.

Clothed in Christ

"For all of you who were baptized into Christ have clothed yourselves in Christ" (Galatians 3:27, NAS).

You may be surprised, as I was, at the result of our personal surveys having to do with church members and salvation.

Such surveys indicate that somewhere between 50 and 90% of all church members are not sure of their salvation. Like Martin Luther, John Wesley and many others who became mighty ambassadors for Christ, some spend many years "serving God" before they experience the assurance and reality of their salvation.

The pastor of a large fashionable church of 1,500 members once reacted negatively when I shared these statistics, doubting that such large percentages of church members lacked assurance of their salvation.

He decided personally to survey his own congregation at the church where he had served as senior pastor for 15 years. To his amazement and shock, more than 75% of the membership indicated they were not sure of their salvation.

The following Sunday, the pastor arranged for the *Four Spiritual Laws* booklet, which contains the distilled essence of the gospel, to be distributed to each member of the congregation. For his sermon he read the contents of the booklet aloud, as the congregation followed him, reading from their own copies of the Four Laws. Then he invited all who wished to receive Christ as their Savior and Lord to read aloud with him the prayer contained in the booklet. Almost the entire congregation joined in the prayer audibly. As a result the church was changed, because changed individuals in sufficient numbers equal a changed church, a changed community and a changed nation.

Have you clothed yourself in Christ?

Bible Reading: Galatians 4:4-7

ACTION POINT: I will not take for granted that I have found faith in Christ simply because I belong to a church, nor will I assume that all church members have assurance of their salvation. I shall encourage all who are not sure to receive Christ and be clothed in His righteousness.

Gift of His Spirit

"This is what God has prepared for us and, as a guarantee, He has given us His Holy Spirit" (2 Corinthians 5:5).

A dynamic young business man sat across from me in my office. By almost every standard of human measure he was an outstanding success in both his business and his religion.

He was one of the leading men in his field of specialty in the world. A highly moral, religious person, he was very active in his church. And yet, he was not sure that he was a Christian.

He wanted desperately — more than anything else in the world — to have real assurance, but he did not know how to go about obtaining it. Step by step, I explained to him from the Bible how he could receive Christ into his life and be sure of his salvation.

Soon we were on our knees in prayer, after which he went on his way rejoicing in the assurance of his salvation to begin a supernatural walk with God.

Many pastors and other Christian leaders, I have discovered, also have this same gnawing doubt about their salvation. One pastor who had preached the Bible-centered gospel for 40 years told me that he was still unsure of his salvation.

The wife of an evangelist confided, "During the past 30 years, my husband and I have introduced thousands of people to Christ, but I have never been sure of my own salvation. Never before have I had the courage to share this concern with anyone, but now I am so desperate that I have come to seek your help."

I explained that we receive Christ as our Savior by faith or on act of the will; then, as a guarantee, He gives us His Holy Spirit.

Bible Reading: 2 Corinthians 5:6-10

ACTION POINT: With God's Holy Spirit as my constant witness, I will daily give thanks to Him for assurance of my salvation.

Your Joy Restored

"Create in me a clean heart, O God: and renew a right spirit within me. Cast me not away from Thy presence: and take not Thy Holy Spirit from me. Restore unto me the joy of Thy salvation: and uphold me with Thy free Spirit. Then will I teach transgressors Thy ways; and sinners shall be converted unto Thee" (Psalm 51:10-13, KJV).

"The Christian owes it to the world to be supernaturally joyful," said A. W. Tozer.

How do we attain that joy?

When we refuse to exhale spiritually by confessing our sins, we are miserable. On the other hand, when we do confess our sins, we experience God's complete forgiveness. He removes our guilt and fills our lives with joy, the kind of joy we will very much want to share with others.

The psalmist also knew this when he wrote: "Create in me a new, clean heart, O God, filled with clean thoughts and right desires... Restore to me again the joy of Your salvation, and make me willing to obey You. Then I will teach Your ways to other sinners, and they — guilty like me — will repent and return to You" (Psalm 51:10,12,13).

There was a time when I allowed moods and circumstances to prevent the joyful launching of a new day with the Lord. As a result, I did not feel that close relationship with Him, that beautiful awareness of His presence that comes from fellowship with Him in His Word and in prayer, and through faithful witnessing of His reality to others.

Without that time with Him, there is no joy and the day often begins and continues in the energy of the flesh. There is no personal awareness of God's presence, and things just seem to go wrong. We can begin every day with that joyful communion with Christ that gives us the assurance of His presence throughout the day. We are the ones who make that choice. God is available; we are the variable.

Bible Reading: Psalm 51:1-9

ACTION POINT: I will begin this day on my knees, praising and rejoicing in the Lord as an expression of my desire to be with Him. I will read His Word and offer prayers of adoration, confession, thanksgiving and supplication. I will ask Him to lead me to others whose hearts He has prepared for this same joyful relationship with God.

Fair in Everything

"The Lord is fair in everything He does, and full of kindness. He is close to all who call on Him sincerely" (Psalm 145:17,18).

A re you afraid to trust the Lord? I find that many people who have had unfortunate experiences in their youth with their parents, especially their fathers, have a reluctance to trust God.

In my talks with thousands of students, I have found a number of young people who have such an attitude problem.

Even the best of earthly parents, at times, are unfair and fail to demonstrate kindness. Yet how wonderful it is to know that our Lord is fair in everything He does and is full of kindness, and He is always close to all who call upon Him sincerely.

Notice that the Scripture promise quoted above is a categorical statement. The psalmist permits no exceptions, even when we are sure we deserved better than we received. Thus we need to claim the promise in God's Word by faith and live by it. Some day we will see events from God's side and recognize the fairness we could not see here.

We often see "as in a glass darkly," but God has perfect 20/20 vision. That's why the attitude of trust alone will help us overcome our feelings that God or the world, is unfair. Only then can we live a supernatural life of daily acceptance of what God sends our way.

Bible Reading: Psalm 145:8-12

ACTION POINT: Today I will put my trust in God and His goodness, no matter how I feel. I will move beyond preoccupation with my disappointments and carry out God's appointments in the certainty that our Lord is fair in everything He does and will enable me to live supernaturally as I continue to trust and obey Him.

Reap What You Sow

"Don't be misled; remember that you can't ignore God and get away with it: a man will always reap just the kind of crop he sows!" (Galatians 6:7).

Steve had just been introduced to this great and exciting law of sowing and reaping. "Is it really true," he asked, "that I will always reap what I sow — and more than I sow — good or bad?"

I was able to assure him, from the authority of Scripture, from experience of 36 years of walking with Christ and by observing closely the lives of many thousands of Christians with whom I have counseled and worked, that the law of sowing and reaping is just as true and inviolate as the law of gravity.

If you want to judge a man, an American humorist once said, you should not look at him in the face but get behind him and see what he is looking at, what he is sowing.

For example, is he looking at God with reverence — or with no deference at all? Does he really believe God means what He says?

A student once asked, "If I give my life to Christ, do I become a puppet?"

The answer is a resounding no! We never become puppets. We have the right of choice; we are free moral agents. God's Word assures us that He guides and encourages us, but we must act as a result of our own self-will. God does not force us to make decisions.

The more we understand the love, the wisdom, the sovereignty, the grace and power of God, the more we will want to trust Him with every detail of our lives. The secret of the supernatural life is to keep Christ on the throne of our lives and delight ourselves in Him as Lord.

We fail in the Christian life when we, as a deliberate act of our will, choose to disobey the leading of the Holy Spirit.

It is a tragedy of the human will that we often think we have a better way than God has for living the Christian life. But do not deceive yourself or allow Satan to mislead you: *God's way is best!*

Bible Reading: Galatians 6:6-10

ACTION POINT: I will seek to sow seeds of love and kindness and faith knowing that as a result I will reap God's best for my life.

One More Reason to Praise

"His presence within us is God's guarantee that He really will give us all that He promised; and the Spirit's seal upon us means that God has already purchased us and that He guarantees to bring us to Himself. This is just one more reason for us to praise our glorious God" (Ephesians 1:14).

To me, this wonderful verse means that, as children of God, we have the ability to obey God's laws if we are filled continually with the Holy Spirit and refuse to obey the old evil nature within us.

In order to live the supernatural life which is available to us through the indwelling Holy Spirit, we must know our rights as children of God. We need to know our spiritual heritage. We must know how to draw upon the inexhaustible, supernatural resources of God's love, power, forgiveness and abundant grace.

The first step is to learn everything we can about God. We also need to know about the nature of man and why he behaves as he does. The best way to learn who God is, who man is and about our rights as children of God is to spend much time — even at the sacrifice of other needs and demands on our schedules — in reading, studying, memorizing and meditating on the Word of God, and in prayer and witnessing.

Paul wrote to the Christians at Rome, "For His Holy Spirit speaks to us deep in our hearts, and tells us that we really are God's children. And since we are His children, we will share His treasures — for all God gives to His Son Jesus is now ours too. But if we are to share His glory, we must also share His suffering" (Romans 8:16,17).

Bible Reading: Ephesians 1:15-23

ACTION POINT: I will acknowledge God's presence, believe His promises and surrender to His special will for me, and thus will I praise Him throughout the day.

God's Home Is Holy

"Don't you realize that all of you together are the house of God, and that the Spirit of God lives among you in His house? If anyone defiles and spoils God's home, God will destroy him. For God's home is holy and clean, and you are that home" (1 Corinthians 3:16,17).

At this writing, I am with the staff at our annual training on the campus of Colorado State University. In addition to the 3,000 United States and Canadian field staff of Campus Crusade for Christ who are here, thousands more are attending music workshops, summer school, numerous conferences and meetings on this campus. Also, the entire Denver Broncos professional football team is here for training.

Throughout the day, from early morning till late at night, the campus is alive with people jogging, roller-skating, playing tennis, walking and other physical activities. These people are disciplining their bodies, keeping them in good physical tone.

Sadly, however, I also witness many people who lack interest in physical well-being by smoking and drinking alcoholic beverages. A stroll down the sidewalks of this beautiful campus will reveal numerous smokers. And, in the early hours, before the clean-up crews go to work, one can see in the gutters the empty beer cans from the previous night's revelry and carousing.

The body of the Christian is the temple of God — Father, Son and Holy Spirit (1 Corinthians 6:19 and 1 Corinthians 3:16,17). For this reason, God asks us to present our bodies as "living sacrifices," holy and righteous, for God could dwell in no less a temple.

Bible Reading: 1 Corinthians 3:11-15

ACTION POINT: I will take especially good care of my body — physically, mentally, spiritually — realizing it is the temple of God's Holy Spirit.

Examples of His Love

"Little children, let us stop just saying we love people; let us really love them, and show it by our actions" (1 John 3:18).

The story is told about two farmers. Every day, one of them would haul pails of water up the steep slope to his terraced field and irrigate his meager crop.

The second farmer tilled the terrace just below, and he would poke a hole in the dyke and let the other farmer's water run down into his field.

The first farmer was upset. Being a Christian, he went to his pastor and asked for advice. The pastor told him to keep on watering as before and to say nothing. So, the farmer returned to his fields and the watering of his crop, but the farmer below him continued to drain off his water. Nothing had changed.

After a few days, the first farmer went to his pastor again. The pastor told him to go a step further — to water his neighbor's crop! So the next day, the farmer brought water to his neighbor's field and watered the crops. After that, he watered his own field.

This went on for three days, and not a word was exchanged between the two farmers. But after the third day, the second farmer came to the first farmer.

"How do I become a Christian?" he asked.

"There is a saying, 'Love your friends and hate your enemies.' But I say: Love your enemies!...If you are friendly only to your friends, how are you different from anyone else? Even the heathen do that. But you are to be perfect, even as your father in heaven is perfect" (Matthew 5:43-48).

Bible Reading: 1 John 3:14-17

ACTION POINT: I will make every effort to demonstrate the love of Christ by the way I act toward others.

His Gifts and Powers

"It is the same and only Holy Spirit who gives all these gifts and powers, deciding which each of us should have" (1 Corinthians 12:11).

As I counsel in the area of Christian service, I find much confusion among many Christians regarding the gifts of the Holy Spirit.

Believers often are so involved in trying to discover or receive additional spiritual gifts that they are not developing and using their known gifts and abilities to do God's will.

For this reason, I caution against going to great lengths to discover one's spiritual gifts. Rather than emphasize gifts, I encourage a person to surrender fully to the lordship of Jesus Christ and appropriate by faith the fullness of the Holy Spirit.

Then, by faith and hard work, while depending on the Holy Spirit, a person can set out with determination to accomplish that to which God has called him.

Paul wrote about this important principle in his letter to the Philippians:

"Dearest friends, when I was there with you, you were always so careful to follow my instructions. And now that I am away you must be even more careful to do the good things that result from being saved, obeying God with deep reverence, shrinking back from all that might displease Him....

"For I can do everything God asks me to do with the help of Christ who gives me the strength and power" (Philippians 2:12; 4:13). This, of course, can be done only if a Christian totally submits himself to the lordship of Jesus Christ and the control of the Holy Spirit.

Bible Reading: 1 Corinthians 12:1-10

ACTION POINT: I'll be more concerned about being yielded to the moment-by-moment direction and control of God's Holy Spirit than about discovering my spiritual gift(s).

As Much As We Need

"But you should divide with them. Right now you have plenty and can help them; then at some other time they can share with you when you need it. In this way each will have as much as he needs" (2 Corinthians 8:14).

I like Paul's emphasis on spiritual equality. In his letter to the church at Corinth, this principle is clearly expressed:

"You can help them...they can share with you...each will have as much as he needs."

Not one of us is a total body within himself; collectively, we are the body of Christ.

The *hand* can accomplish only certain kinds of functions.

The *eyes* cannot physically grasp objects, but they can see them.

The *ears* cannot transport the body like feet can, but ears can hear many sounds.

The hand needs the eye, and the eye needs the hand. All parts of the body need each other in order to function as a healthy body.

Are the parts the same? No. Do they have equality? Yes.

While the Christians at Corinth possessed all the spiritual gifts, they were not glorifying Christ or building up one another. Instead, they were glorifying themselves, glorifying their special gifts, and exercising their gifts in the flesh instead of in the power and control of the Holy Spirit.

Time and again, the apostle Paul stressed to the Corinthians that an atmosphere of godly love, *agape*, must prevail or the exercising of their gifts would be fruitless.

Bible Reading: 2 Corinthians 8:7-15

ACTION POINT: I will be content with my place in the Body of Christ, whether it be large or small, realizing that every part of the body is vitally important in God's kingdom.

Without Me— Nothing

"Abide in Me, and I in you. As the branch cannot bear fruit of itself, except it abide in the vine; no more can ye, except ye abide in Me. I am the vine, ye are the branches: He that abideth in Me, and I in him, the same bringeth forth much fruit: for without Me ye can do nothing" (John 15:4,5, KJV).

As a young man in college and later in business, I used to be very self-sufficient — proud of what I could do on my own. I believed that a man could do just about anything he wanted to do through his own effort, if he were willing to pay the price of hard work and sacrifice, and I experienced some considerable degree of success.

Then, when I became a Christian, the Bible introduced me to a whole new and different philosophy of life — a life of trusting God for His promises. It took me a while to see the fallacy and inadequacy of trying to serve God in my own strength and ability, but that new life of faith in God finally replaced my old life of self-sufficiency.

Now, I realize how totally incapable I am of living the Christian life, how really weak I am in my own strength, and yet how strong I am in Christ. God does not waste our ability and training. We do not lay aside our God-given gifts and talents. We give them back to Him in service, and He multiplies them for His glory.

As Paul says, "I can do all things through him [Christ] who strengthens me" (Philippians 4:13, NAS). In John 15, the Lord stresses the importance of drawing our strength from Him:

"Take care to live in Me, and let Me live in you. For a branch cannot produce fruit when severed from the vine. Nor can you be fruitful apart from Me. Yes, I am the vine; you are the branches. Whoever lives in Me and I in him shall produce a large crop of fruit. For apart from Me, you can't do a thing" (John 15:4,5). Our strength, wisdom, love and power for the supernatural life come from the Lord alone.

Bible Reading: John 15:6-11

ACTION POINT: I will make it a special goal to abide in Christ so that His life-giving power for supernatural living will enable me to bear much fruit for His glory.

Inner Strengthening

"That out of His glorious, unlimited resources He will give you the mighty inner strengthening of His Holy Spirit" (Ephesians 3:16).

In Christ are all the attributes and characteristics promised to His children as the fruit of the Spirit. And the Holy Spirit was given to glorify Christ.

Do you need love?

The Lord Jesus Christ is the incarnation of love. Paul prays that our roots may "go down deep into the soil of God's marvelous love; and may you be able to feel and understand, as all God's children should, how long, how wide, how deep and how high His love really is; and to experience this love for yourselves (though it is so great that you will never see the end of it, or fully know or understand it")" (Ephesians 3:17-19).

Do you need peace?

Christ is the "Prince of Peace." "I am leaving you with a gift," said Jesus, "peace of mind and heart! And the peace I give isn't fragile like the peace the world gives" (John 14:27).

Do you need joy?

Christ is joy.

Do you need patience?

Christ is patience.

Do you need wisdom?

Christ is wisdom.

Are you in need of material possessions so that you can better serve Christ?

They are available in Him, for God owns "the cattle on a thousand hills," and He promised to supply all our needs (Philippians 4:19).

All that we need is to be found in Christ and nowhere else. The supernatural life is Christ, for in Him dwells all the fullness of the Godhead bodily.

Bible Reading: Ephesians 3:17-21

ACTION POINT: Knowing that God's unlimited resources make possible the mighty inner strengthening in my life, I shall focus my attention upon Him through reading His inspired Word and obeying His commands.

Destroying the Devil's Works

"But if you keep on sinning, it shows that you belong to Satan, who since he first began to sin has kept steadily at it. But the Son of God came to destroy these works of the devil" (1 John 3:8).

A young Christian came to inquire of me one day, "How do you account for the fact that so many Christian leaders, many of them famous personalities, pastors and heads of Christian organizations are involved in moral and financial scandals?"

He named several well-known pastors and Christian leaders to illustrate his point.

Sadly I acknowledged his statement to be true. It seems there is an all-out attack of Satan to destroy the credibility of the Christian message. My explanation to him was that our Lord and the apostle Paul dealt with the same problem because, even though the disciples had been with the Lord Jesus three years or more, Judas betrayed Him and the others deserted Him.

The apostle Paul spoke of several who had deserted him. Those included Demas, who loved the present world, and Hymenaeus, Alexander and Philetus, who strayed from the truth.

Only one person can help us live holy lives that will honor our Lord, who came to destroy the works of the devil, and that is the third person of the Trinity — God the Holy Spirit. As long as we cast our ballot for the Spirit in our warfare against the flesh, we can live supernaturally every day in the joy, the wonder, the adventure and the power of the resurrection. It is simply a matter of our will; the decision is ours.

Bible Reading: 1 John 3:4-10

ACTION POINT: "Oh, God, thank You that You sent Your Son to destroy the works of the devil. I will claim the supernatural power of the Holy Spirit so that I may live victoriously and never bring scandal or disgrace to Your name."

His Rich Storehouse

"However, Christ has given each of us special abilities — whatever He wants us to have out of His rich storehouse of gifts" (Ephesians 4:7).

R oger and Len read a popular book on spiritual gifts. Instead of being blessed, they were distressed. They came for counsel.

"What is our gift?" they pleaded, as though I had the ability to immediately discern God's supernatural provision for them.

"First of all," I explained, "you should not be exercised over the undue emphasis on gifts, which has been of somewhat recent origin. For centuries, until recent times, men did not make a great deal of that particular emphasis in the Word of God.

"The emphasis was on the authority of the Scripture, the lordship of Christ, the fullness of the Holy Spirit. Great servants of God were mightily used as preachers, missionaries, teachers and godly laymen, without ever being made particularly aware that spiritual gifts were something that needed to be emphasized. The feeling was, 'Whatever God calls me to do, He will enable me to do, if I am willing to surrender my will to Christ, study the Word of God, obey the leading of the Holy Spirit, work hard and trust God to guide me.' "

I gave them my own testimony of how, though I had been a Christian for more than 30 years and God had graciously used my life in many ways — sometimes my preaching, other times my teaching or administrative gifts, or in the area of helps — I quite honestly did not know my spiritual gift nor did I seek to "discover" my gift. I was very content to know, with the apostle Paul, that I could do all things through Christ who strengthened me, who keeps pouring His power into me.

I showed them a quotation from a book on gifts, in which a famous Christian leader declared that for 25 years he had believed he had a particular gift but recently had cause to question whether he possessed it, and concluded finally that he did not.

My word to you, then, as to Roger and Len, is not to be distressed if you do not know your gift. Simply continue to walk in faith and obedience, make Christ the Lord of every part of your life, be sure you are filled with the Spirit, and hide the Word of God in your heart daily.

Bible Reading: Ephesians 4:1-6

ACTION POINT: For the rest of my life I shall seek the Giver and not the gift, depending upon Him to give me the necessary wisdom and ability and whatever else is needed to accomplish the task which He has called me to do. I shall share this concept with other Christians who are confused over the matter of spiritual gifts.

A Healthy, Growing Body

"Instead, we will lovingly follow the truth at all times — speaking truly, dealing truly, living truly — and so become more and more in every way like Christ who is the Head of His body, the church. Under His direction the whole body is fitted together perfectly, and each part in its own special way helps the other parts, so that the whole body is healthy and growing and full of love" (Ephesians 4:15,16).

I am concerned, as you no doubt are, that God's ideal church, in which the whole body is fitted together perfectly, becomes a reality. And if that is to happen, it will mean that I must become a part of that perfect fit.

Within the body of Christ, each of us has a unique function. True, two people might have similar functions just as a body has two hands that function similarly. But those two hands are not identical. Just try to wear a lefthand glove on your right hand!

The hands have similar functions, not identical functions. You and I might have similar abilities, but we are not identical. We are unique creations of God.

Therefore, we should not look upon our abilities with pride or be boastful of them. On the other hand, we should not be envious or look with disdain on others because of their different abilities.

Spiritual gifts include (1 Corinthians 12): wisdom, knowledge, faith, healing, miracles, prophecy, discerning of spirits, tongues, interpretation of tongues, apostleship, teaching, helping and administration; (Romans 12, additional): leadership, exhortation, giving and mercy.

Bible Reading: Ephesians 4:7-14

ACTION POINT: So that I might fit more perfectly into God's whole body, I will prayerfully seek the leadership of the Holy Spirit to enable me to make a maximum contribution to the body of Christ.

He Listens and Answers

"Mark this well: The Lord has set apart the redeemed for himself. Therefore He will listen to me and answer when I call to Him" (Psalm 4:3).

My 93-year-old mother, has known and walked with the Lord since she was 16. In all the years that I have known her, now more than 60, I have never known her to say an unkind or critical word or do anything that would be contrary to her commitment to Christ, made as a teenage girl.

Hers has been a life of prayer, study of God's Word and worship of Him. The radiance and joy of her godly life has inspired not only her husband and seven children, but also scores of grandchildren and great and great-great grandchildren, and thousands of neighbors and friends.

A few days ago I invited her — for the hundredth time, at least — to come and live with us, knowing that all the rest of the children have made similar invitations. She responded, "No, I prefer to live alone. But I am not really alone, for the Lord Jesus is with me, comforting me, giving me His peace and assurance that He will take care of me."

So she spends her days in prayer, in study of the Word and in being a blessing to all who enter her home, as the love of God flows through her. Only eternity will record the multitudes of lives that have been transformed through her godly example and her dedicated prayers of intercession.

Surely every Christian needs a daily engagement — with priority claim over everything else — to meet the Lord in the secret place if his life is to be a benediction to others.

Bible Reading: Psalm 5:1-7

ACTION POINT: I recognize that if I am going to live a supernatural life, I must set aside time which will take priority over every other consideration. Only a genuine emergency will take precedence over such an engagement of prayer, study of God's Word, worship and praise of my wonderful Lord.

Source of Joy

"So you became our followers and the Lord's; for you received our message with joy from the Holy Spirit in spite of the trials and sorrows it brought you" (1 Thessalonians 1:6).

M ary was so radiant it was as though she had swallowed a light bulb. Wherever she went, there was the radiance of the Lord's presence about her. She literally bubbled over with joy, and whenver she talked about the Lord her words came so quickly they practically tumbled over each other. She was an exciting, contagious person to be around, and many nonbelievers inquired of her, "Why are you so happy? What makes you so different?"

To which, of course, she would always respond by telling them about our wonderful Lord and how He had filled her heart with His joy.

The verse for today clearly indicates that joy comes from the Holy Spirit, who came into this world to glorify Christ. We are told in Galatians also that the fruit of the Spirit is joy, among other things.

When we are filled with the Spirit and thus growing in the fruit of the Spirit — which includes joy — then we will express that joy by singing and making melody in our hearts to the Lord. A happy heart inevitably will be reflected in a joyful countenance.

"I presume everybody has known someone whose life was just radiant," R. A. Torrey said. "Joy beamed out of their eyes; joy bubbled over their lips; joy seemed to fairly run from their fingertips. The gladdest thing on earth is to have a *real* God."

In the words of an unknown poet:

"If you live close to God and His infinite grace,
You don't have to tell; it shows on your face."

Bible Reading: Nehemiah 8:9-12

ACTION POINT: I will not expect to find joy in things, or even in other people primarily, but rather in the source of all joy — God's Holy Spirit. With His help, I will share His supernatural joy wherever I go.

He Prays for You

"Likewise, the Spirit also helpeth our infirmities; for we know not what we should pray for as we ought; but the Spirit itself [Himself] maketh intercession for us with groanings which cannot be uttered" (Romans 8:26, KJV).

P rayer is our mighty force for supernatural living and the most personal, intimate approach to and relationship with God. Through the instrumentality of God's Holy Spirit, we have access to the Almighty, leading the way to supernatural living.

In some theological circles there is much skepticism and hesitancy about the Holy Spirit. We must not forget, however, that Jesus Himself had much to say about the Holy Spirit.

In John's gospel, for instance, Jesus explained to the disciples that it was necessary for Him to leave them in order that the Holy Spirit should come to them. "He shall guide you into all truth...He shall praise Me and bring Me great honor by showing you My glory" (John 16:13,14, LB).

Just as the Holy Spirit transformed the lives of the first-century disciples from spiritually impotent, frustrated, fruitless men into courageous witnesses for Christ, He wants to transform our lives in the same way. We need only to surrender ourselves and by faith we will be filled with His power.

It is the Holy Spirit who draws us to the Lord Jesus whom He came to glorify. He makes the difference between failure and success in the Christian life, between fruitlessness and fruitfulness in our witness. Through His filling of our lives with God's love and forgiveness we are "born again" into the family of God.

And it is the Holy Spirit who not only enables us to pray but who also prays on our behalf, as today's verse clearly points out.

Bible Reading: Romans 8:27-31

ACTION POINT: Today I will visualize, with deep joy and gratitude, the Holy Spirit Himself praying for me, beseeching God on my behalf.

Place of Privilege

"For because of our faith, He has brought us into this place of highest privilege where we now stand, and we confidently and joyfully look forward to actually becoming all that God has had in mind for us to be" (Romans 5:2).

Interesting, is it not, that because of *our* faith, which is really *His* faith imparted to us, He has brought us, you and me, to a place of highest privilege.

What are some of the benefits that constitute this highest privilege?

First, we are justified — considered righteous in God's sight.

Second, we are admitted into His favor and we abide there.

Third, we have the hope and prospect of even higher and richer blessings, in the fullness of His glory, when we are admitted into heaven.

Strange, then, that you and I often chafe at the bit when things become a little rough. At such times as that, I need to remind myself that I do not deserve any better. All the mercies and blessings of God are undeserved — gifts of God's grace ("God's Riches at Christ's Expense," as the apt acrostic expresses it).

What, really, is the "bottom line" of everything that happens to the believer — to you and me? After confessing that we are receiving our just deserts, we must always go back to the all-inclusive promise: "All things are working together for our good." They may not feel good, they may not seem good, they may not even be good, but they are accomplishing good in us.

Bible Reading: Ephesians 3:8-12

ACTION POINT: I will meditate on the rare and high privilege that is mine as a child of God and look forward to becoming all that God wants me to be.

All Men Know What God Wants Them to Do

"But this is the new agreement I will make with the people of Israel, says the Lord: I will write my laws in their minds so that they will know what I want them to do without My even telling them, and these laws will be in their hearts so that they will want to obey them, and I will be their God and they shall be my people" (Hebrews 8:10).

Harry boasted that he was an atheist, that he could not believe in God — that there was no such thing as right and wrong. But as we counseled together, it became apparent that he lived a very immoral life, and the only way he could justify his conduct was to rationalize away the existence of God.

This he was unable to do. As God's Word reminds us, His law is written in our minds, so that we will know what He wants us to do without His even telling us.

A very honest, frank, straightforward counseling session helped Harry to see that he was living a lie, a life of deceit and shame. All of this resulted in making him a very miserable person until he surrendered his life to Christ and became an honest, authentic, transparent disciple of the Lord Jesus Christ.

The Bible says that the mind of natural man is essentially disgusting (Ezekiel 23:17-22), despiteful (Ezekiel 36:5), depraved (Romans 1:28), hardened (2 Corinthians 3:14), hostile (Colossians 1:21) and defiled (Titus 1:15).

In contrast, the Scriptures show that the mind of the Christian is willing (1 Chronicles 28:9), is at peace (Romans 8:6), is renewed (Romans 12:2), can know Christ's mind (1 Corinthians 2:16) and can be obedient (Hebrews 8:10).

Our minds are susceptible to the influence of our old sin-nature and, as such, can pose some dangers to us. As soon as we get out of step spiritually with the Holy Spirit and get our focus off the Lord, our minds begin to give us trouble.

Bible Reading: Hebrews 8:7-13

ACTION POINT: Claiming by faith the help of the Holy Spirit, I will discipline my mind to think God's thoughts as expressed in His holy, inspired Word. In this way, I can be assured of knowing and doing His perfect will.

We Need the Word

"And you will need the helmet of salvation and the sword of the Spirit — which is the Word of God" (Ephesians 6:17).

In my own life, as I have come to know God better and to live more fully in the power and control of the Holy Spirit, my daily devotional Bible reading and study is not a duty or a chore, but a blessing; not an imposition on my time, but an invitation to fellowship in the closest of all ways with our holy, heavenly Father and our wonderful Savior and Lord.

Remember, God delights to have fellowship with us. The success of our studying God's Word and of prayer is not to be determined by some emotional experience which we may have (though this frequently will be our experience), but by the realization that God is pleased that we want to know Him enough to spend time with Him in Bible study and prayer.

Here are some important, practical suggestions for your individual devotional reading and study of the Bible:

1. Begin with a prayer. Ask the Holy Spirit to give you an understanding of God's Word.

2. Keep a Bible study notebook.

3. Read the text slowly and carefully; then reread and take notes.

4. Find out the true meaning of the text. Ask yourself: (a) Who or what is the main subject? (b) Of whom or what is the writer speaking? (c) What is the key verse? (d) What does the passage teach you about Jesus Christ? (e) Does it bring to light personal sin that you need to confess and forsake? (f) Does it contain a command for you to obey? (g) Does it give a promise you can claim?

5. List practical applications, commands, promises.

6. Memorize the Scriptures — particularly key verses.

7. Obey the commands and follow the instructions you learn in God's Word.

Bible Reading: 2 Timothy 3:14-17

ACTION POINT: With His help, I will begin to make time in God's Word — quality time — a priority in my life.

Abounding Therein

"As ye have therefore received Christ Jesus the Lord, so walk ye in Him: Rooted and built up in Him, and stablished in the faith, as ye have been taught, abounding therein with thanksgiving. Beware lest any man spoil you through philosophy and vain deceit, after the tradition of men, after the rudiments of the world, and not after Christ" (Colossians 2:6-8, KJV).

Some years ago, while speaking at the University of Houston, I was told about a brilliant philosophy major. He was much older than most of the other students, having spent many years in the military before he returned to do graduate work.

He was so gifted, so brilliant, so knowledgeable that even the professors were impressed by his ability to comprehend quickly and to debate rationally. He was an atheist, and he had a way of embarrassing the Christians who tried to witness to him.

During one of my visits to the university, I was asked to talk with him about Christ. We sat in a booth in the student center, contrasting his philosophy of life with the Word of God. It was an unusual dialogue. He successfully monopolized the conversation with his philosophy of unbelief in God.

At every opportunity, I would remind him that God loved him and offered a wonderful plan for his life. I showed him various passages of Scripture concerning the person of Jesus Christ (John 1, Colossians 1, Hebrews

1). He seemed to ignore everything I said; there appeared to be no communication between us whatsoever.

A couple of hours passed, and it was getting late. I felt that I was wasting my time and there was no need to continue the discussion. He agreed to call it a day. A friend and staff member who was with me suggested to this student that we would be glad to drop him off at his home on the way to my hotel.

As we got into the car, his first words were, "Everything you said tonight hit me right in the heart. I want to receive Christ. Tell me how I can do it right now." Even though I had not sensed it during our conversation, the Holy Spirit — who really does care — had been speaking to his heart through the truth of God's Word which I had shared with him.

Bible Reading: Colossians 2:1-10

ACTION POINT: I will not depend upon my own wisdom, my personality or even my training to share Christ effectively with others, but I will commit myself to talk about Him wherever I go, depending upon the Holy Spirit to empower me and speak through me to the needs of others.

Poor, Blind and Naked

*"You say, 'I am rich, with everything I want; I don't need a thing!'
And you don't realize that spiritually you are wretched and miserable
and poor and blind and naked"* (Revelation 3:17).

George had come for a week of lay training at Arrowhead Springs. Following one of my messages on revival, in which I explained that most Christians are like the members of the church at Ephesus and Laodicea, as described in Revelation 2 and 3, he came to share with me how, though he was definitely lukewarm and had lost his first love, he frankly had never read those passages, had never heard a sermon such as I had presented and therefore did not realize how wretched and miserable and poor and blind and naked he was.

If there were such an instrument as a "faith thermometer," at what level would your faithfulness register? Hot? Lukewarm? Cold?

Jesus said to the church at Laodicea, "I know you well — you are neither hot nor cold; I wish you were one or the other! But since you are merely lukewarm, I will spit you out of my mouth!" (Revelation 3:15).

Again, I ask you, where does your faithfulness register on that faith thermometer?

The greatest tragedy in the history of nations is happening right here in America. Here we are, a nation founded by Christians, a nation founded upon godly principles, a nation blessed beyond all the nations of history for the purpose of doing God's will in the world. But most people in this country, including the majority of church members, have without realizing it become materialistic and humanistic, all too often worshiping man and his achievements instead of the only true God.

Granted, the opinion polls show meteoric growth in the number of people in America who claim to be born-again Christians. But where does their faith register on the faith thermometer? America is a modern-day Laodicea. We are where we are today because too many Christians have quenched the Holy Spirit in their lives.

Bible Reading: Revelation 3:14-19

ACTION POINT: Realizing that America cannot become spiritually renewed without individual revival, I will humble myself, and pray, and seek God's face, and turn from my wicked ways. By faith I will claim revival in my own heart.

When He's in Control

"But when the Holy Spirit controls our lives, He will produce this kind of fruit in us: . . . self-control" (Galatians 5:22,23).

Sue insisted that she was Spirit-filled, and she frequently challenged others to be filled with the Spirit. But there was no evidence that the Holy Spirit was in control of her life, because she was completely undisciplined in everything she did. She knew nothing about self-control. She knew all about the Holy Spirit, in her mind, but there was no evidence that He was in her life – and in control of her life.

Dr. Henrietta Mears, as director of Christian education at the First Presbyterian Church in Hollywood, had one of the greatest spiritual ministries of her time. Hundreds of young men and women became church members and missionaries under her influence. She lived in a palatial home, owned priceless antiques and dressed beautifully. Most people assumed that she was a woman of great wealth. Actually, she was a person of relatively modest means. She simply knew how to take her regular salary, a modest inheritance, plus savings, and maximize them for God's glory.

For example, she would advise young people, "Do not eat in expensive restaurants where you spend excessively except on rare occasions. Instead,

prepare your own lunch, and over a period of a year you can save enough money by not eating out to take a trip around the world and enrich your spirit, your soul and your cultural sensitivities. Or you can use the money you save to buy something which will enhance the beauty of your home or person."

We see disciplined people all around us in this world. Athletes discipline themselves to strict training, soldiers are drilled in military discipline, artists and writers are disciplined to sharpen their talents through dedicated practice. On the other hand, we also see examples of a lack of discipline in the lives of many people around us.

Whether a person is a Christian or a non-believer, the development of self-control as a quality of character seems to be difficult for most people. Yet we are told in the Bible that the Spirit-filled Christian will exhibit self-control as a part of the fruit of the Spirit.

Bible Reading: 1 Chronicles 28:9-13

ACTION POINT: I acknowledge that to walk in the fullness and control of the Holy Spirit will enable me to demonstrate a life of discipline and self-control. Therefore, by faith, and with the help of the Holy Spirit, I shall live a life of discipline and self-control for the glory of God. Self-control is essential for supernatural living.

No Darkness in Him

"This is the message God has given us to pass on to you: That God is light and in Him is no darkness at all. So if we say we are His friends, but go on living in spiritual darkness and sin, we are lying. But if we are living in the light of God's presence, just as Christ does, then we have wonderful fellowship and joy with each other, and the blood of Jesus His Son cleanses us from every sin" (1 John 1:5-7).

One of the first passages of Scripture that I memorized as a new Christian was the first chapter of 1 John. This passage has been a beacon to me through the years as a simple reminder that in God is light and the only reason that I do not live perpetually in that light is because at times I deliberately sin.

Steve had lost his joy and enthusiasm for Christ, and as a new Christian was perplexed. He could not understand what had happened to him. As we counseled together, it became apparent that he had allowed some of his old natural habit patterns to creep back into his life.

I suggested that he make a list of all the things that were wrong in his life and confess them to the Lord in accordance with 1 John 1:9. A few days later, with joyful enthusiasm he came to share with me how his heart had been kindled afresh with the love of God as he was now walking in the light as God is in the light, having wonderful fellowship with the Lord Jesus Christ.

How does one walk in the light? Do not tolerate unconfessed sin. Meditate upon the Word of God. Spend time in prayer talking to God and letting Him talk to you. Share your faith in Christ with others. Obey the commandments of God.

Are you walking in the light as God is in the light? Are you experiencing the joy of the Lord? Are you constrained by the love of Christ to share Him with others?

Bible Reading: 1 John 1:6-10

ACTION POINT: I shall always seek to walk in the light as God is in the light in order that I may experience wonderful fellowship with my Lord. When I find myself walking in darkness, I shall pause to confess my sins and by faith claim God's forgiveness and cleansing so that I may be restored to once again walk in the light with God.

Cleansed From Sin

"But if we are living in the light of God's presence, just as Christ does, then we have wonderful fellowship and joy with each other, and the blood of Jesus His Son cleanses us from every sin" (1 John 1:7).

A pastor I know had once delighted in studying and preaching the Word of God. In his earlier days, he had been a real soul-winner, but the time came when he no longer spent time reading and studying the Scriptures. He became critical, discouraged and pessimistic. Finally, his personal life and his family fell apart.

At one point, he told me, he was thinking about committing suicide. He could have been spared all of this heartache, tragedy and sorrow if only he had continued to study the Word of God, to meditate on its truths and to obey its commands.

As someone wisely said, "Sin will keep you from God's Word, or God's Word will keep you from sin."

Many of the problems we experience in the Christian life are self-imposed. They are the result of carelessness in the way we walk. The promises of God are true; you can stake your life on them. The way to supernatural living is to walk with God in the light of His presence.

"God is light and in Him is no darkness at all. So if we say we are His friends, but go on living in spiritual darkness and sin, we are lying. But if we are living in the light of God's presence...then we have wonderful fellowship and joy..." (1 John 1:5-7, LB).

Bible Reading: 1 John 2:1-6

ACTION POINT: Claiming the power of the Holy Spirit, I will continue to live in the light of God's presence and explain to those who walk in darkness how they too can walk in the light of God's presence and in joyful fellowship with our risen Savior.

Fullness of Joy

"Thou wilt show me the path of life: in thy presence is fullness of joy; at thy right hand there are pleasures for evermore" (Psalm 16:11, KJV).

"If you have lost the joy of the Lord in your life," someone once observed, "who moved, you or God? For in His presence is fullness of joy."

That saint and prophet of earlier years, A. W. Tozer, suggested several ways for the believer to achieve real joy:

1. Cultivate a genuine friendship with God. He is a Friend who sticks closer than a brother.

2. Take time to exercise yourself daily unto godliness. Vow never to be dishonest about sin in your life, never to defend yourself, never to own anything (or let anything own you), never to pass on anything hurtful about others, never to take any glory to yourself.

3. No known sin must be allowed to remain in your life. "Keep short accounts with God" — never allow unconfessed sins to pile up in your life.

4. Set out to build your own value system based on the Word of God.

Meditate on the Word; practice the presence of God. Set priorities as you realize what is truly important. It will be reflected in the standard of values you set for yourself.

5. Share your spiritual discoveries with others.

Bible Reading: John 15:7-11

ACTION POINT: Knowing that the best witness in the world is a joyful, radiant Christian, I will try to be that kind of believer, trusting the indwelling Holy Spirit to thus empower me and radiate His love and joy through me. I will share my spiritual discoveries with others.

He Protects Worshipers

"He protects all those who love Him, but destroys the wicked" (Psalm 145:20).

Throughout Scripture one is reminded over and over again that when a person obeys Him, God blesses that person. And when a person — or a nation — disobeys Him, God disciplines, just as a loving father disciplines his disobedient child because he loves him, not because of his wrath or any evil intent.

The Israelites, though warned many times that if they disobeyed God He would destroy them, finally had to be destroyed — after numerous warnings and disciplinings (including grievous plagues) — because of their disobedience (Deuteronomy, chapters 8 and 28; Amos, chapter 4). God still disciplines men and nations. It is a sobering thing to disobey God.

Someone has said, "We do not break God's laws, but God's laws break us." If we obey them, we are blessed. If we disobey them, we must suffer the consequences.

Scripture suggests that what applies to individuals and to nations also applies to Christian movements or organizations such as the one with which I have the privilege of serving our Lord. So long as I and the now more than 16,000 full-time and associate staff members continue to obey God, His hand of blessing will remain upon our worldwide efforts. If we disobey Him, He will not only withhold His blessings, but will discipline us as individuals and as a movement.

I pray daily that each one of us may determine to obey God implicitly.

Bible Reading: Psalm 145:14-19

ACTION POINT: Recognizing that the laws of God in the spiritual realm are just as inviolate as the laws of the physical realm, and that God blesses those who obey Him and disciplines those who are disobedient, with the enabling of the Holy Spirit I will seek to express my love for God by living a life of faith and obedience for His glory.

Self-Control Is Better

"It is better to be slow-tempered than famous; it is better to have self-control than to control an army" (Proverbs 16:32).

You and I know from experience that it is not easy to discipline our emotions, our passions or our self-will. In fact, apart from God's help, it is an impossibility.

A lustful person who does not control his thoughts quenches and grieves the Spirit.

An overweight person, because he cannot control his appetite, quenches and grieves the Spirit.

A Christian who places undue emphasis on material possessions quenches and grieves the Holy Spirit.

A gossip who cannot control his tongue quenches and grieves the Spirit.

A husband, wife, or child who fails to live according to the commands of Ephesians chapter 5 quenches and grieves the Holy Spirit.

A student who fails to study adequately because of poor discipline quenches and grieves the Spirit.

Many pages would be required to list all the ways in which lack of self-control quenches and grieves the Holy Spirit.

The spirit, mind and body are the three aspects of our being over which we are told to practice self-control.

What is man's spirit?

It is his immaterial being — man without his body, if you will. The Bible gives many characteristics of the spirit of man. It is that which communicates with the Spirit of God.

Man's spirit is the center of emotions (1 Kings 21:5), the source of passions (Ezekiel 3:14) and the seat of volition or exercise of the will (Proverbs 16:32). Our spirit is subject to divine influence while housed in our mortal body (Deuteronomy 2:30 and Isaiah 19:14), and leaves the body at the time of physical death (Ecclesiastes 12:7 and James 2:26).

Bible Reading: Proverbs 15:1-5

ACTION POINT: Drawing upon this enabling power of the Holy Spirit, I will practice the vital discipline of self-control.

The Lord Forgave You

"Since you have been chosen by God who has given you this new kind of life, and because of His deep love and concern for you, you should practice tenderhearted mercy and kindness to others. Don't worry about making a good impression on them but be ready to suffer quietly and patiently. Be gentle and ready to forgive; never hold grudges. Remember, the Lord forgave you, so you must forgive others" (Colossians 3:12,13).

J. C. Penney, a devout Christian whom I knew personally, built one of America's leading businesses on the principle of the Golden Rule, taught by our Lord:

"Do unto others as you would have them do unto you."

He and other gentle men have developed tenderness and sensitivity to others through their years of maturing, often through many difficult and trying experiences. So should we as Christians seek to develop gentle spirits through the trials and tribulations that God permits us to go through.

Do you lack gentleness in your life?

Do you have a tendency to be arrogant, proud, boastful?

Are you overbearing or even coarse and rude with others?

By faith you can become a gentle person. By faith you can confess your sins and know that they have been forgiven. By faith you can appropriate the filling of the Spirit of Christ. By faith you can practice tenderhearted mercy and kindness to others.

The Lord has commanded us to be gentle people, so by faith we can ask for that portion of the fruit of the Spirit, gentleness and love, and know that He is changing us for the better.

As I have cautioned with regard to other Christlike traits, this is one which usually develops over an extended period of time, usually through the maturing process that comes only with time and trials and sometimes tribulation. Pray that God will give you patience with yourself as you mature into the gentle and humble person He wants you to be.

Bible Reading: Colossians 3:14-17

ACTION POINT: God's promise to me is that He forgives; with His help I will forgive and practice tenderhearted mercy and kindness to others, with the prayer that I may be more and more conformed to the image of my Lord.

The Right Priorities

"Constantly remind the people about these laws, and you yourself must think about them every day and every night so that you will be sure to obey all of them. For only then will you succeed" (Joshua 1:8).

Jim was a driven man. He loved his wife and his four children. But the thing that consumed almost every waking thought was, "How can I be a greater success? How can I make more money? How can I earn the praise of men?"

Through neglect his family began to disintegrate, and he came to me for counsel. His wife was interested in another man; he was alienated from his children. Three were involved in drugs and one had attempted suicide twice.

"Where have I gone wrong?" Jim asked.

I reminded him of the Scripture, "What does it profit a man if he gains the whole world and loses his own soul?"

According to Scripture, a man's priorities are first, to love God with all his heart, his soul and his mind, and then to love his neighbor as himself. Since his closest neighbors are his wife and children, his second priority is his wife. A good marriage takes the Ephesians 5:25 kind of love: "Husbands, love your wives, even as Christ also loved the church," a sacrificial, giving love.

The third priority is his children. He must show love to them, not by giving them *things*, but by giving them *himself*, spending time with them, letting them know they are far more important to him than his business.

A man must love his wife and children unconditionally as God loves him — not when, if, or because they are good and deserve to be loved.

And the fourth priority I discussed with Jim was his business. A man's business must be dedicated to the Lord Jesus Christ.

Jim surrendered his life to Christ. After almost three years of implementing the Bible's priorities, Jim's family again was united in the love of Christ, and God had given Jim and his wife a new-found love for Himself and for each other.

The law of God is clear: When we disobey Him, he disciplines us as a loving father and mother discipline their child, and when we obey Him, He will bless us.

Bible Reading: James 2:1-8

ACTION POINT: I will seek to please the Lord in all that I do, knowing that I will experience His blessings when I obey Him, and His discipline when I disobey Him.

Perfect Harmony

"Most of all, let love guide your life, for then the whole church will stay together in perfect harmony" (Colossians 3:14).

Martha had a very poor self-image. The distress she felt because of her physical appearance was compounded by the guilt of being grossly overweight. She hated herself and was despondent to the point of seriously considering suicide.

I counsel many students and older adults who are not able to accept themselves. Some are weighted down with guilt because of unconfessed sins. Others are not reconciled to their physical handicaps or deformities. Still others feel inferior mentally or socially.

My counsel to such people is this: God loves you and accepts you as you are. The love of God which is shed abroad in our hearts by the Holy Spirit enables us to love ourselves as God made us. We can be thankful for ourselves, loving ourselves unconditionally as God does, and we can love others unconditionally, too.

It is Satan who is the great accuser, causing us to hate ourselves and others. God, having commanded us to love Him with all of our heart, soul, mind and strength, and our neighbor as ourselves, and our enemies, will enable us to do what He commands us to do as we claim His promise.

The great tragedy of many families is that resentment, bitterness and hate overtake their members like an all-consuming cancer, ultimately destroying the unity among husband, wife and children. Love of the husband and wife for each other, and of parents and children for one another, is so basic that it should not need to be mentioned. Yet, sadly and alarmingly, children are alienated from their parents, and even many Christian marriages are ending in divorce — in fact, in greater numbers today than at any other time in history.

God's kind of love is a unifying force. Paul admonishes us to "put on love, which is the perfect bond of unity."

Bible Reading: Colossians 3:18-25

ACTION POINT: Since God commands us to love Him, our neighbors, our enemies and ourselves, today I will claim that supernatural love by faith on the basis of God's command to love and the promise that if I ask anything according to His will, He will hear and answer me.

Ways That Are Right and Best

"He will teach the ways that are right and best to those who humbly turn to Him" (Psalm 25:9).

A guide, taking some tourists through Mammoth Cave, reached a place called "The Cathedral."

Mounting a rock called "The Pulpit," he said he wanted to preach a sermon, and it would be short.

"Keep close to your guide," he said.

The tourists soon found it was a good sermon. If they did not keep close to the guide, they would be lost in the midst of pits, precipices and caverns.

It is hard to find one's way through Mammoth Cave without a guide. It is harder to find one's way through the world without the lamp of God's Word.

"Keep your eye on the Light of the World (Jesus) and use the Lamp of God's Word" is a good motto for the Christian to follow.

Humbly turning to God is one of the most meaningful exercises a person can take. We come in touch with divine sovereignty, and we become instant candidates to discern God's will for our lives.

Humbling ourselves is clearly in line with God's formula for revival:

"If my people, which are called by my name, shall humble themselves, and pray, and seek my face, and turn from their wicked ways; then will I hear from heaven, and will forgive their sin, and will heal their land" (2 Chronicles 7:14, KJV).

Bible Reading: Psalm 25:1-8

ACTION POINT: With the enabling of the Holy Spirit, I will fix my heart and mind on Jesus first and others second, which is true humility.

How to Be Fearless

"The Lord is my light and my salvation; whom shall I fear?" (Psalm 27:1).

The psalmist David did not choose words carelessly — but under divine inspiration — when he spoke of *light* and *salvation.*

Of all the memorials in Westminster Abbey, not one has a nobler thought inscribed on it than the monument to Lord Lawrence — simply his name, with the date of his death, and these words:

"He feared man so little because he feared God so much."

Charles H. Spurgeon gives some helpful insights into Psalm 27:1.

"In the New Testament, the idea which is hinted at in the language of David is expressly revealed as a truth. God does not merely give us His light. He is light, just as He is love in His own uncreated nature.

"'God is light,' John writes in his epistle, 'and in Him is no darkness at all.' When John sought to teach us our Lord's Godhead as clearly and as sharply as possible, he calls Him the 'light,' meaning to teach us that as such He shares the essential nature of the Deity."

How wonderful that we need not live in darkness — in any sense of the word — but that we immediately can have the Light of Life, God Himself, available to us in the person of His indwelling Holy Spirit as well as in His inspired Word. Every prerequisite for the abundant, supernatural life has been made available to us, and access is immediate if we come to Him immediately with our needs.

Bible Reading: Psalm 27:2-6

ACTION POINT: With God's help, I will follow Him who is my light and my salvation. I will have no fear of men or circumstances.

Christ Lives in Me

"I have been crucified with Christ: and I myself no longer live, but Christ lives in me. And the real life I now have within this body is a result of my trusting in the Son of God, who loved me and gave Himself for me" (Galatians 2:20).

After many years of working with thousands of Christians, I am convinced that a person cannot enjoy the supernatural life — which is a believer's heritage in Christ — apart from the proper balance between Bible study, prayer and sharing Christ with others out of the overflow of an obedient, Spirit-filled life.

We need to be able not only to experience this great adventure with Christ ourselves, but also to share this good news with others.

A word of caution and reminder is in order at this point. We become spiritual and experience power from God and become fruitful in our witness as a result of *faith* and faith alone.

The Bible clearly teaches that "the just shall live by faith" Romans 1:17. However, it is equally important to know that good works are the result of faith — "trusting in the Son of God" — and unless there are "good works" there is not faith, for "faith without works is dead" (James 2:17).

Many Christians are confused on this point. They think of works (Bible study, prayer and other spiritual disciplines) as the *means* to, rather than the *results* of, the life of faith. They spend much time in these activities, seeking God's favor and blessing.

They may even attempt to witness for Christ and to obey the various commands of God, thinking that by these means they will achieve supernatural living. But they remain defeated, frustrated, powerless and fruitless.

As you are filled with the Holy Spirit — "Christ living in me" — and walk in His power by faith, the Bible becomes alive, prayer becomes vital, your witness becomes effective and obedience becomes a joy.

Bible Reading: Galatians 2:15-19

ACTION POINT: I will seek to remember that Christ lives in me, in the person of His indwelling Holy Spirit, and thus I have all I need for supernatural living, for victory and joy and peace.

Instruct, Teach, Guide

"I will instruct thee and teach thee in the way which thou shalt go: I will guide thee with Mine eye" (Psalm 32:8, KJV).

As an Eastern monarch, David was familiar with the thought behind this interesting expression: "guide thee with Mine eye."

As he sat in state, David was surrounded by a number of servants who were eager to do his bidding. They constantly fixed their eyes on him, and when David wanted any service done, he rarely needed to speak. Each servant knew his post, and his eyes were dutifully fixed on his master. At a nod or a sign — a turn of the eye — he flew to complete the desired service.

How refreshing to know that our God keeps an eye on each one of us as His children. He knows the way we are going; He knows the way we should take — and with His watchful eye He promises to instruct us and to teach us.

When we become careless and stubborn, and thus are not observing the slightest indications of God's will for us, we require the bit and bridle instead of the guiding eye. Great attentiveness and great desire are presupposed on the part of those who are led.

On some subjects, full directions and plain commands are not always given in the Word of God. In such cases, we must be especially sensitive to the guiding eye.

Similarly, we apply the truth of this passage to the truth of a particular providence. God's guiding us with His eye often indicates to us His will by means of providential events. When we live and walk in the Spirit, by faith, we recognize His guiding eye.

Bible Reading: Proverbs 3:1-6

ACTION POINT: I will try to be more sensitive to God's guiding eye, realizing that I will find proper direction in no other way.

He Gives Attention

"For the eyes of the Lord are intently watching all who live good lives, and He gives attention when they cry to Him" (Psalm 34:15).

A mother and her little 4-year-old daughter were preparing to retire for the night. The child was afraid of the dark, and the mother, on this occasion alone with the child, also felt fearful.

After the light was turned out, the child glimpsed the moon outside the window.

"Mother," she asked, "is the moon God's light?"

"Yes," replied the mother.

"Will God put out His light and go to sleep?"

"No, my child," the mother replied, "God never goes to sleep."

"Well," said the child, with the simplicity of childlike faith, "as long as God is awake, there is no sense in both of us staying awake."

God expects you and me — with that same kind of childlike faith — not only to live good lives but also to cry out to Him in our times of need, knowing that He watches intently and gives attention to our every cry.

Again we have that helpful imagery of guiding eyes, the eyes of Him who rules and reigns over all — who is concerned about each one of His children, and equally concerned about those who have not yet trusted in Him for He is not willing that any should perish.

Bible Reading: Psalm 34:16-22

ACTION POINT: I shall not be afraid to cry out to the Lord when circumstances warrant a call to the Almighty. In the meantime I will devote special time today to worship, praise and thank Him for His goodness to me.

All Who Win Souls Are Wise

"Godly men are growing a tree that bears life-giving fruit, and all who win souls are wise" (Proverbs 11:30).

I have never led anyone to Christ, and I never shall.

However, I have had the privilege of praying with thousands of people who have received Christ as a result of my witness.

When a person receives Christ, it is the work of the Holy Spirit. That is why I cannot boast over much fruit or be discouraged over little fruit.

The responsibility for fruit belongs to the Holy Spirit who works in and through the believer, producing fruit and changing the lives of those who respond favorably to our witness.

The power of our Lord Jesus Christ is available to all who trust and obey Him. We need to "understand how incredibly great His power is to help those who believe Him."

The Lord Jesus commissioned the disciples to go into all the world and preach the gospel, with the promise that He would always be with them.

Bible Reading: Proverbs 11:24-31

ACTION POINT: Today I will consciously draw upon the supernatural resources of the Holy Spirit to obey God's commands for holy living and fruitful witnessing.

We Shall Never Lack

"Even strong young lions sometimes go hungry, but those of us who reverence the Lord will never lack any good thing" (Psalm 34:10).

"When you have nothing left but God," a Christian leader once observed, "then for the first time you become aware that God is enough."

With every command of God is a specific or implied promise to enable us to do what He commands us to do. He always makes it possible for us to fulfill the conditions to obey His commands.

Rarely, will some of us see a check for a million — or even thousands — of dollars. But here is a check for millions of millions, waiting to be cashed by those of us who know and love the Lord, who love Him enough to obey His commands.

Here is a promise of God which is great enough to meet our needs, our wants, even our deepest desires and distresses.

As you and I go through our day, how reassuring it is to know that our reverence for the Lord will be rewarded by provision of every good thing we need. That means the strength, the peace, the courage, the love I need to get me through the decisions, the trials, the testings.

That also means a new consciousness of God's indwelling Holy Spirit, the one through whom I find the supernatural, abundant life. That means a tender conscience toward God, so that I make a supreme effort to avoid yielding to temptation in any way, lest I grieve my wonderful Lord.

Bible Reading: Psalm 34:1-9

ACTION POINT: I shall not be afraid to go to the bank of heaven today and cash a check for all my needs, enabling me to share the supernatural life with all whom my life touches.

Recognizing False Teachers

"Beware of false teachers who come disguised as harmless sheep, but are wolves and will tear you apart. You can detect them by the way they act, just as you can identify a tree by its fruit. You need never confuse grapevines with thorn bushes or figs with thistles (Matthew 7:15,16).

The secular press frequently quoted a famous professor in one of the most prestigious theological seminaries in the world, referring to him as the Protestant theologian of our time. As I talked with two of his students, whom I had the privilege of introducing to Christ, I asked, "What is your impression of Professor So-and-so?" They replied, "If the Bible is true, he is not a Christian."

They went on to explain that he denied the deity of Christ, the authority of Scripture and all the basic tenets of the Christian faith. Yet he was so subtle, so brilliant and profound, that many pastors and Christian leaders who were not biblically oriented were deceived and looked upon him as a great scholar and theologian.

However, after he died, his wife wrote a highly revealing book in which she described his many sexual exploits as well as his other wrongdoings that were inconsistent with what the Bible teaches.

There are many false teachers in the seminaries and pulpits of the world, who represent another master, not our Lord Jesus Christ. They do not preach the inspired Word of God. Often brilliant, loving, gracious, considerate people, they are, nevertheless, well-described by our Lord as false teachers, wolves disguised as harmless sheep.

How can you recognize false teachers? The test is threefold: (1) What is their view of the Lord Jesus Christ? Is He truly the Son of God? Did He die on the cross for our sins? Was He raised from the dead? (2) Do they profess that the Bible is the authority of God, divinely inspired? (3) Do they live lives that are consistent with the teachings of Scripture? Or do they condone practices that are contrary to the Word of God? If they do the latter, beware, for they will rob you of the supernatural resources of God that are available to you.

As you meditate upon the entire passage of scripture for today, ask God to give you a discerning spirit that you may not be deceived by false teachers.

Bible Reading: Matthew 7:13-23

ACTION POINT: I shall meditate upon God's Word and weigh those who profess to be His followers in light of their view of the Lord Jesus Christ, His holy, inspired Word, and how their lives are a witness to what God's Word commands us to be. I will instruct other believers and non-believers alike to be alert to the influence of false teachers.

God Meets Our Needs

"I have been young and now I am old. And in all my years I have never seen the Lord forsake a man who loves Him; nor have I seen the children of the godly go hungry" (Psalm 37:25).

Tom had been a humble follower and servant of the Lord Jesus Christ from his youth. He had learned of our Lord at the family altar in his modest home. Through the urging of his father and mother, he mastered and memorized large portions of Scripture. By his teenage years he was preaching, and after a brief time of study in a Bible institute he became an evangelist. His work was largely in the smaller rural churches. His speech was never eloquent nor was he distinguished and cultured in his appearance and demeanor, but he was a man of God. Wherever he went, hearts were strangely warmed as he spoke the truths concerning our wonderful Savior.

Now he had reached the ripe age of ninety. His hair was snow white and a bit long, but always neat. His ministry had covered over seventy years, and in that period he had come to know heartache, sorrow, adversity and poverty (especially during the depression years). He had performed many wedding ceremonies, had spent long nights at the bedside of the sick and had preached many funeral sermons. In obedience to his Lord, he had ministered to the widows and orphans, the poor and imprisoned. On this occasion, as he was coming to the climax of a rich and overflowing life, a radiant adventure with God — yes, the supernatural life — he reminisced. As he recalled some of the heartaches and tragedies, he said, "You know, not one single time in all my years have I seen the Lord forsake a man who loved Him, nor have I seen the children of the godly go hungry. Of course, I have seen Christians suffer, and I've been with them in their sorrow. But there's something different about the life of the one who walks with God. There's serenity, a peace. And then almost miraculously, while the unglodly often go hungry, God meets the needs of His children as He promised.

"Yes," he said in conclusion, "you can trust God and His Word. He never fails to keep His promise."

Bible Reading: Psalm 37:26-34

ACTION POINT: Knowing that I can trust God to meet my every need no matter what happens, I shall seek first the kingdom of God. Through the enabling of the Holy Spirit, I will live a godly life, a supernatural life for the glory of my Savior, and I will tell others how faithful and trustworthy He is.

He Will Take Care of Us

"He will take care of the helpless and poor when they cry to Him; for they have no one else to defend them" (Psalm 72:12).

Some time ago, a French tourist set out to cross St. Bernard's Pass by himself. When he got caught in the fog near the top, he sat on a rock and waited for one of the famous St. Bernard dogs, which have rescued thousands of lost travelers, to come and attend to him. But none came.

When the fog cleared away, he managed to reach the hospice. There he let it be known that he thought the dog a rather overrated animal.

"There I was," he said, "for at least six hours, and not one came near me."

"But why," exclaimed one of the monks, "did you not ring us up on the telephone?"

Then he explained to the astonished tourist that the whole of the pass is provided with shelters at short distances from each other — all in direct phone communication with the hospice. When the bell rings, the monks send off a dog loaded with bread, wine and other comforts.

The dog goes straight to the proper shelter. The system saves the hounds their former duty of patrolling the pass on the chance of a stray traveler being found, and as the pass is under deep snow for about eight months of the year, this entailed hard and often fruitless labor.

Many people in need of spiritual help have not yet realized there is One who will hear and answer directly the troubled cries for help.

Bible Reading: Psalm 72:13-19

ACTION POINT: Remembering that we "have not because we ask not," I'll remember to call on a kind heavenly Father today and whenever I have a need.

Obedience Releases the Power

"For the Lord says, 'Because he loves me, I will rescue him; I will make him great because he trusts in my name. When he calls on Me I will answer; I will be with him in trouble, and rescue him and honor him' " (Psalm 91:14,15).

Pete was the playboy type. He believed that Christ was in his life and that he had eternal life and would go to heaven when he died, but he was not willing to "go all the way with the Lord." He wanted to live the "good life," he said. One day perhaps he would make a total commitment of his life to Christ, but not now. He had all kinds of physical and emotional problems, but somehow he was never able to make the connection that the fact that his life was miserable was because of his disobedience to God.

All of God's supernatural resources are latent within us waiting for us, as an act of the will by faith, to release that power. This explains the difference between impotent, fruitless, defeated Christians and those who are buoyant, joyful, victorious and fruitful in magnificent ways for the glory of God. Both are indwelt by the same God and possess the same supernatural power, but one for whatever reason — lack of knowledge, lack of faith, disobedience — fails to release the power while the other — knowledgeable, dedicated, obedient, faithful — releases the power.

John 14:21 is another way of stating Psalm 91:14,15. Jesus said, "He that hath My commandments, and keepeth them, he it is that loveth Me: and he that loveth Me shall be loved of My Father, and I will love him, and will manifest Myself to him."

We demonstrate that we love God when we obey Him. And when we trust and obey Him, all the supernatural resources of deity are released in our behalf. He literally heals our bodies, our minds and our spirits and enables us to live the supernatural life.

Bible Reading: Psalm 91:7-13

ACTION POINT: I will acknowledge Jesus daily as the Lord of my life and demonstrate my love by obeying His commandments. In so doing, I can be assured that He will be with me in trouble and deliver me and honor me as He promised.

The Godly Shall Flourish

"But the godly shall flourish like palm trees, and grow tall as the cedars of Lebanon. For they are transplanted into the Lord's own garden, and are under His personal care. Even in old age they will still produce fruit and be vital and green" (Psalm 92:12-14).

John Vredenburgh preached in a Somerville, New York church for many years, often feeling that his ministry was a great failure even though he preached the gospel faithfully. His death came amidst discouragements, and even some of his members wondered about his success and effectiveness as a minister.

Not long after his death, however, spiritual revival came to Somerville. On one Sunday alone, 200 people came to Christ — most of whom dated their spiritual stirrings from the ministry of John Vredenburgh.

Faithfulness and persistence are great virtues in the service of Jesus Christ. "Pay Day, Some Day" was a significant theme and message of that great Southern Baptist pastor, R. G. Lee — and since God's timing is always perfect, it surely will come in good time.

"Even in old age they will still produce fruit." Though the outward man may be perishing, the inward man is renewed day by day. When the outward ear grows deaf, the inward man hears the voice of God. When the eye grows dim, the mind is enlightened with God's Word.

When the flesh becomes weak, we are "strengthened with might in the inner man." Older Christians look toward heaven, where they again shall see family and friends; meanwhile, they share their maturity and good judgment with others, knowing that God still rewards the faithful. Until that dying breath, the supernatural life on earth can continue.

Bible Reading: Psalm 92:7-11

ACTION POINT: Knowing that even in old(er) age my life can produce fruit, I will persevere and remain faithful to our Lord and His commands.

Faithful of the Land

"Mine eyes shall be upon the faithful of the land, that he may dwell with Me: he that walketh in a perfect way, he shall serve Me" (Psalm 101:6, KJV).

My mind immediately turns to the faithful minister of the gospel, the Sunday school teacher, the Christian worker as I read this verse of Scripture with its glorious promise.

Christian leaders are, indeed, included in this conditional promise. But many others may have a part as well. When that construction worker, a believer, who hears blasphemy on the job dares to speak up for his Lord, his act shall not go unnoticed and unrewarded.

That man who is scrupulously honest in his business, in the face of countless opportunities to be otherwise and in the face of competition and opposition that would seek to wipe him out, likewise shall have his reward.

That homemaker who cuts no corners, but completes the drudgery of housework with love and joy and peace, shall rejoice too in that day when the faithful are rewarded. That young person who dares swim upstream against the tide of humanism, the drug culture, the careless, the indifferent, also shall be rewarded.

It is remarkable, too, that God rewards His children for good works which He makes possible by giving the grace and ability to perform them! He gives us grace, then smiles on us because we exercise the very grace that is a gift from Him.

Bible Reading: Psalm 101:1-5

ACTION POINT: I will do what is right, regardless, and be faithful in every task I am called upon to do.

Freedom From Fear

"He does not fear bad news, nor live in dread of what may happen. For he is settled in his mind that Jehovah will take care of him" (Psalm 112:7).

Sarah was a hypochondriac, a bundle of nerves, plagued by all kinds of fears — fears that she would become ill, fears that she would have an accident, fears that something would happen to her husband or children or that they would experience financial reverses. Her every conversation was negative. And of course, her attitude alienated her from others, and the more isolated she found herself, the more fearful she became.

Completely absorbed with her own problems, she was seriously thinking of committing suicide when a Christian couple moved in next door to her. They began to demonstrate the love of God and share the good news of His forgiveness in Jesus Christ. Few people had taken an interest in Sarah, but this godly, Christian couple, especially Mary, the wife, embraced her with understanding, compassion and a loving heart.

Together they began to study the Bible and after a brief time, Sarah received Christ and began to grow as a Christian. She began to memorize Scripture and took great delight in hiding large quantities of the Word in her heart. Now her mind and her conversation were saturated with the things of God — His attributes, His holiness, His love — and His promises became a joyful reality to her.

A year had passed when one day she remarked to me with great enthusiasm, "I have been liberated. Christ has set me free. I seldom think of my own problems anymore, but find my mind absorbed with God and His truth, and how I might reach out in love and compassion to others as Mary reached out to me in my desperate need."

Sarah was no longer afraid. The fears that had plagued her were gone, because it was settled in her mind that Jehovah would take care of her and her family. No matter what happened, she knew that she could trust a loving, gracious, holy, righteous God, who had become her very real heavenly Father. Jesus Christ had become more real to her than her own flesh and blood.

Bible Reading: Psalm 112:1-6

ACTION POINT: I will seek to know more and more about my Lord by hiding His Word in my heart and meditating upon His many attributes. For I am convinced that He will watch over me, protect and care for me so that nothing can happen to me that He does not allow for my good.

The Best Counsel

"The godly man is a good counselor because he is just and fair and knows right from wrong" (Psalm 37:30,31).

Mary had gone to several psychologists and psychiatrists, and even religious leaders, seeking help, but no one had been able to help her. Consequently, she had been committed to a mental institution. Now, in desperation her family had come to seek help.

It did not take long to discover the root of her problem — she was plagued with a deep sense of guilt. Mary had been sexually promiscuous as a teenager, and prior to that she had been violated by her step-father who had taken advantage of her when she was a very young girl.

All of this tormented her greatly, but no one had taken her to the Word of God to help her understand that she did not have to carry the burden of her own sin. There is forgiveness. Scripture teaches that if we confess our sins, God is waiting to forgive and cleanse us.

There are three things we need to know about confession. First, the word "confess" means, in the original Greek language, "to agree with." If I agree with God concerning my immorality, stealing, dishonesty, whatever it may be, I am saying, "Lord, I know it is sin." Second, we know from Scripture that Christ has paid the penalty for our sins

by shedding His blood on the cross. And third, we must repent, which means we change our attitude toward that sin. This results in a change of action. When we do this, we have the promise that what we confess, God forgives, and He cleanses us from all unrighteousness.

When Mary understood the truth of God's promise, she and I knelt together and by faith she surrendered all of her guilt and frustration to Christ, who died for her, and she claimed God's forgiveness.

Only God could liberate her from the darkness and gloom of Satan's kingdom and bring her into the kingdom of light — the kingdom of our Lord Jesus Christ. Mary sensed God's immediate liberation and began to rejoice in the assurance of forgiveness and eternal life with Christ. She became a radiant, joyful and victorious witness for our Savior.

Bible Reading: Psalm 37:32-40

ACTION POINT: Not only will I seek the counsel of godly men and women, but I will, with God's help, become a godly person myself. I will saturate my mind with the truth of His holy Scripture, so that I will know what is right and wrong according to the Word of God, and I will then be able to give wise counsel to others.

Overflowing Blessings

"Lord, I am overflowing with Your blessings, just as You promised" (Psalm 119:65).

As the father of Dr. Harry Ironside, famous Christian leader, pastor and author, lay dying, he seemed to have a recurring view of the descending sheet which Peter saw in a vision.

"A great sheet and wild beasts," he mumbled, over and over, "and...and ...and."

The next words would not come, so he would start over again.

"John," a friend whispered to him, "it says, 'creeping things.' "

"Oh, yes," the dying man said, "that's how I got in — just a poor, good-for-nothing creeping thing. But I got in, saved by grace."

And considering the fact that each one of us, in ourselves, outside the Lord Jesus Christ, is but a poor creeping thing saved by grace, we must marvel anew as we overflow with His blessings.

What an exalted place we can have! Children of God, heirs of God, joint heirs with Christ, indwelt by His Holy Spirit, we are recipients of eternal life, given supernatural, abundant life as we yield ourselves to Him.

God has dealt well with each one of His children. He has given us work to do — to serve Him is to reign. He has given us provision. He has given us encouragement. He has given us many tokens of the pay we shall receive at the end of life's journey. He has dealt with us according to His Word.

Even the testings and trials are for a divine purpose: to conform us to His image; to make us more Christlike. Truly, we are on the winning side; how important it is that we tell men and women, boys and girls, around us each day, that they too can be on the winning side.

Bible Reading: Psalm 119:66-72

ACTION POINT: I will make a special effort to count my blessings today, and in deep gratitude share the good news of the gospel with others.

Preserved From the Enemy

"Though I walk in the midst of trouble, thou wilt revive me: thou shalt stretch forth thine hand against the wrath of mine enemies, and thy right hand shall save me" (Psalm 138:7, KJV).

Robert Bruce, the famous emancipator of Scotland, was fleeing from his enemies. He sought refuge in a cave.

Hot on his trail, his enemies reached his hideout where they saw that a spider had built a web over the mouth of the cave. His pursuers, concluding that he could not have entered without first destroying the web, turned around and went on their way.

"Oh, God," Bruce prayed, "I thank Thee that in the tiny bowels of a spider you can place for me a shelter, and then send the spider in time to place it for my protection."

"God works in mysterious ways His wonders to perform," and whatever is necessary to protect His children from their enemies will be done.

All of life's journey is summed up in that one work "walk." Constant action, movement onward, never stationary, always on the move. Life is not simply a walk; often it is a walk "in the midst of trouble." Since sin came into the world, pleasure is mixed with pain. Trials and conflict often seem to mar the pathway.

To the trusting, confident believer in Christ, however, there is certain renewal and deliverance. Christ's indwelling Holy Spirit, given full control, guarantees victory and joy and abundant life — supernatural life.

Bible Reading: Psalm 138:1-6

ACTION POINT: I will see God's protecting hand in my walk with Him today and proclaim His faithfulness to others.

We Can Have Real Peace

"So now, since we have been made right in God's sight by faith in His promises, we can have real peace with Him because of what Jesus Christ our Lord has done for us" (Romans 5:1).

When Arthur DeMoss, one of my very best friends and one of our Lord's choicest servants, went to be with the Lord, as the result of an unexpected heart attack, all of us were shocked. The word reached me in Austria, where I was meeting with our European staff. Immediately, I flew back to the United States for the memorial service.

As I participated in that service, I looked over the large audience, about half of whom had been introduced to Christ through the ministry of this man whom we had all come to honor.

In the crowd, I saw one face that stood out — a face that was the most radiant of all. It was Art's widow, Nancy. She was sitting in the front row with their seven children. Her radiant countenance was a demonstration to me of the supernatural joy and peace which God gives in such times of extreme grief.

Nancy and Art were the greatest of lovers and friends. They had been deeply in love since their courtship and were almost inseparable whether in the building of the business, in the rearing of their family or in their burden for evangelism and the souls of men.

Yet, in this time of Nancy's greatest sorrow, the evidence that she was filled with the Spirit radiated from her countenance. She was experiencing the supernatural peace of God — love's security, which is available to all of God's children.

Bible Reading: Romans 5:2-11

ACTION POINT: I will claim by faith God's peace — not only for me but also for family and friends in need of such peace — and seek to introduce others to the One who is the Prince of Peace.

First Step to Wisdom

"How does a man become wise? The first step is to trust and reverence the Lord! Only fools refuse to be taught" (Proverbs 1:7).

In 1787, the Constitutional Convention was on the verge of total failure. The issue: whether small states should have the same representation as large states.

From the wisdom of his 81 years, Benjamin Franklin recalled the Scripture which says, "Except the Lord build the house, they labor in vain that build it" (Psalm 127:1), and in this hopeless situation, he offered a suggestion.

"Gentlemen," he said, "I have lived a long time and am convinced that God governs in the affairs of men. If a sparrow cannot fall to the ground without His notice, is it probable that an empire can rise without His aid?

"I move that prayer imploring the assistance of heaven be held every morning before we proceed to business." God heard their prayers and the conflict was soon resolved. To this day, all legislative sessions continue to be opened with prayer, with God's blessing.

"Reverence of the Lord is the beginning of knowledge" reads the Modern Language translation of this verse — a preamble to wise living a good motto for life.

Someone has said, "The eternal task of religion is the conquest of fear." Men fear many things — bacteria, losing their jobs, being dependent in old age, giving offense to their neighbors, war, failure, death.

Fear (worshipful reverence) of God represents a different kind of fear — the kind a child shows toward wise and loving parents when he shuns acts of disobedience to avoid both grieving those parents whom he loves and suffering the inevitable discipline which follows disobedience. Perhaps if we feared God more, we would fear everything else less.

Bible Reading: Proverbs 1:8-16

ACTION POINT: My fear and reverence of God is the beginning of supernatural living and will result in worship of Him — by walk as well as by talk.

Practicing the Presence of God

"How precious it is, Lord, to realize that You are thinking about me constantly! I can't even count how many times a day Your thoughts turn towards me. And when I waken in the morning, You are still thinking of me!" (Psalm 139:17,18).

Our sons, Zac and Brad, have helped me to understand, in some small measure, the truth of this promise, for in the course of a single day, I will lift them up in prayer many times. I am finite, but God is infinite. My love for our sons is limited, but His love is inexhaustible and unconditional. It is because of God's love in my heart that I am able to love my sons unconditionally, even as He loves me.

What a comforting, encouraging thought, that the omnipotent Creator, God, who possesses all power and control of creation, loves me enough that He is constantly thinking about me. When I allow Him to do so, He talks to me, expressing His love, wisdom and grace from His Word, through divine impressions and the counsel of wise and godly friends. His eyes run to and fro throughout the whole earth to make Himself strong and mighty in my behalf (2 Chronicles 16:9).

Just as He is constantly thinking about me, I have been admonished to pray without ceasing. To talk to Him, to think about Him all the time — as difficult as it may sound — is a joyful reality to those who practice the presence of God. Is that the kind of relationship you are experiencing day by day? If not, it can be.

Bible Reading: Psalm 139:1-10

ACTION POINT: Mindful that God loves, cares and thinks about me constantly, I shall seek to live the supernatural life by practicing His presence, by praying without ceasing and by claiming His supernatural power by faith.

Long, Satisfying Life

"If you want a long and satisfying life, closely follow my instructions" (Proverbs 3:2).

A famous children's specialist declared, "When it comes to a serious illness, the child who has been taught to obey has four times the chance of recovery that the spoiled and undisciplined child has."

Every parent should consider well the implications of that statement. We have all been taught that one of the Ten Commandments was for children to obey their parents.

But it is doubtful that many of us have ever considered that obedience might mean the difference between the saving or losing of a child's life.

The hymnwriter who said that we should "trust and obey, for there's no other way to be happy in Jesus" well knew what he was saying. A "long and satisfying life" certainly would be synonymous with a "happy life."

Many Christians have every intention of following God's instructions — without ever really knowing what those instructions are. That is why it is supremely important for every believer to spend time in God's Word, the book of instructions for Christians.

Are you one of those who truly want a long and satisfying life? Then, are you willing to follow God's instructions for your life? Are you willing to familiarize yourself thoroughly with His instructions so that you will have no difficulty knowing and following them?

Bible Reading: Proverbs 3:1-8

ACTION POINT: I will follow closely God's instructions in order that I may live a long and satisfying life.

Give Him the First Part

"Honor the Lord by giving Him the first part of all your income, and He will fill your barns with wheat and barley and overflow your wine vats with the finest wines" (Proverbs 3:9,10).

"Yes, I tithe," said John D. Rockefeller, Sr., "and I would like to tell you how it all came about.

"I had to begin work as a small boy to help support my mother. My first wages amounted to $1.50 per week. The first week after I went to work I took the $1.50 home to my mother and she held the money in her lap and explained to me that she would be happy if I would give a tenth of it to the Lord.

"I did," Rockefeller said, "and from that week until this day I have tithed every dollar God has entrusted to me. And I want to say if I had not tithed the first dollar I made I would not have tithed the first million dollars I made.

"Tell your readers to train the children to tithe, and they will grow up to be faithful stewards of the Lord."

As R. G. Le Tourneau observed years ago, "We do not give to God because it pays, but it does pay to give to God and to serve Him faithfully." Without any question, God honors faithful stewardship — of time, energy, money, all that we have and are.

The importance of tithing is one of the first lessons I learned as a new Christian. Now I realize that that is only the beginning, because everything that I enjoy has been entrusted to me by a gracious, loving Father, who expects me to maximize all that he has put into my hands; therefore, tithing must be followed by offerings, based on the clear Word of God that as we sow we reap. The more we give back to God, the more He will entrust to us, but we are to give with a cheerful heart out of a deep sense of gratitude for all that God has given to us.

Bible Reading: Malachi 3:8-12

ACTION POINT: God will have the first fruits of my life, the first part of my money, my time, my talent, my energy.

Wisdom Brings Peace

"Wisdom gives a good, long life, riches, honor, pleasure, peace" (Proverbs 3:16,17).

High up in the Andes Mountains stands a bronze statue of Christ — the base of granite, the figure fashioned from old cannons — marking the boundary between Argentina and Chile.

"Sooner shall these mountains crumble into dust," reads the Spanish engraving, "than Argentines and Chileans break the peace sworn at the feet of Christ the Redeemer."

Peoples of these two countries had been quarreling about their boundaries for many years, and suffering from the resultant mistrust.

In 1900, with the conflict at its highest, citizens begged King Edward VII of Great Britain to mediate the dispute. On May 28, 1903, the two governments signed a treaty ending the conflict.

During the celebration that followed, Senora de Costa, a noble lady of Argentina who had done much to bring about the peace, conceived the idea of a monument. She had the statue of Christ shaped from the cannons that had been used to strike terror into Chilean hearts.

At the dedication ceremony, the statue was presented to the world as a sign of the victory of good will. "Protect, Oh Lord, our native land," prayed Senora de Costa. "Ever give us faith and hope. May fruitful peace be our first patrimony and good example its greatest glory."

The monument stands today as a reminder that only Christ — the Prince of Peace — can bring real peace to the world. And that refers as much to individual peace as it does to national and international peace.

Bible Reading: Proverbs 3:18-23

ACTION POINT: Like Solomon of old, I shall seek the wisdom that brings a good, long life, riches, honor, pleasure and the lasting peace that comes from God's indwelling Holy Spirit.

Wait Patiently and Confidently

"But if we must keep trusting God for something that hasn't happened yet, it teaches us to wait patiently and confidently" (Romans 8:25).

During my college days, I was not a believer. Only in retrospect can I appreciate in some measure the testimony of one of my professors, who was the head of the education department.

He and his wife were devout Christians. They had a mongoloid child, whom they took with them wherever they went, and I am sure that their motivation for doing so — at least in part — was to give a testimony of the fruit of the Spirit, patience and love.

They loved the child dearly and felt that God had given them the responsibility and privilege to rear the child personally as a testimony of His grace, rather than placing her in a home for retarded children. The Bible teaches us that God never gives us a responsibility, a load or a burden without also giving us the ability to be victorious.

This professor and his wife bore their tremendous burden with joyful hearts. Wherever they went, they waited on the child, hand and foot. Instead of being embarrassed and humiliated, trying to hide the child in the closet, they unashamedly always took her with them, as a witness for Christ and as an example of His faithfulness and sufficiency.

They demonstrated patience and love by drawing upon the supernatural resources of the Holy Spirit in their close, moment-by-moment walk with God. Because of the working of the Holy Spirit in their lives, they were able to bear their trials supernaturally without grumbling or complaining. This is not to suggest that every dedicated Christian couple would be led of God to respond in the same way under similar circumstances. In their case, their lives communicated patience.

Bible Reading: Romans 8:18-24

ACTION POINT: Knowing that God's Holy Spirit indwells me and enables me to live supernaturally, I will claim by faith the fruit of the Spirit (Galatians 5:22,23) with special emphasis on patience for today and every day.

Real Life, Radiant Health

"I have been crucified with Christ; and I myself no longer live, but Christ lives in me. And the real life I now have within this body is a result of my trusting in the Son of God, who loved me and gave Himself for me" (Galatians 2:10).

George Muller was asked the secret of his fruitful service for the Lord. "There was a day when I died," he said, "utterly died."

As he spoke, he bent lower and lower until he almost touched the floor.

"I died to George Muller," he continued, "his opinions, preferences, tastes and will — died to the world, its approval or censure — died to the approval or blame even of my brethren and friends — and since then I have studied only to show myself approved unto God."

With that kind of obedience to God and His inspired Word, it is small wonder that that great man of faith, George Muller, saw God perform miracle after miracle in his behalf, helping to support hundreds and even thousands of orphans simply by trusting God to provide.

Men and women of the world today would pay literally millions of dollars for the real life and radiant health promised in Proverbs 4:20-22 to the believer for simple faith and trust in God. "Listen, son of mine, to what I say. Listen carefully. Keep these thoughts ever in mind; let them penetrate deep within your heart, for they will mean real life for you, and radiant health." To me, these verses encourage reading, studying, memorizing and meditating upon the Word of God.

Being crucified with Christ and hiding His Word in our hearts will not only keep us from sin, but it will also promote *real life* and *radiant health* for us, which we will want to share with others.

Bible Reading: Proverbs 4:23-27; 5:1,2

ACTION POINT: By faith, I will recognize that I have been crucified with Christ and will keep His thoughts in my mind throughout this day, meditating on His promises and faithfulness.

Our Treasuries Filled

"My paths are those of justice and right. Those who love and follow Me are indeed wealthy. I fill their treasuries" (Proverbs 8:20,21).

"How does it feel to be a millionaire?" someone once asked the maker of Pullman cars, George M. Pullman.

"I have never thought of that before," replied Pullman, "but now that you mention it, I believe I am no better off — certainly not happier, than when I did not have a dollar to my name and had to work from daylight to dark.

"I wore a good suit of clothes then, and I only wear one suit at a time now. I relished three meals a day then a good deal more than I do three meals a day now. I had fewer cares, I slept better and may add that I believe I was generally far happier in those days than I have been many times since I became a millionaire."

As Pullman learned, true wealth is not found in earthly riches. The heart can never be fully satisfied with anything of the world; besides, the world passes away. True wealth is found in the knowledge of Christ and of His great salvation, and in the possession of the abiding riches which He bestows on all who believe in Him.

True wealth has to do with spiritual health — inner peace, clear conscience and sins forgiven. That man, woman or young person with abiding faith in Christ, who is yielded to the control of God's indwelling Holy Spirit, has true wealth — the supernatural life.

Bible Reading: Proverbs 8:22-31

ACTION POINT: I'll begin to look more to the "Bank of Heaven" for my true wealth.

Walk in the Light

"Later, in one of His talks, Jesus said to the people, 'I am the Light of the world. So if you follow me, you won't be stumbling through the darkness, for living light will flood your path" (John 8:12).

The living room of our home was dark when I quietly slipped a key into the lock and opened the door one night, walking slowly and softly so as not to awaken Vonette and our sons who were very young. Though they had been trained to put away their toys, somehow in the rush to get ready for bed that night they had left cars and a train and other favorite playthings scattered throughout the living room.

You guessed it! I stepped on one with wheels that almost threw me to the floor before I could regain my balance. Many a person has broken a leg or an arm under similar circumstances, and some have even fallen and hit their heads on sharp objects, resulting in a fatal accident.

So it is in the spiritual realm. If we insist on walking in the darkness, we will inevitably stumble and take risks that can greatly jeopardize our spiritual health and, in some cases, lead to our spiritual death by cutting ourselves off from God.

Jesus said, "I am the light of the world. He that followeth me shall not walk in darkness." In the first epistle of John we are told, "God is light, and in Him is no darkness at all. If we say that we have fellowship with Him, and walk in darkness, we lie and do not tell the truth. If we walk in the light, as God is in the light, we have fellowship one with another and the blood of Jesus Christ, God's Son, cleanses [and keeps on cleansing] us from all sin."

There is only one person who qualifies to be the light of the world. That is Jesus. So how do we follow Him? What does it mean to walk in the light? Basically, it means that there is no unconfessed sin. It means that we are filled with the Holy Spirit, that we are feasting upon the Word of God and obeying His commands which include sharing our love for Christ with others.

Bible Reading: 1 Thessalonians 5:4-8

ACTION POINT: Through the enabling of the Holy Spirit, I shall walk in the light with Christ who is the light of the world, and reflect His light in such an attractive way that those who walk in darkness will be drawn to the light as moths are drawn to a burning candle.

How to Stay Pure

"How can a young man stay pure? By reading Your Word and following its rules" (Psalm 119:9).

I can live a pure life if I follow God's Word. That seems to be the clear import of the psalmist's message in this verse. And if that is true — and I have no doubt it is — then certain things surely should follow.

I will begin today by determining to know His Word and to obey it. Simple logic would dictate that I cannot and will not obey His Word if I am not familiar with it.

In a day when immorality is rampant and divorce is becoming commonplace even among Christians, how important it is that I seek to keep my life pure. Surely I cannot expect to be used of God in a supernatural way to help fulfill the Great Commission unless I am pure. And there seems to be no better way to accomplish that desired end than by reading, studying — even memorizing — His Word, and then, through the enabling of the Holy Spirit, by claiming God's promises and obeying His commandments.

Earlier (Day 18) we mentioned the importance of hiding God's Word in our hearts, that we might not sin against Him (Psalm 119:11). Again I would emphasize the value of committing to memory many verses — and even chapters — from the Word of God. In that way, we will have them stored in our minds so that God can bring them to our minds in time of special need and can use them to enable us to live supernaturally.

Basic to living the supernatural life is this matter of spending time in God's Word, which is quick and powerful.

Bible Reading: Psalm 119:10-16

ACTION POINT: Today I will spend quality time in the Word of God and begin to memorize favorite passages, especially Psalm 119.

Life-giving Fruit

"Godly men are growing a tree that bears life-giving fruit, and all who win souls are wise" (Proverbs 11:30).

"The monument I want after I am dead," said Dwight L. Moody, "is a monument with two legs going around the world — a saved sinner telling about the salvation of Jesus Christ."

When a young minister asked the Duke of Wellington whether he did not consider it useless to attempt to evangelize India, the Iron Duke sternly replied:

"What are your marching orders, sir?"

No doubt one of Satan's greatest weapons of deceit in the world today is that of procrastination. Tomorrow I am going to become a soul-winner. Next month, after an evangelistic training program, I will become a great witness. As soon as I finish seminary or Bible college, I'll begin sharing the good news of the gospel.

But "today is the day of salvation, now is the accepted time," declares the Word of God. Sensitivity to God's Holy Spirit — dwelling within to give me supernatural ability — will enable me to tell others what Christ means to me, and what He has done for me.

In God's economy, the truly wise person is that one who is redeeming the time, buying up every opportunity to share his faith, refusing to put off that which he knows should become a natural, every-day, moment-by-moment part of his life. Wonder of wonders, God even promises to put the very words in our mouths, if we ask Him, as we go in His name.

Bible Reading: 2 Corinthians 5:11-17

ACTION POINT: I will do what God leads me to do this day to bear life-giving fruit.

Abound With Blessings

"A faithful man will abound with blessings, but he who hastens to be rich will not go unpunished" (Proverbs 28:20, RSV).

"Years ago when my children were small," declared a godly Baptist layman in South Carolina, who was secretary and treasurer of a large cotton mill corporation, "my salary was too small for my actual needs. Strive as I would I could not keep out of debt.

"This became a heavy cross to me, and one night I was unable to sleep. I arose and went to my desk, where I spent some time in prayer to God for help and guidance. Then I took a pen and paper and wrote out a solemn contract with my heavenly Father."

Continuing, the layman said, "I promised Him that no matter what testings or trials came I would never turn back. Also, that no matter how pressing my obligations I would scrupulously tithe my income. Next I promised the Lord that if He would let me make a certain salary I would pay two-tenths, then if I made a certain larger salary I would pay three-tenths.

"Finally I named a larger salary, which was far beyond anything I had ever hoped to earn, and told the Lord if I ever reached such a salary I would give him one-half of my income. For many years it has been my privilege to give one-half of my income to the Lord."

This verse warns the man who is so determined to accumulate personal wealth that he robs God of that which is rightfully His. That man will not go unpunished, God promises. May he help us to give cheerfully of that which He entrusts to us.

Bible Reading: Proverbs 28:21-28

ACTION POINT: Whatever I give to the Lord, His servants and His work will be done cheerfully and generously, as He has prospered me.

Bring Forth Much Fruit

"Verily, verily, I say unto you, Except a corn of wheat fall into the ground and die, it abideth alone: but if it die, it bringeth forth much fruit" (John 12:24, KJV).

Alex was distressed over his constant failure to live the Christian life victoriously.

"I am always failing," he said. "I know what is right, but I am simply not able to keep the many commitments, resolutions and rededications that I make to the Lord almost daily. What is wrong with me? Why do I constantly fail? How can I push that magic button which will change my life and make me the kind of person God wants me to be, and the kind of person I want to be?"

I turned with him to review Romans 7 and 8, and discussed with him how all of us experience this conflict when we walk in our own strength. But the victory is ours as we walk in the Spirit. It is impossible to control ourselves and be controlled by the Holy Spirit at the same time.

Perhaps you have had that same problem and wondered why your life was not bringing forth much fruit. Christ cannot be in control if you are on the throne of your life. So you must abdicate — surrender the throne of your life to Christ. This involves faith.

As an expression of your will, in prayer, you surrender the throne of your life to Him, and by faith you draw upon His resources to live a supernatural life, holy and fruitful.

The command of Ephesians 5:18 is given to all believers: We are to be filled, directed and empowered by the Holy Spirit, continually, moment by moment, every day. And the promise of 1 John 5:14, 15 is made to all believers: When we pray according to God's will, He hears and answers us.

The person who walks by faith in the control of the Holy Spirit has a new Master. The Lord Jesus said, "He who does not take his cross and follow after Me is not worthy of Me" (Matthew 10:38, NAS). "Unless a grain of wheat falls into the earth and dies, it remains by itself alone; but if it dies, it bears much fruit" (John 12:24, NAS).

Bible Reading: John 12:25-32

ACTION POINT: Because my deep desire is to "bear much fruit," I will surrender afresh to God's Holy Spirit so that He might endow me with supernatural life and enable me to bear much fruit for His glory.

Praise Brings Results

"And at the moment they began to sing and to praise, the Lord caused the armies of Ammon, Moab, and Mount Seir to begin fighting among themselves, and they destroyed each other!" (2 Chronicles 20:22).

The armies of Ammon, Moab and Mount Seir had declared war on King Jehoshaphat and the people of Judah. So Jehoshaphat called the people together and prayed, "Oh, our God. Won't You stop them. We have no way to protect ourselves against this mighty army. We don't know what to do but we are looking to You."

Then the Lord instructed the people, "Don't be afraid, don't be paralyzed by this mighty army for the battle is not yours, but God's! Tomorrow, go down and attack them!...But you will not need to fight. Take your places; stand quietly and see the incredible rescue operation God will perform for you" (2 Chronicles 20:15-17).

After consultation with the leaders of the people, Jehoshaphat determined that there should be a choir, clothed in sanctified garments and singing the song, "His Lovingkindness Is Forever," leading the march. As they walked along praising and thanking the Lord, He released His mighty power in their behalf.

One of the greatest lessons I have ever learned about the Christian life is the importance of praise and thanks-giving. The greater the problem, the more difficult the circumstances, the greater the crisis, the more important it is to praise God at all times, to worship Him for who He is; for His attributes of sovereignty, love, grace, power, wisdom and might; for the certainty that He will fight for us, that He will demonstrate His supernatural resources in our behalf.

As in the case of Jehoshaphat and the people of Judah when they began to praise God and He caused the three opposing armies to fight against each other and destroy one another, God will fight for us if we trust and obey Him. There is no better way to demonstrate faith and obedience than to praise Him and to thank Him, even when our world is crumbling around us and the enemy is threatening to destroy. God honors praise. Hebrews 13:15 reminds us, "With Jesus' help, we will continually offer our sacrifice of praise to God by telling others of the glory of His name."

Bible Reading: Psalm 136: 1, 21-26

ACTION POINT: Today I will continue to praise God and give thanks to Him for who He is. When difficulties arise, I will praise Him all the more and thank Him for His faithfulness. I will depend upon the supernatural resources of God which enable me to live the supernatural life, regardless of the circumstances.

The Most Vital Food

"Your words are what sustain me; they are food to my hungry soul. They bring joy to my sorrowing heart and delight me. How proud I am to bear Your name, O Lord" (Jeremiah 15:16).

In my earlier years — as perhaps was true of yours — one thing that seemed to sustain me more than anything else was food: three square meals a day, and sometimes something in between. Food is still vital — I would not understate its value — but I have found something far more vital to my happiness and success as a believer in Christ.

Now, I can truly say with the weeping prophet, Jeremiah, that the very words of God are what really sustain me. They are food to my hungry soul. And they accomplish immeasurable good in my life, and thus in the lives of thousands of people whom I am privileged to meet throughout the world.

God's Word brings joy to my sorrowing heart. Why? Because it has an answer — *the* answer — to every need, every burden, every problem I will face this day, and in the days to come. Furthermore, it will provide the answers for others whom I contact.

God's Word truly delights me, as it did Jeremiah. When I need encouragement, I turn to the Psalms. When I need practical wisdom for daily decisions, I turn to the Proverbs of Solomon. And so on with every kind of need I face.

All of this being true — God's Word sustaining me, being food to my hungry soul, bringing joy to my sorrowing heart, and delighting me — "How proud I am to bear your name, O Lord!"

Bible Reading: Jeremiah 15:15-21

ACTION POINT: My spiritual food must take priority over all other considerations in my life.

Everything Is Possible

"Jesus looked at them intently, then said, 'Without God, it is utterly impossible. But with God everything is possible' " (Mark 10:27).

"An hour in prayer can give the believer enough power to overcome the second most powerful force in the universe," sagely declared an anonymous observer.

God's Word gives us many "exceeding great and precious promises" that confirm the truth of this wise observation — and the truth of the scriptural promise that with God everything is possible. One of these precious promises declares, "They that wait upon the Lord shall renew their strength" (Isaiah 40:31, KJV).

Sometimes renewed strength — spiritual strength, God's strength — is all we need to face the problem or difficulty or testing or trial that confronts us.

In the gigantic tasks God has given us to do in the work of Campus Crusade for Christ, often it is the confirmed realization that with God everything is possible that keeps us going on, trusting God to do that which no man could possibly do.

God's indwelling Holy Spirit, making possible the supernatural life, constantly empowers and enables us to reach out and attempt great and mighty things for God — always an outreach that involves the needs of others more than our own personal needs, as great as they may seem to be at times.

Bible Reading: Mark 10:23-27

ACTION POINT: "Dear Lord, give me a heart like Yours — one that reaches out to the ends of the earth, and the end of the block, with the good news of the gospel, always believing that nothing is impossible with Your help."

Faith Can Grow

"His lord said unto him, Well done, thou good and faithful servant: thou hast been faithful over a few things, I will make thee ruler over many things: enter thou into the joy of thy lord" (Matthew 25:21, KJV).

At one stage of my spiritual growth, I was able to trust God for a soul — and He answered that prayer by leading me to one person whose heart He had prepared. Through the years God has increased my faith to trust Him for 6 souls then 20, 50, 100, 1000, 1 million, 100 million souls! Always He has honored my faith and obedience. Now I pray for a billion souls and, by faith I believe that a billion will be harvested for the glory of God.

God has not changed; I have changed.

I believe that God deals with us in a similar way with regard to spiritual fruit. As we continue to trust God to develop in us all the various love traits, He honors that faithfulness because we are obeying Him by doing what He commands us to do.

Faithfulness is that trait of the Holy Spirit (faithfulness — love) that makes faith a living reality every day in the life of the believer who is living supernaturally. As we continue to walk in the power, love and wisdom of the Holy Spirit, we learn to develop greater confidence in the Lord Jesus Christ, in His Word, in our rights as children of God and in the ability of the indwelling Holy Spirit to empower and control our lives.

Faithfulness can be compared to an athlete's conditioning. A marathon runner does not begin training by running great distances. Instead, he starts with short runs. Then, as his body becomes more conditioned, he increases the distance of his runs until he reaches the full distance of the marathon.

Faithfulness in the life of a Christian also develops over an extended period of time spent in "conditioning." As we learn to trust God in small things, our faith grows and grows until we are able to trust Him in greater things.

God rewards us for our faithfulness, and each time we see Him respond favorably, He reaches out to us through His Holy Spirit and increases our faith to trust Him for even greater things.

Bible Reading: Matthew 25:14-20

ACTION POINT: I will seek to cultivate this fruit of the Spirit by being faithful to the calling God has entrusted to me.

In the World to Come

"And Jesus replied, 'Let me assure you that no one has ever given up anything — home, brothers, sisters, mother, father, children, or property — for love of Me and to tell others the Good News, who won't be given back, a hundred times over, homes, brothers, sisters, mothers, children and land — with persecutions! All these will be his here on earth, and in the world to come he shall have eternal life' " (Mark 10:29,30).

What a wonderful promise. God will return to you and me a hundred times over what we invest for Him and His kingdom.

I believe that millions of Christians like ourselves are awakening to the fact that we must be about our Father's business. As I observe God's working in the lives of people around the world through many movements, I am persuaded that the greatest spiritual awakening since Pentecost has already begun.

Jesus said, "Go. . .and make disciples in all nations." In order to make disciples, we must be disciples ourselves. Like begets like. We produce after our own kind.

The man who is committed to Christ, who understands how to walk in the fullness of the Spirit, is going to influence others and help to produce the same kind of Christians. Jesus said, "If anyone wishes to come after Me, let him deny himself, and take up his cross daily, and follow Me" (Luke 9:23).

For some, such a call to discipleship may sound too hard. However, in these verses Jesus tells us that we must be willing to give up everything. That this promise has been fulfilled in the lives of all who seek first Christ and His kingdom has been attested to times without number — not always in material things, of course, but in rewards far more meaningful and enriching.

Bible Reading: Luke 9:23-26

ACTION POINT: Realizing that God has promised manifold gifts, persecutions, eternal life in exchange for faithfulness and commitment to Him, I vow to make that surrender real and meaningful in my life every day.

You Cannot Outgive God

"For if you give, you will get! Your gift will return to you in full and overflowing measure, pressed down, shaken together to make room for more, and running over. Whatever measure you use to give — large or small — will be used to measure what is given back to you" (Luke 6:38).

R. G. Le Tourneau was one of God's great businessmen. He wrote a book, entitled *God Runs My Business.* Though he had little formal training, he became one of America's leading industrialists, developing and securing patents for many major improvements in earth-moving equipment. He gave away millions of dollars, and he founded a wonderful Christian college which bears his name. I had known and admired him for many years, but one of my most memorable experiences with him was at his plant in Longview, Texas. As we chatted, I was captivated by this exuberant, joyful layman who was overflowing with the love of God, still creative in his later years, and always proclaiming the truth that you cannot outgive God — the more you give away the more you receive. He had discovered a law of the universe.

The giving of the tithe (ten percent of our increase) is an Old Testament principle. The New Testament principle of giving is expressed in this passage: "The more you give, the more you will receive." I personally do not believe that that involves indiscriminate giving, but rather that we should prayerfully evaluate all the various opportunities that are available to further the cause of Christ and His kingdom.

New Testament concept makes clear that everything belongs to God. We are custodians, stewards, of that which is entrusted to us for only a brief moment of time. Three-score and ten years (or possibly a little more), and then all that we possess will pass on to another. We are not to hoard, nor are we to pass on large estates to our heirs. That which is entrusted to God's children is given to them to be used while they are still alive. We are to care for our own, and make provision for their needs, but all that is entrusted to us beyond that amount should be spent while we are still alive, while we can guarantee proper stewardship.

Bible Reading: 2 Corinthians 8:1-6

ACTION POINT: Mindful of this spiritual principle, that everything belongs to God and He has entrusted me with the privilege and responsibility of being a good steward, I will seek every opportunity to invest all the time, talent and treasure available to me while I am still alive, for the enhancement of the kingdom of God.

You've Already Won

"Dear young friends, you belong to God and have already won your fight with those who are against Christ, because there is someone in your hearts who is stronger than any evil teacher in this wicked world" (1 John 4:4).

"I am afraid of Satan," a young minister once told me.

"You should be afraid of Satan," I responded, "if you insist on controlling your own life. But not if you are willing to let Christ control your life. The Bible says, 'Greater is He who is in you than he who is in the world.' "

My friend lived in a city where one of the largest zoos in the world was located.

"What do you do with lions in your city?" I asked.

"We keep them in cages," he replied.

"You can visit the lion in its cage at the zoo," I explained, "and it cannot hurt you, even if you are close to the cage. But stay out of that cage, or the lion will make mincemeat out of you."

Satan is in a "cage." He was defeated 2,000 years ago when Christ died on the cross for our sins. Victory is *now* ours. We do not look forward to victory, but we move *from* victory, the victory of the cross.

Satan has no power except that which God allows him to have. Do not be afraid of him, but do stay away from him. Avoid his every effort to tempt and mislead you. Remember, that choice is up to you.

Bible Reading: 1 John 2:1-6

ACTION POINT: I will with God's help, stay out of Satan's "cage," choosing rather to enlist God's indwelling Holy Spirit to fight for me in the supernatural battle against the satanic forces which surround me.

How to Save Your Life

"And He said to them all, If any man will come after Me, let him deny himself, and take up his cross daily, and follow Me. For whosoever will save his life shall lose it: but whosoever will lose his life for My sake, the same shall save it" (Luke 9:23,24, KJV).

Martin Luther once told the maidens and housewives of Germany that in scrubbing floors and going about their household duties they were accomplishing just as great a work in the sight of heaven as the monks and priests with their penances and holy offices.

In the 15th century, a woman — Margery Baxter — had said the same thing couched in different terms.

"If ye desire to see the true cross of Christ," she said, "I will show it to you at home in your own house."

Stretching out her arms, she continued, "This is the true cross of Christ, thou mightest and mayest behold and worship in thine own house. Therefore, it is but vain to run to the church to worship dead crosses."

Her message was plain: *holiness is in our daily service.*

Your life and mine are worshiping Christ today to the degree that we practice the presence of God in every minute detail of our lives throughout the day. We are taking up our cross when we shine for Jesus just where we are, obediently serving Him and sharing His good news with others.

If you and I want to save our lives, we do well to lose them in obedient service to the Lord Jesus Christ, allowing His indwelling Holy Spirit to work in us and through us.

Bible Reading: John 12:23-26

ACTION POINT: I will take up my cross today — shining just where He puts me at this point in my life.

Real Freedom

"If the Son therefore shall make you free, you shall be free indeed" (John 8:36, KJV).

A dedicated, but defeated, young missionary returned from the field devastated because of his failure; first, to live the Christian life; and second, to introduce others to the Savior. He came to my office for counsel.

I explained to him that the Christian life is simply a matter of surrendering our lives to the risen Christ and appropriating the fullness of God's Holy Spirit by faith. "Relax," I said. "Let the Lord Jesus Christ live and love through you. Let Him seek and save the lost through your life."

He became very impatient with me. "You dilute and distort the gospel," he insisted. "It really costs to serve Jesus. I have made great sacrifices on the mission field. I have worked day and night. I struggled. It has cost me my health — though I am prepared to die for Christ — but you make it too easy, and I cannot accept what you are saying." He left my office in anger.

Later he called for another appointment, saying, "I don't agree with you, but there's a quality in your life that I want for myself, and I'd like to talk further."

Again I explained, "The just shall live by faith. All the supernatural resources of God are available to us by faith, not by our sacrifice and good works — though good works must follow faith, for faith without works is dead."

As we talked, his attitude began to change. Then some days later I received a letter filled with praise, worship and adoration to God as he described the miracle that had taken place in his life. He had discovered the liberating truth of the principle that God's grace is available to us by faith. The Christian life is supernatural. No individual is capable of living it apart from the Lord Jesus Christ. Jesus explains it in John 15:4,5: "As the branch cannot bear fruit of itself, except it abide in the vine, no more can ye, except ye abide in Me. I am the vine, ye are the branches... without Me ye can do nothing."

It is His supernatural life, in all of its resurrection power, released through the ministry of the Holy Spirit, that enables us to live supernatural lives for the glory of God. Only then can we be free, for the Son alone can liberate us.

Bible Reading: Romans 8:1-6

ACTION POINT: By faith, I shall act upon my rights as a child of God and claim the supernatural power of the Son of God. Knowing that He has already set me free, through His death and resurrection, I am confident that He will enable me to experience that freedom, moment by moment, so that I may live the supernatural life to which I have been called.

PROMISES — DAY 164

Produce Lovely Fruit

*"You didn't choose Me! I chose you! I appointed you to go and pro-
duce lovely fruit always, so that no matter what you ask for from
the Father, using My name, He will give it to you"* (John 15:16).

Some time ago I asked a leading
theologian and dean of faculty of
a renowned theological seminary if he
felt that one could be a Spirit-filled person without sharing Christ as a way of
life.

His answer was an emphatic, "No!"

On what basis could he make such
a strong statement? The answer is obvious. Our Savior came to "seek and
to save the lost" and He has "chosen
and ordained" us to share the good
news of His love and forgiveness with
everyone, everywhere.

To be unwilling to witness for Christ
with our lips is to disobey this command just as much as to be unwilling
to witness for Him by living holy lives
is to disobey His command. In neither
case can the disobedient Christian expect God to control and empower his
life.

There are those who say, "I witness
for Christ by living a good life." But
it is not enough to live a good life.
Many non-Christians live fine, moral,
ethical lives.

According to the Lord Jesus, the only
way we can demonstrate that we are
truly following Him is to produce fruit,
which includes introducing others to
our Savior as well as living holy lives.
And the only way we can produce fruit
is through the power of the Holy Spirit.

Bible Reading: John 15:7-15

ACTION POINT: My part of the "bargain" is to share the good news which
will produce lovely fruit; God's part is to provide the wisdom, love and power,
through the enabling of the Holy Spirit, to be a fruitful witness. "Lord, help
me to be faithful in my part, knowing You will be faithful in Yours."

The Simple, Wonderful Message

"He brought them out and begged them, 'Sirs, what must I do to be saved?' They replied, 'Believe on the Lord Jesus and you will be saved, and your entire household' " (Acts 16:30-31).

The story is told of a man who was very fond of the famous general, Robert E. Lee. He was eager for his four-year-old son to admire and respect this great, southern, Civil War general as much as he did. So every day, as they strolled through the park near their home, they would stop in front of the statue of General Lee astride his beautiful horse, Traveler, and the father would say to his little David, "Say good morning to General Lee," The little lad would dutifully wave his hand in obedience to his father's instructions and say, "Good morning, General Lee." Months passed and one day, as they again stood in front of the statue of General Lee, the father said, "Say good morning to General Lee," which the boy did. But as they walked on through the park together, David asked, "Daddy, who is that man riding General Lee?"

One of the biggest problems we have in life is communication. To David's young mind the horse was more important than the rider. We all have a tendency to filter information through our own experiences. What I say is not necessarily what you hear, and what you say may not be what I hear. This is true even in communicating the gospel.

The most joyful news ever announced is found in Luke 2:10,11: " 'Don't be afraid!' the angel said. 'I bring you the most joyful news ever announced, and it is for everyone! The Savior — yes, the Messiah, the Lord — has been born tonight in Bethlehem!' " Yet that simple message has been diluted and profaned through the centuries.

One evening, I presented this message to a very mature, intelligent layman.

"Does it make sense?" I inquired.

It was as though a light suddenly went on and, for the first time, he understood what the gospel was all about. "Of course it does," he answered.

"Would you like to receive Christ right now?"

"Of course I would. If what you say is true, I should think everyone would want to know Christ."

If Spirit-filled, trained communicators properly presented the gospel, the majority of people would want to receive Christ.

Bible Reading: John 1:9-14

ACTION POINT: I will seek to present the good news of God's love and forgiveness through Jesus Christ in such a logical, joyful, Spirit-filled way that those who hear will want to know my wonderful Savior. And I will trust God to use me to train other Christians as well to be better communicators of the greatest news the world has ever heard.

We Are Kings

"The sin of this one man, Adam, caused death to be king over all, but all who will take God's gift of forgiveness and acquittal are kings of life because of this one man, Jesus Christ" (Romans 5:17).

Jack protested angrily, "Why should I be held accountable for the sin of Adam? Why should I be judged and condemned to eternal punishment because of the disobedience of someone who lived centuries ago? I resent that his action should involve me." I asked my young student friend if he remembered the infamous Japanese attack on Pearl Harbor followed by the declaration of war by then President Franklin Delano Roosevelt. "Yes," he said, "I'm a student of history and I remember that event very well." I reminded Jack that every able-bodied man who was of age was automatically conscripted to join the United States Army to do battle against Japan. "Yes," he said, "I know."

"Don't you think it unfair, following your logic, that the President of the United States should make a decision that would affect young men like yourself? Remember that tens of thousands of them died on the field of battle. Was that fair?"

"Well," he replied, "that was the only decision that could be made. We had to protect our homeland. We had been attacked and had to defend ourselves."

"So it was with Adam," I explained. "The wisdom of the Almighty Creator was attacked by Satan in the Garden of Eden and the battle was lost when Adam and Eve, the epitome of God's creation, surrendered to Satan's tempting lies. God, in His sovereignty, wisdom and grace caused the results of the disobedience of Adam to be borne by the rest of us in the human race. But the judgment of God which demands penalty for sin was intercepted by God's love. While we were yet in our sins God proved His love for us by sending the Lord Jesus Christ to die for us. Now, through accepting God's free gift by faith, we can become kings of life because of this one man, Jesus Christ."

Simply stated, one man, Adam, through his disobedience to God, introduced sin into the world, and one man, Jesus Christ, through his obedience to God, paid the penalty for that sin for all who would believe and trust in Him.

Bible Reading: Romans 5:14-21

ACTION POINT: Christ has overcome the sin I inherited from Adam by liberating me from the king of death, and making me a king of light. As an expression of my deep gratitude for His love and grace, I will seek every opportunity to communicate this good news to others who still live in darkness that they, too, may enjoy the abundant supernatural life which I now enjoy.

He Forgets Our Sins

"And then he adds, 'I will never again remember their sins and lawless deeds' " (Hebrews 10:17).

We were seated at the breakfast table, talking about the exciting adventure of the Christian life. Chuck and Mary were just discovering new facets and understanding of the life in Christ.

"Can you tell us in a few words what should be our objective as Christians?" they asked me.

In very brief summary, I replied, "The Christian life is the process of becoming in our experience through the enabling of the Holy Spirit what we already are in God's sight, in order to bring maximum glory, honor and praise to His name."

Christ gave Himself to God for our sins — as one sacrifice for one time. Then He sat down at the place of highest honor at God's right hand. For by that one offering He made forever perfect in the sight of God all those whom He is making holy.

I am perfect in God's sight, because in His sight there is no such thing as time and space. Let me hasten to add: I know that I am not perfect in my experience. That is a process which takes time, knowledge of God and His Word, and growth in faith in order to claim these truths as reality in our lives.

I am perfect in God's sight because He sees me in Christ, and in Christ, who is perfect and without sin, He sees me without spot or blemish. Someone has referred to this great experience of being crucified, baptized and enthroned with Christ as a different life altogether. As we are reminded in 2 Corinthians 5:17 (KJV), "Therefore if any man be in Christ, he is a new creature: old things are passed away; behold, all things are become new."

Bible Reading: Hebrews 8:8-12

ACTION POINT: Because God has forgiven and forgotten all my sins and lawless deeds, I will now, through the enabling of His Holy Spirit, receive His forgiveness and cleansing and never again be burdened with those sins of the past. I will claim my new supernatural life in Christ for the glory of God. Because this is such great good news, I will not keep it to myself. I must tell others.

Spiritually Minded

"For to be carnally minded is death; but to be spiritually minded is life and peace" (Romans 8:6, KJV).

I believe the truth of this verse may speak to a common cause of depression among Christians who allow their minds to dwell on ungodly thoughts and/or over-introspection.

Paul writes: "I advise you to obey only the Holy Spirit's instructions. He will tell you where to go and what to do, and then you won't always be doing the wrong things your evil nature wants you to.

"For we naturally love to do evil things that are just the opposite from the things that the Holy Spirit tells us to do, and the good things we want to do when the Spirit has His way with us are just the opposite of our natural desires" (Galatians 5:16,17).

Our minds are suceptible to the influence of our old sin-nature and, as such, can pose real dangers to us. As soon as we get out of step with the Holy Spirit and get our focus off the Lord, our minds begin to give us trouble.

"The Christian life is really simple," I heard a pastor say recently. "It's simply doing what we're told to do." And he is right. We will be spiritually minded, not carnally minded, if we obey the simple commands of God's Word.

Bible Reading: Romans 8:5-11

ACTION POINT: Through the enabling of the Holy Spirit, I will give the spiritual mind priority over the carnal mind in my life.

He Gave His Son

"Since He did not spare even His own Son for us but gave Him up for us all, won't He also surely give us everything else?" (Romans 8:32).

George was very faithful in his Christian walk. In fact, he had a little black book in which he recorded all of his activities for each day. These included daily devotions, note-taking, verses to be memorized, appointments to be kept and every activity of his life. Outwardly he seemed so perfect that I, as a young Christian, wanted to be like him. Then one day he had a nervous breakdown. As he told me later, the last thing he did before he went to the hospital was to throw away his little black book and tell his wife he never wanted to see it again. Without realizing it, he had become very legalistic in his relationship with God rather than accepting, by faith, what God had already done for him. While in the hospital he began to recall some of the thousands of verses which he had memorized through the years. It was then that he relaxed enough to allow the Holy Spirit to illumine his mind to comprehend the importance of living by faith.

As Paul writes to the Galatians in the third chapter: "What magician has hypnotized you and cast an evil spell upon you? For you used to see the meaning of Jesus Christ's death as clearly as though I had waved a placard before you with a picture on it of Christ dying on the cross. Let me ask you this one question: Did you receive the Holy Spirit by trying to keep the Jewish laws? Of course not, for the Holy Spirit came upon you only after you heard about Christ and trusted Him to save you. Then, have you gone completely crazy? For if trying to obey the Jewish laws never gave you spiritual life in the first place, why do you think that trying to obey them now will make you stronger Christians?"

I ask you again: Does God give you the power of the Holy Spirit as a result of your trying to obey His laws? No, of course not. He gives that power when you believe in Christ and fully trust Him. The greatest heresy of the Christian life is legalism; and yet, it inevitably seems to attract dedicated, committed Christians. They are happy to accept salvation as a gift of God by faith. But like the Galatians, they insist on earning their way thereafter.

We must never forget that salvation is a gift of God which we receive by faith. Nothing can be earned. If we believe God, we will want to work to please Him, not to earn His favor.

Bible Reading: Romans 8:33-39

ACTION POINT: I will invite the Holy Spirit to protect me from becoming legalistic in my walk with Christ. Having received salvation by faith, I shall claim each day's blessings by faith as I live the supernatural life.

All Is Ours

"So don't be proud of following the wise men of this world. For God has already given you everything you need. He has given you Paul and Apollos and Peter as your helpers. He has given you the whole world to use, and life and even death are your servants. He has given you all of the present and all of the future. All are yours, and you belong to Christ, and Christ is God's" (1 Corinthians 3:21-23).

A famous scholar and statesman called me aside to offer his counsel. "As the head of a great worldwide Christian student movement," he said, "you should be more scholarly, more of a philosopher. Your approach is too simple. Your critics and even some of your friends feel that your writings and your speaking should be more profound as befits one of your stature and position." He continued in this vein for some time. I heard him out, prayerfully asking God to give me the wisdom to respond.

When he finished I said to him, "There was a time when I wanted to impress people with my intellect, my learning. I spent many years in graduate school including two theological seminaries where I had the privilege of sitting at the feet of some of the most learned theologians of our time."

I confessed to him that there was a period in my student life when I became intoxicated with learning and could have spent the rest of my life in the ivory tower. Then it occurred to me in a very definite, dramatic way that one of the reasons the Christian message was not better understood by every Christian and the reason the Christian church was making such little impact upon a worldly society was that many theologians, and consequently their students, pastors and missionaries, had complicated the good news of God's love and forgiveness. I reminded my friend that Jesus, the greatest teacher of all, taught in such a way that the masses, largely illiterate and unlearned, heard Him gladly. I went on to explain that I had made a concerted effort all through my ministry to try to communicate clearly by eliminating big words and philosophical and theological jargon, the kind of "Christianese" that does not communicate except to those who are familiar with the usage.

This famous scholar seemed to understand for the first time the importance of following the example of our Lord and other great teachers through the centuries who sought to communicate clearly to the masses.

Bible Reading: 1 Corinthians 3:16-20

ACTION POINT: Remembering that God has given me everything I need, I will look to Him to guide my steps and enable me to live the supernatural life. I will also keep the message simple as I communicate the good news of God's love in Christ.

Not in Vain

"Therefore, my beloved brethren, be ye steadfast, unmoveable, always abounding in the work of the Lord, forasmuch as ye know that your labour is not in vain in the Lord" (1 Corinthians 15:58, KJV).

"Do not let your belief of these truths be shaken," the apostle Paul was saying to the Corinthian believers. "They are most certain, and of the utmost importance."

In the context, you will remember that Paul had just been talking about the resurrection, and now he wanted them to be steadfast believers of this great truth. The person who has no belief in the afterlife — the resurrection — is of all men most miserable. His motto is: "Eat, drink and be merry, for tomorrow we die."

Paul also exhorts believers to be immoveable in their expectation of being raised incorruptible and immortal. Christians should never lose sight of this hope of the gospel:

"The only condition is that you fully believe the Truth, standing in it steadfast and firm, strong in the Lord, convinced of the Good News that Jesus died for you, and never shifting from trusting Him to save you. This is the wonderful news that came to each of you and is now spreading all over the world. And I, Paul, have the joy of telling it to others" (Colossians 1:23).

Having determined to remain steadfast and unmoveable for the rest of their lives, believers then are ready with God's help to labor faithfully for the Lord, knowing that such labor is not in vain.

Bible Reading: 1 Corinthians 15:51-57

ACTION POINT: Drawing by faith upon the supernatural resources of the Holy Spirit, I will keep my expectation and my hope steadfast and unmoveable, continuing my service for the Lord with the confident assurance that it will not be in vain.

More Than We Could Hope For

"Now glory be to God who by His mighty power at work within us is able to do far more than we would ever dare to ask or even dream of infinitely beyond our highest prayers, desires, thoughts, or hopes" (Ephesians 3:20).

Few verses describe the supernatural life better than does this powerful promise. On hundreds, if not thousands, of occasions I have meditated upon this truth and have been inspired to claim increasingly great and mighty things for the glory of God because of the inspiration contained in this Word. Think of it, the omnipotent Creator, God, who created the heavens and the earth and the vastness of all the hundreds of millions of galaxies, has come to take up residence within us! Our bodies have become His temple. That omnipotent, divine, supernatural, inexhaustible resource of power dwells within every believer.

How much power? Far more than we would ever dare to ask or even dream of! Let your mind race, your prayers be without limit, and yet, whatever you believe, whatever you think, whatever you pray for, God's power is infinitely beyond it all.

I have come to the conclusion, after many years of serving our wonderful Lord, that there is nothing too big for us to attempt for the glory of God. If our hearts and motives are pure, if what we do is according to the Word

of God, He hears, and is able to do more than we ask or even think.

For example, is it God's will that the Great Commission be fulfilled? Of course. It is His command. We read further in 2 Peter 3:9 that God is not willing that any should perish but that all should come to repentance and has, according to verse 15 of this chapter, delayed His return in order that more people might have a chance to hear.

Let your mind soar over the vastness of the earth, where there is a continuing population explosion, and each generation is faced with another billion or more souls to pray for. I challenge you to believe God for the entire world to be blanketed with His love and forgiveness.

I am presently praying for a billion souls to come to Christ before A.D. 2000, and on the basis of what we are now seeing, God is putting His plan together through many members of the Body of Christ cooperating under many umbrellas, including Here's Life, World, to see that prayer fulfilled.

Bible Reading: Ephesians 3:13-19

ACTION POINT: Today I will let my mind soar and my prayers expand. I will ask the Holy Spirit to give me the faith to comprehend the magnitude of God's purpose in my life and never be satisfied with anything less than the reality of this great promise, Ephesians 3:20, in my life.

Cleansing From Sin

"If we confess our sins, He is faithful and just to forgive us our sins, and to cleanse us from all unrighteousness" (1 John 1:9, KJV).

Henry was experiencing difficulty in communicating with God. "It seems as though He is far away from me," he said, "and no matter what I do I am not able to make contact with Him."

Henry was weighted down with problems and concerns that robbed him of his joy, his radiance and even his physical strength. He was a Christian and wanted to be a man of God but had become careless in his walk with Christ, and in the process had lost his first love.

If that condition describes you as well, it is quite likely that you have allowed sin to short-circuit your relationship with God. The mighty overflow of His power has been cut off, and you are no longer walking in the light as God is in the light. This is expressed in this great epistle of 1 John.

King David knew that experience because he had disobeyed God and, as recorded in Psalm 32, would not admit that he had sinned. As a result, his dishonesty made him miserable and filled his days with frustration.

If the light has gone out in your life and you are conscious of the same kind of experience to which King David refers, may I encourage you to take a sheet of paper, make a list of everything you know is wrong in your life, as the Holy Spirit directs you, and confess your sins to God.

As you make your list, claim the promise of 1 John 1:9. The word *confess* means "to agree with," "to say along with." You are saying to God, "I acknowledge that what I am doing is wrong. I know Christ's death on the cross paid the penalty for these sins. I repent." To repent means genuinely to change your mind, which results in a change of action.

As a result of this change, you no longer do those things that grieve or quench the Spirit, and you desire to honor Him every moment of every day of your life through faith and obedience. Then, whenever sin enters your life, you engage in spiritual breathing.

Bible Reading: Proverbs 28:10-14

ACTION POINT: Today I will make a list of everything the Holy Spirit calls to my mind that is short-circuiting His power in my life, and I will genuinely confess them before God.

Protected From Satan

"But the Lord is faithful: He will make you strong and guard you from satanic attacks of every kind" (2 Thessalonians 3:3).

As a lad I grew up in a rural community on a ranch five miles from the nearest town. I received the first seven years of my formal education in a one-room, country school. I was often the only student in my class and there were never more than three of us. It was not unusual for some big bully to pick on a student smaller than himself and fights would ensue.

I had been taught never to run from a fight because that was not the manly thing to do and so I sometimes found myself in such a situation. I was encouraged by a brother, several years older, who would stand by to insure that the fighting was fair and that I would not be taken advantage of. The Lord Jesus Christ is our elder brother. He stands by to help us, to make us strong and guard us from the attacks of Satan who is like the big bully.

Two thousand years ago Satan was defeated at the cross. He has no control over us except that which God allows and which we by our disobedience and unbelief enable Him to have. Why then, you may ask, does the average Christian have such a tough time living the Christian life? It is because he does not understand that the battle has already been won! Victory is ours and nothing can touch us or harm us whether we are criticized, persecuted or even martyred for the sake of the kingdom, for we are not of this world. We are citizens of the heavenly kingdom. While here on this earth, Christ will envelop us and surround us with His supernatural peace and power, turning tragedy to triumph, heartache and sorrow to joy. This is our heritage if only we keep on trusting and obeying Him.

Bible Reading: 2 Thessalonians 3:1-5

ACTION POINT: I will remember that Jesus Christ is not only my Savior and Lord, but my older brother and that He will protect me against satanic attacks of every kind. The battle has already been won! Through His enabling supernatural resources, I will live a supernatural life for His glory today.

He Never Fails nor Forsakes

"Stay away from the love of money; be satisfied with what you have. For God has said, 'I will never, never fail you nor forsake you' " (Hebrews 13:5).

Malcolm Muggeridge, one of England's leading intellectuals, came to our Christian Embassy headquarters for lunch one day. Together we talked about the things of God — the Christian adventure. On that day, he offered little hope for the future of the Western world.

"We are," he said, "like a pan of frogs in cold water placed over a low flame. As the flame warms the water, the frogs relax. And by the time the water is boiling, it is too late for them to jump out of the pan. They are boiled alive. In contrast, if the frogs were placed in boiling water, they would leap out instantly."

He continued by explaining that the average person in America and in Western Europe was being destroyed by materialism, the love of money and the love of things. People are greedy and are grasping for more than they have. Our appetites know no bounds; we have become insatiable.

As a result, no doubt there is more vital Christianity in Eastern Germany than in Western Germany, in Poland than in Italy, in the Soviet Union than in England. The Christians who are willing to pay the price of persecution in these countries have learned to seek first the kingdom of God and His righteousness and to be satisfied with what they have.

With the apostle Paul, they are able to say, "I have learned, in whatsoever state I am, therewith to be content" (Philippians 4:11, KJV). You will observe that the admonition was to stay away from the *love* of money. There is nothing wrong with money. Thank God for able, dedicated, godly men and women to whom God has given the ability to make money, but who recognize that there is no satisfaction or fulfillment in making money. It is in the stewardship of that which God has entrusted to them that they find fulfillment and true meaning to life.

Bible Reading: Ephesians 5:1-5

ACTION POINT: With the certainty that God will never, never fail me nor forsake me, I will seek to find fulfillment and meaning in my life in Christ and not in materialism. I will encourage others to do the same today.

Crown of Life

"Blessed is the man that endureth temptation: for when he is tried, he shall receive the crown of life, which the Lord hath promised to them that love Him" (James 1:12, KJV).

In Christian art, the crown is usually pictured entwined with the cross. This suggests that endurance of trial leads to victory, as the above verse indicates.

Temptation often comes at our weakest — rather than our strongest — moments. When we have reached the limit of our love and our patience, for example, we are tempted to be unlike Christ in one way or another. Remember, Jesus' temptation began after forty days of fasting.

People usually are impressed — favorably or unfavorably — when they see how we act under pressure. It is possible for one weak act to spoil a whole lifetime of witness.

The beatitude, or blessing, in Matthew 5:10; says, "Blessed are they which are persecuted for righteousness' sake: for theirs is the kingdom of heaven" (KJV). The crown of life is promised to those who successfully stand up under the testing of their faith. The Christian life is a spiritual conflict from the moment of birth until we go to be with the Lord. The flesh wars against the Spirit and the Spirit against the flesh. There is absolutely no hope for victory until one discovers the availability of the supernatural resources of the indwelling Holy Spirit.

A young student who came to me for counsel said, "I have given up. I can't live the Christian life. There is no hope for me."

"Good," I replied. "At last you have recognized that you cannot live the Christian life. Now there *is* hope for you, for the Christian life is a supernatural life and the only one who can live it is Jesus Christ Himself."

Surrender your life totally, completely to Him and recognize moment by moment, day by day, that the Holy Spirit is the only one who will enable you to endure temptation. By faith you must draw upon His supernatural resources to live a supernatural life. Only then will you be victorious and fruitful for the glory of God.

Bible Reading: James 5:7-11

ACTION POINT: Today and every day I will remember to draw upon the supernatural resources of the indwelling Christ who will enable me to be victorious over temptation and to live the supernatural life as a testimony to His faithfulness.

Knowledge and Wisdom

"But the wisdom that comes from heaven is first of all pure and full of quiet gentleness. Then it is peace-loving and courteous. It allows discussion and is willing to yield to others; it is full of mercy and good deeds. It is wholehearted and straightforward and sincere" (James 3:17).

"**D**onkeys laden with books," a phrase in rabbinical literature, is descriptive of those who know much but still remain fools.

Another expression says that "knowledge is power." True, but how is the knowledge used — beneficially or malevolently? That is a vitally important question. We have more knowledge than ever before, but few would claim that we have more wisdom.

Going faster and farther, we may be still going astray. Just as grapes are not picked from a bramble bush, neither can the good life be harvested from sowing wild oats.

For a nation of people, many of whom are "educated beyond their intelligence," as an anonymous wit once observed, America sorely lacks a sufficiency of men with real wisdom — that which is given by the Lord Himself.

In our modern education, we seem to be preoccupied with the accumulation of knowledge, to the neglect of that wisdom which alone can save us from the misuse of knowledge.

William Lyon Phelps, famous English professor at Yale University and a godly statesman, once said, "If I could choose between a knowledge of the Bible and a college education, I would readily choose the knowledge of the Bible."

If we lack wisdom, God's wisdom, we need only ask of Him and He will grant it when we ask in faith, according to His promise in James 1:5.

Bible Reading: James 3:13-18

ACTION POINT: In order to live a supernatural life I'll look for divine wisdom from the proper source — God, His Word, and His indwelling Holy Spirit.

Everything You Do

"But if anyone keeps looking steadily into God's law for free men, he will not only remember it but he will do what it says, and God will greatly bless him in everything he does" (James 1:25).

Jim expressed his displeasure with the Epistle of James.

"I agree with Martin Luther," he said. Bothered by the apparent contradiction between James and Paul, Luther for a long time rejected the Epistle of James. Later, however, he had become satisfied that it was a part of the inspired Scripture.

"I am no longer under law, but under grace," Jim continued. "I feel free to do whatever I want to do, knowing that I have already found favor in God's sight through what Christ has accomplished for me on the cross."

Having been reared in a very legalistic church, he was now liberated. And, he said, the rest of his life he would emphasize the importance of grace and faith.

I endeavored to explain to him that he was allowing the pendulum of his life to swing to the other extreme. There had to be balance. "Faith without works is dead." The extreme of either view leads to heresy. Trying to please God and earn salvation through works alone is impossible; it is an insult to God and leads nowhere.

But believing that Christ's death on the cross had paid the penalty for all of our sins and that now we are free to live any way we like and do anything we want to do without any thought of obedience is also heretical. Throughout the Scriptures, from Genesis through Revelation, obedience is important. Our Lord emphasized that fact in John 14:21, "He that hath my commandments, and keepeth them, he it is that loveth me" (KJV).

We prove that we love Him by our actions, by our obedience. In this verse for today we have the promise, "God will greatly bless him [the believer] in everything he does," when he obeys God's commands.

Bible Reading: 1 Peter 2:9-12

ACTION POINT: Since the supernatural life of the Christian is a life of good works, I will demonstrate my faith by my good works, for faith without works is dead. I will share this truth with someone who is living in the bondage of legalism.

Strength to the Humble

"But He gives us more and more strength to stand against all such evil longings. As the Scripture says, God gives strength to the humble, but sets Himself against the proud and haughty" (James 4:6).

Dr. A. B. Simpson, leader of the Christian and Missionary Alliance at its inception, wisely said years ago: "Humility is not thinking meanly of yourself; it is not thinking of yourself at all."

Under that rigid definition, not many of us would qualify as being truly humble — nevertheless, the statement contains a great deal of truth, for it is a goal toward which we should all strive.

No real progress is made toward God in any person's life — believer or unbeliever — without this special characteristic of humility. One proof of that is found in the familiar verse:

"If My people, which are called by My name, shall humble themselves, and pray, and seek my face, and turn from their wicked ways; then will I hear from heaven, and will forgive their sin, and will heal their land" (2 Chronicles 7:14, KJV).

Even before we pray, before we seek His face, before we turn from our wicked ways, we must humble ourselves. Why? Because we are in no position to meet any of these other three criteria without first humbling ourselves.

Every Christian who seeks to advance in a holy life must remember well that humility is the most important lesson a believer has to learn. There may be intense consecration, fervent zeal and heavenly experience, yet there also may be an unconscious self-exaltation. True humility must come from God.

Bible Reading: James 4:7-10

ACTION POINT: Remembering that pride is the root sin from which all others grow, I will humble myself and with the assistance of the Holy Spirit I will stay so busy helping, praying for and encouraging others that pride cannot take root in my life.

Inspiration of God

"All scripture is given by inspiration of God, and is profitable for doctrine, for reproof, for correction, for instruction in righteousness" (2 Timothy 3:16, KJV).

Recently, it was my privilege to be chairman of a national congress on the Bible, which was held in San Diego, California. Thousands of Christian leaders came from across the nation and from other countries. More than fifty leading scholars addressed the various plenary and seminar sessions.

We were there to affirm our confidence that the Word of God is holy, inspired and without error. God's Word is unlike any other book ever written. It is full of power and transforms the lives of all who read and obey its commandments. Many scholars read it without understanding, while others with little or no formal education comprehend its truths and are transformed in the process because they walk with God in humility and in the fullness and control of the Holy Spirit.

The story is told of a famous actor who attended a party one evening. A minister, who was also present, asked him if he would be kind enough to recite the 23rd Psalm. The actor, a famous and eloquent star of stage and screen, agreed on one condition — that the minister, a man in his eighties who had served God faithfully and humbly for half a century, would also recite the psalm.

The minister agreed, and the actor began. The words came like beautiful music, and everyone was enthralled at his beautiful presentation of the 23rd Psalm. A standing ovation greeted him at the finish.

Then the minister stood. He was not polished or eloquent. But as he began to recite the 23rd Psalm, a holy hush fell over his listeners and tears began to fill their eyes. When he finished, there was no applause — only silence. The actor stood to his feet. "I have reached your eyes and your ears and your emotions," he said. "But this man of God has reached the very depths of your being."

Bible Reading: 2 Peter 1:19-21

ACTION POINT: I will seek to become so familiar with God's Word, and obedient to its precepts, that my life will reflect its teachings. I will encourage others to join me in this great adventure of getting to know God and His holy, inspired Word.

Anything Is Possible

"Jesus said unto him, If thou canst believe, all things are possible to him that believeth" (Mark 9:23, KJV).

"My doing all depends on thy believing" is what Jesus really said to the desperate father of the demoniac boy. And it is what He says to you and me today.

The Lord sought to bring forth faith in that struggling soul, and — through pain and travail — it came to birth. Realizing that the solution rested not upon God's power but upon his own faith, the man became conscious of conflicting principles and delivered himself of a noble utterance:

"Lord, I believe; help Thou mine unbelief.

Mystery of mysteries: even the very faith that we must exercise to bring down the power of God is a gift from God Himself. But some conditions are laid down before we receive that gift of faith.

"Faith comes by hearing and hearing by the Word of God."

When I spend time in God's Word — whether reading, studying, memorizing or meditating — that faith is being built up in me. Not faith in myself, not faith in a routine, but faith in the almighty ruler of heaven and earth.

That physical illness; that unsaved loved one; that financial need; that faltering relationship; that broken home — whatever the need might be — the solution is as close as the Word of God, for our dependence upon it, and upon the God of the Word, brings the faith that unlocks the solution to every need.

Bible Reading: Mark 9:24-29

ACTION POINT: I shall believe God today for every need I face, at the same time building up my faith in Him by feasting on His Word.

Power for Healing

"Is anyone sick? He should call for the elders of the church and they should pray over him and pour oil upon him, calling on the Lord to heal him. And their prayer, if offered in faith, will make him well; and if his sickness was caused by some sin, the Lord will forgive him" (James 5:14,15).

Many years ago the principal of a missionary school in Hong Kong asked me to address the student body the following day. He and others involved in the school had prayed for years for revival to come to the student body and faculty. "God has impressed me," he said, "that you are to be His instrument for that revival." God encouraged my heart and gave me such a sense of great excitement and anticipation that I could hardly go to sleep that night.

But early in the morning, some kind of serious amoebic illness struck me and I could hardly get out of bed. Believing that God was going to use me in spite of my illness, though, I claimed His supernatural power and was dressed and ready when the principal arrived to take me to the anticipated meeting. A famous Asian evangelist who, for several years, had been ill with a mysterious disease that even the finest medical specialists were unable to diagnose had also gotten out of his sickbed, to be my interpreter.

Here we were, two very sick men delivering a message on revival. However, I had hardly spoken more than a sentence or two when I felt the supernatural healing touch of God upon me. The power was reflected in my message and God did send revival, not only to the students and faculty, but also to this speaker.

Later, as we rejoiced together, the principal asked if I would join in praying for my interpreter who was still very ill. We gathered around and laid hands on him – the principal, his wife and I. By faith we claimed his healing and I went on my way. Within days the man was miraculously restored to fullness of health and within weeks was on his first evangelistic speaking tour in several years, proclaiming the good news of God's love and forgiveness through Jesus Christ.

Unfortunately, the major denominations have left the emphasis on healing to some who have prostituted this great truth, cheapened it, and made it a laughing matter, not only among evangelical believers, but in the secular world at large. Though many for whom we pray are not healed – else no one would die – we must remember that it is a privilege and power available to believers that we can claim for the glory of our risen Savior.

Bible Reading: James 5:13-18

ACTION POINT: I will pray in faith for those who are ill and claim God's supernatural healing power in their behalf.

Finished With Sin

"He personally carried the load of our sins in His own body when He died on the cross, so that we can be finished with sin and live a good life from now on. For his wounds have healed ours!" (1 Peter 2:24).

Following one of my messages a young woman in her early 20's asked for counsel. She was weighted down with her guilt and sin. In fact, she was so distraught that she would not look me in the eye. All the while I was counseling her she was under such deep conviction that all that I could see was the top of her head.

I asked, "Do you believe that Jesus Christ is the Son of God?" She nodded in the affirmative. "Do you believe that He died on the cross for your sins?" Again she responded affirmatively. "Would you like to invite Him into your life and ask Him to cleanse you with His precious blood, which He shed on the cross for your sins, and make you a new creature in Christ?" Again, she nodded. Together we knelt in prayer and through her sobs she surrendered to Christ, acknowledging the wickedness and filth of a life of gross immorality. She confessed to God her disobedience of her father and mother whose hearts had been broken by her prodigal ways.

After some time on our knees it was obvious that God had touched her, had forgiven and cleansed her. The sobbing had passed and now she was at peace. The Spirit within me bore witness that she had become a new creature in Christ. As we stood to our feet, she looked at me with her eyes still glistening with tears and her face radiant with joy. She now knew the reality of our promise for today. Jesus had taken the load of her sins on His own body and she was now cleansed. With His wounds He had healed her and now she could live a life for the glory of God.

Who, but Jesus, could work such a miracle? Is it any wonder that those who know Him in this way want, like the apostle Paul, to tell everyone who will listen about Him? He alone can forgive our sin and liberate us from the darkness and gloom of Satan's kingdom.

Bible Reading: 1 Peter 2:21-25

ACTION POINT: With great joy and deep gratitude I will praise the Lord that He has taken upon Himself the load of my sin and through His death on the cross has paid the penalty which I could never have paid through my own effort. As an expression of my gratitude and through the enabling of the Holy Spirit, I commit myself to live a good life, a supernatural life that will glorify my God and Savior.

Mercy and Grace

"Let us therefore come boldly unto the throne of grace, that we may obtain mercy, and find grace to help in time of need" (Hebrews 4:16, KJV).

Though prayer has been a vital, integral part of my life since I became a Christian, I am always discovering new challenges and new facets of prayer. I find one of the most powerful, exciting and fulfilling privileges God has given to man to be that of prayer based on the authority of God's Word.

Man instinctively prays, even if only to false gods built of sticks and stones. Whenever he is faced with tragedy, heartache, sorrow or danger, he prays.

There is a serious danger in this "ignorant" kind of praying, however. It is a well-established fact of philosophy and history that man always assimilates the moral character of the object he worships. People who have prayed to gods of blood, fire and war have become militaristic, ruthless and sadistic.

This same principle applies to the Christian, who can pray to the one true God. "As we behold His [Christ's] face, we are changed into the same image from glory to glory." This explains the scriptural emphasis of praying worshipfully to the only true, righteous, holy and loving God.

In spite of this potential metamorphosis, however, the lives of few Christians are characterized by the supernatural. Many Christians today are impotent and fruitless compared to those of the first century. This is because the average Christian spends so little time at the throne of grace, so little time beholding the face of our Lord. And, as a result, he does not really believe that mercy and grace are available to enable him to live a supernatural life.

Bible Reading: Hebrews 3:1-6

ACTION POINT: Knowing I can come boldly to the throne of grace and receive mercy, cleansing, forgiveness and help for my every need, challenge and opportunity — from my Lord Jesus Himself, our great high priest — I will spend more time in His presence and not be satisfied with an impotent, fruitless life.

Peace of Heart and Mind

"I am leaving you with a gift — peace of mind and heart! And the peace I give isn't fragile like the peace the world gives. So don't be troubled or afraid" (John 14:27).

A stricken widow stood beside the coffin of her husband. She said to a friend, "There lies my only earthly support, my most faithful human friend, one who has never failed me; but I must not forget there lies also the will of God, and that will is perfect love."

By faith, she saw good and blessing, remembering the promise of God, "I know the plans that I have for you...plans for good..." (Jeremiah 29:11).

As the Prince of Peace, Jesus gives peace of heart and mind, truly one of the greatest and most remarkable gifts we can receive. In the midst of trial and testing, His perfect peace is a supernatural blessing far exceeding even such coveted gifts as good health, for with His inner peace we have everything we need.

How do we obtain that kind of peace? First, it is the fruit of the Spirit. "Love, joy, *peace*..." As we are yielded to Him and controlled by the Holy Spirit, the fruit of peace is being cultivated in our lives moment by moment, day by day.

Second, "Thou wilt keep him in perfect peace whose mind is stayed on Thee" (Isaiah 26:3, KJV); "As he thinketh in his heart so is he" (Proverbs 23:7, KJV). It is a fact of life that we become in our attitudes and actions like that which most dominates our thoughts. That explains the dramatic moral and spiritual deterioration resulting from the influence of immoral television programming. When the Lord is given His proper priority in our lives, His perfect peace will reign in our hearts.

While it is true that all such blessings are gifts of God and cannot be earned or merited, it is equally true that we can deliberately choose to cooperate with God's Holy Spirit by yielding ourselves to Him and thus cultivating the fruit of peace.

Bible Reading: Isaiah 26:1-5

ACTION POINT: By faith I shall claim God's promised peace for today and every day. I shall ask the Holy Spirit to help me concentrate my heart's gaze on the Lord Jesus Christ, the Prince of Peace, and I will encourage someone else to do the same.

Rescue From Temptation

"So also the Lord can rescue you and me from the temptations that surround us, and continue to punish the ungodly until the day of final judgment comes" (2 Peter 2:9).

Charles G. Finney was one of America's most outstanding evangelists. One day while he was still a young lawyer, he sat in his village law office in the state of New York. It was early in the day, and the Lord began to deal with him.

"Finney," an inner voice asked, "what are you going to do when you finish your course?"

"Put out a shingle and practice law."

"Then what?" the voice persisted.

"Get rich."

"Then what?"

"Retire."

"Then what?"

"Die."

"Then what?"

This time the words came tremblingly, "The judgment."

Young Finney ran for the woods half a mile away. As he prayed, he vowed that he would not leave until he had made his peace with God. After a long struggle, he discovered that he could not resist God's call, and he came out of the woods that evening with the high purpose of living the remainder of his life to the glory of God, enjoying Him forever.

Like that great preacher and evangelist you and I can be rescued from the temptations of the world so that we will not resist any clear call from God.

Bible Reading: 2 Peter 2:10-17

ACTION POINT: When the world tries to squeeze me into its mold, I'll not resist the clear call from our Lord Jesus Christ to follow Him.

He Keeps His Promises

"Understand, therefore, that the Lord your God is the faithful God who for a thousand generations keeps His promises and constantly loves those who love Him and who obey His commands" (Deuteronomy 7:9).

Torn between the desire to surrender his life to the Lord and the desire to be his own person, Tom gave vent to his frustration.

"I want to be a good Christian," he said, "but I'm afraid of God and what He might do to change my plans. You see, I have great plans for my life and I don't want to end up wasting it.

"For example, I don't want to marry someone with whom I would be miserable or risk my opportunities for a successful business career."

I asked Tom, as I have often asked others, "Do you really believe that God loves you?"

"Yes," he replied — and that is the general response. Then I reminded him that Jesus Christ so loved him that He was willing to die on the cross for his sins.

"Do you believe that He died for you?"

"Yes," Tom agreed, and that also is the general reply.

Then, my final question, "Don't you think that you can trust the omnipotent Creator God, who so loved you that He sent His only begotten Son, who Himself loved you so much that He was willing to die on the cross for your sins, that you may have a full and abundant life here on earth and for all eternity?"

Tom's response was, "I'd never thought of it that way before. Of course I can trust Him, and I will."

Together we knelt in prayer, and God touched his life in such a dramatic way that he has since been used to introduce many thousands to our Savior.

Bible Reading: Deuteronomy 7:6-8,10-13

ACTION POINT: Today I will surrender my will to do the will of God in all things, because I know that He is a God of love, wisdom, compassion and concern who wants the very best for me. I will share this good news with other Christians who are reluctant to surrender their wills to Him and with nonbelievers who have not yet entered into the joy and excitement of the supernatural life.

Riches in Glory

"And it is He who will supply all your needs from His riches in glory, because of what Christ Jesus has done for us" (Philippians 4:19).

God has faithfully met the needs of this great worldwide ministry since its inception. He met our needs when there were only two of us — Vonette and I — on the staff. He meets our needs today (1983) with more than 16,000 full-time and associate staff members serving in most communities of America and in 151 other countries.

He met our needs when our budget was a few thousand dollars a year. He continues to meet our needs when our budget is approximately $100 million a year. During this exciting, incredibly rich and rewarding adventure with our gracious Lord, we have never had an extra dollar at the end of any day. We get only what we need — and no more.

During these years, there have been many dramatic demonstrations of His faithfulness, when He has led us to undertake major and frequently expensive projects. He has always supplied the funds to pay for what He orders. We have learned many lessons concerning God's faithfulness.

First, whatever He leads us to do He will enable us to do by supplying the manpower, the finances and the know-how — oftentimes dramatically — if we continue to trust and obey Him.

Second, "we have not because we ask not" (James 4:2, KJV).

Third, we do not receive when our motives are impure.

But of this we can be sure: if our hearts are pure, our motives are pure and we do what we do for the glory of God — to help fulfill the Great Commission through the winning and discipling of men for Christ throughout the world — we can always be assured that God will supply our needs. Not to do so would be a contradiction of His attributes, for the idea of the Great Commission began with our Lord.

Bible Reading: 2 Corinthians 9:6-11

ACTION POINT: I will examine my heart to determine my motives and relate my needs to the scriptural commands with the confidence that God will supply all of my needs from His riches in glory, because of what Christ Jesus has done for me. I will thank Him in advance for meeting my needs, and encourage others to trust Him also. This is a part of my commitment to supernatural living.

Claiming Forgiveness

"But, dearly loved friends, if our consciences are clear, we can come to the Lord with perfect assurance and trust, and get whatever we ask for because we are obeying Him and doing the things that please Him" (1 John 3:21,22).

What a marvelous promise — unfortunately, a promise which few Christians are able to claim. Why? Because they do not have a clear conscience in regard to their sin and when they come to God, they cannot come with confidence that He will hear and answer them. As God's Word reminds us in Psalm 66:15, if I regard iniquity in my heart, the Lord will not hear me. How wonderful to know that whatever sins have been committed, the shedding of Christ's blood and His death on the cross have paid the penalty for them all. If we confess our sin of pride, lust, jealousy, gossip, dishonesty, greed, whatever it may be, we can by faith claim His forgiveness. Remember that, if we agree with God concerning our sin, if we recognize that Christ's death on the cross has indeed paid the penalty for that sin, and if we repent or change our attitude, which results in a change of our action, we can know that we are forgiven. However, if there is no change of attitude and action, obviously there has been no true confession and therefore no forgiveness and cleansing.

If you have truly confessed your sins, you can come now into the presence of God with great joy and a clear conscience and have perfect assurance and trust that whatever you ask for, you will receive because you are praying according to the will and the Word of God.

Bible Reading: 1 John 3:18-24

ACTION POINT: One of the qualifications for supernatural living is a clear conscience. Therefore, by God's grace I will keep my heart and motives pure through the practice of spiritual breathing knowing that when I breathe spiritually (exhale — confess, inhale — appropriate the promise), I can come into God's presence with a clear conscience and expect to receive answers to my prayers.

Rescued From Darkness

"For He has rescued us out of the darkness and gloom of Satan's kingdom and brought us into the kingdom of his dear Son" (Colossians 1:13)

A famous general invited me to his office. He was hungry for God and eager to become a Christian. Yet as we counseled together, he seemed reluctant to pray. I inquired as to his reluctance, and he said, "I don't understand myself. I want to receive Christ, but I can't."

I turned to Colossians 1:13,14 and asked him to read it aloud. Then I asked him to tell me what he thought it meant. The light went on. Suddenly he realized that he was a member of Satan's kingdom, and Satan was trying to hinder his being liberated from darkness and gloom into the glorious light of the kingdom of God's dear Son. Satan did not want him to receive Christ into his heart.

As soon as this man realized he was a member of Satan's kingdom, he was ready to pray and receive Christ into his life so that he would then become a member of God's kingdom.

I, too, was once in Satan's kingdom — not a very pleasant thought, but true. And so were you if you are a Christian. Every person born into this world is a part of Satan's kingdom; all who are not now experiencing the saving grace and love of Christ are a part of his kingdom.

It is God the Holy Spirit who enables men to comprehend spiritual truth. It is God the Holy Spirit who liberates men from darkness into light. It is God the Holy Spirit who is responsible for the new birth that brings men into the kingdom of God.

When we go out to witness, it is not enough to know God's plan. It is not enough to know the Four Spiritual Laws. It is not enough for us to be nicely groomed and properly scented. We need to go in the power of God's Holy Spirit. He alone can change men.

Bible Reading: Ephesians 6:10-13

ACTION POINT: My first concern in everything I do and every contact I make today will be that the power of God's Holy Spirit will be operative in my life, so that others will see His supernatural qualities in my life and want to join me in following Him.

We Are Held Securely

"No one who has become part of God's family makes a practice of sinning, for Christ, God's Son, holds him securely and the devil cannot get his hands on him" (1 John 5:18).

"I am enjoying my new-found liberty. I know that I am a Christian. I know that I am going to heaven, but for the moment I want to do my own thing. I recognize that the Lord may discipline me for the things that I am doing which the Bible says are wrong. I was reared in a very strict, legalistic Christian family and church and I have never enjoyed life before, but now I am having a ball. I don't see anything wrong with drinking and sex and the other so-called sins that I have been told all my life were so terribly wrong."

Do you believe that person is a Christian? Of course I have no way of judging, but according to the Word of God it is quite likely that this person has never really experienced a new birth. Can you imagine a beautiful butterfly going back again to crawl in the dirt as it did as a caterpillar?

It is possible, of course, for a Christian, one who has experienced new life in Christ, to sin, and even to continue in sin for a period of time, but never with a casual, flippant indifference to God's way as this person expressed.

In the second chapter of the same epistle, the writer says the same thing in different words: "How can we be sure that we belong to Him? By looking within ourselves: are we really trying to do what He wants us to? Someone may say, 'I am a Christian; I am on my way to heaven; I belong to Christ.' But if he doesn't do what Christ tells him to, he is a liar. But those who do what Christ tells them to will learn to love God more and more. That is the way to know whether or not you are a Christian. Anyone who says he is a Christian should live as Christ did" (1 John 2:3-6).

Though it is not possible for us in this life to know the perfection that our Lord experienced, there will be that heartfelt desire to do what He wants us to do. Therefore, anyone who is a child of God will not make a practice of sinning. Those who are so inclined should consider the possibility that they could be forever separated from God on judgment day.

Bible Reading: 1 John 5:16-21

ACTION POINT: I am assured of my own salvation through faith in Christ which is demonstrated by the transformation of my attitudes and actions. I will encourage professing Christians, whose lives do not reflect God's desires, to appropriate by faith the fullness of the Holy Spirit and His power in their daily walk so that they, too, can have the assurance of their salvation and their place in God's special kingdom.

Strength Out of Weakness

"And he said unto me, My grace is sufficient for thee: for my strength is made perfect in weakness. Most gladly therefore will I rather glory in my infirmities, that the power of Christ may rest upon me" (2 Corinthians 12:9, KJV).

On thousands of occasions, under all kinds of circumstances, I have found God's promise to be true in my own experiences and in the lives of multitudes of others.

Charles Spurgeon rode home one evening after a heavy day's work. Feeling very wearied and depressed, he suddenly recalled the Scripture, "My grace is sufficient for thee."

Immediately he compared himself to a tiny fish in the Thames river, apprehensive lest its drinking so many pints of water in the river each day might drink the Thames dry. Then he could hear Father Thames say, "Drink away, little fish, my stream is sufficient for thee."

Then he pictured a little mouse in Joseph's granaries in Egypt, afraid lest its consumption of the corn it needed might exhaust the supplies and it would starve to death. Then Joseph would come along and sense its fear, saying "Cheer up, little mouse, my granaries are sufficient for thee."

He thought of himself as a mountain climber reaching the lofty summit and dreading lest he might exhaust all the oxygen in the atmosphere. Then he would hear the Creator Himself say, "Breathe away, O man, and fill thy lungs ever. My atmosphere is sufficient for thee."

"Then," Spurgeon told his congregation, "for the first time in my life I experienced what Abraham must have felt when he fell upon his face and laughed."

What kinds of needs do you have today? Are they needs for which our heavenly Father is not sufficient? Can you trust Him? Is there anyone who has proven himself to be more trustworthy?

Bible Reading: 2 Corinthians 12:1-10

ACTION POINT: In every type of need, burden and problem I face today — whether my own or that of someone else — I will count on the sufficiency of Christ to handle it, and to enable me to live supernaturally.

He Gives Good Gifts

"And if you hardhearted, sinful men know how to give good gifts to your children, won't your Father in heaven even more certainly give good gifts to those who ask Him for them?" (Matthew 7:11).

"Daddy, we love you and want to do only that which pleases you."

Do you know what I would do if my sons expressed their love for me and their trust in me in this way?

"I love you, too," I would tell them, as I put my arms around them and gave them a big hug. "I appreciate your offer to do anything I want. Your expression of love and faith is the greatest gift you can give me."

As a result, I am all the more sensitive and diligent to demonstrate my love and concern for them.

Is God any less loving and concerned for His children? Of course not. He has proven over and over again that He is a loving God. He is worthy of our trust. Further, He has the wisdom and power to do for us far more than we ever are able to do for our children.

"If you then, being evil, know how to give good gifts to your children, how much more shall your Father who is in heaven give what is good to those who ask Him?" (Matthew 7:11, NAS).

By our attitudes and actions, most of us say to God, "I don't love You. I don't trust You."

Can you think of anything that would hurt you more deeply, coming from your children? The average Christian is a practical atheist living as though God does not exist. Even though we give lip service to Him, we often refuse to trust and obey His promises as recorded in His Word.

Bible Reading: Matthew 7:7-11

ACTION POINT: Knowing that God wants to give me a supernatural, abundant life, I will trust and obey Him today in all that I do.

Spirit of His Son

"And because we are His sons God has sent the Spirit of His Son into our hearts, so now we can rightly speak of God as our dear Father" (Galatians 4:6).

What would you say is the most sacred privilege and indescribable honor of your entire lifetime? If you are a Christian and you rightly understand the meaning of our verse for today, you will agree that nothing compares with presenting your body to the Holy Spirit to be His dwelling place here on earth.

Wherever I am in the world, whether speaking in meetings, reading the Bible, praying, counseling, attending various conferences, alone in my hotel room or enjoying the company of my dearly beloved wife and family, I am always keenly aware that my body is a temple of God and there is no higher privilege.

I am reminded of the Virgin Mary's response to the angel's announcement that she would conceive a child by the Holy Spirit. "Oh, how I praise the Lord! How I rejoice in God my Savior, for He took notice of this lowly servant girl and now generation after generation forever shall call me blessed of God, for He the mighty one has done great things to me.

"His mercy goes on from generation to generation to all who reverence Him," she continues in triumphant, joyful expression of her grateful heart.

We too should praise and give thanks to God constantly for the privilege of being chosen to be a temple in which He dwells here on earth. As one meditates upon this fact, one becomes intoxicated with the realization that the infinite, omnipotent, holy, loving, righteous God and Father, Son and Holy Spirit, now dwell within us who have received Him.

There are many believers who are not fully aware of the significance of this fact, because, though they as believers in Christ possess the Holy Spirit, the Holy Spirit does not possess all of them. Ours is the indescribable privilege of presenting our bodies to Him as a living sacrifice, as temples in which He will dwell. Only then, will we have the power to live the abundant, supernatural life promised to those who yield their hearts and lives to the control of the Holy Spirit.

Bible Reading: Galatians 4:7-14

ACTION POINT: As often as the thought comes to mind today, I will acknowledge the fullness and control of God's Holy Spirit in my life. I will also encourage other Christians to claim by faith the fullness and power of the Holy Spirit for their lives.

Awards for Faithfulness

"Stop being afraid of what you are about to suffer — for the devil will soon throw some of you into prison to test you. You will be persecuted for 'ten days.' Remain faithful even when facing death and I will give you the crown of life — an unending, glorious future" (Revelation 2:10).

I find this a very timely word of caution, for we live in a day when it appears that the enemy is making his last fling. I would not attempt to set dates, for it may be years, decades or even centuries before the culmination of all things.

But the fact remains that committed believers are facing persecution and testing as perhaps seldom before. You and I may be called upon to suffer for the cause of Christ. By faith, we are not to fear, knowing that an "unending, glorious future" awaits us.

This promise might apply equally to the physical suffering we encounter from time to time as a part of the natural order of things. If we can accept such suffering as part of God's plan for us — one of the "all things" of Romans 8:28 that is working together for our good — we will be among those victors who are able to "count it all joy."

As we consider these possibilities, we may be optimistic, even cheerful, knowing that we are already on the winning side — more than conquerors. And we need not be afraid, for "God has not given us the spirit of fear, but of power, and of love, and of a sound mind."

Bible Reading: Revelation 2:8-11

ACTION POINT: I will count on God's promise of Romans 8:28 to do only that which is good for me, regardless of the circumstances. He will enable me to live supernaturally.

The Lord Will Pay

"Remember, the Lord will pay you for each good thing you do, whether you are slave or free" (Ephesians 6:8).

When I proposed to Vonette I told her that I loved her dearly, and I wanted her to be my wife. I promised to do everything I could to make her happy and that she would always be the most important person in my life. But I further explained that my first allegiance was to the Lord, for I had already made that commitment to Him and could not and would not violate that promise to follow Him whatever the cost. She agreed, and we were married on those conditions.

My love for Vonette is far greater today because Jesus Christ is first in my life, and her love for me is far greater because He is first in her life. Our relationship is infinitely richer and more meaningful than it would have been had she been master of her life, and I the lord of my life, or if we had made each other first in our lives and the Lord Jesus Christ second.

The apostle Paul, writing under the inspiration of the Holy Spirit, is affirming the promise of our Lord recorded in Matthew 6:32,33, "Your heavenly Father already knows perfectly well what you need and He will give it to you if you give Him first place in your life and live as He wants you to."

In the context of this verse in Ephesians, Paul is dealing with family relationships — authority within the family. If we can grasp the concept of God as our paymaster, it will make a vast difference in the way we respond to the authority of men.

Christ knows everything you endure; He gives you your full portion of all that He owns. He is really the one for whom you are working. Wherever you are working, you may have assignments and responsibilities which you do not enjoy. But if Christ is truly the one for whom you work, then you will undertake His assignments cheerfully.

If we choose to be rebellious, we face the danger of a reward from our paymaster that might not be at all to our liking. Let us be about our Father's business — willingly, joyfully, enthusiastically.

Bible Reading: Ephesians 6:1-7

ACTION POINT: Though I may have a boss or leader who tells me what to do, and when to do it, I will always remember that my first allegiance is to the Lord Jesus Christ, and by putting Him first, even above my loved ones who surround me, I can serve others with greater joy, confidence and enthusiasm.

No Hurt in Second Death

"Let everyone who can hear, listen to what the Spirit is saying to the churches: He who is victorious shall not be hurt by the Second Death" (Revelation 2:11).

I find great comfort in the promises of God's Word, and this is another that makes a positive assurance to us: we shall not be hurt by the Second Death.

But just what is meant by the term *Second Death?* It would seem to mean that the conqueror shall not have anything to fear in the future world. The punishment of hell is sometimes called death — not in the sense that the soul will cease to exist, but because death is the most fearful thing we know about, and there is a striking similarity in many respects between death and future punishment.

As death cuts us off from life, so the second death cuts one off from eternal life. Death puts an end to all our earthly hopes, and the second death to all hope forever. Death is accompanied by terrors and alarms, which are only faint emblems of the coming terror in the world of woe.

This promise of no harm for us in the second death really is all that is necessary to sustain us in our trials. Nothing else is needed to make the burdens of life tolerable but this assurance that the end of our earthly journey will bring us to the close of suffering. No power can harm us beyond the grave.

We have no promise that we shall not die, but we do have this glorious assurance that nothing beyond that will ever hurt us. Meanwhile, we are expected to listen — and to be faithful.

Bible Reading: John 8:21-25

ACTION POINT: Knowing that nothing beyond the grave will ever hurt me, I will make this present life count for Christ and His kingdom.

Glory Will Be Ours

"Yet what we suffer now is nothing compared to the glory he will give us later" (Romans 8:8).

In Sydney, Australia, a taxi driver to whom I witnessed became very angry.

"I was in World War II," he exploded, "and I saw thousands of people die. I don't want to have anything to do with a God who allows war."

"Don't blame God for war and the slaughter of millions of people," I explained. "War is the result of man's sin. Man does what he does because of his selfishness and pride. God does not desire that man should destroy men. God is not in favor of war. But sickness, death, earthquakes, tornadoes, floods are all a part of God's judgment because of man's sin, because of man's disobedience to His commands.

The problem of suffering is a mysterious one, but for the Christian there is a good, logical answer. All creation waits patiently and hopefully for that future day when God will resurrect His children. On that day, thorns and thistles, sin and death and decay — the things that overcome the world will all disappear at God's command.

The world around us then will share in the glorious freedom from sin which God's children enjoy. Even the things of nature, animals and plants which now suffer deterioration and death, await the coming of the time of this great glory.

We Christians — though we have the Holy Spirit within us as a foretaste of future glory — also groan to be released from pain, heartache, sorrow and suffering. We too wait anxiously for that day when God will give us full rights as His children, including the new bodies He has promised us — bodies that will never suffer again, and that will never die.

Bible Reading: Romans 8:24-27

ACTION POINT: I will rejoice in the certainty that glory is ahead for me as a believer, and as a result I am willing to joyfully endure whatever suffering comes my way. I will also encourage others in their times of sorrow to consider God's love and plan for them, and will help them to understand the scriptural reason for man's suffering.

Worthy of Trust

"What is faith? It is the confident assurance that something we want is going to happen. It is the certainty that what we hope for is waiting for us, even though we cannot see it up ahead" (Hebrews 11:1).

Frequently, individuals make gifts of property or stocks and bonds to the ministry of Campus Crusade for Christ. I am notified by our legal department that the papers have been received, confirming our ownership. Then, on the basis of their word, I consider the value and the potential sale of these properties in light of our budget for this worldwide ministry.

Can you imagine? I make decisions involving literally millions of dollars based upon a word or a memo. I do not see the stocks and bonds. I do not visit the property. I do not even see the papers. But I can take the word of my associates, whom I have learned to trust, and, predicated on their recommendations, I can determine how many missionaries we can send to the field.

That is what faith is all about. I have faith in my beloved colleagues because they have demonstrated themselves to be trustworthy. How much more should I have faith in our loving, holy, gracious, God and Father who has demonstrated His faithfulness and trustworthiness innumerable times? How much more should I believe His holy, inspired Word — His many promises?

However, God's promises do not become reality unless we act upon them, claiming them in faith, any more than the word of my associates would be of any value unless I acted upon that information.

Vast resources of heaven are available to us. We appropriate them by faith. Consider the following illustration: Suppose I have $1,000 in the bank. I go to the bank with a check for $100 in my hand. I hand it to the teller, get on my knees and begin to beseech the teller to cash my check for $100. This would seem unusual to the teller and to all who might observe me for that is not the way to cash a check. Rather, I place it before the teller with the assurance that I have ten times the amount of the check on deposit and therefore without any hesitancy can expect my check to be cashed.

So it is with the bank of heaven. I know that the promises of God are faithful and true. God does not lie. God is worthy of my trust and, therefore, whatever He promises, He will perform if only I will trust and obey him.

Bible Reading: Psalm 119:89-96

ACTION POINT: Today I will claim the promises of God by faith with the joyful assurance that whatever God promises, He is faithful to perform. I will claim His supernatural resources for supernatural living.

All Things for Our Good

"And we know that all that happens to us is working for our good if we love God and are fitting into His plans" (Romans 8:28).

I waited and prayed in the chapel at the Loma Linda Hospital. My beloved wife, Vonette, had been in major surgery for four hours. Three weeks before, while I was in Brazil, she had gone to our doctor for a physical examination and he had informed her that she had a large growth that could be malignant.

Though he wanted to operate at once, the doctor agreed at Vonette's insistence to wait until I returned from a tour of several Latin American countries. Vonette called to give me the doctor's report while I was in Rio de Janeiro. Naturally I wanted to return home at once. However, she assured me that she would be all right and encouraged me not to interrupt the meetings since they had the potential of ultimately helping to train hundreds of thousands of Christians to help reach millions for our Lord throughout all of Latin America (which they have subsequently done through a great Here's Life movement in each of those countries).

We prayed together over the telephone, praising God for His faithfulness to us in the past. As an expression of our faith and an act of obedience to His holy, inspired Word, we thanked Him for this opportunity to trust Him, even though at the moment it seemed very difficult. Then as we praised and gave thanks to the Lord, His supernatural peace flooded our hearts. God always honors faith and obedience.

During the following weeks we continued to praise and thank God as we both continued to speak and witness for Him personally and at many meetings, recognizing that we are His servants, and that the Master is responsible for the welfare of His servants.

After the surgery the doctors assured us that the operation was a success and that there was no malignancy. We continue to thank and praise the Lord for His goodness to us. We know that, if we love God, all things really do work together for our good regardless of the circumstances and regardless of the outcome. Why did God allow us to go through this experience? In order that we would be reminded of His faithfulness and learn to love, trust and obey Him.

Bible Reading: Romans 8:29-34

ACTION POINT: Since I love God and am fitting into His plans, I will, by faith, count all things as working together for my good today and will thank God and praise Him in obedience to His command. I will encourage others to do the same, to trust and obey God as an expression of the supernatural life.

In the Book of Life

"Everyone who conquers will be clothed in white, and I will not erase his name from the Book of Life, but I will announce before My Father and His angels that he is Mine" (Revelation 3:5).

Perhaps you have rejoiced — as I have — at the reminder that our names are written in the Lamb's Book of Life, God's heavenly record of the redeemed.

Here are two more promises to the conqueror, the overcomer, the victorious Christian — one having to do with future reign, the other with our security in Him.

Not only to the believers in Sardis who should be victorious, but also to those in every age and every land, lies the hope — indeed the promise — of appearing with Christ in white robes expressing holiness and joy in that future day when He shall rule and reign on this earth.

If you are a believer in Christ, your name is in that book which contains the names of those who are to live with Him throughout eternity. Not to have our names erased, of course, means that the names will be found there on the great day of final account, and forever and ever.

What better way could we use our time today — and tomorrow — and the next day — than to add names to the Book of Life, by faithfully witnessing to others about the good news of the gospel? Our privilege and responsibility is to share; God's Holy Spirit does the work of convicting and saving.

Bible Reading: Revelation 3:1-6

ACTION POINT: "Dear Lord, help me to add names to Your Book of Life by sharing my faith in You at every possible opportunity."

His Spirit Tells Us

"That is what is meant by the Scriptures which say that no mere man has ever seen, heard or even imagined what wonderful things God has ready for those who love the Lord. But we know about these things because God has sent His Spirit to tell us, and His Spirit searches out and shows us all of God's deepest secrets" (1 Corinthians 2:9,10).

For many years, on every populated continent, I have asked millions of Christians this question: "What is the greatest thing that has ever happened to you since you became a Christian?"

The answer invariably has been: "To experience the reality, power, control and fruit of the Holy Spirit." There is no other truth that so transforms the life of the Christian and enables him to be fruitful for the glory of God.

Two strangers were viewing the Niagara whirlpool rapids one day and one said to the other, "Come and I'll show you the greatest unused power in the world."

Taking him to the foot of Niagara Falls, he said, "There is the greatest unused power in the world!"

"Oh, no my friend," came the reply, "not so. The greatest unused power in the world is the Holy Spirit of the living God."

Christ's strength is given to us through the Holy Spirit to meet our every need. How do we receive that strength, that supernatural power?

As Christians, we have that potential within us, in the person of God's Holy Spirit, but sin hinders the working of the Holy Spirit in our lives.

By confessing all our known sin and appropriating that supernatural power of the Holy Spirit within us, we can, by faith, be filled and continue to be filled with the power of the Holy Spirit. Then, according to God's Word, the Holy Spirit ministers to our every need.

When we by faith are filled with the Holy Spirit, He guides us, empowers us, makes us holy, bears witness in our lives, comforts us, gives us joy, gives discernment, bears fruit in and through our lives and gives us spiritual gifts for the building up of the Body of Christ.

Bible Reading: 1 Corinthians 2:11-16

ACTION POINT: I will by faith appropriate the greatest unused power in the world today, the supernatural power of God's indwelling Holy Spirit who enables me to live a supernatural life. I will share with someone today how he, too, can live a supernatural life.

Glorious Future

"As for the one who conquers, I will make him a pillar in the temple of my God; he will be secure, and will go out no more; and I will write my God's Name on him, and he will be a citizen in the city of my God — the New Jerusalem, coming down from heaven from my God; and he will have my new Name inscribed upon him" (Revelation 3:12).

You and I shall some day be in that beautiful temple in Jerusalem — New Jerusalem — to rule and reign with the King of kings and Lord of lords forever and forever.

Can you see it now? While we do not know — and need not know — all the incidental details and circumstances, we know enough from God's holy Word to know that some day we shall be with Him, never to be separated. That is cause for shouting and rejoicing.

And we need not be terrified by the condition that we must be conquerors before we qualify for any of these promised blessings. Has He not told us that we are already "more than conquerors?"

Here again we have that promise of the *new name*, thought by some to be the very name of Christ Himself — certainly worthy of attainment, whatever its true meaning.

To be "heirs with God and joint-heirs with Christ" holds all the wonderful promise that the human mind can imagine. Just to be with Him is enough; to know that He adds blessing upon blessing as we rule and reign with Him — that is unparalleled joy indeed.

Bible Reading: Revelation 3:7-13

ACTION POINT: With a quick look at the future, I'll do my best to make this day all that God intends for me, especially in my outreach to others.

We Are His Friends

"And since, when we were his enemies, we were brought back to God by the death of His Son, what blessings He must have for us now that we are His friends, and He is living within us!" (Romans 5:10).

Marilyn had a very poor self-image. She hated the way she looked and felt that her personality was so bad that she could never expect to have true friends. She was concerned especially about marriage. How could she ever find a man to love her since she was so unattractive (in her thinking).

I was able to help her see how much God loved her, and how great was His blessing for her as a child of God. The supernatural life-style was available to her, and she was the one to determine whether or not she would measure up, as an act of the will by faith, to what God had called and enabled her to be. Her part was simply to trust and obey Him.

With God's help, she determined to be that kind of person, the kind of person God had created her to be.

We who are Christians can see ourselves as God sees us and through the enabling of the Holy Spirit become what we are in His sight. With the eyes of love, He sees us covered with the blood of Christ, which was shed on the cross for our sins, and, as expressed in Hebrews 10, He sees us as holy, righteous and totally forgiven. He holds nothing against us. The penalty for our sins has been paid — once and for all. There is nothing which we can add.

Now we have the privilege of becoming in our experience what we are already in God's sight.

Bible Reading: Romans 5:11-15

ACTION POINT: Through the enabling of the Holy Spirit, I will begin to see myself as God sees me: loved, forgiven, holy, righteous, spiritually mature, aggressive and fruitful for the glory of God. Today I will live by faith the supernatural life which is my heritage in Christ.

Can't Keep on Sinning

"The person who has been born into God's family does not make a practice of sinning, because now God's life is in him; so he can't keep on sinning, for this new life has been born into him and controls him — he has been born again" (1 John 3:9).

I am sobered by the very thought that, having served the Lord for more than 30 exciting, wonderful, fruitful years, I might yet dishonor His name and bring disgrace to His cause. I know what has happened to other brothers and sisters in Christ — some of whom had apparently at one time been Spirit-filled Christian leaders, and I know that I too could fail the Lord if I do not continue to trust and obey Him. Even the apostle Paul lived in reverential fear that he might dishonor the name and cause of our Lord.

"So be careful. If you are thinking, 'Oh, I would never behave like that,' let this be a warning to you. For you too may fall into sin. But remember this: The wrong desires that come into your life aren't anything new and different. Many others have faced exactly the same problems before you. And no temptation is irresistible.

"You can trust God to keep the temptation from becoming so strong that you can't stand up against it, for He has promised this and will do what He says. He will show you how to escape temptation's power so that you can bear up patiently against it" (1 Corinthians 10:12,13).

For many years it has been my prayer, as I pray on the offensive, "Oh, God, if there is a possibility that I may dishonor or disgrace Your name by becoming involved in a moral, financial or any other kind of scandal that would discredit my ministry and nullify my love and witness for You, I would rather You take my life first before such a thing could happen."

The Scripture warns all believers that any one of them, too, could fall. No one reaches the place of spiritual maturity or perfection where he can say, "I don't need the Lord's help any more." The only one who can enable us to live victorious lives is the Lord Jesus Christ Himself.

Bible Reading: 1 John 2:21-29

ACTION POINT: At the very first sign of yielding to Satan in any way, large or small, I will remind the Lord of my utter dependence on Him and I will claim by faith His power to live a supernatural life.

On the Throne Beside Him

"I will let everyone who conquers sit beside Me on My throne, just as I took my place with My Father on His throne when I had conquered" (Revelation 3:31).

C an you imagine such glorious majesty as that which is promised in this verse?

In Revelation, Christ is frequently pictured as being on a throne, both in heaven and during His return to earth. More unusual is this promise to overcomers that, just as Christ is seated with God on His throne, they will sit on their thrones with Christ, but this is in keeping with the reward of a crown as described in chapter 2, verse 10.

In Mark 10:35-45, in response to the request of James and John that they be allowed to sit at His right and left in glory, Jesus replied that this was not in His power to grant. On the contrary, He reminded them that they were to be, like Him, the "servant of all."

Matthew 19:28 presents quite a different view, with Jesus telling His disciples that when the Son of man sits on His glorious throne, those who have followed Him "will also sit on twelve thrones, judging the twelve tribes of Israel."

In Luke's parallel passage (22:30), the disciples are to eat with Christ at His table and also to sit on thrones judging the twelve tribes — a joyful combination similar to the one presented in Revelation 3:21. The promise that the overcomers will rule is to find its glorious fulfillment in their millenial reign with Christ (Revelation 20:4).

In our daily walk with Christ, this view of His grace and love and majesty should spur us on to holy living — to supernatural living.

Bible Reading: Acts 2:30-36

ACTION POINT: I will strive to express my gratitude and appreciation for God's wonderful provision for His children by living my life in such a way that all that I do and say will be pleasing to Him.

Promise of the Spirit

"And Peter replied, 'Each one of you must turn from sin, return to God, and be baptized in the name of Jesus Christ for the forgiveness of your sins; then you also shall receive this gift, the Holy Spirit. For Christ promised Him to each one of you who has been called by the Lord our God, and to your children and even to those in distant lands!' " (Acts 2: 38,39).

The most important truth that I or anyone else could share with Christians is to help them understand the person and ministry of the Holy Spirit. My own life was dramatically transformed when by faith I claimed the fullness and power of the Holy Spirit.

"One day in New York — what a day!" declared Dwight L. Moody. "I can't describe it. I seldom refer to it. It is almost too sacred to name. I can only say God revealed Himself to me. I had such an experience of love that I had to ask Him to stay His hand.

"I went to preaching again. The sermons were no different. I did not present any new truth. Yet hundreds were converted. I would not be back where I was before that blessed experience if you would give me Glasgow."

The Holy Spirit is the key to revival. He is the key to revival because He is the key to supernatural living, and apart from living supernaturally — living in the fullness of the Holy Spirit — the believer has no power to introduce others to Christ and help fulfill the Great Commission.

The Holy Spirit is convicting many Christians of their lethargy, their coldness of heart and unbelief, the loss of their first love. A spiritual Mount St. Helens is about to erupt, spreading the good news of the love and forgiveness of our Lord Jesus Christ far and wide through our land and the world. We shall see a resurgence in evangelism and a zeal unparalleled in church history as we endeavor — in the power of the Holy Spirit — to help fulfill the Great Commission.

Bible Reading: Acts 2:32-37

ACTION POINT: I shall ask the Holy Spirit to empower and control my life so that I may be a part of a mighty spiritual awakening to help fulfill the Great Commission, beginning in my home, community and church in obedience to the Lord's command.

We Help Conquer Satan

"They defeated him by the blood of the Lamb, and by their testimony; for they did not love their lives but laid them down for Him" (Revelation 12:11).

Down through the years, you and I have lauded and applauded the martyrs — and rightly so.

These heroes of the faith — like Chester Bitterman of the Wycliffe Bible Translators, one of the latest in a long line of martyrs — preferred death to disloyalty to God and to Christ. Their testimony literally was written in blood.

Truly, "they did not love their lives but laid them down for Him." And by so doing, they became partners with God and with Christ in defeating the enemy of men's souls, Satan. Satan is to be conquered not only by the blood of the Lamb, but also by reason of the testimony of the martyrs.

T. E. McCully, father of missionary martyr Ed McCully, who, along with Jim Elliot, Pete Fleming, Nate Saint and Roger Youderian, lost his life to the Auca Indians on January 8, 1956, made a sage observation about the great sacrifice these young men had made.

"Sometimes," he said, it's harder to be a living sacrifice than it is to be a dead sacrifice." And this hits us all right where we live, in our walk with Christ today. The daily grind, the commitment and recommitment, the enduring of trial and testing — all of this takes a daily sacrifice. This is an opportunity for our lives to be a "sacrifice of praise" to our God.

Bible Reading: Revelation 12:7-12

ACTION POINT: Claiming the power of the Holy Spirit by faith, I will seek to be a living sacrifice, so that my life will be part of Satan's defeat.

Will He Be Ashamed?

"And anyone who is ashamed of Me and My message in these days of unbelief and sin, I, the Messiah, will be ashamed of him when I return in the glory of My Father, with the holy angels" (Mark 8:38).

Dr. Charles Malik, once president of the General Assembly of the United Nations, and I — along with others — were invited to a very prestigious meeting in Washington, D.C. Present were some of the most distinguished leaders in our nation and from other countries.

In the course of his remarks, Dr. Malik emphasized his conviction that there were no human solutions to the problems that face mankind. Only Jesus Christ could help us as individuals and as nations.

As a young businessman, I was tremendously impressed to think that one of the world's leading scholars and statesmen would speak so boldly and courageously of his faith in Christ. Following the meeting, I introduced myself to him and expressed to him my appreciation for his courage in speaking out so boldly for Christ.

I had heard others — politicians, statesmen, scholars — speak of faith in God and the Bible and the church in general terms. But few, in those days, ever spoke of their faith in the person of the Lord Jesus Christ. I shall never forget his response.

"I am sobered by the words of my Lord," he said, quoting today's verse, Mark 8:3.

Perhaps you are one who loudly acclaims, "No, I could never be ashamed of my wonderful Lord." But the familiar axiom is true: *actions speak louder than words.* If we are truly unashamed of our Savior, we will look for every opportunity to share the good news of His great love.

Bible Reading: Psalm 31:1-5

ACTION POINT: I will not be ashamed of my Lord and Savior Jesus Christ, but will trust the indwelling Holy Spirit to witness through me.

Everything I Need

"Because the Lord is my Shepherd, I have everything I need!" (Psalm 23:1).

A minister telephoned his sermon topic to his local newspaper one day.

"The Lord Is My Shepherd," he said.

"Is that all?" he was asked.

"That's enough," the pastor replied.

The weekend church page carried his sermon topic as: "The Lord Is My Shepherd — That's Enough."

Thoroughly satisfied with the meaning of the expanded title, he used it as his subject on Sunday morning — to the delight and great benefit of his congregation.

Surely the truth of this familiar verse, when properly assessed, should delight and benefit each one of us. Who but our wonderful Lord could serve as such a faithful shepherd? And what better description is there of His loving care for us than that which is implied in the word *shepherd*?

With Him as our Shepherd, what else could we possibly need? He has promised to be our daily provision, our healer, our all in all. Truly nothing happens to the genuine believer without the knowledge and permissive will of our heavenly Father.

Bible Reading: Psalm 23:1-6

ACTION POINT: "Dear Lord, help me to see You today as my Shepherd — gracious caretaker and friend, provider of everything I could ever possibly need."

Help for Hard Times

"He cares for them when times are hard; even in famine, they will have enough" (Psalm 37:19).

I recall that, in the early 1930's during the time of the great depression in America, many people experienced hard times. It was not always easy to fully appreciate the fact I know now to be true: God always cares for His children.

"When times are hard" can refer not only to the material, but also to the physical and the spiritual. And during any of these times — whether in poverty, poor health or the spiritual doldrums — our great God always cares for us.

In Bible times, God often proved the truth of the assertion that He cares for His people in periods of famine. And no doubt multitudes of sufferers around the world today would attest to that fact, in spite of their suffering.

When physical suffering is involved, it is not always easy to see the hand of God. But one sure way to increase faith is to exercise the sacrifice of praise — praise to our wonderful God for the positive fact that "all things do work together for our good if we love God and are called according to His purpose."

When spiritual poverty is concerned, we need only retreat to that time and place in our lives where we wandered away from God, whatever degree of wandering that involves, whether large or small. "Blessed are they that hunger and thirst after righteousness, for they shall be filled."

Bible Reading: Psalm 37:16-22

ACTION POINT: At all times of difficulty in my life — spiritual, material, physical — I will look for God's hand of blessing in the joyful assurance that He cares for me.

It All Belongs to Him

"For every beast of the forest is mine, and the cattle upon a thousand hills" (Psalm 50:10, KJV).

Gently chiding a Christian worker for praying that God might give him a second-hand car to use in his service for the Lord, Dr. A. W. Tozer reminded the man:

"God owns the cattle on a thousand hills, and the Cadillacs, too. Why not ask Him for the best?"

That same principle might apply to many areas of our lives today. If we truly believe that "according to your faith, be it unto you," then it is imperative that we trust God for greater things than normally we might.

Motive, of course, is supremely important in our asking from God. If the thing asked is clearly for God's glory, to be used in His service, the motivation is good. If pride or any other motive plays a part in the decision, then we do well to think twice before asking great things from God.

What man owns, we do well to remember, we own under God. And God has never given to man the absolute proprietorship in any thing. Nor does He invade our rights when He comes and claims what we possess, or when He in any way removes what is most valuable to us.

God owns all things — let's leave to Him the right to do whatever He wishes with the things He owns.

Bible Reading: Psalm 50:7-15

ACTION POINT: Since my receiving is "according to my faith," I will with proper motive for His glory believe God in a large manner this day — for whatever needs may arise.

He Does Such Wonders

"I will cry to the God of heaven who does such wonders for me" (Psalm 57:2).

I cannot begin to count the times, even during just one 24-hour day, that I lift my heart in praise, worship and adoration and thanksgiving to God in heaven. I begin the day by acknowledging His lordship of my life and inviting Him to have complete control of my thoughts, my attitudes, my actions, my motives, my desires, my words; to walk around in my body, think with my mind, love with my heart, speak with my lips and continue through me to seek and save the lost and minister to those in need. Throughout the day I bring before Him the personal needs of my family. I pray for the extended family of Campus Crusade for Christ staff and their families and for all those who support this ministry through their prayers and finances. I pray for business and professional people, that God will bless their finances as well as their lives so that they can continue to help support this and other ministries for His kingdom.

As I look through the mail, I breathe a prayer to God for some staff member, friend, associate or supporter who is hurting, needing encouragement, strength and peace. At all of my many daily conferences, I will begin and close with a brief word of prayer claiming the promise of God-given wisdom for the matters we shall be discussing, for supernatural discernment that will enable me to see through all the intricacies of the problems presented. When the phone rings, I breathe a silent prayer and often a vocal one at the appropriate time with that person on the other end of the line who is in distress, whether from family problems or work-related difficulties.

In between, I pray alone and with others for the hundreds of different people, events and circumstances that involve the worldwide ministry of Campus Crusade for Christ and the ministry of His Body throughout the world.

Bible Reading: Psalm 57:1-11

ACTION POINT: Recognizing that prayer is as vital to my spiritual life as air is to my physical being, I will pray without ceasing and in all things give thanks to our God in heaven who does such wonders for me.

He Can Help!

"O my people, trust Him all the time. Pour out your longings before Him, for He can help!" (Psalm 62:8).

"I have no faith in this matter," a minister said to an evangelist, "but I see it is in the Word of God and I am going to act on God's Word, no matter how I feel."

The evangelist smiled. "Why, that is faith!" he said.

The Word of God is the secret of faith. "Faith cometh by hearing, and hearing by the Word of God." We do not attain or achieve faith; we simply receive it as we read God's Word.

Many a child of God is failing to enjoy God's richest blessings in Christ because he fails to receive the gift of faith. He looks within himself for some quality that will enable him to believe, instead of "looking unto Jesus, the author and finisher of our faith."

In the words of an anonymous poem published by *War Cry:*

He does not even watch the way.
    His father's hand, he knows,
Will guide his tiny feet along
    The pathway as he goes

A childlike faith! A perfect trust!
    God grant to us today,
A faith that grasps our Father's hand
    And trusts Him all the way.

Bible Reading: Psalm 62:1-7

ACTION POINT: I will be wise in the ways of God today by looking for help from the One whom I know I can trust.

Authority Over the Enemy

"And I have given you authority over all the power of the Enemy"
(Luke 10:19).

By nature I am a very shy, reserved person. But I can look the world in the face and say, "I'm a child of the King. There is royal blood in my veins."

Because of our identification with Christ, we are no longer ordinary people. The authority of God is available to those who believe in Christ. What a promise!

"Authority over all the power of the Enemy!" That is His promise, but it is something you and I must claim each time we face the enemy. We are to believe this; it is an intellectually valid fact. It is not exercising positive thinking and blindly hoping for the best; rather, it is claiming and leaning on the promises of God by faith.

Supernatural authority belongs to the believer, and there is a difference between authority and power. A policeman standing at a busy intersection has no physical power that would enable him to stop cars coming from all directions. But that little whistle he blows and the uniform he wears represent authority, and because of that authority the drivers know they had better stop.

You and I have authority — given to us by the Lord Himself — over all the power of the enemy. he may tempt us; he may attack us; he may sorely try us. But victory is assured us as we continue to trust and obey our Lord and claim by faith His supernatural resources for our strength.

Bible Reading: Luke 10:20-24

ACTION POINT: Because I have been given all authority over the enemy, by faith I will exercise that authority in behalf of others as well as myself, believing God for ultimate victory in each situation.

Never Too Busy

"He will listen to the prayers of the destitute for He is never too busy to heed their requests" (Psalm 102:17).

As a relatively young Christian businessman, I was deacon of the First Presbyterian Church of Hollywood. I was asked to be the chairman of all of our deputation ministry involving more than 100 college- and post-college-age men and women who dedicated their lives to serving Christ in the hospitals, jails and skid row missions.

On many occasions it was my responsibility and privilege to speak at various mission meetings attended by hundreds of destitute winos, alcholics, drug addicts and others who had lost their way and were now in desperate need of help, physically and spiritually. God always ministered to me as well as to them for I seldom spoke to such a group without my own heart being deeply stirred. Inevitably I found myself reaching out to these men, poor, dejected, discouraged, many of whom had not bathed for months, and yet I found myself embracing them in the name of Jesus, pleading with them to allow Him to turn the tragedy of their lives into His eternal triumph. Many did and with life-changing results.

But unfortunately, there were far more who refused Christ. I am reminded of one with whom I pleaded to surrender his life to Christ and receive the gift of God's grace. He had, through the ravages of drink, lost his wife, his children, his business and even his health. He had absolutely nothing left, but his response to my insistence that he receive Christ was, "I cannot, I have too much to give up." I could hardly believe my ears! God was waiting with arms outstretched, eager to embrace him with His love and forgiveness, to transform his life. Let us never forget that this is God's desire for *every person* for He is not willing that *any* should perish, but that *all* should come to repentance.

Bible Reading: Psalm 102:18-28

ACTION POINT: Today I will encourage others, rich and poor, old and young, all who are spiritually destitute, to turn to God, who loves and forgives, that they, too, may experience eternal and supernatural life.

To Seek and to Save

"For the Son of man is come to seek and to save that which was lost" (Luke 19:10, KJV).

The Word of God clearly teaches that He wants His children to live supernaturally, especially in the area of living holy lives and bearing much fruit since that is the reason our Lord Jesus Christ came to this world.

Through the years I have prayed that my life and the ministry of Campus Crusade for Christ would be characterized by the supernatural. I have prayed that God would work in and through us in such a mighty way that all who see the results of our efforts would know that God alone was responsible, and give Him all the glory.

Now as I look back — marveling at God's miraculous working in our behalf — I remember earlier days which were also characterized by praise and glory to God, even though I was not privileged then to speak to millions or even thousands. At one point in our ministry, about the only understanding supportive listener I could find was my wife.

Vonette and I used to live mostly for material pleasures. But soon after our marriage we made a full commitment of our lives to the Lord. Now it is our desire (1) to live holy lives, controlled and empowered by the Holy Spirit (2) to be effective witnesses for Christ, and (3) to help fulfill the Great Commission in our generation to the end that we may continue the ministry which our Lord began as He came to "seek and to save the lost."

Bible Reading: Luke 19:1-9

ACTION POINT: I determine to bring my priorities in line with those of my Lord and Savior, who came to seek and to save the lost and to encourage others to do the same.

Praying in His Will

"This is the confidence which we have before Him, that, if we ask anything according to His will, He hears us. And if we know that He hears us in whatever we ask, we know that we have requests which we have asked from Him" (1 John 5:14,15, NAS).

A very dedicated church member, who came to me for counsel concerning her prayer life, said, "I pray all the time, but I don't seem to get any answers. I have become discouraged and I wonder if God really answers prayer."

I showed her this wonderful promise and asked, "First of all, do you pray according to the will of God?" This was a new thought to her.

"What do you mean?" she inquired. I explained by reminding her what God's Word says. How do our requests relate to the Word of God and to the desires which He places in our hearts? As we read in Psalm 37:4, if we delight ourselves in the Lord, He gives us the desires of our hearts, and in Philippians 2:13 Paul states that it is God who works in us both to will and to do His good pleasure. For example, we can always know that we are praying according to the will of God and the Word of God when we pray for the salvation of souls, for God is not willing that any should perish, but that all should come to repentance. We can pray for the maturing of believers because God wants all of us to be conformed to the image of Christ. We can also pray for

all the needs of our brothers and sisters materially, emotionally, and most of all, spiritually — because God's Word promises that He will supply all of our needs according to His riches in glory in Christ Jesus.

One can know that selfish prayers for "me, myself and only my interests" are not likely to be heard because we are to seek first God's kingdom.

If we want to receive blessings from God for ourselves, we must forget ourselves and help others find their fulfillment. In the process, God will meet our needs. This does not suggest that we should not give attention to our own needs and to the needs of our loved ones, but rather we are not to seek *only* that which is for our personal best.

No prayer life can be effective without a thorough knowledge and understanding of God's Word, the basis from which we can know the will of God and thus pray with assurance that our prayers will be answered.

Bible Reading: 1 John 3:22-24

ACTION POINT: I will saturate my mind with the Word of God and seek to know and do His will so that when I pray, my prayers will have ready answers.

His Mighty Power Within

"Last of all I want to remind you that your strength must come from the Lord's mighty power within you" (Ephesians 6:10).

W hen my saintly mother became a Christian at 16, she immediately determined to become a woman of God with the help of the Holy Spirit. She devoted her life to my father and to the rearing of seven children.

Through the years, as I have observed her attitudes and actions closely, I have never seen her do anything that reflected negatively on the Lord.

As a result, my life has been greatly affected in a positive way. There is no question in my mind that everything God has done and ever will do in and through me will be, in no small measure, a result of those unique, godly qualities of my mother, and especially of her prayers.

In today's world, there often is considerable criticism of the woman who finds her fulfillment as a wife, mother and homemaker, as though such roles are demeaning to the woman. The popular thought is that there is something better, such as a professional career.

I would not minimize the fact that there are gifted women who should be involved in business and professional life, but in most cases this would be a secondary role compared to the privilege of being a mother, especially a godly Christian mother in whose life the fruit of the Spirit is demonstrated.

What I can say about my mother, I believe my sons can say about theirs, for Vonette has demonstrated those same godly, Christlike qualities toward them as a mother — and, as a wife, toward me.

These two examples underscore a wonderful, basic truth of supernatural living: As we continue to live supernaturally, walking in the power and under the guidance and control of the Holy Spirit, the personality and character of Christ become more and more a part of us.

Bible Reading: Ephesians 6:11-20

ACTION POINT: When I need special strength — whether physical, emotional or spiritual — I will claim by faith the Lord's mighty power within me to meet the need.

Trusting Means Safety

"Fear of man is a dangerous trap, but to trust in God means safety" (Proverbs 29:25).

One of the delegates attending a lay institute for evangelism protested that he was not going to go out into the community to share his faith, something he had never done before. I assured him that he was not required to go; it was simply an optional assignment. But I explained that if he would go along and observe a more mature witnessing Christian, he would learn something and would feel greater freedom in the future to witness on his own. Again he expressed his fear, but he did go, and God marvelously used him and his witnessing partner to introduce two people to Christ. He came home absolutely radiant, joyful, overflowing with thanksgiving and praise to God. He came to me immediately to say, "I am so glad that I went. I would have missed one of the greatest blessings of my life had I not gone. Thank you so much for encouraging me to go."

The number one barrier to witnessing in the Christian life is the fear of man. Think of the contradiction. it never occurs to the average Christian that not to witness is to disobey God, and the consequences can be devastating to his spiritual life. Therefore the average Christian risks offending God for fear of offending man.

It is interesting that there are 365 "fear nots" in the Bible — one for every day in the year. And yet there is one fear in particular that thwarts effective witnessing for Christ more than any other — the fear of man.

It would not be a distorted picture to envision thousands — and even millions — of believers caught in that dangerous trap referred to by the psalmist. And what a deadly snare!

Martin Luther, years ago, found a solution to this deadly enemy:

And though this world, with devils filled,
  Should threaten to undo us,
We will not fear, for God has willed
  His truth to triumph through us.
    The prince of darkness grim —
    We tremble not for him;
    His rage we can endure,
    For lo! his doom is sure,
    One little word shall fell him.

Our trust must be in God whose indwelling Holy Spirit helps us not only to trust Him, but also to share the good news of the gospel with others.

Bible Reading: Proverbs 29:19-24

ACTION POINT: With God's help, I will share His love and forgiveness with others with the confidence that having called me to be His witness, He will enable me and will prepare the hearts of those to whom I go.

PROMISES – DAY 221

True Spiritual Life

"Only the Holy Spirit gives eternal life. Those born only once, with physical birth, will never receive this gift. But now I have told you how to get this true spiritual life" (John 6:63).

A businessman called to ask if he could bring one of his associates to talk to me about receiving Christ. As the three of us talked together, it became apparent that the businessman who had arranged the meeting was not a Christian either. So after his friend had received Christ, I asked him if he believed that Jesus Christ was the Son of God.

"Yes," he said.

"Do you believe that He died for your sins?"

"Of course."

"Have you ever received Him into your life as your Savior and Lord?"

"No," he said, "I haven't."

"Wouldn't you like to do so?"

"Yes," he said, "I would. But I have been waiting for that peculiar time when God would speak to me in a very emotional way."

He explained that this was the way his mother had become a Christian, and he felt that this was the way he should become a Christian, too.

Once again I reviewed very simply the plan of salvation, explaining that only the Holy Spirit gives eternal life and there may or may not be an emotional experience accompanying the moment of salvation. I explained that salvation is a gift of God, which we receive by faith on the basis of His promise.

So together we prayed, and though I had explained that he should not expect any emotional experience, God graciously touched him in a very dramatic way emotionally, contrary to my own experience and that of the majority of people with whom I counsel and pray.

Bible Reading: John 6:60-65

ACTION POINT: Realizing that no one can enter the kingdom of God apart from a spiritual birth, I will today pray for many opportunities to share the good news of God's love and forgiveness in Christ with others.

Perfect Peace

"He will keep in perfect peace all those who trust in Him, whose thoughts turn often to the Lord" (Isaiah 26:3).

John shared how, during the serious illness and death of his beloved Agnes, God had enveloped him with His perfect peace. Tom spoke with moistened eyes, of how God filled his heart with peace when he lost his job of more than 25 years. Roger and Kim shared how they experienced perfect peace in the loss of their darling two-year-old who had just died of leukemia. Peter had just received the solemn word from his doctor that he had no more than six months to live. What joy, soon he would see his Lord and witness perfect peace!

How can these things be?

Because the Prince of Peace dwells within the heart of every believer and He promised, "Peace I leave with you, My peace I give unto you: not as the world giveth, give I unto you. Let not your heart be troubled, neither let it be afraid" (John 14:27, KJV). God is waiting to pour out His supernatural peace upon all who will trust and obey Him.

In my experience with thousands of businessmen, laymen and students, I have discovered an interesting fact. In a time of crisis when one's world is crumbling, wealth, fame, power, position, glory, are not important any more. It is inner peace that every man longs for and for which he would gladly give his fortune. But remember that perfect peace comes only to those who walk in faith and obedience. Such peace is not the experience of those who live self-centered lives, violating the laws of God.

Bible Reading: John 14:27-31.

ACTION POINT: As a candidate for God's perfect peace, I will meditate upon His laws and through the enabling of His Holy Spirit, seek to obey His commands.

He Will Uphold Us

"Fear not, for I am with you. Do not be dismayed. I am your God. I will strengthen you; I will help you; I will uphold you with My victorious right hand" (Isaiah 41:10).

An obsolete Army transport plane was filled with people from various parts of the world. We flew, at the invitation of the president of a third world country, for a dedication ceremony of a historic sight. But it was not until we were crowded into the plane and ready to take off that we observed that there were no seatbelts. In fact there were not even enough seats for all the guests. It was quite an unusual experience at best. Yet, I was able to claim this assuring promise that God gave to Isaiah and gives to all of his children who trust and obey Him.

Many times in my trips to various parts of the world, I have encountered difficulties, opposition, problems and challenges. In such times as these, I have needed and claimed the promises of God.

God's banquet table is full to overflowing. Not only can we be free from fear, but we can also be encouraged knowing that He is our God and thus he will strengthen and help and uphold us with His victorious right hand. If you and I come to such a banquet table as this and come away with only crumbs, we should not blame the one who has prepared the table. He has made all things possible for us and given us all things in Him. Even if your task today is simply to perform routine duties, you may approach them without fear, even of boredom, knowing that God is with you.

Bible Reading: Isaiah 41:1-9

ACTION POINT: Claiming this marvelous promise from God's word, I will not fear, but will claim with joyful confidence His faithful promise to meet my every need, knowing that I am complete in Him who will enable me to live the supernatural life.

A Blameless Watchman

"If you refuse to warn the wicked when I want you to tell them, You are under the penalty of death, therefore repent and save your life — they will die in their sins, but I will punish you. I will demand your blood for theirs. But if you warn them and they keep on sinning, and refuse to repent, they will die in their sins, but you are blameless — you have done all you could" (Ezekiel 3:18,19).

One of the most sobering messages I find in all the words of God is this terrible warning found in the book of Ezekiel. God commanded Ezekiel to warn the people of Israel to turn from their sins. Some would argue that this has no application for the Christian. I would disagree. In principle this is exactly what our Lord commands us to do — to go and make disciples of all nations, to preach the gospel to all men, to follow Jesus and He will make us to become fishers of men.

It is a sobering thing to realize that all around us there are multitudes of men and women, even loved ones, who do not know the Savior. Many of them have never received an intelligent, Spirit-filled, loving witness concerning our Savior. Who will tell them? There are some people whom you and I can reach whom nobody else can influence.

I am writing this day's devotion while in Amsterdam where I am speaking at an international gathering of Christian evangelists. During the course of my days here I have talked with many taxi drivers, maids, waiters and other employees of the hotel. Only one professed to be a believer and we had good fellowship together. Some were openly defiant, even angry at the name of Jesus. But in each case I have shared the gospel, constrained by the love of Christ out of a deep sense of gratitude for all that He has done for me, and as an act of obedience to His command to be His witness.

I pray that God will give me a greater sense of urgency to warn men that unless they turn to Christ they will die in their sins. I do not want to be responsible because I failed to warn them. They must know that there is a heaven and a hell and that there is no other name under heaven given among men whereby we must be saved but the name of our Lord Jesus Christ.

Bible Reading: Ezekiel 3:15-21

ACTION POINT: I will ask the Holy Spirit to quicken within my heart, out of a deep sense of gratitude for all He has done for me and from a desire to obey our Lord's commands, a greater sense of urgency to be His witness and to warn men to turn from their wicked ways and receive Christ, the gift of God's love.

A Matter of the Will

"If any man will do His will, he shall know of the doctrine, whether it be of God, or whether I speak of Myself" (John 7:17, KJV).

At the conclusion of an address I gave at M.I.T., a skeptical young man approached me. He said, "I am a scientist, I can't believe anything that I can't see. I must be able to go into the laboratory and test a proposition or a theory. I must prove its authenticity before I will believe and accept.

"Religion," he said, "is a matter of faith. It has no substance, and as far as I'm concerned no validity."

I turned to the seventh chapter of John, verse 17 — our Scripture portion for today — and asked him to read it aloud.

"Do you understand what Jesus is saying here?" I asked.

"Well, I'm not sure," he replied. "What is your point?"

"Your problem is not your intellect, but your will. Are you willing to do what God wants you to do? Are there relationships in your life that you're not willing to surrender in order to do the will of God? Are there moral problems, problems of integrity that you are not willing to relinquish?"

An odd expression came over his countenance.

"How did you know?" Then he said, "I'd like to talk to you privately." Later, as we sat together alone, he poured out his heart to me. He said, "I know that what you're saying is true. I know that there's a God in heaven, and I know that Jesus Christ is His Son and that He died on the cross for me.

"But," he said, "there is sin in my life. I have been living with a young woman without the benefit of marriage for the last couple of years. Today you have exposed me for what I really am — a fraud, a sham, a hypocrite, and I want with God's help to terminate my present relationship with this young woman and receive Christ into my life."

I am happy to report that, soon after, he and the young woman both surrendered their lives to Christ and were married. Together they are making their lives count for the glory of God.

Bible Reading: John 7:14-18

ACTION POINT: Today I will confess — and turn from — all known sin that keeps me from knowing and doing the will of God. I will also share this message with others.

Whatsoever You Desire

"For verily I say unto you, That whosoever shall say unto this mountain, Be thou removed, and be thou cast into the sea; and shall not doubt in his heart, but shall believe that those things which he saith shall come to pass; he shall have whatsoever he saith. Therefore I say unto you, What things soever ye desire, when ye pray, believe that ye receive them, and ye shall have them" (Mark 11:23,24, KJV).

How big is your God? If the Holy Spirit were to withdraw from your life and from the fellowship of your local church, would He be missed? In other words, is there anything supernatural about your life or the local church where you have fellowship with other believers?

A skeptic, contrasting the actor and Christian worker, gave this evaluation: The actor presents fiction as though it were true. The Christian worker all too often presents truth as though it were fiction.

A militant atheist attacked Christians with this accusation: "You say that your God is omnipotent, that He created the heavens and the earth. You say that He is a loving God who sent His only Son to die on the cross for the sins of man and on the third day was raised from the dead. You say that through faith in Him one could have a whole new quality of life, of peace, love and joy; a purpose and meaning plus the assurance of eternal life. I say to you that is a lie and you know it, because if you really believe what you say you believe, you would pay whatever price it took to tell everyone who would listen. What you claim is without question the greatest news the world has ever heard, but it couldn't be true or you would be more enthusiastic about it. If I believed what you believe, I would sell everything I have and use every resource at my command to reach the largest possible number of people with this good news."

Unfortunately, the critics and the skeptics have good reason to find fault with us. It is true that, if we really believed what we say we believe, we would be constrained, as was the apostle Paul, to tell everyone who would listen about Christ, mindful that there is nothing more important in all the world that we could do. At the same time we would claim our rights as children of God, drawing upon the supernatural resources of God.

Bible Reading: Mark 11:20-26

ACTION POINT: I will seek to know God better by studying His Word and meditating upon His attributes so that His supernatural qualities will become more and more a part of my life for the glory and praise of His name.

Shine Like the Sun

"And those who are wise – the people of God – shall shine as brightly as the sun's brilliance, and those who turn many to righteousness will glitter like stars forever" (Daniel 12:3).

Did it ever occur to you that as a child of God you are to radiate in your countenance the beauty and glory of God? Have you ever considered the inconsistency of having a glum expression while professing that the Son of God, the light of the world, dwells within you?

Proverbs 15:13 reminds us that a happy face means a glad heart; a sad face means a breaking heart.

When missionary Adoniram Judson was home on furlough many years ago, he passed through the city of Stonington, Connecticut. A young boy, playing about the wharves at the time of Judson's arrival, was struck by the missionary's appearance. He had never before seen such a light on a man's face.

Curious, he ran up the street to a minister's home to ask if he knew who the stranger was. Following the boy back, the minister became so engaged in conversation with Judson that he forgot all about the lad standing nearby.

Many years later that boy – unable to get away from the influence of what he had seen on a man's face – became the famous preacher, Henry Clay Trumbull. One chapter in his book of memoirs is entitled, "What a Boy Saw in the Face of Adoniram Judson."

A shining face – radiant with the love and joy of Jesus Christ – had changed a life. Just as flowers thrive when they bend toward the light of the sun, so shining, radiant faces are the result of those who concentrate their gaze upon the Lord Jesus Christ.

May we never underestimate the power of a glowing face that stems from time spent with God. Even as Moses' countenance shone, may your face and mine reveal time spent alone with God and in His Word.

Bible Reading: Matthew 5:13-16

ACTION POINT: I will spend sufficient time with the Lord each day to insure a radiant countenance for the glory of God and as a witness to those with whom I have contact each day.

Perfect Healing

"Jesus' name has healed this man — and you know how lame he was before. Faith in Jesus' name — faith given us from God — has caused this perfect healing" (Acts 3:16).

This is another of the great "3:16" verses of the Bible — with a truth and a promise that you and I need probably every day of our lives. Jesus claimed "all authority in heaven and earth" (Matthew 28:18). "In Him dwelleth all the fullness of the Godhead bodily" (Colossians 2:9, KJV; see also 1:15-19).

There is great power in the name of Jesus. Throughout Scripture that fact is emphasized. And I have seen it illustrated in miraculous ways through the film *Jesus,* which has been used of God to introduce tens of millions of men, women, young people and children to Christ in most countries of the world.

The promise, equally clear, is that if we exercise faith in that wonderful name of Jesus — faith that is a gift from God — we can see healing, both physical and spiritual.

I sit in astonishment often as I try to comprehend such great love that would give us the very gifts He requires of us — faith, in this instance. We need not conjure up such faith; it is made available on simple terms: "Faith comes by hearing, and hearing by the Word of God."

And we may appropriate this truth and this promise today.

Bible Reading: Acts 3:12-18

ACTION POINT: "Dear Lord, I dare to believe that You are still the same yesterday, today and forever, so I can trust you to heal, and to enable me to live a supernatural life.

Joy and Gladness

*"And the Lord will bless Israel again, and make her deserts blossom;
her barren wilderness will become as beautiful as the Garden of Eden.
Joy and gladness will be found there, thanksgiving and lovely songs"*
(Isaiah 51:3).

When the editors of a Christian publication came to Arrowhead Springs sometime ago to interview me, the discussion turned to the subject of problems in the Christian life. They were skeptical when I explained my way of handling difficult circumstances, potential sources of anxiety and frustration.

As you will note from this verse in Isaiah, thanksgiving is a spiritual way of singing to the Lord. As we sing with a thankful heart, we receive the joy of the Lord in return.

So it was that I explained to the editors: "Many years ago I learned to obey God's command to be thankful in all things as an act of faith. And since I am assured from God's Word that He rules in the affairs of men and nations, that He is all-wise, all-powerful and compassionate and that He loves me dearly, I would be very foolish indeed to worry about my problems, cares and tribulations even for a few moments. I cast them upon the Lord as soon as they are brought to my attention.

"For example, I can list at least 25 major problems that I have given to the Lord today — some of which would crush me and destroy my effectiveness if I tried to carry them myself."

Then I recalled an earlier week beset with illness, surgery and bereavement for loved ones and friends. "But," I told them, "I chose to obey the Lord's command to give them all to Him, and to retain a thankful spirit."

Bible Reading: Ephesians 5:18-21

ACTION POINT: I will trust God's Holy Spirit to establish a thankful spirit in my heart and life today and every day as a way of life.

Subduing the Enemy

"At that time Samuel said to [the Israelites], 'If you are really serious about wanting to return to the Lord, get rid of your foreign gods and your Ashtaroth idols. Determine to obey only the Lord; then He will rescue you from the Philistines' " (1 Samuel 7:3).

As I was reading and meditating upon the Word of God this morning, the thought struck me forcefully that this passage relates to multitudes of defeated, frustrated Christians today who feel that they have lost contact with God. They are puzzled as to why He has withdrawn His blessing from them, but the reason, in most cases, is very simple.

Throughout the history of Israel, the people alternately obeyed God and disobeyed Him. When they obeyed, He blessed, and when they disobeyed, He disciplined. At this particular time the Lord seemingly had abandoned them. It was because, as Samuel explained, they were worshiping foreign gods and idols. "If you will only obey God," he counseled, "He will rescue you from the Philistines."

So they destroyed their idols and worshiped the Lord, and then a miracle happened. Samuel invited all of Israel to come to Mispah and said, "I will pray to the Lord for you." As they gathered there, the Philistine leaders heard about it and mobilized their army to attack. Of course, the Israelites were terribly frightened, but God spoke with a mighty thunder from heaven, and the Philistines were thrown into terrible confusion. Israel surrounded them, and subdued them, and the Philistines did not invade Israel again for the remainder of Samuel's life.

Enemies can take many forms, but their intent is always to destroy. What are the Philistines in your life? Lust, pride, jealousy, materialism, financial indebtedness, physical illness, resentments, antagonism, criticism, discrimination? Do you feel that God has forsaken you?

Why not look into the mirror of God's Word? Ask the Lord to reveal the idols of your life, then turn away from then. Confess your sins and claim God's victory over those areas of life that are destroying you.

Bible Reading: 1 Samuel 7:1-12

ACTION POINT: I will carefully examine my life to see if I am harboring any idols that would cause the Spirit of God to be grieved and quenched. I will destroy any that I find, and will confess my sins and appropriate God's fullness to live a supernatural life for His glory.

Guardian Angels

"For the angel of the Lord guards and rescues all who reverence Him"
(Psalm 34:7).

For many years my travels have taken me from continent to continent, to scores of countries each year. I have traveled under all kinds of circumstances, not a few times faced with danger. But always there was peace in my heart that the Lord was with me and I was surrounded by His guardian angels to protect me.

In Pakistan, during a time of great political upheaval, I had finished a series of meetings in Lahore and was taken to the train station. Though I was unaware of what was happening, an angry crowd of thousands was marching on the station to destroy it with cocktail bombs.

The director of the railway line rushed us onto the train, put us in our compartments and told us not to open our doors under any circumstances — unless we knew that the one knocking was a friend. The train ride to Karachi would require more than 24 hours, which was just the time I needed to finish rewriting my book *Come Help Change the World.*

So I put on my pajamas, got in my berth and began to read and write. It was not until we arrived in Karachi some 28 hours later that I discovered how guardian angels had watched over us and protected us. The train in front of us had been burned when rioting students had lain on the track and refused to move. So the train ran over them and killed them. In retaliation, the mob burned the train and killed the officials.

Now we were the next train and they were prepared to do the same for us. But God miraculously went before us and there were no mishaps. We arrived safely in Karachi to discover that martial law had been declared and all was peaceful. A Red Cross van took us to the hotel and there God continued to protect us. When the violence subsided we were able to catch a plane out of Karachi for Europe.

Bible Reading: Isaiah 63:7-9

ACTION POINT: Today I will make a special point of expressing my gratitude to God for assigning guardian angels to watch over me, protect and help me in my time of trouble. I will not take for granted the protection that many times in the past I have overlooked, not recognizing God's miraculous, divine intervention, enabling me to live a supernatural life.

A New Creature

"As it is written, There is none righteous, no, not one: There is none that understandeth, there is none that seeketh after God. They are all gone out of the way, they are together become unprofitable; there is none that doeth good, no, not one" (Romans 3:10-12, KJV).

At the conclusion of one of my messages at a pastor's conference, a pastor stood to take issue with me concerning a statement that I had made. I had said that there is a great hunger for God throughout the world, and that more people are now hearing the gospel and receiving Christ than at any time since the Great Commission was given almost 2,000 years ago.

"How can you say that," he objected, "when the Scripture clearly teaches that no man seeketh after God?"

"That is exactly what the Bible teaches," I responded, "and I agree with the Word of God 100 percent, but do not forget that — though in his natural inclination man does not have a hunger for God — the Holy Spirit sends conviction and creates within the human heart a desire for the Savior."

As Jesus put it, "No one can come to Me unless the Father who sent Me, draws him" (John 6:44, NAS). There are three things that we can learn about the human race from this passage. First, no one is righteous. Second, no one understands the things of God; and third, no one seeks God. What a contrast between what man is like in his natural state and what man becomes at spiritual birth when he is liberated from the darkness and gloom of Satan's kingdom and ushered into the light of God's glorious kingdom through Jesus Christ. That man becomes a new creature. Old things are passed away and behold all things become new.

What a contrast between the natural and the supernatural. The natural man must depend upon his own resources, his own wisdom, to find meaning and purpose in life, inevitably resulting in a life of conflict, discord and frustration. But the one who trusts in God has the privilege of drawing upon the supernatural resources of God daily; resources of joy, peace, love; resources that provide meaning and purpose, assurance of eternal life.

Most people live lives of quiet desperation in self-imposed poverty because those of us who know the truth of the supernatural are strangely silent. God forgive us.

Bible Reading: Romans 3:13-20

ACTION POINT: With God's help I refuse to remain silent any longer, but will seek to proclaim "the most joyful news ever announced" (Luke 2:10,11), to all who will listen in order that others may join me in living the supernatural life.

His Ways Will Satisfy

"Don't copy the behavior and customs of this world, but be a new and different person with a fresh newness in all you do and think. Then you will learn from your own experience how His ways will really satisfy you" (Romans 12:2).

"The trouble with living sacrifices," someone has well said, "is that they keep crawling off the altar."

That may be true. We "crawl off the altar" when we sin, and the only way to put ourselves back on the altar is to breathe spiritually – confess our known sins in accordance with the promise of 1 John 1:9 and appropriate the fullness of the Holy Spirit as we are commanded to do by faith (Ephesians 5:18).

When we do this, we will be living supernaturally and our lives will produce the fruit of the Spirit in great abundance.

Only by being filled with the Spirit, and thus realizing the fruit of the Spirit, can spiritual gifts be effectively utilized in witnessing and building up the Body of Christ.

We begin by totally yielding ourselves by faith to Christ in a full, irrevocable surrender to His lordship.

"He died once for all to end sin's power, but now He lives forever in unbroken fellowship with God. So look upon your old sin-nature as dead and unresponsive to sin, and instead be alive to God, alert to Him, through Jesus Christ our Lord.

"Do not let sin control your puny body any longer; do not give in to its sinful desires. Do not let any part of your bodies become tools of wickedness, to be used for sinning; but give yourselves completely to God – every part of you – for you are back from death and you want to be tools in the hands of God, to be used for His good purposes" (Romans 6:10-13).

Bible Reading: Romans 12:3-8

ACTION POINT: Knowing that God's ways will really satisfy me, I will seek first His kingdom, resist the devil at his every appearance and watch with joy as he flees.

Put God to the Test

"Oh, put God to the test and see how kind He is! See for yourself the way His mercies shower down on all who trust in Him" (Psalm 34:8).

S am wanted to receive Christ, but he was reluctant. Somehow, he just could not bring himself to make that necessary commitment of the will to exercise his faith and receive Christ. Because of unfortunate experiences in his youth, he had a distorted view of the goodness of God.

I encouraged him to make his commitment, but he still hesitated. Finally, I turned to that wonderful promise of our Scripture for today and asked him to read it. As he read, the Holy Spirit gave him the faith to believe that he could trust God.

Put God to the test. Taste and see how good and kind He is. Sam discovered that day, and for the rest of his life, the faithfulness and the goodness and the kindness of God.

Do you have reservations, uncertainties, fears about the trustworthiness of God? If so, I encourage you to place your trust in Him, and you will find, as millions have found, and as I have found, that God is good, faithful and true.

Similarly, you and I can put God to the test and find a friendly haven in the midst of enemy territory. More important, perhaps, is the certainty we can have that God does hear and answer our prayers — in situations where He and He alone knows the end from the beginning and can provide deliverance.

How vital to the supernatural life to know that we have immediate access to the God of the universe, the very one who alone can guarantee victory and deliverance.

Bible Reading: 1 Peter 2:1-5

ACTION POINT: Realizing that, as a believer, I am constantly in "enemy territory," I will trust God and encourage others to trust Him moment by moment for deliverance, for I know that He is just and kind and good. He is a loving, heavenly Father whom I can trust. I will encourage others to put God to the test and see how kind He is, to discover for themselves His mercies that He showers on all who place their trust in Him.

He Does Glorious Things

"Thank the Lord for all the glorious things He does; proclaim them to the nations. Sing His praises and tell everyone about His miracles" (Psalm 105:1,2).

How long has it been since you have taken time to meditate upon and list all the glorious things the Lord has done for you and how long has it been since you have shared them with your family, your neighbors or even strangers? Of course, your list may differ from that of your neighbors or of fellow believers in your local church or from mine. But among those glorious things that He has done are: He has, by His Holy Spirit, drawn us all to Himself; He has created within our hearts a hunger for His love; and through faith in Christ we have become His children; our sins have been forgiven and we now have the joy of living every moment of every day in vital union and fellowship with Him — all this with the certainty that we shall spend eternity with Him. Mere human words could never express the gratitude that wells up within one's heart at the thought of God's great gifts. The word "alleluia" is universal and is spoken in all languages as an expression of praise to God and no word is more appropriate.

My personal list of blessings also includes a godly, praying mother who lived her Christianity and dedicated me to Christ before I was born, and followed me — as she did all her other children — with her daily prayers; a wonderful father whom I had the privilege of introducing to Christ after I became a Christian and seeing him begin to experience that peace which comes from knowing Christ; a godly wife who loves the Lord Jesus Christ and shares my commitment to serve Him as our Lord and Master whatever the cost, wherever He leads us.

I thank Him for sons who love Him, and who have committed their lives to serving Him wherever He leads; a daughter-in-law who shares the love and conviction of her husband; a marvelous staff of thousands of godly men and women who seek first the kingdom of God and his righteousness; and hundreds of thousands of co-laborers who undergird me and this ministry.

The glorious things that He has done are without number. Yes, we must sing His praises and tell everyone about His miracles. We must proclaim the glorious things He has done to all the nations!

Bible Reading: Psalm 113

ACTION POINT: Today I will meditate upon the glorious things God has done for me and I will sing His praises and tell everyone about His miracles. I will give my prayer and financial support to helping proclaim His greatness to all the nations of earth.

Reverence Brings Reward

"If you belong to the Lord, reverence Him; for everyone who does this has everything he needs" (Psalm 34:9).

Roger had a heart for God. He wanted to be everything the Lord wanted him to be. But he was troubled over how to achieve the balance between being what God wanted him to be and doing what God wanted him to do.

As we talked together I reminded Roger that everything flows from our relationship with the Lord — that He has to be primary. In Matthew 4:19, Jesus says, "Follow me, and I will make you fishers of men." As we follow Him, He enables us to become fishers of men.

"If ye abide in Me, and My words abide in you, ye shall ask what ye will, and it shall be done unto you" (John 15:7, KJV). "Out of the heart are the issues of life" (Proverbs 4:23, KJV). That which is most on our hearts will be most on our lips. If we love the Lord Jesus with all our heart, soul, mind and strength, it will be impossible for us to remain silent.

At the same time, obedience is a confirmation of our walk with the Lord. Jesus said, "He that hath My commandments, and keepeth them, he it is that loveth Me: and he that loveth Me shall be loved of My Father, and I will love him, and will manifest Myself to him" (John 14:21, KJV).

One of the most important commandments of our Lord is that we lead holy lives. Another is that we be fruitful in our witnessing for Christ. There is no substitute for reverence, worship, praise, adoration.

As we remember to reverence God by enlisting His guiding hand *before* we get into a predicament, He reaches out in love and extends a protecting hand in the midst of the trouble as we again invoke His divine care. If I am to live the supernatural life today, it will require divine enabling, and I must remain yielded to God's indwelling Holy Spirit.

Bible Reading: Psalm 34:10-15

ACTION POINT: I will worship God today as a demonstration of my love and trust for Him by spending quality time with Him in His Word and in prayer, and helping others to understand the importance of reverence for and worship of God.

Free Gift

"For the wages of sin is death, but the free gift of God is eternal life through Jesus Christ our Lord" (Romans 6:23).

One night I was speaking to several hundred men gathered in a skid row mission for an evangelistic meeting. I had been invited to bring the address and as always my heart was deeply stirred when I realized that these men needed the Lord so very much. In the spiritual sense, though, their lot was no worse than the leaders of the city, for all have sinned and come short of the glory of God, and the wages of sin is death whether one is rich or poor, old or young, sick or well. It makes no difference. The wages of sin is death.

In an effort to communicate to these men the love of God and His free gift of eternal life through faith in Jesus Christ our Lord, I pulled a ten-dollar bill from my pocket and said, "The first person who comes to take this from my hand, can hve it as a free gift." This was my way of illustrating God's gift of grace. Out of the hundreds of people seated before me, not a single person moved as I extended the bill, repeating several times, "The first one who will come and take this bill from my hand can have it."

Finally, a middle-aged man, shabbily dressed like the rest, stood timidly to his feet and with an inquiring expression said, "Do you really mean it?" I said, "Sure, come and get it; it is yours."

He almost ran to grasp it and he thanked me. The rest of the crowd began mumbling, as if to say, "Why didn't I have the faith to go and accept the gift?"

This gave me a marvelous opportunity to emphasize that we do not earn God's love. He loves us unconditionally — not because of who we are, but because of who He is. God proved His love for us in that while we were all wretched sinners, He sent His only begotten Son to die on the cross for us and to give to all men who will receive Him the gift of eternal life. Oh, what an attractive gift. Who could refuse to accept such a wonderful gift?

Bible Reading: Romans 6:17-22

ACTION POINT: I will trust the Lord to help me make His offer of this marvelous free gift, the gift of His only begotten Son who is eternal life, so attractive that no one can refuse to accept it.

Anyone Who Calls

"Anyone who calls upon the name of the Lord will be saved" (Romans 10:13).

I have been privileged to counsel personally thousands of people — men, women, young people, children — about their spiritual needs. The experiences that remain uppermost in my heart and mind have a direct bearing on this verse.

Helping people to see their truly desperate plight outside of saving faith in Jesus Christ is sometimes difficult, but what a reward awaits those who become aware of their condition. No matter what their background — criminal, alcoholic, self-righteous or whatever — uninformed people need to recognize the fact that they are lost without Christ.

Accomplishing that purpose is a long step toward their genuine conversion, for I have heard many thousands come to the place where they do indeed "call upon the name of the Lord" and they are saved.

If you can help your loved one, neighbor or friend — or even a total stranger — to become sufficiently alarmed about their eternal welfare that they call on the name of the Lord, you have come a long way toward bringing that person to Christ in a saving relationship.

Some people are bothered by the simplicity of the gospel. I am grateful that it is so simple that anyone can understand, believe, and receive. The promise of this verse is emphatic: "Anyone who calls upon the name of the Lord *will be saved.*" Let's believe it and share it.

Bible Reading: Romans 10:14-17

ACTION POINT: I will not let the utter simplicity of the gospel keep me from sharing the Good News that we need only call upon the name of the Lord to be saved.

He Fulfills God's Promises

"Jesus Christ, the Son of God––– isn't one to say 'yes' when he means 'no.' He always does exactly what He says. He carries out and fulfills all of God's promises, no matter how many of them there are and we have told everyone how faithful He is giving glory to His name" (2 Corinthians 1:19,20).

From Genesis to Revelation the Word of God contains thousands of promises which we as believers in Christ can claim. We are reminded in Matthew 28:18 that all authority in heaven and earth has been given to Him, and in Colossians 2:2,3 that God's great secret plan now at last made known is Christ Himself; that in Him lie hidden all the mighty untapped treasures of wisdom and knowledge, "For in Christ there is all of God in a human body; so you have everything when you have Christ, and you are filled with God through your union with Christ" (Colossians 2:9,10).

So make a list of all the promises of God that apply to you, and claim those promises in the name of the Lord Jesus Christ. For "He always does exactly what He says. He carries out and fulfills all of God's promises." Begin to live supernaturally by drawing upon the supernatural resources of God, claiming His promises by faith.

Bible Reading: 2 Corinthians 1:15-19

ACTION POINT: I refuse to live the typical Christian existence. I want my life to be characterized by the supernatural, so by faith in the name of the Lord Jesus Christ, I will claim those promises which will enable me to live supernaturally as a testimony that I serve the Lord Jesus Christ.

To Be Approved

"Study to show thyself approved unto God, a workman that needeth not to be ashamed, rightly dividing the word of truth" (2 Timothy 2:15, KJV).

M ost all of my adult life has been centered around the university world — as a student, a teacher, and one who works with students, professors and administrators in the intellectual realm. I count many of the leading scholars of our time as beloved friends, yet if I had to choose between a Ph.D. from the most prestigious university in the world and a thorough knowledge of and comprehension of the Word of God, I would gladly choose the latter. Fortunately, it is not necessary to choose because one can have both academic training and a knowledge of God's Word.

A recommendation which I have made to our two sons and to thousands of our staff and students with whom we work is that degrees are very important in today's world, but they will not only be meaningless and worthless in terms of eternity, but can contribute to one's moral and spiritual disintegration unless at the same time one is studying to show himself approved unto God. In all of our academic pursuits and in our commitment to excellence in the business and professional realms, we must be careful to give God and His Holy inspired Word their rightful place in our daily schedule. Ultimately, it is our knowledge of God learned through the study of Scripture and our response to Him that makes all the difference in our life-style. It makes the difference in the choosing of our mate, in the rearing of our children, in the choosing of our friends, our business or professional career, in all of our attitudes and actions and in the contribution which we make to society. Let us give priority to priorities, the highest of which is to seek after God through the diligent study of His holy revelation to man and to encourage others to join with us in rightly dividing the word of truth.

Bible Reading: 2 Timothy 2:19-25

ACTION POINT: With God's help I will seek not only to be a student of God's Word but also to acquire the ability to teach His Word to others.

No Abuse Tolerated

"So shall they fear the name of the Lord from the west, and His glory from the rising of the sun. When the enemy shall come in like a flood, the Spirit of the Lord shall lift up a standard against him" (Isaiah 59:19, KJV).

A prominent secular columnist and a businessman were united in their efforts to destroy a well-known godly Christian leader. It seemed that they would stoop to whatever mischief was necessary to accomplish their goal: Discredit this man of God.

One day they were warned of the danger of attacking God's anointed. They were shown that they were not simply attacking an individual, but they were actually tempting God, because this man was His servant and it was God's responsibility to take care of him. The warning was given in these words, "If I were you, I'd be petrified with fear because you are not attacking a man, but a servant of God. I'd be afraid of what God would do to me to punish me if I were guilty of doing what you are doing."

They laughed at such a warning, but only a few hours later one of them was killed in a tragic accident. The other was very sobered by this dramatic demonstration of how God protects His own.

I agree with the man who gave the warning. In fact, I would hate to be a critic or an enemy, not just of a godly Christian leader, but of any child of God who seeks to live a holy life because that individual can be assured that God will fight for him. Whenever a person who desires to please the Lord with all of his attitudes and actions and desires and motives is attacked, the Spirit of the Lord will raise up a standard against the adversary.

If you are a man or woman of God, I would be scared to death to criticize you, or to find fault with you, or to attack you in any way. All who belong to the Lord Jesus Christ have been purchased with His own precious blood, and He will not tolerate the abuse of His blood-purchased followers.

Bible Reading: Isaiah 59:16-21

ACTION POINT: With God's help, I will guard my tongue, my attitudes and actions concerning other believers, following the admonition, "Judge not, that you be not judged" (Matthew 7:1). I will seek to love all men as an expression of the supernatural life-style.

Protection From Accidents

"The good man does not escape all troubles — he has them too. But the Lord helps him in each and every one. God even protects him from accidents" (Psalm 34:19,20).

Jerry was a new Christian and for the first time was hearing about the importance of the Spirit-filled life. His was a logical question, put to me following one of my lectures on a large university campus.

"Does the Spirit-filled Christian have problems, testings, temptations like the nonbeliever and the disobedient Christian?" he asked.

"No," I replied, "the Spirit-filled Christian does not have the same kind of problems that the nonbeliever and the carnal Christian have, because most of the problems we experience in life are self-imposed. The Spirit-filled person is one who seeks to do the will of God and lives by faith, drawing upon the supernatural resources of God the Holy Spirit for every attitude, motive and desire of his life."

There may be problems, such as loss of loved ones, financial reverses, illness and disappointments. The Spirit-filled Christian does not escape all troubles. But the Lord is always there with him, undergirding, helping, inspiring, motivating, encouraging, imparting to him wisdom — physical, mental and spiritual resources. Even when tragedy, heartache, sorrow and disappointment come, the Spirit-filled person knows that God is still in control.

Therefore, by faith and obedience to the command of 1 Thessalonians 5:18, he can say, "In all things I give thanks."

We can know that God helps us in each and every trouble and that He even protects us from accidents.

Bible Reading: Psalm 35:1-9

ACTION POINT: Today I will look for opportunities to remind myself and my friends that our loving God and Father is working in and through every problem we face each day, so that we might mature and become more like our Lord Jesus Christ.

Power Over Nations

"To everyone who overcomes — who to the very end keeps on doing things that please Me — I will give power over the nations. You will rule them with a rod of iron just as My Father gave Me the authority to rule them; they will be shattered like a pot of clay that is broken into tiny pieces. And I will give you the Morning Star!" (Revelation 2:26-28).

I marvel at the numerous promises made to the overcomer, the one "who to the very end keeps on doing things that please Me." Now we are even promised power over the nations, as we rule and reign with our heavenly Father in that coming day.

As I ponder this verse, I see in a very few words the key to the entire Christian life — the one thing alone that will keep us victorious today, tomorrow and throughout our lives. Again, it is that significant clause: "who to the very end keeps on doing things that please Me."

Lest you think that is an over-simplification of the victorious Christian life, can you think of anything else God requires of us? And He even provides His Holy Spirit as an indwelling reminder of the daily victory He makes possible. This is the supernatural life.

Earlier, we are told of a conquering Christ who will rule the nations of the earth with a rod of iron. This promise tells us that Christ will turn this power over to the conqueror — the overcomer — and his victorious companions in death.

Bible Reading: Psalm 2:1-12

ACTION POINT: I will trust the Lord to make being an overcomer a reality for me as a way of life — by the power of His indwelling Holy Spirit.

He Gives Us a New Song to Sing

"He has given me a new song to sing, of praises to our God. Now many will hear of the glorious things He did for me, and stand in awe before the Lord, and put their trust in Him" (Psalm 40:3).

Jim was big man on campus, president of his fraternity and an atheist. He ridiculed all those who professed faith in God, especially the Christians in his fraternity house.

I was invited, over his objections, to speak at one of their weekly meetings. A number of the fraternity brothers were active in Campus Crusade and insisted that I come even though Jim resented the idea. Yet, upon completion of my message, he was one of the very first to respond and, after further counsel, received Christ. He became one of the most joyful, radiant, contagious, fruitful witnesses for Christ on the entire campus.

He had a new song to sing, a song of praise to God who had liberated him from a life of decadence and deceit. Now his heart fairly burst with joy as he developed a strategy to help reach every key student for Christ on a great university campus.

There is no greater joy in life than that of sharing Christ with others, and there is no greater joy that comes to another than that which comes with the assurance of salvation when one receives Christ into his life.

Would you like to be an instrument of God to cause others to sing praises to Him? Then tell them the glorious things He has done for you and for them, and encourage them to place their trust in Christ.

Bible Reading: Psalm 40:4-8

ACTION POINT: Today I will seek every opportunity to encourage others to receive Christ so that they can join with me in singing a new song of praise to our God, and together we will share the glorious things He does for us when we place our trust in Him.

None of These Diseases

"And said, If thou wilt diligently hearken to the voice of the Lord thy God, and wilt do that which is right in His sight, and wilt give ear to His commandments, and keep all His statutes, I will put none of these diseases upon thee, which I have brought upon the Egyptians: for I am the Lord that healeth thee" (Exodus 15:26, KJV).

Prior to a recent minor operation the surgeon came to my hospital room for prayer and to explain the nature of the hernia correction. He explained, "It is God alone who heals. It is my responsibility, along with my staff, to treat and care for you."

In his excellent book, *None of These Diseases,* Dr. S. I. McMillen abundantly amplifies and proves the point of this promise: that if we always do that which is right in God's sight, at the very least our health will be greatly improved.

This highly qualified physician contends that most of our physical problems are caused by stress, but the person who is doing that which is right in God's sight is not likely to be continually under stress — at least not the kind of stress that impairs one physically.

"I am the Lord that healeth thee." And He is the same yesterday, today and forever. That would indicate that His healing is available for all today — which of course brings up the sticky question of method and means.

Whatever our persuasion about this, the fact remains that if we really do believe that it is God who heals, then it should follow that He would be our first resource in time of physical need. And it may well be that His direction would take us to the physician. But He alone would be the healer.

Bible Reading: Exodus 15:22-26

ACTION POINT: As I approach each task today, I will make a conscious effort to be concerned about doing that which is right in God's sight.

Not by the Law

"Now do you see it? No one can ever be made right in God's sight by doing what the law commands. For the more we know of God's laws, the clearer it becomes that we aren't obeying them: His laws serve only to make us see that we are sinners. But now God has shown us a different way to heaven — not by 'being good enough' and trying to keep His laws, but by a new way (though not new, really, for the Scriptures told about it long ago). Now God says He will accept and acquit us — declare us 'not guilty' — if we trust Jesus Christ to take away our sins. And we all can be saved in this same way, by coming to Christ, no matter who we are or what we have been like. Yes, all have sinned; all fall short of God's glorious ideal; yet now God declares us 'not guilty' of offending Him if we trust in Jesus Christ, who in His kindness freely takes away our sins" (Romans 3:20-24).

One of my greatest concerns through the years, especially for those who are involved in Christian ministry around the world, has been the problem of legalism. In my opinion, legalism is the greatest heresy of Christianity. The reason legalism is so dangerous is that it is extremely subtle in its appeal. It is attractive even to the most sincere Christians, who are genuinely seeking to please God by determining to be "good enough" and to "earn God's favor" through the good works of their self-effort.

How often there has been a tendency to forget "the just shall live by faith," and "without faith it is impossible to please God." There is a strong tendency to work hard in the flesh in order to please God. But if we trust Jesus Christ to take away such sins in our lives, He is faithful to do so, as He promised.

Bible Reading: Romans 3:25-31

ACTION POINT: Today I will remind myself often that the law is merely a way to show me that I am a sinner. By faith, I will trust Christ and accept His grace and forgiveness. By faith, I will draw upon the mighty resources of God to live the supernatural life, which is my heritage in Christ.

Blessed Are the Humble

"Blessed are the poor in spirit for theirs is the kingdom of heaven" (Matthew 5:3).

A young Christian leader, who was probably more impressed with himself than he should have been, shared with me one day how he had difficulty in being humble about all of his talent. He was a better than average speaker and a reasonably gifted singer, he had a good mind and personality, and in his heart of hearts he knew that as a Christian he should be humble.

He said, "I spend many hours on my knees asking God to make me humble." I responded, "I can save you a lot of prayer time in that regard if you are interested." He assured me that he was. Whereupon I explained to him that every gift he possessed — personality, good mind, his ability to sing, speak, and other qualities — were all gifts of God and could be taken from him at any moment by a brain tumor or car accident or plane crash or any of a thousand different things. Furthermore I reminded him that Scripture admonishes us to humble ourselves.

"Humility is perfect quietness of heart," Andrew Murray said. "It is to have no trouble. It is never to be fretted or irritated or sore or disappointed. It is to expect nothing, to wonder at nothing that is done to me. It is to be at rest when nobody praises me and when I am blamed or despised. It is to have a blessed home in the Lord, where I can go in and shut the door and kneel to my Father in secret, and am at peace as in a deep sea of calmness when all around and above is trouble."

Few Christians achieve such high standards, nevertheless it is an objective toward which we all should strive as long as we live, following the example of our Lord recorded in Philippians, chapter 2.

To be poor in spirit implies not only that we have a humble opinion of ourselves, but also that we recognize that we are sinners and have no righteousness of our own; that we are willing to be saved only by the grace and mercy of God; that we are willing to serve where God places us, to bear the burdens He allows and to stay in His hands and admit that we deserve no favor from Him.

As commonly interpreted, the word "blessed" means "happy." You and I are assured of happiness when we are making conscious strides toward humility. All of this becomes possible as we yield to God's indwelling Holy Spirit.

Bible Reading: Matthew 5:17-20

ACTION POINT: With the help of the Holy Spirit I will consciously humble myself, asking Him to enable me to love God with all my heart, soul, mind and strength and my neighbor as myself as an act of humility and as a major factor in achieving the supernatural life.

The Mind of Christ

*"For who hath known the mind of the Lord, that he may instruct Him?
But we have the mind of Christ"* (1 Corinthians 2:16, KJV).

The first thing I do when I awaken each morning is to kneel before my Lord in humility, meditate upon His attributes, and praise, worship and adore Him.

The last thing I do before I go to bed at night is to kneel in prayer, to praise, worship and give thanks to Him. Thus, my first thoughts are automatically of Him when I awaken, because all night long my subconscious mind has been meditating upon Him.

Every morning of every day, I acknowledge His lordship. I gladly surrender control of my life to Him, acknowledging my dependence upon Him. Then, by faith, I claim His mind and His wisdom for direction in every detail of my life. I trust Him to influence and control my attitudes, my motives, my desires, my thoughts and my actions.

In different words and ways, I remind Him that I am a suit of clothes for Him and that He can do anything He wants in and through me. I invite Him to walk around in my body. I ask Him to think with my mind, to love with my heart, to speak with my lips, to lead me wherever He wants me to go, to seek and save the lost through me.

We should study the Word of God daily and diligently, determining as an act of the will to pattern our lives according to His commands and His example. We begin to experience the reality and the availability of the mind of Christ when we literally saturate our minds with His thoughts and spend much time meditating upon His Word.

Bible Reading: 1 Corinthians 2:9-15

ACTION POINT: Consciously and deliberately I will begin each day by inviting Christ to walk around in my body, think with my mind, love with my heart, speak with my lips and continue to "seek and to save the lost" through me.

Happy Are the Mourners

"Blessed are they that mourn for they shall be comforted" (Matthew 5:4).

During my days of agnosticism and early inquiry into the Christian faith, I was not aware of my sin. I had come to believe that Jesus Christ was the Son of God, that He died on the cross for the sins of man but somehow it had not dawned on me that I was that bad. My life-style was not much different from that of the average church member. And, though my life was far from exemplary, in my own estimation I was a pretty decent fellow. As a matter of fact, I had some problems with all the talk about the cross and the shedding of blood. It seemed offensive to my aesthetic nature.

I was willing to believe that Jesus was the greatest influence, the greatest teacher, the greatest leader, the greatest example that man had ever known. And if He had to die on the cross to make a point, I did not think it was important enough to be made an issue. In fact, the thing that was really important to me was the fact that according to the Bible and the historical evidence, Jesus lived a very wonderful life dedicated to helping others. Then one day — I shall never forget the time and place, though I have forgotten the exact passage — as I read the Bible I was suddenly gripped with the necessity of Christ dying on the cross for *my* sins. I finally realized that without the shedding of blood there is no forgiveness of sin, that I had fallen far short of the glory of God and that I deserved death. I realized that there is nothing in me that merited His love, His grace, His forgiveness, His cleansing. I found myself on my knees in tears, deeply conscious of my unworthiness and, for the first time in my life, I understood the true meaning of the cross and the reason He shed His blood for me.

Soon after that I was elected to the board of deacons of my church and was called upon to serve communion. I shall never forget that experience. I found myself weeping as I served the wafers representing His broken body and the grape juice representing His blood that was shed for the sins of all men, for *my* sins, because now His death on the cross meant everything to me. A hymn, which had once been offensive to me, now became one of my favorites: "What can wash away my sin? Nothing but the blood of Jesus. What can make me whole again? Nothing but the blood of Jesus. Oh precious is that flow that makes me white as snow. No other fount I know. Nothing but the blood of Jesus." I believe that this is what Jesus had in mind when He said, "Blessed are they that mourn for they shall be comforted."

Bible Reading: Jeremiah 31: 10-14

ACTION POINT: I will not ignore my sins, but will mourn over them by confessing, repenting, and, through the discipline of spiritual breathing, walking constantly in the light as a model of the supernatural life.

The Supernatural Power of God's Love

"For I am persuaded that neither death, nor life, nor angels, nor principalities, nor powers, nor things present, nor things to come, nor height, nor depth, nor any other creature, shall be able to separate us from the love of God, which is in Christ Jesus our Lord" (Romans 8:38,39, KJV).

More than anything else, I was drawn to Christ because of His love for me. The Bible says that Christ proved His supernatural love for us by coming "to die for us while we were still sinners."

Because of that great love, which draws me to Him and causes me to want to please Him and to love Him in return, I learned how to love supernaturally. In more than 30 years of counseling thousands of people about interpersonal conflicts, I do not know of a single problem that could not have been resolved if those involved had been willing to accept and respond to God's love for them, and to love others as an act of the will by faith, as God commands.

Such a statement may sound simplistic and exaggerated, yet I make it after carefully reviewing in my mind all kinds of conflicts between husbands and wives, parents and children, neighbors, friends and enemies.

Think of it! Christ's forgiveness is so great and compassionate that He will not allow anything or anyone to condemn us or separate us from His supernatural love. Even though He is "holy, blameless, unstained, separated from sinners, and exalted above the heavens," He still loves us and cleanses us from all unrighteousness. He gives us absolute assurance that nothing can ever "separate us from the love of God, which is in Christ Jesus our Lord."

Bible Reading: Romans 8:32-37

ACTION POINT: I determine to express my gratitude to God for His great love for me by loving Him in return and by loving by faith *everyone* with whom I have contact today. With the help of the Holy Spirit, I will demonstrate that love by gracious acts of the will.

Happiness for the Meek

"The meek and lowly are fortunate! for the whole wide world belongs to them" (Matthew 5:5).

When you think of the word "meek," does the name Casper Milquetoast or some other similar figure come to your mind? True meekness in no sense means or implies spinelessness. In truth, genuine meekness is patience in the face of injuries, insults, abuse and persecution, whether physical or mental. It is not cowardice or a surrender of our rights. Rather it is the opposite of anger, malice, prejudice or resentment.

Meekness today is seen in the actions of believers who allow God to be their defense instead of making an effort to avenge real or imagined hurts. It is patience in the midst of extreme difficulties or humility under fire, as described in 1 Corinthians 13. It hardly even notices when others make a mistake.

Certainly this is one of the major charcteristics of our Lord who claimed to be gentle and humble at heart. Matthew 11:28,29: "Come to Me, all who are weary and heavy-laden, and I will give you rest. Take My yoke upon you, and learn from Me for I am *gentle and humble* in heart, and you shall find rest for your souls" (Matthew 11:28,29, NAS).

The meek, like our Lord, are those who have remarkable, controlled strength and are calm and peaceful when all around there is confusion and chaos. These are the ones who will inherit the earth, who will be sought out as leaders. They are the ones who will help to build a better world.

Bible Reading: James 4:5-10

ACTION POINT: Dear Lord, I pray that you will help me to be meek as You count meekness. Give me a right reaction to insult and injury, real or imagined, to demonstrate strength under control following the example of my Lord.

Covered With His Love

"Long ago, even before He made the world, God chose us to be His very own, through what Christ would do for us; He decided then to make us holy in His eyes, without a single fault — we who stand before Him covered with His love" (Ephesians 1:4).

On every continent and in scores of countries, I have asked thousands of people, including Muslims, Hindus, Buddhists, communists and atheists: "Who is the greatest person who ever lived? Who has done more good for mankind than anyone else?"

Among knowledgeable people, the answer is always the same, "Jesus of Nazareth."

Born nearly 2,000 years ago, His coming had been foretold for centuries by the great prophets of Israel. The Old Testament, written by many individuals over a period of 1,500 years, contains more than 300 references concerning the promised Messiah. All of these prophecies have been fulfilled in the birth, life, ministry, death and resurrection of Jesus. They could not have referred to anyone else.

That in itself is conclusive evidence of God's personal and supernatural intervention in history. Jesus' coming into this world was no accident, and we who trust Him are covered by His love.

What a beautiful picture — *covered with His love!*

"All the armies that ever marched and all the navies that were ever built, and all the parliaments that ever sat, and all the kings that ever reigned, put together have not affected the life of man upon this earth as has that one solitary life," declared an anonymous observer in reflecting upon the life of Jesus Christ.

Bible Reading: Ephesians 1:5-14

ACTION POINT: Throughout this day I will picture myself embraced by the arms of the Almighty, His love covering and comforting me. I will share His love and faithfulness with others.

Blessed Are the Merciful

"Blessed are the merciful: for they shall obtain mercy" (Matthew 5:7, KJV).

If you and I have a desire to imitate God, seldom do we accomplish that purpose more than in the practice of showing mercy. God delights in nothing more than in the exercise of showing mercy.

One of the clear prerequisites to real happiness is this display of genuine mercy. Surely God has given us the supreme example, by giving His only Son to die in our place. That is mercy beyond comprehension, beyond description.

The world speaks often of having someone at its mercy. In a very real sense, God has us at His mercy — but He chose to be merciful and make a way of escape for us. The decision to take that way is ours.

To the degree that we show mercy to the poor, the wretched, the guilty — to that degree we are like God. And if He keeps us here on earth to be conformed more and more to His image, how important it is that we trust Him — by His indwelling Holy Spirit — to make us merciful.

When we do something to glorify God, like giving a cup of cold water in His name, in obedience to His commandments and with a desire that He should be honored, He will consider it as done unto Him and reward us accordingly.

The lesson is clear: the merciful shall obtain mercy. And who among us is not a candidate for more of God's mercy?

Bible Reading: Luke 6:31-36

ACTION POINT: "Dear Lord, with Your great mercy as the supreme example, I resolve to allow your Holy Spirit to show mercy through me."

How to Test Your Experience: I

"Talk with each other much about the Lord, quoting psalms and hymns and singing sacred songs, making music in your hearts to the Lord. Always give thanks for everything to our God and Father in the name of our Lord Jesus Christ. Honor Christ by submitting to each other" (Ephesians 5:19,20).

Mary was one of those ardent, faithful church members — a Sunday school teacher, choir member and active participant in a home Bible study — who just assume they are filled with the Holy Spirit because they do everything their pastor or Christian leader asks of them.

"Why has no one, up to now, ever told me that I needed to be filled with the Holy Spirit?" she asked me just after I had publicly suggested that very thing.

To help Mary better understand her own spiritual condition, I read to her the above passage from Ephesians. Then I asked her several questions relating to that portion of Scripture.

"Are you talking about Christ to others? Is your heart filled with melody to the Lord? Do you spend time in God's Word daily? Do you have a thankful spirit? Do you submit to others in the Lord?"

Mary hesitated only a moment. "If these are evidences of a Spirit-filled life, I must not be controlled by the Holy Spirit. But I would like to be. What should I do?"

With great delight and joy I shared appropriate Scriptures with her, and together we bowed in prayer as she claimed by faith the fullness and control of the Holy Spirit in her life. Surrendering to the lordship of Christ, turning from all known sin, hungering and thirsting after righteousness, she now knew with certainty that she was filled with the Spirit. Being filled with the Spirit is not a once-and-for-all decision, but a way of life in which we claim the fullness of the Spirit moment by moment, day by day, by faith.

Bible Reading: Colossians 3:12-17

ACTION POINT: I will honestly compare myself with the evidences of the supernatural, Spirit-filled life listed in the fifth chapter of Ephesians. If these are not true in my life, I will claim by faith the fullness and control of God's Holy Spirit, and ask Him to make these qualities a reality in my daily relationships with the Lord, with my loved ones and with others.

How to Test Your Experience: II

"You wives must submit to your husbands' leadership in the same way you submit to the Lord. . . . And you husbands, show the same kind of love to your wives as Christ showed to the church when He died for her, to make her holy and clean, washed by baptism and God's Word. . . .

"Children, obey your parents; this is the right thing to do because God has placed them in authority over you. Honor your father and mother. . . .

"And now a word to you parents. Don't keep on scolding and nagging your children, making them angry and resentful. Rather, bring them up with the loving discipline the Lord Himself approves, with suggestions and godly advice" (Ephesians 5:22,25,26; 6:1-4).

When a dear Christian friend came to me for counsel one day, he and I agreed that something was obviously wrong in his relationship with Christ.

"Do you know for sure that you are filled with the Holy Spirit?" I asked.

"Yes, I know all about the Holy Spirit and I know that I am filled."

"Here's a good test," I suggested. Then I read him the above passage from Ephesians, whereupon the Holy Spirit helped him to realize, as he compared with this passage the daily reality of his walk with Christ, that he was not truly filled with the Holy Spirit. He was honest and confessed that he did not even begin to love his wife as Christ loved the church, nor did he have a good relationship with his children, but he wanted to measure up to the scriptural standard in both cases.

As we bowed together in prayer, by faith he claimed the fullness of the Holy Spirit, and God gave to him a joyful new relationship with Christ and with his wife and children, as well as with everybody else around him.

Bible Reading: Colossians 3:18-25

ACTION POINT: I will meditate on this passage from Ephesians 5. If these experiences are not real in my life, I will claim by faith the fullness and control of God's Holy Spirit and ask Him to make them a reality in my daily relationship with the Lord, with my loved ones and with all others.

Happy Are the Pure in Heart

"Blessed are the pure in heart for they shall see God" (Matthew 5:8, KJV).

Jesus had a flashpoint against the hypocrisy of the Pharisees. They professed to be something they were not. Externally they did everything right, adhering meticulously to all the details of the law. yet He referred to them as being "whitewashed tombs" internally, and being "full of dead men's bones." Thus, obviously, the "pure in heart" did not apply to the Pharisees, according to His view of them.

In John 14:21, Jesus says, "The one who obeys Me is the one who loves Me and because he loves Me My Father will love him and I will too and I will reveal Myself to him." That is another way of saying what He said in the verse in Matthew above. The pure in heart shall see God because He will reveal Himself to those who obey, and only the pure in heart obey.

If God seems impersonal to you, far off and unreachable, you may want to look into the mirror of your heart to see if anything there would grieve or quench the Spirit, short-circuiting His communication with you.

You may be sure of this promise of God: The pure in heart will experience the reality of His presence within.

If for some reason this is not your experience, God has made provision whereby you can have vital fellowship with Him. Breathe spiritually. Exhale by confessing your sins, and inhale by appropriating the fullness of God's Spirit. Begin to delight yourself in the Lord and in His Word, asking God to give you a pure heart, and you may be assured that God will become a reality to you.

Bible Reading: Psalm 18:20-26

ACTION POINT: Because I desire to have a close personal relationship with God and to live a supernatural life, I will keep my heart pure before Him.

Blessed Peacemakers

"Is there any such thing as Christians cheering each other up? Do you love me enough to want to help me? Does it mean anything to you that we are brothers in the Lord, sharing the same Spirit? Are your hearts tender and sympathetic at all? Then make me truly happy by loving each other and agreeing wholeheartedly with each other, working together with one heart and mind and purpose" (Philippians 2:1,2). "Happy are those who strive for peace — they shall be called the sons of God" (Matthew 5:9).

Few individuals are more pleasing to our Lord than those who seek to promote peace. He is our great example since He is the author of peace. He is called the Prince of Peace, and He promises, "Peace I leave with you, My peace I give unto you: not as the world giveth, give I unto you. Let not your heart be troubled, neither let it be afraid" (John 14:27, KJV).

When you and I think of peacemakers today, we think perhaps of national leaders who have made great efforts toward international peace, or of negotiators who have served as intermediaries, attempting to eliminate strife between management and labor.

But more is involved in this beatitude — certainly more of a spiritual nature. You may know, or have known, as I have, members of churches whom the Lord has been able to use as peacemakers — those who calm fears and help to unruffle feathers when the inevitable quarrels arise.

Peacemaking is something that requires work. It does not come easily.

Basically, man is hostile toward himself, toward his neighbor and toward God. The peacemaker is one who can build bridges of love and understanding and trust.

Friends, neighbors, men of influence, lawyers, physicians, may do much to promote peace, and certainly homemakers within families can make a great difference in the harmony of a home. Long and deadly arguments can be resolved by a simple expression of love and a kind word at the right moment.

Our strife-worn world, from the individual home to the international centers of influence, is in need of children of God who are peacemakers — committed to being ambassadors of the Prince of Peace.

Bible Reading: 2 Corinthians 13:11-14.

ACTION POINT: Through the enabling of God's Holy Spirit, I will seek ways to become a peacemaker in building bridges of love, trust and understanding where there is now conflict, discord and even hate.

A New Quality of Life

"When the Holy Spirit, who is truth, comes, He shall guide you into all truth, for He will not be presenting His own ideas, but will be passing on to you what He has heard. He will tell you about the future. He shall praise Me and bring Me great honor by showing you My glory. All the Father's glory is Mine: this is what I mean when I say that He will show you My glory" (John 16:13-15).

Steve asked me the question, "What is my Number 1 priority as a Christian? I want to be a man of God, so I need counsel as to what I am to do first." This is a good question for every Christian to ask.

The answer is simply: to glorify God. Jesus tells us how we can best do this in John 15:8, "By this is My Father glorified, that you bear much fruit, and so prove to be My disciples" (NASB). Or, as the Living Bible states it, "My true disciples produce bountiful harvests. This brings great glory to My Father."

The Holy Spirit has come to be a witness to our Lord Jesus. When the Spirit controls our lives, we too will be witnesses for Him.

Witnessing for Christ with our lips is not only a natural result of being filled and controlled by the Holy Spirit, but also is a necessary act of obedience if we are to continue to experience the fullness of the Holy Spirit.

That which is most on our hearts is most on our lips, so if we truly love Christ, we will want to share Him with others. But God does not want or need the witness of individuals whose carnal lives fail to give credibility to their testimonies.

The greatest experience that has ever happened to any believer is to know Jesus Christ personally as Savior and Lord, to be forgiven of his sins and to have assurance of eternal life.

Therefore, the most important thing we can do to help another person is to introduce him to Christ. Only the Holy Spirit can empower us to live holy lives and be fruitful witnesses for Christ.

Bible Reading: John 14:16-26

ACTION POINT: I will ask the Holy Spirit to glorify God through the quality of my life and the witness of my words, as a demonstration of the supernatural life that I have received from God.

The Bond of Love

"Let me assure you that no one has ever given up anything — home, brothers, sisters, mother, father, children, or property — for love of Me and to tell others the Good News, who won't be given back, a hundred times over, homes, brothers, sisters, mothers, children, and land — with persecution! All these will be his here on earth, and in the world to come he shall have eternal life" (Mark 10:29,30).

Having admonished His disciples to follow Him even at the cost of leaving everything — including mothers and families — behind, Christ is now affirming His consistency with the disciples. Obviously He loved His own mother dearly — one of His last acts before He died on the cross was to be sure that the apostle John would take care of her. Yet the bond of love which Jesus felt toward His disciples, a bond which continues today toward those who truly seek Him with all their hearts, transcends even the bond of love which one experiences in flesh-and-blood relationships, unless those relationships are also rooted in the love of Christ.

Romans 5:8 explains the basis for this bond. The love of God is shed abroad in our hearts through the Holy Spirit, and the Holy Spirit ignites the hearts of true disciples with supernatural love, (*agape*) in action. That bond of love builds a spiritual family relationship that transcends all others, a relationship that is truly supernatural. In this way our Lord fulfills His promise that everything that is given up to follow Him will be given back a hundred times over in this life.

Bible Reading: Matthew 12:46-50

ACTION POINT: In every way I will seek to obey the commands of my Father in heaven with the certainty that greater bonds of love will unite my heart with many brothers and sisters. This will demonstrate to the world the validity of the revolutionary, supernatural power of the love of God ignited in our hearts through the Holy Spirit.

The Church Will Prevail

"You are Peter, a stone; and upon this rock I will build my church; and all the powers of hell shall not prevail against it" (Matthew 16:18).

You and I can truly rejoice: no matter how weak and ineffective our church may seem to be at times, the fact remains that "all the powers of hell shall not prevail against it." Remarkably fulfilled to this date, this promise has the Word of God Himself to back it up.

Sometimes, we see the human frailties of one another in the church — which will always be there — and we forget for the moment the great strengths that are present: the Word of God; fellow believers who are fully committed to the Lord; genuine worship of our heavenly Father.

Primarily, we have the promise that the church is God's instrument for worship and instruction of His children. It is a rallying place for believers; a powerhouse of prayer; a training school for sharing our faith.

A parallel to this promise has to do with the Word of God. Men have tried to destroy it down through the ages, but it remains the all-time best seller and so shall it ever be. Men have tried to count the church down and out many times, never with any degree of success whatsoever. And so shall that ever be, as well.

Rejoice: all the plots, stratagems and machinations of the enemy of the church shall never be able to overcome it. You and I, meanwhile, can do our part to help make the church all that God intends for it to be.

Bible Reading: Hebrews 12:21-24

ACTION POINT: I will praise God for His protecting hand over the church, and do all in my power, the Holy Spirit enabling, to keep it strong and triumphant — the center of spiritual revolution.

Are You Bearing Fruit?

"By this is My Father glorified, that you bear much fruit, and so prove to be My disciples" (John 15:8, NAS).

Early in my Christian life, I had little faith as I prayed for one person, who by God's grace received Christ. My faith grew and I could pray for two, who received Christ. The more I understood the attributes of God and experienced His blessing on my witness for Him, the more I could trust Him.

As our Campus Crusade for Christ staff grew in number and we trained more and more students and laymen, we began to pray for millions to receive Christ. God honored our faith and prayers with many millions of recorded decisions for our Savior in more than 150 countries of the world.

Now that we are helping to train millions of Christians on every major continent, associated with thousands of churches of all denominations and various other Christian organizations, I have the faith to pray for a billion souls to receive Christ. As I have come to know our Lord Jesus Christ better, I have learned to trust Him more. I now believe that He will do great and mighty things through me and through others as we live by faith the supernatural Christian life. Faith is like a muscle; it grows with excercise. The more we see God do in and through the lives of His children, the more we expect Him to do. Please note God does not change — He is the same yesterday, today and forever. We are the ones who change as we mature in faith.

How do you know that you are a true disciple? That you are glorifying God? By bearing much fruit. But what kind of fruit? The fruit of your holy life and the fruit of your Spirit-anointed lips must be in balance.

Some Christians concentrate on Bible study and prayer, seeking to honor God. Others concentrate on much Christian activity. Every time the church door opens, they are there. Yet neither type of person is experiencing God's best.

Remember, we glorify God when we bear *much* fruit. Too many Christians are satisfied with modest efforts and modest results. Yet the better we know God and the more we are acquainted with His Word, the more we have fellowship with Him and grasp His vision and His burden for all people throughout the world.

Bible Reading: John 15:4,5,12

ACTION POINT: I determine, through the enabling of the Holy Spirit, that I will glorify God by bearing much fruit through both the witness of my life and the witness of my lips.

How to Find Your Life

"For anyone who keeps his life for himself shall lose it; and anyone who loses his life for Me shall find it again" (Matthew 16:25).

From all outward appearances Tom and Mary were the ideal couple. They lived in a beautiful mansion. They possessed several fine cars — more than they needed. Both of them dressed elegantly and they entertained lavishly. They were the life of the party and everything seemed too good to be true. And it was.

Beneath the facade they were miserable creatures, though outwardly they seemed to be loving and considerate of each other. I soon learned that they had great resentments and deep-seated antagonisms toward each other. Their quarrels had become more frequent, sometimes exploding into temper tantrums, and sometimes resulting in physical abuse. They had tried in a number of ways to find happiness and fulfillment, including several around-the-world trips. But the harder they had tried, the more miserable they had become.

It was in this context that I shared with them the importance of surrendering their lives to Christ and inviting Him to be their Savior. I counseled them to lose themselves, as His representatives, in bringing happiness into the lives of others.

Receiving Christ was not so hard for them to do. They both realized they were sinners and needed a Savior. But they had lived such selfish lives for so long that it was not easy for them to begin to consider others as the Scripture admonishes. After a time they did begin to work with elderly people in convalescent homes and with prisoners through the ministry of the local church. On occasion, they gave their testimony at the skid row mission.

With the passing of time, the miracle happened and that illusive goal of happiness, fulfillment and satisfaction became a reality. In losing their lives, they truly found them in service to others in the name of Christ. They found the abundant life which He promised and for which they had sought so long.

God's loyalty has been proven over and over again. In reviewing my own experiences, and in observing the lives of many others, I have become aware that the individual who seeks happiness never finds it, but the one who is committed to taking happiness to others always finds it. And he also finds meaning, purpose, joy and peace in the process.

Bible Reading: Matthew 16:24-27

ACTION POINT: I am determined to experience the reality of this promise by surrendering the control of my life to Him and demonstrating my commitment through serving others.

Maturity — In His Timing

"But when the Holy Spirit controls our lives He will produce this kind of fruit in us: love, joy, peace, patience, kindness, goodness, faithfulness, gentleness and self-control" (Galatians 5:22,23).

One of my dear friends had a 25-year-old son who had never grown past the baby stage mentally or physically. He had greeted the birth of his beautiful baby boy with great joy, but his joy turned to heartache and sorrow with the passing of years as his son never matured.

Unfortunately and tragically, many Christians never pass the baby or childhood stages. Think of the heartache and sorrow that God experiences when He looks upon those of His children who have never matured, though they have been Christians for many years.

Martha, a new Christian, approached me with this question, "With all my heart I want to be a woman of God, but I do not experience the consistency of Galatians 5:22,23 in my life. What is wrong?"

Maybe you are asking the same question. If so, it will be helpful for you to understand that the Christian life is a life of growth. Just as in our physical lives we begin as babies and progress through childhood into adolescence, young adulthood and mature adulthood, so it is in our spiritual lives.

The Holy Spirit takes up residence within every believer at the moment of new birth. The growth process is greatly accelerated when a believer consciously yields himself to the lordship of Christ and the filling and control of the Holy Spirit. A believer who is empowered by the Holy Spirit and is a faithful student of God's Word, who has learned to trust and obey God, can pass through the various stages of spiritual growth and become a mature Christian within a brief period of time. Some Spirit-filled Christians demonstrate more of the fruit of the Spirit within one year than others who have been untaught, uncommitted believers for 50 years.

Bible Reading: Romans 5:1-5

ACTION POINT: I am determined that I will become a spiritually mature Christian, in whose life the fruit of the Spirit will be demonstrated. Through the enabling of the Holy Spirit I will dedicate myself to prayer, reading the Word and witnessing, and living a life of obedience.

If Two Agree

"I also tell you this — if two of you agree down here on earth concerning anything you ask for, My Father in heaven will do it for you" (Matthew 18:19).

Some of the richest experiences of my life have occurred in the practice of meeting with one or two individuals to pray specifically for definite things. The Scripture promises that one person can defeat 1000 but two can defeat 10,000 (Deuteronomy 32:30).

I believe that same principle holds in prayer. When individuals pray together, agreeing concerning a certain matter — assuming, of course, that they are praying according to the Word and will of God — the mighty sources of deity are released in their behalf.

Some interpret this verse to refer to church discipline, rejecting the claim that I am making in principle that there is great power, supernatural power, released when God's children unite together in prayer. We have not because we ask not (James 4:2). Whatsoever we shall ask in prayer, believing, we shall receive (Matthew 21:22). If we ask anything according to God's will, He hears and answers us (1 John 5:14). If we ask anything in Christ's name, He will do it (John 14:14).

When two or more individuals unite and together claim these promises concerning a certain matter, whatever it may be, they should expect answers. That is in accordance with God's promise and God does not lie.

Bible Reading: Matthew 18:15-20

ACTION POINT: I will seek opportunities to unite with others to pray specifically concerning the needs of individual believers or my church or missions around the world, and we will expect answers in accordance with God's promise.

Power to Witness

"But ye shall receive power, after the Holy Ghost is come upon you: and ye shall be witnesses unto Me both in Jerusalem, and in all Judea, and in Samaria, and unto the uttermost part of the earth" (Acts 1:8, KJV).

While I was speaking to a group of theological students in Australia, one young man became very angry and argumentative when I emphasized the importance of witnessing for Christ daily as a way of life and explained that disobedient Christians cannot be Spirit-filled. Not to witness for Christ is to disobey our Lord's specific command. Therefore, any Christian who does not regularly share his faith in Christ cannot walk in the fullness of the Holy Spirit.

"I work day and night to maintain good grades," he declared. I don't have time to witness while in seminary. I can witness after I become a pastor."

Many Christians make similar excuses for their lack of witness, but none are valid. Some say they do not have the gift of evangelism. Others say they are still preparing for the day when they will be witnesses. Some pastors believe it is the responsibility of their members to witness, and they are to preach and teach the Word. Yet the Bible clearly teaches that all believers are to be witnesses with their lives and with their lips. It is a command of God.

On thousands of occasions we have found that pastors, students and laymen who have never introduced anyone to our Lord become fruitful witnesses when they learn how to live a Spirit-filled life and are taught how to share their faith in Christ with others. The apostle Paul, who was a Spirit-filled witness, shares in Colossians 1:28 how everywhere we go we are to tell everyone who will listen about Christ.

Bible Reading: Luke 24:45-49

ACTION POINT: Today — and every day — I will ask the Holy Spirit to direct me to those whose hearts He has prepared, and to anoint and empower me to speak convincingly, lovingly and effectively of our Savior.

He's in the Midst

"For where two or three gather together because they are Mine, I will be right there among them" (Matthew 18:20).

What better proof is there of the fact that Jesus is God, that He is omnipresent? As you and I gather with our little groups — whether two or three, or 200 — Jesus is there in the midst. And at the same time that wonderful promise applies to similar groups in Africa, Israel, China and anywhere else!

This general assertion is made to support the particular promise made to his apostles in verse 19. Those who meet in His name can be sure He is among them.

An omniscient, omnipotent God — and His Son Jesus Christ — are omnipresent (everywhere present at the same time)! What a glorious truth! Let your imagination soar: among the Masai tribe in Kenya, Africa, or the Quechua Indians in Ecuador — if they are meeting in that name which is above every name, even Jesus Christ our Lord, He is right there meeting with them.

Equally important, you and one or two friends meeting together in His name *can* have the assurance that He is right there meeting with you as well. And you can feel His presence — especially as you acknowledge the fact that He is there and begin to worship Him for who and what He is.

Joy of joys, God and Jesus Christ who meet with missionaries and national believers on the field and with church leaders in their councils also meet with you and me today.

Bible Reading: Acts 20:32-38

ACTION POINT: I will look for new opportunities to invoke His presence in my midst by fellowshipping with other believers in His name.

The Key to Real Joy

"Remember what Christ taught and let His words enrich your lives and make you wise; teach them to each other and sing them out in psalms and hymns and spiritual songs, singing to the Lord with thankful hearts. And whatever you do or say, let it be as a representative of the Lord Jesus, and come with Him into the presence of God the Father to give Him your thanks" (Colossians 3:16,17).

As I travel and speak throughout the world, I meet many individuals who are caught up in the emotionalism of a religious experience which they attribute to the Holy Spirit. They live from experience to experience, with little knowledge of what the Bible teaches. As a result, they seldom grow past the baby stage. They are seeking and talking about their experiences with the Holy Spirit instead of the Lord Jesus, forgetting that the Holy Spirit came to glorify Christ.

At the other extreme, I find that most Christians seldom mention the Holy Spirit. The supernatural life is a life of balance.

Notice the close parallel between Ephesians 5:18-20 and Colossians 3:16,17. The Spirit-filled person and the one whose mind and heart are saturated with the person and the Word of Jesus Christ will be joyful and thankful, and he will do all as a testimony of love to Him who is our Lord and Savior.

We can no more live a joyful, abundant, fruitful, victorious, supernatural life apart from the Word of God than we can do so apart from the Spirit of God. They are like the two wings of an airplane; a plane cannot fly with only one wing. Neither can we live balanced, victorious lives if we do not invest time in reading, studying, memorizing and meditating on God's Word, while at the same time depending on the Holy Spirit, who inspired its writing centuries ago, to illuminate its truth to our minds and hearts.

Bible Reading: 1 Corinthians 10:31-33

ACTION POINT: Today — and every day — I will claim the Holy Spirit's power to enable me to read, study, memorize and meditate on God's holy, inspired Word with comprehension. I will claim by faith the help of the Holy Spirit to live in accordance with the teaching of God's revealed truth. With His help, I will live a balanced, Spirit-controlled, supernatural life.

We Can Obey All

" 'Sir, which is the most important command in the laws of Moses?'
Jesus replied, ' "Love the Lord your God with all your heart, soul,
and mind." This is the first and greatest commandment. The second
most important is similar: "Love your neighbor as much as you love
yourself." All the other commandments and all the demands of the
prophets stem from these two laws and are fulfilled if you obey them.
Keep only these and you will find that you are obeying all the others' "
(Matthew 22:36-40).

Steve came for counsel. "I want with all my heart to be a man of God," he said. "Can you tell me how I can please the Lord and be everything He wants me to be? You have walked with the Lord for many years. Surely you have learned some lessons that would help me." I turned to this passage, and we read it and discussed it together.

"Jesus has answered your question, Steve," I said to him. "If you keep these two commandments, all the others and all the demands of the prophets will be fulfilled." We turned to Exodus 20:1-17 and reviewed the Ten Commandments.

"You see, Steve, if you love God with all your heart, you will have no other god before Him. You will not take the name of the Lord your God in vain. You will remember the sabbath day to keep it holy. If you love your neighbor as yourself, you will honor your father and mother. You will not murder, commit adultery, steal, lie or covet that which belongs to your neighbor."

Think what would happen if every person who professes to be a follower of Jesus Christ would truly obey the two great commandments. Not only would the Ten Commandments be fulfilled, but so would the Golden Rule and every other command of God. The great miracle would result. The moral, spiritual and even the economical problems that plague the nations of the world would be resolved almost overnight.

This kind of love is the fruit of the Holy Spirit. For the supernatural love of God (*agape*) is spread abroad in our hearts through the Holy Spirit. It is only as we walk in the fullness of the power of the Holy Spirit, fully surrendered to the lordship of Jesus Christ, that we can fulfill these commandments.

Bible Reading: Mark 12:28-34

ACTION POINT: Through the supernatural enabling power of the Holy Spirit, I will love God with all my heart, soul, mind and strength and my neighbors as myself, knowing that as I do so, I will be fulfilling and obeying all the other laws.

His Word Remains Forever

"Heaven and earth will disappear, but my words remain forever" (Matthew 24:35).

A re you not glad there is something that will remain forever, steadfast and true?

In a day of change and turmoil, the promise is made that the Word of God will stand forever. The significance of that guarantee is monumental, incredible. It is not just that a book shall remain in print; rather, it is that the multitudinous truths contained in that book likewise will remain in effect, steadfast and true.

Long after heaven and earth have passed away God's holy Word will continue to endure.

That should mean much to you and me in our daily walk. God's promise, "All things work together for good," to the believer is just as true today as it was when it was written centuries ago.

In fact, every one of the promises in the Word of God — including the 365 referred to in this daily devotional — is bona fide, guaranteed by the God of the universe, the Creator of all things. That alone should strengthen our faith to know that we can trust Him supremely with our lives and everything concerned with them.

When all else fails, when hope is almost gone, we can come back to the Word of God, which is "quick and powerful and sharper than a two-edged sword." It will have the answer for every problem, every burden, every need we face.

Bible Reading: Matthew 24:36-42

ACTION POINT: I will place my complete confidence in God's unchanging Word and will rest upon His faithful promises to all believers for supernatural living.

Ask What You Will

"If ye abide in Me, and My words abide in you, ye shall ask what ye will, and it shall be done unto you" (John 15:7, KJV).

When Campus Crusade for Christ began at the University of California, Los Angeles, in 1951, our first act was to organize a 24-hour prayer chain. Around the clock, scores of men and women interceded for UCLA students and faculty. God answered prayer in a remarkable way, as His Spirit touched the entire campus.

Thirty-one years later, more than 16,000 full-time and associate staff members of Campus Crusade for Christ in more than 150 countries and protectorates are teaching millions of others the importance of prayer, with revolutionary spiritual results and many millions receiving Christ.

Prayer has always been the breath, life, vitality, strength and power of the Christian. Beginning with our Lord, who spent much time in prayer, and continuing with the disciples and fruitful, Spirit-filled Christians through the centuries, prayer remains a major emphasis in the life of every believer.

History records no mighty men or women of God whose lives were not characterized by prayer, nor any great spiritual movements, awakenings or revivals that were not preceded by prayer. James 4:2 reminds us, "Ye have not, because ye ask not."

It is not enough to pray; we must pray according to the Word and will of God. For that reason, understanding and obeying our Scripture assignment for today is crucial. We must abide in Christ and allow His Word to abide in us before we are qualified to pray. God's Word reminds us, "And this is the confidence that we have in Him, that, if we ask any thing according to His will, He heareth us; And if we know that He hear us, whatsoever we ask, we know that we have the petitions that we desired of Him" (1 John 5:14,15, KJV).

Bible Reading: Matthew 7:7-11

ACTION POINT: From this day forth I will seek, through the enabling of the Holy Spirit, to abide in Christ and have His Word abide in me. As I discover God's Will through the diligent study of his Word and the leading of His Holy Spirit, I will pray more intelligently and thus can expect answers to my prayers.

So He May Forgive Us

"And when ye stand praying, forgive, if ye have aught against any: that your Father also which is in heaven may forgive you your trespasses" (Mark 11:25, KJV).

Y ou and I have a way by which we can be absolutely certain of God's forgiveness. It is two-fold.

First, we must be sure that we have forgiven anyone and everyone against whom we may have anything or hold any resentment.

Second, we must believe His word unquestioningly — and his Word does indeed tell us we will be forgiven when we ask under these conditions.

Most familiar, of course, is the glorious promise of 1 John 1:9, "If we confess our sins, He is faithful and just to forgive us our sins, and to cleanse us from all unrighteousness" (KJV).

Though today's verse uses the word *stand* in reference to praying, Scripture clearly states that the posture in prayer was sometimes standing and sometimes kneeling. God, however, looks on the heart rather than on our position as we pray.

If the heart is right, any posture may be proper. All other things being equal, however, the kneeling position seems more in keeping with the proper attitude of humility and reverence in our approach to God. (Physical condition, of course, sometimes makes this inadvisable or impossible.)

Most important, we are to forgive before we pray. That much is certain.

Bible Reading: Matthew 6:9-15

ACTION POINT: I will examine my heart throughout the day to be sure I have forgiven any who should be forgiven — before I pray.

The Holy Spirit Will Speak

"But when you are arrested and stand trial, don't worry about what to say in your defense. Just say what God tells you to. Then you will not be speaking, but the Holy Spirit will" (Mark 13:11).

Have you ever had the experience of trying to say a word for the Lord, just sharing your faith, and breathing a prayer for guidance — then marveling as the Lord Himself, by His indwelling Holy Spirit, put the very words in your mouth that needed to be said?

Such has been my experience — many times. And I marvel and rejoice each time. On some occasions, I have addressed crowds of varying sizes, often not only feeling totally inadequate but also concluding my message of the evening with the feeling that I had been a poor ambassador of Christ. Then, someone has approached me after the service and thanked me for saying just the word he needed at that moment.

We serve a faithful God. That neighbor who needs a word of encouragement — ask the Lord to give you the right words to say to him or her. That correspondent hundreds of miles away — trust God for His message to him or her through you.

Certain conditions must prevail, of course, before the Holy Spirit can speak through us. But they are easily met. I must come with a clean heart, surrendered to the Holy Spirit, with my sins forgiven, having forgiven other people, holding no resentment or ill feeling against anyone. "If I regard iniquity in my heart, the Lord will not hear me" (Psalm 66:18, KJV).

Let us trust God and His indwelling Holy Spirit for the very words of counsel we should say to a loved one or friend today.

Bible Reading: Acts 2:1-4

ACTION POINT: I will trust God and His Holy Spirit to put the very words in my mouth this day that need to be said to others whose lives I touch.

Helping the Church

"The Holy Spirit displays God's power through each of us as a means of helping the entire church" (1 Corinthians 12:7).

A friend once asked me, "Are all the spiritual gifts for today?" and "How can I discern my spiritual gifts?"

He had been reading a number of books with conflicting views on gifts and had heard sermons — some encouraging him to discover his gifts and others saying the gifts are not for today. He was woefully confused.

I shared with this friend that I have been a Christian for more than 35 years and have known the reality of the fullness of the Spirit for more than 30 years. I explained that I have seen God do remarkable — even miraculous — things in and through my life throughout the years.

Yet, I have not felt the need to "discover" my gifts, because I believe that whatever God calls me to do He will enable me to do if I am willing to trust and obey Him, work hard and discipline myself.

The Holy Spirit obviously controls and distributes all the gifts. So when I am filled, controlled and empowered with the Holy Spirit, I possess all of the gifts potentially. God will give me any gift I need.

I went on to tell my young friend that some of the gifts of the Spirit are supernatural enhancements of abilities common to all men, wisdom for instance.

Other gifts, such as healing, are granted by the Holy Spirit to only a select few.

But the gifts differ in another way, too. Some are instantaneous, and others are developmental in nature. Primarily, we need to remember that whatever God calls us to do, He will enable us to do. "For it is God who works in you, both to will and to work for His good pleasure" (Philippians 2:13, NAS).

Bible Reading: 1 Corinthians 12:24-31

ACTION POINT: I will dwell on God's ability to do in and through me whatever He calls upon me to do, rather than to spend precious time seeking to discover my spiritual gifts.

Because You Believe

"You believed that God would do what He said; that is why He has given you this wonderful blessing" (Luke 1:45).

So much of the life you and I live as Christians depends on simple belief. Do we really trust God to do what He says He will do?

This particular verse, of course, concerns Mary. No doubt she was chosen to be the mother of Jesus because of the faith God knew she possessed. In any case, God honored that faith by bestowing upon her the highest privilege any mother could have.

Even taken out of context, the meaning is the same: If we truly believe God will do what He says, the wonderful blessing He promises will be ours. And that applies to every area of our lives — spiritual, physical, material.

What is your greatest need today? If you are a housewife and mother, it may be for patience and love. If you are a business or professional man or woman, it may be for wisdom or strength or courage. If you are a student, it may be for persistence, commitment, application.

In all probability, you cannot think of a circumstance or situation which is beyond the ability of God to control. The promises of God are both general and specific, so that they will meet the need of every heart and life.

We may expect a great blessing from God today. Why? Because we are going to believe He will do what He said.

Bible Reading: Luke 1:39-44

ACTION POINT: "Dear Lord, I will believe you for supernatural living in every situation and circumstance of my life this day.

Greater Works Than He Does

"In solemn truth I tell you, anyone believing in Me shall do the same miracles I have done, and even greater ones, because I am going to be with the Father. You can ask Him for anything, using My name, and I will do it, for this will bring praise to the Father because of what I, the Son, will do for you" (John 14:12, 13).

For many years, during and after seminary, I asked leading theologians, pastors and students, "What does this passage mean? How can I and other believers do the same miracles that our Lord did when He was here in the flesh — and even greater ones?"

Surely there had to be some mistakes in the translation of this passage, for I saw little evidence of this supernatural power in the lives of the Christians around me or in my own life.

But I had wrongly interpreted what Jesus said. I was thinking only of the miracles of physical healing. God still heals the sick, and almost daily I pray that He will touch the ailing bodies of ill ones. God sometimes heals them miraculously, though mostly He works through the skill of surgeons and the miracle of modern medicine.

Yet, while physical healing is certainly valid and very desirable, I realize more and more that a greater miracle is the miracle of new birth. For the body that is healed will one day die, but the person who is introduced to Christ and experiences salvation will live forever.

The main reason our Lord came to this earth was to "seek and save the lost," not primarily to perform miracles of physical healing. Frequently, we are privileged to experience the reality of our Lord's promise as He enables us to "seek and save the lost" in greater numbers than He did while He was here in the flesh.

For example, in 1980, during the Korean Here's Life World Evangelization Crusade we saw more than one million people indicate salvation decisions during the week.

Bible Reading: Matthew 21:21, 22

ACTION POINT: Beginning today, I will claim, in the name of Jesus, that He who dwells within me, who came to seek and to save the lost and is not willing that any should perish, will do even greater miracles in and through my life than He did while here in the flesh. By faith, I will experience and share the supernatural life of Christ with others.

The Key to Blessing

"He replied, 'Yes, but even more blessed are all who hear the Word of God and put it into practice' " (Luke 11:28).

If you and I could know only one rule that would guarantee us real happiness, no doubt this should be it. Because the meaning of this promise is the same in or out of context, we shall share briefly the out-of-context guarantee contained therein.

Man's chief happiness — his, or her, highest honor — is to obey the Word of God. No earthly honor or achievement can compare with the blessing, meaning in and fulfillment that come from obeying the Word and Will of God.

Implicit in putting into practice — or obeying — the Word of God is the matter of *knowing* the Word of God. This, of course, implies reading, studying, meditating upon and even memorizing the Scriptures. If we are neglecting this phase of the Christian life, we are omitting a vitally important part of spiritual nurture, without which it is impossible to live a supernatural life.

Something about the Word refreshes, cleanses, uplifts the heart and soul of each one of us when we spend time in its pages. God made it — and us — that way. No matter how many times we may have read the Word of God, even the entire Bible, there is something remarkably fresh and new about it every time we read it.

If somehow we lack the discipline to do what we know we should about the Word, we may pray ceaselessly for the Holy Spirit to illumine its truths to our minds and apply them to our lives.

Bible Reading: James 1:22-25

ACTION POINT: I will not neglect God's Word but will consider it a necessary ingredient to the life of the Spirit — supernatural living.

He Gives Special Abilities

"Now God gives us many kinds of special abilities, but it is the same Holy Spirit who is the source of them all" (1 Corinthians 12:4).

The late Dr. William Evans, famous Bible teacher and pulpit orator, was one of the most eloquent preachers I have ever heard. He serves as an example of a person who developed his spiritual gift.

Dr. Evans shared with me how he believed as a young man that he had been called of God to be a preacher. But he spoke in a high, squeaky, English cockney accent that was not particularly pleasant to the ear and certainly not conducive to preaching the most "joyful news ever announced."

So when young Evans told Dwight L. Moody (under whose ministry he had been influenced for Christ) about his calling to be a preacher, Moody unhesitatingly advised him, "Forget it! You don't have the ability to speak, and no one would listen to you."

But William Evans determined that he would become a great preacher for the glory of God. So, like Demosthenes of old, he began to practice speaking with pebbles in his mouth and to practice deep diaphragmatic breathing.

After several years, he developed a deep, resonant, bass voice — one of the most beautiful speaking voices I have ever heard. Wherever he went, congregations would pack the pews to hear him preach.

William Evans was an example of Philippians 2:13 in action. Did he have the spiritual gift of preaching? Of course he did! But it did not come to him overnight. He had to work long and hard, by faith, and in the power of the Holy Spirit, to develop his spiritual gift.

Philippians 2:13 reminds us that whatever God calls us to do He will enable us to do. Be assured that you do not need to depend on your own abilities to serve Him.

Bible Reading: 1 Corinthians 12:5-11

ACTION POINT: Instead of spending fruitless time searching for my spiritual gifts, I will depend on the Holy Spirit to guide me, apply myself diligently to excel in whatever He leads me to do and trust God for a fruitful life and witness.

Yours Is the Kingdom

"So don't be afraid, little flock. For it gives your Father great happiness to give you the Kingdom" (Luke 12:32).

Do you like the picture, as I do, of being a part of God's little flock? That makes Him our shepherd, of course, and it makes us His sheep. How apt a picture!

Often, I am sure, most of us must seem to wander like lost sheep — not knowing which way to turn. It is at such times, in particular, that I need to see the Lord Jesus Christ as my great Shepherd, tenderly watching over me in the midst of every kind of heartache and burden.

In Judea, it was common to see men tending sheep, looking over the flocks by day and by night. The shepherd watched over them, defended them, provided for them, led them to green pastures and beside still waters.

Jesus was — and is — the Good Shepherd. His flock was relatively small. Few really followed Him, compared to the multitude who ignored Him. Though small in number, they were not to fear because God was their Friend. He would provide for them. He purposed to give them the kingdom, and they had nothing to fear.

Today, we are a part of a large and growing flock with a great and loving Shepherd. Just to know that He watches over us — cares for us — is joy supreme.

Bible Reading: Luke 12:28-34

ACTION POINT: During the day I will deliberately look up into God's heaven several times to see that great Shepherd of the sheep, the Lord Jesus Christ.

He Honors the Humble

"For everyone who tries to honor himself shall be humbled: and he who humbles himself shall be honored" (Luke 14:11).

At times I am respectfully amused at the repetition of certain themes in the Word of God — repeated over and over again so that you and I will not forget the importance of the message. This is one of those principles.

Many missionaries have given up honor, acclaim and success at home in obedience to God's call upon their lives. Perhaps to their surprise, God has honored them in many ways despite the fact that they purposely gave up all rights to such honor.

In every field of endeavor, the principle is true. Most men who seek genuine acclaim are thoroughly humbled along the way. Conversely, most people who humble themselves as a part of their commitment to Jesus Christ and His service are eventually honored.

I have seen this truth fulfilled on numerous occasions in the work of Campus Crusade for Christ to which the Lord has called me. Many young people have stepped into unsung roles of service for their Master. God has honored them not only with fruit for their hire, but also with a measure of acclaim they never would have achieved otherwise.

It is a part of God's plan to abase the proud and raise up the humble. Our goal should be committed service for the Savior. We should let Him take care of the honoring and the humbling.

Bible Reading: Matthew 23:5-12

ACTION POINT: I'll recognize anew today that the only good thing about me — and about any believer — is the reality of my relationship with the Lord Jesus Christ through the indwelling person of the Holy Spirit.

Bread of Life

"Jesus replied, 'I am the Bread of Life. No one coming to Me will ever be hungry again. Those believing in Me shall never thirst'" (John 6:35).

What would it be like never to be hungry — never to be thirsty?

Even in affluent America, you and I — and perhaps most people — have felt the pangs of hunger and thirst, if only for a brief period. Jesus is telling us here that, spiritually speaking, we need never be hungry or thirsty again.

But how is that possible?

As the bread of life — the support of spiritual life — His doctrines give life and peace to the soul.

In Eastern countries, especially, there are vast deserts and often a great lack of water. By nature, the soul is like a traveler wandering through such a desert. Thirsting for happiness, seeking it everywhere and finding it not, he looks in all directions and tries all objects — in vain.

St. Augustine expressed this hunger for God in the following prayer, "Thou hast made us for Thyself, O God, and our hearts are restless until they find their rest in Thee."

When we drink of the water that is Christ, we become satisfied — and need never thirst again. As we continue to grow in grace, which comes only by feasting on His Word, we find a never-ending pattern of satisfaction with Him and all that concerns Him.

The principle is clear: As you and I feed on the Word of God and its rich truths, we are satisfying a spiritual hunger and thirst that could never be satisfied otherwise. Hungering and thirsting after righteousness, on the other hand, is also a daily necessity if we are really to grow in grace. The truths are not contradictory, but are complementary.

Bible Reading: Matthew 5:1-6

ACTION POINT: My daily manna and drink shall come from the living Word, our Lord Jesus Christ, and His holy inspired written word, the Bible, enabling me to live the supernatural life.

Trusting Is God's Gift

"Because of His kindness you have been saved through trusting Christ. And even trusting is not of yourselves; it too is a gift from God. Salvation is not a reward for the good we have done, so none of us can take any credit for it" (Ephesians 2:8,9).

Joe had asked Jesus to come into his life many times but was never sure of his salvation. "How can I be sure I'm a Christian and will go to heaven when I die?" he asked.

I explained that it was not enough to ask Jesus to come to live within us and forgive our sins. We must believe that He will do exactly what He promised to do. By faith, we must be able to say, "I know that Jesus is the Son of God, that He died on the cross for my sins, that He was raised from the dead and that He will come into my life and change me if I ask Him to. I know that He will make me His child and never leave me because all of these are promises from God's holy, inspired Word. Therefore, I believe the promise of Ephesians 2:8,9 — that I attain salvation through trust in Christ."

Through the years I have seen thousands of individuals profess faith in Christ after hearing or reading John 1:12, (KJV) "But as many as received Him, to them He gave the right to become children of God," and Revelation 3:20, where Jesus promised, "Behold, I stand at the door and knock; if any one hears My voice and opens the door, I will come in to him" (NAS). But not everyone with whom I have prayed has received assurance of salvation. The reason? It is not enough to ask Christ into our lives; we must *believe* His promise, "For by grace you have been saved through faith" (Ephesians 2:8, NAS).

Bible Reading: 1 Peter 1:3-9

ACTION POINT: Have I been asking Jesus Christ into my life frequently through the years, but am not sure He is there, not sure of eternal life, or that I would go to heaven if I died today? If so, I will pray, "Right now, Lord Jesus, whatever may have taken place in my life prior to this moment, I want to declare that I believe in You as my Savior and wish to follow You as my Lord. So, for the last time, I invite You to come into my life. Forgive my sins; cleanse me; make me the kind of person You want me to be. By faith in You and in the authority of Your inspired Word, I now acknowledge that You live within me, and I believe Your promise, 'I will never desert you, nor will I ever forsake you.'* Therefore, I will never insult You by asking You to come into my life again, but will hereafter thank You daily that You indwell me, that I have eternal life and that through the enabling of Your power I can live a supernatural life. *Hebrews 13:5, NAS.

He Has Not Deserted Me

"And He who sent Me is with Me — He has not deserted Me — for I always do those things that are pleasing to Him" (John 8:29).

If we have a conscience free of offense, and if we have evidence that we please God, it matters little if men oppose us or what others may think of us. "Enoch, before his translation, had this testimony — that he pleased God."

It would not be fair for you or me to profess ignorance in this matter of pleasing God. If we had never known before, we know now that it comes from doing always those things He commands — which of course are the things that please Him.

Jesus is saying here, among other things, that God is with Him in the working of miracles. Though men had forsaken and rejected Him, yet God stayed by Him and worked in and through Him.

In the same way, God has made it possible for us to please Him by giving us His Holy Spirit to indwell, enable and empower us for service. With the available enablement, we are without excuse in the matter of doing the "greater things" He has promised for those who love and serve Him.

What better goal for today, tomorrow and all our coming days than to seek to please Him?

Bible Reading: John 8:25-28

ACTION POINT: So that Christ might be magnified in my body, whether by life or by death, I will seek to do only those things today which please Him.

You Will Be Different

"Therefore, if any man be in Christ, he is a new creature; old things are passed away; behold, all things are become new" (2 Corinthians 5:17, KJV).

A prominent businessman, elder in a prestigious church, was impatient with "narrow-minded, born-again Christians." "I am a Christian," he said, "but I have never been born again, and frankly I'm not interested. We emphasize more important issues in my church."

When I read the third chapter of John with him and explained that there is only one kind of biblical Christian, the one who is "born again," and that no other kind of "Christian" can enter into the kingdom of God according to the words of Jesus, the light suddenly went on. With this new insight he readily received Christ as his Savior and Lord.

A caterpillar is an ugly, hairy, earthbound worm — until it weaves a cocoon about its body. Then an amazing transformation takes place. Out of that cocoon emerges a beautiful butterfly — a new creature, able to live on another plane, to soar into the heavens. So it is with man.

John 3 records Jesus' explanation of how one becomes a new creature. Nicodemus, a ruler of the Jews who tried to adhere meticulously to every detail of the law, had come to Jesus for counsel.

"'Rabbi, we know that You have come from God as a teacher; for no one can do these signs that You do unless God is with him.' Jesus answered and said to him, 'Truly, truly, I say to you, unless one is born again, he cannot see the kingdom of God'" (John 3:2,3, NAS).

Puzzled, Nicodemus asked, "How can a man be born when he is old? He cannot enter a second time into his mother's womb and be born, can he?" (John 3:4, NAS). Then Jesus explained that physical birth alone does not qualify anyone to enter the kingdom of God. Since His is a spiritual kingdom, we must experience spiritual birth.

Bible Reading: Romans 6:4-14.

ACTION POINT: I will read John's gospel, chapter three, meditating especially on the first eight verses, and will consider again my relationship with the Lord. If I should die today, I want to be sure I would go to heaven, and through the enabling of the Holy Spirit I want to begin living the supernatural life.

See God's Glory

"Jesus saith unto her, 'Said I not unto thee, that, if thou wouldest believe, thou shouldest see the glory of God?'" (John 11:40, KJV).

How wonderful to behold the glory of God! And in varying degrees you and I have the capability and opportunity of doing that very thing!

Jesus here, of course, is talking to Martha about her brother Lazarus, whom He was just about to raise from the dead. The message is plain: "Because you believed, Martha, you will see the glory of God in the raising of Lazarus."

Because you and I dare to believe God today, against all evidence and appearances to the contrary, He will let us see something of His glory. Just what is meant by that?

Most scholars agree that the glory of God, in this context at least, refers to the power and goodness displayed in the resurrection. That holds endless possibilities of fulfillment.

Amazing, isn't it, that the simple matter of believing often is so difficult for the *believer,* as we are called? "Ye receive not, because ye ask not." "According to your faith be it unto you." "Ye receive not because ye ask amiss."

May our Lord increase our faith by driving us into His Word, since "faith comes by hearing, and hearing by His Word."

Bible Reading: John 11:35-44

ACTION POINT: I truly desire to experience the glory of God in my life. To this end I will, through the enabling of the Holy Spirit, live a life of faith and obedience.

You Can Be Sure

*"And how can we be sure that we belong to Him? By looking within
ourselves: are we really trying to do what He wants us to? Someone
may say, 'I am a Christian; I am on my way to heaven; I belong to
Christ.' But if he doesn't do what Christ tells him to do, he is a liar.
But those who do what Christ tells them to will learn to love God
more and more. That is the way to know whether or not you are a
Christian. Anyone who says he is a Christian should live as Christ
did"* (1 John 2:3-6).

I frequently counsel with people who
assure me that they are Christians,
but their life-styles betray their profession. In fact, Jesus refers to this kind
of person in His parable of the wheat
and tares (Matthew 13:24-30).

"I never knew you; depart from me,"
He will say to people whose profession
of Christian faith is insincere (Matthew
7:23, NAS). According to the Word of
God, these people are confused, and we
do them a great injustice if we do not
hold before them the mirror of God's
Word. Our Scripture portion today is
one of the most effective passages to
help open their eyes.

If there has not been a difference in
your life-style since you professed faith
in Christ; if, even in your failure and
sin — and we all fail and sin at times
— you do not have a desire to obey
God and live a life pleasing to Him, it
is quite possible that the new birth has
not taken place in your life. Test
yourself if you are not sure; if you have
not done so, you can experience the new
birth simply by receiving Christ into
your heart today. This applies more
directly to carnal Christians.

Bible Reading: 1 John 3:18-24

ACTION POINT: To be absolutely certain of my relationship with Jesus
Christ, I will take spiritual inventory of my life and seek to ascertain whether
my life-style is consistent with that of the true believer and follower of Christ.

Path of Blessing

"You know these things — now do them! That is the path of blessing" (John 13:17).

These words of Jesus are as binding on us who follow Him today as they were on the disciples who actually heard Him speak them.

You will remember the setting. Jesus had just washed the feet of His disciples as an example of servanthood that He wanted them to observe and to learn. And that is the lesson we do well to ponder: service for others.

Except for the good we can do others, in the power and with the enabling of God's Holy Spirit, what really is the purpose of our being left here on earth? And miracle of miracles, when we do that which is right— serve others, in Christ's name — our own personal problems seem minor and relatively unimportant.

Loneliness and depression have their quickest cure in the realm of helping others. No matter what our problem — physical, spiritual or material — it is quite likely we can find others whose plights are worse. By giving of ourselves in their behalf, we forget about our own troubles, which are usually resolved in the process.

Simple, is it not, that we are to do those things the Lord commands us to do? When we read and study His Word, we can find out just what they are.

Bible Reading: John 13:12-16

ACTION POINT: I will not be content with just admiring the example Jesus has set before us, but will seek to obey His commands to be a doer of the Word as well.

Never Alone

"No I will not abandon you or leave you as orphans in the storm. I will come to you" (John 14:18).

"I feel so alone," Bev said, "with my husband gone and all my children married. Sometimes I can hardly bear the pain, the anguish. At times it's as though I am about to suffocate — I am so lonely!"

Bev was in her late 70s. Her husband was dead, and the other members of her family had become involved in their own careers and activities. Though they loved her, they were so busy they seldom saw her to express that love.

I shared with her the good news of the one who loved her so much that He died on the cross for her and paid the penalty for her sins, the one who promised to come to her and, once He came, never to leave her.

There in the loneliness of her living room, she bowed with me in prayer and invited the risen living Christ to take up residence in her life, to forgive her, to cleanse her, to make her whole, to make her a child of God. When she lifted her face, her cheeks were moist with tears of repentance and her heart was made new with joy.

"I feel so different," she said. "Already I feel enveloped with the sense of God's presence, His love and His peace."

As the months passed, it became increasingly evident that she was not alone. He who was with her had been faithful to His promise never to leave her.

Do you feel deserted, alone, rejected? Do you have problems with your family, work, school or health? Whatever may be your need, Jesus is waiting to make His presence as real to you as if He were with you in his physical body.

There are five things that I would encourage you to do to enhance the realization of His presence. (1) Meditate upon His Word day and night. (2) Confess all known sin. (3) Aggressively obey His commandments. (4) Talk to Him about everything as you would to your dearest friend, as indeed He really is. (5) Tell everyone who will listen about Him so that they too can experience with you the supernatural life which comes only from allowing the supernatural power of the indwelling Christ to be reflected in and through you.

Bible Reading: Psalm 68:3-6

ACTION POINT: In order to enhance the Lord's presence in my life, I will practice the five recommendations knowing that as I walk in this vital personal relationship with the risen Christ, the supernatural qualities that characterize His life will become more and more apparent in mine.

Still Present With You

"In just a little while I will be gone from the world, but I will still be present with you. For I will live again — and you will too" (John 14:19)

In this one verse the whole gospel story is expressed, for Jesus is speaking on the day before His death, foretelling just what will happen then and thereafter.

And what He has to say should bring renewed joy and comfort and peace to our hearts in the midst of a chaotic world that perhaps includes an element of chaos even in the home or at the office or in the classroom.

Yes, He was gone from the world to assume His rightful position at the right hand of His heavenly Father — after His death and resurrection. Now He is present with us in the person of His indwelling Holy Spirit, who lives within every believer. And to the extent we give Him control of our hearts and lives, He empowers and enables us to live a supernatural, abundant life.

He prophesies His resurrection — "I will live again" — the joyous truth of which makes possible His final promise to His disciples, "You will live too."

Jesus is saying, in effect, that the life of the Christian depends on that of Christ. They are united, and if they were separated, the Christian could not enjoy spiritual life here nor eternal joy hereafter. But He lives! And because He lives, we too shall live — forever, with Him throughout the endless ages of eternity!

Bible Reading: Romans 5:6-11

ACTION POINT: Because Jesus died, arose and now lives at God's right hand while at the same time living in me, I can live the abundant, *supernatural* life today, and forever!

You Are Indwelt by God Himself!

"Haven't you yet learned that your body is the home of the Holy Spirit God gave you, and that He lives within you? Your own body does not belong to you" (1 Corinthians 6:19).

The Bible teaches that there is one God manifested in three persons — Father, Son and Holy Spirit — and that God lives within everyone who has received Christ.

One of the most important truths I have learned as a Christian is that this omnipotent, holy, righteous, loving, triune God — our heavenly Father, our risen Savior and Holy Spirit, Creator of heaven and earth — comes to dwell within sinful man at the moment he receives Christ! And, through Christ's blood, sinful man is made righteous at the moment of the new birth!

Meditate with me upon what this means. When you fully grasp that the God of love, grace, wisdom, power and majesty dwells within you, it will revolutionize your life. That might well be, for you, the beginning step of a supernatural life. Recognizing that God's Holy Spirit dwells within you waiting to release His matchless love and mighty power is absolutely awesome.

You are His temple, and if you invite Him to, He will actually walk around in your body, think with your mind, love with your heart, speak with your lips and continue to seek and save the lost, for whom He gave His life 2,000 years ago. Incredible! Incomprehensible to our finite minds, this truth is so clearly emphasized in the Word of God and demonstrated in the lives of all who trust and obey Him that there can be no doubt. If you have received Christ, God — Father, Son and Holy Spirit — now indwells you and your body has become His temple.

Bible Reading: Acts 2:37-40

ACTION POINT: I will begin every day by acknowledging that my body is a temple of God. I will invite the Lord Jesus Christ to walk around in my body, think with my mind, love with my heart, speak with my lips and continue to seek and save the lost through me. I will invite the Holy Spirit to empower and enable me to live a holy, supernatural life and be a fruitful witness of God's love and grace — that my life will bring praise, honor, worship and glory to God the Father.

He Brings You Comfort

Jesus said, "But I will send you the Comforter — the Holy Spirit, the source of all truth. He will come to you from the Father and will tell you all about Me" (John 15:26).

For years I was among the more than 95 percent of church members who, according to various surveys, are not knowledgeable concerning the person and ministry of the Holy Spirit. Then God, in His gracious love and wisdom, showed me how simple it is to release His power into and through my life by faith, just as years before I had received assurance of my salvation by faith.

If I had only one message to proclaim to the Christian world, it would be this: how to know and experience, moment by moment, day by day, the reality of the fullness and power of the Holy Spirit. Everything that has to do with the Christian life involves God the Holy Spirit, the third person of the Trinity.

We are born again through the ministry of the Spirit (John 3). The Holy Spirit inspired men of old to record the holy, inspired Word of God (2 Peter 1:21). Only those who are filled, controlled and empowered with His presence can comprehend what He communicated to those writers centuries ago, which is the message that He has for us today (1 Corinthians 2:14).

We cannot live holy lives apart from the Holy Spirit, for He alone can produce the fruit of the Spirit (Galatians 5:22,23) in our lives. We cannot pray intelligently unless the Holy Spirit enables us, for He makes intercession for us with groanings too deep for words (Romans 8:26). We have no power to witness for Christ apart from His power (Acts 1:8). Only the Holy Spirit can enable us to live a supernatural life.

Bible Reading: John 14:16-21

ACTION POINT: I determine to learn everything I can about the Holy Spirit. I will refer to the concordance in my Bible and study every reference to Him in the Scriptures, and ask my pastor, or other spiritual leaders in whom I have confidence, to recommend books on the person and ministry of the Holy Spirit. I will not be satisfied with anything less than the love, joy, peace, victory and power that comes from living daily in the fullness of the Holy Spirit.

His Life in Us

"Jesus said, 'I will only reveal Myself to those who love Me and obey Me. The Father will love them too, and We will come to them and live with them. Anyone who doesn't obey Me doesn't love Me' " (John 14:23,24).

Millions of Christians throughout the world profess their love for Christ each week by attending church services, singing songs, studying their Bibles, attending prayer meetings, etc. Yet, all the talk in the world will never convince anyone that you or I truly love the Lord unless we obey His commandments.

How can we know His commandments unless we study His Word? When we study His Word, how can we comprehend what He is saying unless the Holy Spirit illumines our minds and teaches us? It is God the Holy Spirit who inspired the writing of His holy Word through holy men. He alone can help us understand the true meaning of the Scripture and enable us to obey His commands.

Thus, the reality of Christ abiding in us is made possible through a supernatural enabling of the Holy Spirit who came to glorify Christ and through whose indwelling presence the Lord Jesus will reveal Himself to us.

Is Jesus Christ a reality in your life? If not, it is quite likely that you are not demonstrating your love for Him by studying His Word and obeying His commandments.

Bible Reading: John 14:15-22

ACTION POINT: With the help of the Holy Spirit who enables me to live the supernatural life, I will endeavor to demonstrate my love for Christ by studying His Word and obeying His commandments.

God's Word Works

"As the rain and snow come down from heaven and stay upon the ground to water the earth, and cause the grain to grow and to produce seed for the farmer and bread for the hungry, so also is My Word. I send it out and it always produces fruit. It shall accomplish all I want it to, and prosper everywhere I send it" (Isaiah 55:10,11).

An angry student leader confronted me at the conclusion of my message to a student meeting at UCLA. "You have no right to impose your views upon these students," he exclaimed. "You will confuse them. They are easily influenced and might respond to some of your religious views which I totally reject."

I learned that he was the Communist leader on the campus and did not believe in God or the Scriptures. I invited him to our home for dinner and as we ate, we talked about many things of a general nature, nothing controversial. After we had finished our dessert, I reached over and picked up my Bible and said that I would like to read something very important to him. He resisted, saying, "I don't want to hear anything from the Bible. I don't believe it. It is a ridiculous book filled with all kinds of myths, contradictions and exaggerations."

I would have, made similar statements during my years of agnosticism. Not because I knew such statements to be true, but because I was simply parroting what others had told

me — I did not really know the facts.

I said, "If you don't mind, I would like to read you something anyway," and so I turned to John 1:1. "In the beginning was the Word, and the Word was with God, and the Word was God" (KJV). I continued through the 14th verse. Then I turned to Colossians 1 and Hebrews 1, reading similar portions identifying Christ as the Creator, the visible expression of the invisible God. I concluded with 1 John 2:22,23.

As I read each passage, he asked if he could read it for himself. The initial flash of anger soon turned to interest and then to acceptance and finally he was like a repentant child experiencing the warmth and love of the Father's embrace. He surrendered all resistance. As he stood to leave that evening, I asked him to sign our guest book. He wrote his name, address and these words: "The night of decision."

Bible Reading: Isaiah 55:6-13

ACTION POINT: Today I will share a portion of God's Word with someone who does not know our Savior with the prayer that he, too, will come to know Him and experience with me the supernatural life which is our heritage in Christ.

Life's Greatest Investment

"And anyone who gives up his home, brothers, sisters, father, mother, wife, children, or property, to follow Me, shall receive a hundred times as much in return [in this life], and shall have eternal life" (Matthew 19:29).

I can tell you on the authority of God's Word and from personal experience and observation that this promise is true. From my own commitment — made more than 30 years ago — and after having spoken with hundreds of Christian leaders and humble servants of God around the world, and observed the thousands whom I have counseled, I do not know of anyone whom God is using in any significant way who would say that this spiritual law has not been true in his life.

The time to invest your time, talent and treasure for Christ and His kingdom is now. The powerful tide of secular humanism, atheism, materialism, communism and other anti-God forces is threatening to engulf the world. From the human perspective, on the basis of what I see and hear, I could be very pessimistic about the future freedom of mankind.

On the contrary, I am very optimistic, not on the basis of what I see and hear, but on the basis of what I believe God is saying to my heart and of what I am observing that He is doing throughout the world. I am constantly reminded and assured, "Greater is He that is in you, than he that is in the world" (1 John 4:4, KJV). Satan and his demonic forces were defeated 2,000 years ago.

Do you want a safe formula for success? Then recognize and practice the following:

First, remember that everything entrusted to our care actually belongs to God. We are His stewards here on earth.

Second, God does not want us to hoard His blessings.

Third, "As you sow, you reap."

Fourth, invest generously — above the tithe in time, talent and treasure.

Fifth, invest supernaturally — by faith.

Bible Reading: Matthew 25:35-40

ACTION POINT: Recognizing myself as God's steward, I will prayerfully seek to learn what He would have me do to maximize my life for His glory through the investment of my time, talent and treasure.

A Greater Harvest

"He has already tended you by pruning you back for greater strength and usefulness by means of the commands I gave you" (John 15:3).

My friend was in the process of pruning his vineyard, and it appeared to me — in my limited knowledge of vineyards — that the pruning was too severe. Only the main stump remained. I inquired, "Why have you pruned the vine back to just the main stump?"

"Because," he said, "that is the way to ensure that it will produce a greater harvest. Otherwise the nourishment flowing up through the roots would be dissipated in keeping the vines alive. It could not produce the maximum number of grapes."

It is my regular prayer that God will keep both me as an individual and the movement of which I am a part well pruned that we may not waste time, energy, talent and money producing beautiful foliage with no fruit. Our subjection to that pruning can be either voluntary or reluctant. How much better it is for us to invite the Lord to do the pruning than to have the pruning forced upon us over our protests.

The best possible way to cooperate in God's pruning is to study His Word. Memorize and meditate upon His truths, obey His commandments and claim His promises. Jesus taught the disciples personally, by word and model, over a period of more than three years. Yet, Judas betrayed the Lord and committed suicide and the others denied Him and deserted Him at the cross. It was not until the Holy Spirit came upon them at Pentecost that their lives were really transformed and the things He had taught them became a reality to them.

The same Holy Spirit who transformed their lives and gave them the courage to die as martyrs proclaiming God's truth dwells within you and me. He wants to bear much fruit through us as He did through them. I encourage you to make that time, when you study the commands that Jesus gave us and apply His truths to your heart, the most important part of your day.

Bible Reading: John 15:1-5

ACTION POINT: I will cooperate with the Holy Spirit in the pruning process of my life by spending much time studying, memorizing and meditating on the Word of God, applying its truths to my life as I claim the supernatural resources of the living Christ for supernatural living.

No Longer Slaves

"And you are My friends if you obey Me. I no longer call you slaves, for a master doesn't confide in his slaves; now you are My friends, proved by the fact that I have told you everything the Father told Me" (John 15:14,15).

How many really close friends do you and I have? Not many, I think you will agree, for a close friend is one in whom you confide regularly, who knows you just as you are and loves you just the same.

So it is with our heavenly Friend, the one who "sticks closer than a brother." And how do we earn the right to become that kind of intimate friend? Simply by obeying His commands, "which are not grievous," but really are necessary to keep us in the straight and narrow path and to give us a happy, blessed life.

In a sense, of course, we are still His bondslaves, His servants, but He deigns to call us His friends if we love Him enough to obey His commands. And He proves His friendship by sharing with us all that the Father has shared with Him. What greater Friend could we have?

Jesus not only called His disciples friends, but He also treated them as friends. He opened His mind to them, made known His plans and acquainted them with the plan of His coming, His death, His resurrection and ascension. He followed this proof of His friendship with the actual title of *friend*.

Oh, that you and I might see Him today truly as our Friend — one who sticks closer than a brother or sister or mother or father.

Bible Reading: John 15:11-17

ACTION POINT: As I take inventory of my real friends today, I will especially include the one Friend above all friends, the Lord Jesus Christ, the source of the supernatural life which God has commanded me to live.

He Can Be Found

"And ye shall seek Me, and find Me, when ye shall search for Me with all your heart" (Jeremiah 29:13, KJV).

Halfhearted efforts, I have found from personal experience, seldom bring success and victory. The difference between a successful person and a failure is that the successful person is always willing to do more than the unsuccessful person is willing to do.

In spiritual matters, in particular, this is true, as evidenced scores of times in the Word of God. This is one of the most expressive of those passages that major on this theme.

Another is: "Blessed are they that hunger and thirst after righteousness, for they shall be filled" (Matthew 5:6, KJV).

But one point needs to be made abundantly clear: This promise is not only to the unbeliever, though it is often taken that way. It applies equally to the believer, who may be searching after God for a variety of reasons.

The key word here, of course is *heart.* "As [a man] thinketh in his *heart,* so is he" (Proverbs 23:7, KJV). "Out of the abundance of the *heart* the mouth speaketh" (Matthew 12:34, KJV).

What do you need from God today? Wisdom? Peace? Courage? Love? To find God in such a real way that you know He is meeting that need for you, you must really mean business with Him. Then He will indeed do business for you.

A doubter, or an unbeliever, reading this has a wonderful assurance: He can find God if he truly seeks Him with his whole heart.

Bible Reading: Jeremiah 29:10-14

ACTION POINT: I'll begin right at home by personally seeking God for myself *with my whole heart,* and I will remind others how God can be real to them.

Reasons for Trials

"He... comforts and strengthens us in our hardships and trials. And why does He do this? So that when others are troubled, needing our sympathy and encouragement, we can pass on to them this same help and comfort God has given us" (2 Corinthians 1:3,4).

For two years, Annette had suffered through the agony of her beloved husband's terminal cancer. Meanwhile, their only son had been drawn into drug addiction through the influence of an undesirable group of students in the local high school. She was devastated. Her whole life was filled with heartache and sorrow. She had nothing to live for. Then a neighbor told her of Jesus — how He could give her peace of heart and peace of mind and could provide the purpose she needed in her life. He could even change her son.

So Annette received the wonderful gift of God's love, the Lord Jesus Christ, and began to pray for her son. At first he was antagonistic, but gradually he became aware of the dramatic transformation in his mother, and in answer to her prayers, along with those of her new-found friends in the local church, he too came to worship the Savior and make Him Lord of his life.

In the meantime, Annette was suffering great financial difficulty because of the huge doctor and hospital bills and her lack of ability to work during her husband's illness. But God wonderfully comforted and strengthened her so that now she can witness joyfully of His gracious mercy and faithfulness in her behalf. She and her son are ministering effectively to others who are experiencing heartache and tragedy similar to those which once plagued them.

Are you experiencing difficulties, sorrows, heartaches, disappointments? Ask the Lord to show you how to translate them into victories so that He can use you to be a blessing to those around you who are experiencing similar difficulties.

Bible Reading: 2 Corinthians 1:3-7

ACTION POINT: Knowing that God is faithful in His love and wisdom, I will trust the indwelling Holy Spirit for the power to accept the trial or adversity I face today, and will expect God to use it to comfort and help someone else through me.

Our Great Privilege

"And don't you realize that you also will perish unless you leave your evil ways and turn to God?" (Luke 13:3).

Today I sought to share the love and forgiveness of God through Jesus Christ with a taxi driver who reacted impatiently when I handed him a book which I had written, entitled "Jesus and the Intellectual." He flung it aside in contempt. I have seldom met anyone who appeared to be more angry and resentful of God than he was. I felt impressed to say to Him what Jesus said to the Galileans, "It is a matter of life and death what you do with Jesus Christ. There is a heaven and there is a hell. God loves you and cares for you. He wants you to come to Him and receive the gift of His only begotten Son through whom you can have forgiveness, life abundant and life eternal." From all appearances he could not have cared less.

That warning to the Galileans many years ago applies equally to nations and individuals today. If one truth in the Word of God is made abundantly clear, it is this: Repent or perish.

"It is because of this solemn fear of the Lord, which is ever present in our minds, that we work so hard to win others. God knows our hearts, that they are pure in this matter, and I hope that, deep within, you really know it too" (2 Corinthians 5:11).

As Christians we have the awesome responsibility and great privilege to tell everyone who will listen about Christ. Most of us would take great risk to save the life of a drowning child or to snatch up a toddler from the path of an automobile. Yet, most everyone who is living today will be dead in 100 years or less, but all men will live in heaven or hell for eternity. How much more important it is to tell men and women who are perishing without Christ of the loving Savior who cares and who is waiting to forgive if only they will surrender their lives to Him!

We must warn them and if we do not know how, it behooves us to learn how to share our faith. One method of witnessing is the use of the Four Spiritual Laws booklet. Anyone is capable of sharing this booklet with others — if not vocally, at least by handing it to someone.

If you are hesitant to witness vocally, why not begin by distributing literature like the Four Spiritual Laws booklet?

Bible Reading: Luke 13:1-5

ACTION POINT: I resolve with God's help, to begin to distribute Christian literature, especially the Word of God and materials that will help individuals to make definite commitments of their lives to Jesus Christ as Savior and Lord.

You Will Be Saved

"For if you tell others with your own mouth that Jesus Christ is your Lord, and believe in your own heart that God has raised Him from the dead, you will be saved" (Romans 10:9).

M any years ago, God clearly led me in the preparation, planning and production of a little booklet called the *Four Spiritual Laws*. Still widely used today, its total volume of copies to date might well be second only to the Bible itself. More than a billion copies have been distributed and one can reasonably conclude that many millions have received Christ as a result of reading its message.

In something so succinct, it of course was impossible to include all of the appropriate Scriptures under each of the four laws. This verse for today, Romans 10:9, is one of those that might have been used with Law Four, for it fits in well with the wording:

"We must individually *receive* Jesus Christ as Savior and Lord; then we can know and experience God's love and plan for our lives."

The three passages used (John 1:12; Ephesians 2:8,9; Revelation 3:20) clearly direct the seeker after God. And of course this verse in Romans clearly confirms all that the other passages affirm.

Two conditions precede salvation, the apostle Paul is saying to the church in Rome: (1) "Tell others with your own mouth that Jesus Christ is your Lord," and (2) "Believe in your own heart that God has raised Him from the dead." Simple, yet significant and meaningful, are these two preparatory steps.

As you share your faith with others today and in the days to come, recall with joy these two simple conditions that must be met.

Bible Reading: Romans 10:8-13

ACTION POINT: "Dear Lord, I thank You with all of my heart for the simplicity of the gospel and, with the enabling of the Holy Spirit, I will share this good news with all who will listen.

You Will Rejoice

"You have sorrow now, but I will see you again and then you will rejoice; and no one can rob you of that joy" (John 16:22).

Once you and I truly experience the joy of the Lord, no one can rob us of that joy!

That does not mean that we will never experience disappointment, sorrow or grief; but it does mean that deep down underneath it all is the joy that comes as a gift from God, the fruit of the Spirit. And that is the kind of joy that no one can take away.

Underneath the tears, the heartache, lies the calm, sweet peace that God gives *to those who walk in faith and obedience*. And that is a part of the joy that He promises.

Jesus' promise to see His disciples again, of course, refers to after the resurrection. "You will be so firmly persuaded that I have risen," He says to them, "and that I am the Messiah, that neither the threats nor the persecutions of men will ever be able to shake your faith, or produce doubt or unbelief and thus take away your joy."

Jesus' prediction, as we know, was remarkably fulfilled, for after He revealed Himself to them following the resurrection, not one of the apostles ever doubted for a moment that He had risen from the dead. No trial or persecution was able to shake their faith — so that their joy remained.

You and I have certainties of faith that are unshakable, and thus they produce joy — joy that will remain forever and ever.

Bible Reading: John 16:20-24

ACTION POINT: I will remember to praise and thank God for the unshakable joy that He alone gives.

More Than You Need

"God is able to make it up to you by giving you everything you need and more, so that there will not only be enough for your own needs, but plenty left over to give joyfully to others" (2 Corinthians 9:8).

One of the greatest discoveries that I have ever made in the Christian life is the law of sowing and reaping. Paul explains, beginning in his second letter to the Corinthians with the sixth verse of Chapter 9, "If you give little, you'll get little. A farmer who plants just a few seeds will harvest only a small crop, but if he plants much, he will reap much. Everyone must make up his own mind as to how much he should give. Don't force anyone to give more than he really wants to, for cheerful givers are the ones God prizes" (2 Corinthians 9:6,7).

I have several friends and colleagues who have joined with me in claiming this marvelous promise of God and in every case the blessings are abundant. People with modest incomes are able not only to give large sums of money, but also to enjoy a life-style that one could hardly expect even from individuals whose salaries were much more than theirs. It is a "loaves and fishes" kind of demonstration of God's faithfulness. You cannot outgive God. As someone put it, "I give to God by the spoonsful and He returns to me shovelsful."

Most believers have never discovered the joy and excitement of Christian stewardship. Always remember that God's graces are bestowed upon us, not that we may hoard them, but that we may pass them on to others.

The same principle of giving also applies to the giving of our time and our talent to the proclamation of the gospel. The more we give, the more we receive. Was God giving you an extra portion of love today, of joy, of patience, of encouragement, or peace? Pass it on. Has something exciting happened to you? He may have given that extra supply for you to pass on to others in need. By the same token, if your supply in any of these things is lacking, you need only ask. With your motivation of wanting to share with others, God will not delay in responding to your request.

Bible Reading: 2 Corinthians 9:6-11

ACTION POINT: In order to be a faithful steward of that which God has entrusted to me, I shall seek to share with others a generous portion of all that He gives to me, with special emphasis on the good news concerning our Lord Jesus Christ and the supernatural life which He gives.

A Prosperous Land

"If my people who are called by My name humble themselves and pray, and seek My face and turn from their wicked ways, then I will hear from heaven, will forgive their sin, and will heal their land" (2 Chronicles 7:14).

On April 29, 1980, 500,000 men and women gathered on the Washington Mall to fast and pray and claim this promise of God.

For years, I have had a growing conviction in my heart that, because the Supreme Court ruled that Bible reading and prayer in our schools is unconstitutional, our nation has turned more and more away from God — immorality has become the "new morality"; homosexuality has become the "alternate life-style"; drug addiction and alcoholism are no longer treated as evil; even violent criminals are being declared "not guilty by reason of insanity." The decaying of our society is evident on all sides.

One of the more alarming, documented facts is that the Soviet Union has been accelerating its production of armaments of war, including nuclear weapons. And through a massive move toward peace through disarmament and through neglect on the part of our leaders, we have allowed our military power to disintegrate to the point of vulnerability.

During the late '60s and '70s I genuinely believed that unless God supernaturally met with us and we repented as a nation and turned from our sin, the boast of Nikita S. Khrushchev, former head of the Soviet Union, "We will bury you!" could well come true. For this reason I agreed, along with Pat Robertson, founder and president of Christian Broadcasting Network, and John Gimenez, to cosponsor that great gathering on the Washington Mall.

As 500,000 people spent the day from early in the morning until late in the afternoon, praying, fasting and crying out to God, I sensed that God lifted my load. And, as I sat on the platform joining with my brothers and sisters from all over America, including millions who were joining with us in prayer over radio and television, God lifted the burden that had been on my heart for at least fifteen years. He gave me the assurance that the promise of 2 Chronicles 7:14 would be fulfilled as a direct result of our gathering on that day.

Since that time, there has been no question in my mind but what God heard our prayers and laid the groundwork for a dramatic turnaround in our nation.

Bible Reading: Leviticus 26:3-12

ACTION POINT: Claiming the promise of 2 Chronicles 7:14, I will pray for God's supernatural release of blessing and power upon this nation, that we might experience a continuous revival from each individual in the smallest community of America to our leaders in the halls of Congress, the Supreme Court and the White House.

When We Commit

"Commit everything you do to the Lord. Trust Him to help you do it and He will" (Psalm 37:5).

Janet remained after the student meeting for counsel.

"How can I commit everything I do to the Lord?" she inquired. "What is involved in a total commitment?"

I explained that mere words can be superficial and shallow, and even insulting to God. It is the commitment of our intellects, our emotions and our wills to do the will of God in every situation with the faith that we can, as He promised, trust Him to help us do whatever He calls us to do.

Sometimes I wonder if we really know the meaning of the word *commitment.* Paraphrasing an anonymous source:

We sing "Sweet Hour of Prayer" and are content with five or ten minutes a day. We sing "Onward Christian Soldiers" and wait to be drafted into His service. We sing "O For a Thousand Tongues to Sing" and don't use the one we have.

We sing "I Love to Tell the Story" but never witness to the love of Christ personally. We sing "We're Marching to Zion" but fail to march to worship or Sunday school. We sing "Cast Thy Burden on the Lord" and worry ourselves into a nervous breakdown.

We sing "The Whole Wide World for Jesus" and never invite our next-door neighbor to consider the claims of Christ. We sing "O Day of Rest and Gladness" and wear ourselves out traveling or cutting grass or playing golf on Sunday. We sing "Throw Out the Lifeline" and content ourselves with throwing out a fishing line.

Consistency is a wonderful word for the believer in Christ. Add to that the word *commitment* and you have a rare combination of supernatural enablements that result in a triumphant, fruitful life.

Bible Reading: Proverbs 3:5-10

ACTION POINT: Today I will commit everything I do to the Lord and trust Him to help me do what He calls me to do. Since He has called me to be His witness, I will trust Him to enable me to share His love and forgiveness through Christ with someone else today.

You Will Have Life

"But these are recorded so that you will believe that He is the Messiah, the Son of God, and that believing in Him you will have life" (John 20:31).

What a message you and I have to share. That is why John wrote this entire Gospel, so that we, first of all, might believe, but then also that we might share the good news with all who will listen.

"These are recorded" — the miracles presented in this gospel — so that we might believe. The goal of the book is two-fold: (1) to prove that Jesus was (is) the Messiah and (2) that all those who look at the proof might be convinced and thus find eternal life.

The miracles, facts, arguments, instructions and conversations — all are directed toward that end. John's goal (to demonstrate that Jesus is the Messiah), if kept steadily in view, will throw much light on the book. The argument is unasnswerable, framed after the strictest rules of reasoning, infinitely beyond the skill of man, and having throughout the clearest evidence of demonstration.

All Scripture is given to us for a purpose. The purpose of this particular passage is crystal clear; hence it demands some kind of response from those of us who truly believe. To know the truth is not enough. We must act on it, trusting the Lord of the harvest to make us sensitive and alert to the spiritual needs of those around us.

Bible Reading: John 3:9-15

ACTION POINT: I will seek to be sensitive to the spiritual needs of all with whom I have contact.

A Place Prepared for You

"And if I go and prepare a place for you, I will come again, and receive you unto Myself, that where I am, there ye may be also" (John 14:3, KJV).

Recently my 93-year-old father went to be with the Lord. Though I was saddened to realize that I would never see him again in this life, and I shed a few tears of sorrow for myself, at the same time I rejoiced in the knowledge that to be absent from the body is to be present with the Lord.

My father is now rejoicing in the presence of our wonderful God and Savior. One day I shall join with him, my mother (who is still living at 93), all my brothers and sisters who have declared their faith in Christ, and multitudes of other loved ones, friends and saints to spend eternity in that place where "eye hath not seen, ear hath not heard...what God hath prepared for those who love Him."

"I cannot think what we shall find to do in heaven," mused Martin Luther. "No change, no work, no eating, no drinking, nothing to do."

"Yes," responded a friend, " 'Lord, show us the Father, and it sufficeth us.' "

"Why, of course," said Luther, "that sight will give us quite enough to do!"

Joy of joys, you and I not only have been given purpose and power for living the supernatural, abundant life — by the indwelling Holy Spirit — but we have also been promised a place in His presence when this life is over. And, as Luther realized, we will then worship Him face to face throughout the endless ages of eternity.

We need not know exactly what heaven will be like; we need only know who will be there — our Lord Jesus Christ Himself. That assurance and anticipation should motivate us to live the kind of supernatural life that burdens and concerns us about the needs of others, moment by moment, day by day.

Bible Reading: John 14:27-31

ACTION POINT: Today I will meditate on the glory and beauty of my heavenly Father and my eternal home where I shall worship and have fellowship with my Lord throughout eternity. I will encourage loved ones, friends and strangers alike to prepare to go there also when their work on earth is done.

Judging the World

"For He has set a day for justly judging the world by the man He has appointed, and has pointed Him out by bringing Him back to life again" (Acts 17:31).

Why does God command men and women to repent? And why does He expect you and me to relay His message to them?

The answer is simple: because "He has set a day for justly judging the world." And if people refuse to be penitent and thus become pardoned, they must be condemned.

"Justly," of course, can be interpreted: "according to the rules of strict justice." And who will do the judging? The man God has appointed – His only Son, Jesus Christ; the one He has pointed out to us clearly by bringing Him back to life again.

Jesus, you will remember, declared that He would judge the nations (John 5:25,26 and Matthew chapter 25). God confirmed the truth of those declarations by raising Him from the dead – giving His sanction to what the Lord Jesus had said, for surely God would not work a miracle in behalf of an impostor.

What comfort and help can you and I receive from these truths today? Surely, this is a reminder that God is still on the throne; He is in control; nothing is going on in the world without His knowledge and consent.

Further, we are reminded of God's justice, which assures us that He will always do right in behalf of His children. That falls right in line with Romans 8:28, of course, which concerns all things working together for our good.

Bible Reading: Psalm 9:7-10

ACTION POINT: World turmoil will not upset me, for I know the God who sits on the throne – and who rules over all.

He Welcomes You

"Come unto Me, all ye that labour and are heavy laden, and I will give you rest. Take My yoke upon you, and learn of Me; for I am meek and lowly in heart: and ye shall find rest unto your souls. For My yoke is easy, and My burden is light" (Matthew 11:28-30, KJV).

Several years ago I had the privilege of meeting with a world-famous theologian. This great scholar had denied the deity of Christ and had taught thousands of seminarians who had studied under him that Jesus was only a great man and a great teacher. He was not God incarnate, and surely could not forgive sin and provide rest to His followers. Yet, in a unique way God had created a hunger in his heart for truth and for two years he had done an in-depth study of the life of Jesus.

As we met together in his office, he asked, "What do you tell a student when he asks you how to become a Christian?"

When I realized he was sincere, I proceeded to explain why I believe Jesus Christ is the Son of God and why all men everywhere need Him as their Savior and Lord, and how anyone who wants to can receive Him.

"I am persuaded," he said after a while, "that no honest person who is willing to consider the overwhelming evidence for the deity of Christ can deny that He is the Son of God."

This great scholar, who had denied the deity of Christ all his life and encouraged millions of others to think likewise, bowed in prayer and received Christ into his life as Savior and Lord.

Jesus Christ stands out clearly as the one supernaturally unique figure in all of history. He is incomparable. He invites all who will to experience His love and forgiveness. "Come unto Me." He welcomes "all you that labour and are heavy laden, and I will give you rest . . . My yoke is easy, and My burden is light."

Bible Reading: Matthew 11:23-27

ACTION POINT: Through the enabling of the Holy Spirit, I will seek to make sure that every loved one, every friend, every contact I make today is fully aware of the fact that God loves him, that Jesus Christ died for him and will welcome him into His family through a simple act of faith. I will tell him that He offers peace and rest — from life's burdens — to all who follow Him in faith and obedience.

Prayer Has Great Power

"Admit your faults to one another and pray for each other so that you may be healed. The earnest prayer of a righteous man has great power and wonderful results" (James 5:16).

"I can take my telescope and look millions and millions of miles into space," said the great scientist Sir Isaac Newton, "but I can lay it aside and go into my room, shut the door, get down on my knees in earnest prayer, and see more of heaven and get closer to God than I can assisted by all the telescopes and material agencies on earth."

Among many other things, the carnal Christian is characterized by a poor prayer life. The spiritual Christian, on the other hand, is charcterized by an effective fruitful prayer life.

Prayer is simply communicating with God by listening as well as talking. The acrostic ACTS is helpful in recalling the various components of effective prayer, though the order is not necessarily rigid.

"A" is for *adoration* — worship of God, first for who He is; and second for all of His benefits. He alone is worthy of our adoration and praise.

"C" stands for *confession*. "If we confess our sins, He is faithful and just to forgive us our sins, and to cleanse us from all unrighteousness." Sometimes this component should take priority, especially for the unbeliever and the disobedient believer, because God does not hear the prayers of the disobedient until they confess. "If I regard iniquity in my heart, the Lord will not hear me" (Psalms 66:18, KJV).

"T" is for *thanksgiving* — gratitude to God for His blessings.

"S" represents *supplication* — expressing our petitions to God for individuals and specific things and events.

Bible Reading: James 5:13-18

ACTION POINT: I will claim great power and wonderful results for supernatural living by a righteous life and by giving priority to prayer. I will remember to bring my adoration, confession, thanksgiving and supplication to God throughout the day.

You Can Trust Him

"So don't worry at all about having enough food and clothing. Why be like the heathen? For they take pride in all these things and are deeply concerned about them. But your heavenly Father already knows perfectly well that you need them, and He will give them to you if you give Him first place in your life and live as He wants you to" (Matthew 6:31-33).

As a young businessman, I was strongly attracted to the material things of the world and worked very hard to achieve success. But when I became a Christian, I could not ignore the logic of Christ's command, "Seek ye first the kingdom of God and His righteousness" (Matthew 6:33, KJV).

I made my commitment to obey His command. Since that day so many years ago, I have sought to be obedient to that command. The Lord has graciously and abundantly blessed me with the fulfillment of the promise of His supernatural provision which follows:

"Your heavenly Father already knows perfectly well (the things you need), and He will give them to you if you give Him first place in your life and live as He wants you to."

God is trustworthy, and the obedient, faithful Christian soon learns that he, like the psalmist of old, can proclaim:

"I have never seen the Lord forsake a man who loves Him; nor have I seen the children of the godly go hungry" (Psalm 37:25).

Bible Reading: Matthew 6:25-30

ACTION POINT: Resting on the absolute certainties of the Word of God, I will refuse to worry about anything today (recognizing that *concern* involves others, while *worry* involves only myself). "All things work together for good to them that love God..." (Romans 8:28). "My God shall supply all your need..." (Philippians 4:19). By trusting these and other promises from God's Word, I have no reason to worry.

How to Obey God's Laws

"So now we can obey God's laws if we follow after the Holy Spirit and no longer obey the old evil nature within us" (Romans 8:4).

A re you not glad that the Word of God makes things so simple?

If we really want to obey God's laws, His resources are available to us. First and foremost, the Holy Spirit abides within to guide us. While it is true that we have all of the Holy Spirit at the time of our conversion, we cannot expect the full blessing and power of God until the Holy Spirit has full control of all of us.

As we appropriate the fullness of His Holy Spirit by faith, we are supplied with supernatural power to obey God's laws. That supernatural power, even, is contingent upon our cooperation in that we must not only commit ourselves to the Holy Spirit but we must also be familiar with the Word of God if we are indeed to obey its commands.

Obedience is a key word in the Christian life. This verse points it out quite clearly, for we either obey God's laws or we obey the old evil nature. The choice is ours as we are controlled and empowered by the Holy Spirit.

Someone has well pointed out that all of life, really, is nothing more nor less than a series of choices. The secret of the successful Christian life is in making the right choices. And even the wisdom to make the right choices is available — as a gift from God.

That leaves us, you and me, without excuse. We can, if we choose, through the enabling of the Holy Spirit, obey God's laws and thus accomplish His purpose for us as believers.

Bible Reading: Galatians 5:16-26

ACTION POINT: Drawing upon the supernatural resources of the Holy Spirit I choose to obey God's laws rather than yield to the pull of my old evil nature.

No Other Savior

"There is salvation in no one else! Under all heaven there is no other name for men to call upon to save them" (Acts 4:12).

As a young skeptic, I had difficulty believing in the resurrection, for I could not believe in the supernatural. But as I became aware of the uniqueness of Jesus and of the different quality of life that was His, I was forced to reconsider the biblical claim to His resurrection.

Since it is a matter of historical fact that the tomb in which His dead body was placed was empty three days later, I set out to discover if the tomb could have been empty on any other basis than the biblical claim that He had been raised from the dead. In my research, I learned that there were three different theories explaining the empty tomb.

First, it was proposed that He was not really dead but had fainted from loss of blood on the cross, and that He recovered in the cool of the tomb (this notion is today expounded by certain skeptics under the name of the "swoon theory"). Second, it was conceivable that Jesus' body was stolen by His enemies; or third, that it was stolen by the disciples.

Experience and logic have forced me to discount all three of these theories as impossibilities. First, Jesus could never have moved the stone or escaped from the guards in His weakened condition. Second, Jesus' enemies had no reason to steal His body since they did not want to give credence to a belief in His resurrection. Even if they had stolen the body, they could simply have produced it to discount the resurrection.

Third the disciples who deserted Jesus at His trial and crucifixion were the same men who, having seen Him after His resurrection, spent the rest of their lives telling everyone who would listen, even at the cost of their lives, that Jesus was alive. Ask yourself this question, "Would the disciples be willing to die as martyrs propagating a lie?"

Christianity alone has a living Savior; in Him alone is salvation.

Bible Reading: Romans 10:9-13

ACTION POINT: Several times today, as the Holy Spirit prompts me, I will remember to thank God for the gift of His Son as my personal Savior and will tell someone else that Jesus is alive and wants to be his Savior, too.

Claiming the Promise

"But when I am afraid, I will put my confidence in You. Yes, I will trust the promises of God. And since I am trusting Him, what can mere man do to me?" (Psalm 56:3,4).

Raymond and Martha were active church members and gave generously to the needs of their fellowship. But their real security, as Raymond shared, was largely in monetary holdings. After working hard for many years to build a financial empire, they had nothing to worry about. They were on "Easy Street" and could do anything for the rest of their lives, confident of being able to pass on a sizeable fortune to their children and grandchildren.

But at this point, Raymond turned over the reins of his business to a trusted employee who, through mismanagement and embezzlement, coupled with a severe economic depression, was able to destroy in approximately two years what had taken Raymond more than thirty years to accumulate.

Devastated and fearful, Raymond and Martha turned to God and His Word. As they claimed God's promises, the Savior whom they had professed to know but had not really known, became a reality in their lives. They became joyful, radiant and victorious. Though they had lost almost everything materially, they had, in the process, gained all that was really important. Now their trust was in the Lord who filled their lives with His love and grace. They passed on God's blessing to others, including me.

Bible Reading: Psalm 25:4-10

ACTION POINT: I will not wait until personal tragedy, physical illness, financial reverses, heartache or sorrow cross my path, but will place my confidence in the Lord and in his Word and begin now to draw upon His supernatural resources to live a full and meaningfdul life for His glory.

Chosen to be Glorified

"And having chosen us, He called us to come to Him; and when we came, He declared us 'not guilty,' filled us with Christ's goodness, gave us right standing with Himself, and promised us His glory" (Romans 8:30).

A famous Christian leader insisted to me that anyone could lose his salvation. I asked him if he felt that he would ever lose his. Quickly, he replied, "Absolutely not. I am sure I will not lose my salvation."

Can we lose our salvation? Personally, I believe there is too much controversy over this issue. Some fear that the individual who has assurance of salvation and knows that he will spend eternity with God might have a tendency to compromise his conduct, which would result in disobedience to God and would be an insult to Christ and His church. Others think that the individual who does not live like a Christian — although he professes faith in Christ — has never experienced the new birth, does not have eternal life and will be forever separated from God.

It is quite likely that the person who insists on "doing his own thing" — going his own way while professing to be a Christian — is deceived and should be encouraged to look into the mirror of God's Word. For if his salvation is real, the evidence should proclaim it.

The caterpillar which goes through a metamorphosis to become a butterfly, lives like a butterfly, not a caterpillar. In the same way, the man or woman who has experienced new life in Christ will witness to it in his life.

Our beginning Scripture deals with seven marvelous truths: (1) He chose us. (2) He called us. (3) We came. (4) He declared us not guilty. (5) He filled us with Christ's goodness. (6) He gave us a right standing with Himself. (7) He promised us His glory.

For centuries, man has been mystified by predestination and eternal security. One famous theologian put it this way: "How would it be a source of consolation to say... that whom God foreknew, He predestinated, and whom he predestinated, He called, and whom He called, He justified, and whom He justified might fall away and be lost forever?"

We should praise and worship God because of His promises to all who receive Him that He will never leave them nor forsake them (Hebrews 13:5).

Bible Reading: Ephesians 1:3-6

ACTION POINT: I will meditate upon the truths in this marvelous Word from God. And as an expression of my gratitude for the privilege of living a supernatural life, I will praise and thank God constantly for His goodness and will encourage other believers to do the same.

Before We Even Call

"I will answer them before they even call to Me. While they are still talking to Me about their needs, I will go ahead and answer their prayers!" (Isaiah 65:24).

Allenby's Bridge, which spans the Jordan River, was built to honor the man whom God used to lead the miraculous conquest of Jerusalem without the firing of a single gun.

Allenby recalled how, as a little boy when he used to lisp his evening prayers, he was taught to repeat after his mother the closing part of the prayer:

"And, O Lord, we will not forget Thy ancient people, Israel. Lord, hasten the day when Israel truly shall be Thy people and shall be restored to Thy favor and to their land."

"I never knew then," Allenby said at a reception in London, "that God would give me the privilege of helping to answer my own childhood prayers."

Even more wonderful than that kind of divine providence is the truth expressed in Isaiah 65:24 (KJV): "Before they call, I will answer." I have seen this promise fulfilled many times in the global program of Campus Crusade for Christ. Even during the time we have prayed for desperate needs — financial and otherwise — God was already laying it upon the hearts of His faithful people to respond.

What a great comfort to know that we serve that kind of God!

Bible Reading: Isaiah 65:18-25

ACTION POINT: Even as I pray for the needs of others and myself today, I will remember the power and faithfulness of God who has already begun to answer even before I ask.

Living the Godly Life

"As God's messenger I give each of you God's warning: Be honest in your estimate of yourselves, measuring your value by how much faith God has given you" (Romans 12:3).

A newly appointed director of affairs for our ministry came to me for counsel after being given his assignment. "Tell me," he inquired, "what are the biggest problems that I will encounter in my new area of responsibility?"

"Three major ones," I responded. "First, pride, the problem that caused Satan to seek a place of authority over God Himself, resulting in his expulsion from the heavenly kingdom. Since creation, man's greatest problem has been pride — thinking more highly of oneself than one ought to think.

"Your second problem will be materialism — the desire to accumulate wealth, to live the good life, to keep up with the Joneses with better houses, cars, clothes, and security.

"And the third problem will be sex, the temptation to immorality. Man's second greatest drive after self-preservation is sex. In the marriage bond, sex is one of the most beautiful of the God-given privileges. But out of marriage, it results in grieving and quenching the Spirit and, ultimately, in the discipline of God. Therefore, be faithful to the wife that God has given you and love her as Christ loved the church, (Ephesians 5:25).

"Keep yourself humble by God's power. Seek the simple life and be motivated and constrained by the love of God for the souls of men, rather than for the good things of this world."

This is my counsel to all of our staff. It is my message to all Christian leaders and to all who seek to live godly lives.

The highways and byways of the world are littered with men and women of great talent and ability who are no longer being used of God. The fire has gone out of their hearts; the smile is gone from their faces. They harvest no fruit for the kingdom. They have fallen, thinking more highly of themselves than they ought to think, after the example of Satan, the author of pride.

God's Word admonishes us to think soberly, wisely, prudently and modestly. The faith which we each have is a gift from God, measured by Him. That fact alone should produce in you and me a true humility, changing any feeling of pride to one of gratitude. The truly humble person regards God as the source of all blessings.

Bible Reading: Ephesians 4:1-6

ACTION POINT: When the temptation comes to think more highly of myself than I ought to think, with God's help I will remember that everything I have is a gift of His grace. I will humble myself before God and man and, by faith, live a supernatural, godly life, dedicated to the extension of His kingdom.

Satisfies God's Requirements

"Love does no wrong to anyone. That's why it fully satisfies all of God's requirements. It is the only law you need" (Romans 13:10).

E arly in my Christian life, I was troubled over the command to love God so completely, as I mentioned in yesterday's reading. How could I ever measure up to such a high standard? Then He showed me how to love by faith.

We are to love God. We are to love our neighbors. We are to love our enemies. We are to love our family members. And we are to love ourselves with God's kind of love, by faith.

Since the greatest commandment is to love God, we are to give Him our first love, never allowing anyone or anything to come before Him. And supernaturally, we are to express the *agape* kind of love to others — a love no less in its quality and magnitude than that which we express toward God.

In the same way, God loves all His children perfectly. He loves you and me just as much as He loves His Son, the Lord Jesus Christ (John 17:23).

The person who has not yet learned to love God and to seek Him above all else and all others is to be pitied. Such a person is only denying himself the blessings that await all who love God with all their heart, soul and mind.

It is natural for us to fulfill the command to love our neighbors as ourselves if we truly love God in the way mentioned above. If we are properly related to God, vertically, we will be properly related to our fellow man, horizontally.

Bible Reading: 1 Corinthians 13

ACTION POINT: By faith I will claim God's love — for Him, for my neighbors, for myself, for my enemies — and as a result do only good, which is a result of supernatural living.

Wonderful Friendship

"God will surely do this for you, for He always does just what He says, and He is the one who invited you into this wonderful friendship with His Son, even Christ our Lord" (1 Corinthians 1:9).

You and I do not always prove faithful, but the apostle Paul wants us to know, by way of his letter to the believers in Corinth, that our God will surely do what He has promised; in this case, make us "blameless in the day of our Lord Jesus Christ" (verse 8).

The apostle wants the Corinthians to know that they can depend upon the faithfulness of God, who had begun a good work among them, and certainly would see them through to the end. He did the inviting; He would do the keeping.

Christians are able to participate with Christ in several ways. First, in His trials and sufferings, for we are subjected to temptations and trials similar to His: "But rejoice, inasmuch as ye are partakers of Christ's sufferings" (1 Peter 4:13, KJV).

Second, in His feelings and views (Romans 8:9).

Third, in His heirship to the inheritance and glory which awaits Him: "And if children, then heirs; heirs of God, and joint-heirs with Christ" (Romans 8:17, KJV).

Fourth, in His triumph in the resurrection and future glory: "Ye which have followed Me, in the regeneration when the Son of man shall sit on the throne of His glory, ye also shall sit upon twelve thrones, judging the twelve tribes of Israel" (Matthew 19:28, KJV).

Are you not glad for that kind of friendship?

Bible Reading: 2 Thessalonians 3:3-5

ACTION POINT: When I look for a faithful friend, my first thought will be of Christ Himself, who truly qualifies as my very best friend.

Abundant, Supernatural Life

"Even so, consider yourself to be dead to sin but alive to God in Christ Jesus" (Romans 6:11, NAS).

My friend Randy had given up on the Christian life. He said, "I have tried, but failed so many times; nothing seems to work. God doesn't hear my prayers, and I am tired of trying. I've read the Bible, prayed, memorized Scripture, and gone to church. But there is no joy and I don't see any purpose in continuing a life of shame and hypocrisy, pretending I am something that I'm not."

After listening to his account of his many failures and defeats, I began to explain the ministry of the Holy Spirit. He interrupted me with, "I know all about the Holy Spirit. I've read everything that I can find, everything you and others have written — and nothing works for me."

My thoughts turned to Romans, chapter 6. I asked him, "Randy, are you sure you're a Christian?"

"Yes," he answered. "I'm sure."

"How do you know."

"By faith," he responded. "The Scripture promises, 'For by grace are you saved through faith, that not of yourselves, it's a gift of God, not of works, lest any man should boast.' I know I'm saved."

"Why," I asked him, "do you trust God for your salvation, but do not believe in His other promises concerning your rights as a child of God?"

I began to read from Romans 6 and reminded Randy that every believer has available to him the mighty, supernatural power of the risen Christ. With the enabling of the Holy Spirit, the believer can live that supernatural life simply by claiming his rights through an act of his will. The same Holy Spirit who inspired Ephesians 2:8 and 9 inspired Romans 6, and, by faith, we can claim that sin no longer has control over us and that the mighty power of the resurrection is available as promised.

That day, God touched Randy's life, his spiritual eyes were opened and he began, by faith, to live in accordance with his God-given heritage.

Bible Reading: Romans 6:12-18

ACTION POINT: Today, by faith, I will claim the truths of Romans 6. As an act of my will, I surrender the members of my body as instruments of righteousness unto God, to live that abundant, supernatural life, which is my heritage in Christ. Enabled by the Holy Spirit, I will encourage other believers to claim their kingdom rights, and non-believers to join this adventure with the risen Savior.

Overwhelming Love

"But despite all this, overwhelming victory is ours through Christ who loved us enough to die for us" (Romans 8:37).

Today I prayed with a beloved friend who is dying of cancer. As he and his precious wife and I held hands, we lifted our voices in praise to God, knowing that He makes no mistakes, that "all things work together for good to those who love Him," and that He is fully aware of my brother's body riddled with pain as a result of cancerous cells that are on a warpath. Together we claimed that victory which comes from an unwavering confidence in Christ's sufficiency.

The victory comes, of course, through Christ who loved us enough to die for us. Such love is beyond our ability to grasp with our minds, but it is not beyond our ability to experience with our hearts. God's love is unconditional and it is constant. Because He is perfect, His love is perfect, too.

The Scriptures tell of a certain lawyer who asked Jesus, "Sir, which is the most important command in the law of Moses?"

Jesus replied, "You shall love the Lord your God with all your heart, soul and mind. This is the first and greatest commandment. The second most important is similar: Love your neighbor as much as you love yourself."

The question may come to your mind: "Why does God want our love?" From a human standpoint, this could appear selfish and egotistical. But God, in His sovereignty and love, has so created man that he finds his greatest joy and fulfillment when he loves God with all his heart and soul and mind, and his neighbor as himself.

Early in my Christian life, I was troubled over the command to love God so completely. But now the Holy Spirit has filled my heart with God's love. And as I meditate on the "overwhelming victory" that He gives us, I find my love for Him growing.

Bible Reading: Romans 8:35-39

ACTION POINT: His great love and "overwhelming victory" for me prompts me to respond with supernatural love for Him and for others.

He Gives the Victory

"But thanks be to God, which giveth us the victory through our Lord Jesus Christ" (1 Corinthians 15:57, KJV).

In our busy lives, yours and mine, there are days when victory seems an impossibility. Heartaches, trials, burdens, or just the ordinary cares of the day, all seem foreign to the idea of being victorious.

And yet the fact remains that we are "more than conquerors" even when we do not feel like it. God graciously allows His children to be human and to express our doubts and fears when suffering and pain and testing and trial seem to overwhelm us.

"I have to be very honest," confessed Joyce Landorf, well-known Christian author and speaker, during a long period of illness. "One of the things I have learned from severe pain is that I have felt totally abandoned by God. I didn't think He'd let that happen to me, but He has.

"And maybe the feeling of abandonment when pain is at its writhing best. . .maybe that"s what makes it so sweet after the pain goes and the Lord says, 'I was here all the time. I haven't left you. I will never forsake you.' Now those words get sweeter to me because I know what it has felt like to not feel His presence."

We do not have all the answers, but we know one who does. And that is where our victory begins — acknowledging (1) that God is a God of love, one who never makes a mistake, and (2) He will never leave us or forsake us.

Bible Reading: Romans 7:18-25

ACTION POINT: I will consider myself a victor, whatever may transpire, because I serve the victorious one.

His Great Love for Us

"But God showed His great love for us by sending Christ to die for us while we were still sinners" (Romans 5:8).

A dear friend and Christian leader from another country hated and resented his father, who was an alcoholic. Through the years, my friend had been humiliated and embarrassed by his father's conduct. He wanted nothing to do with him.

As he grew more and more mature in his faith, and the Christlike qualities began to develop in his life, he began to realize that his attitude toward his father was wrong. He knew well that God's Word commanded him to love and honor his mother and father, with no conditions.

Then he began to comprehend and experience the truth of loving by faith after a message which he had heard me give. As a result, he went to his father and, as an act of the will, by faith — because at that point he did not honestly feel like doing so — he expressed his love.

He was amazed to discover that his father had been hurt for years because he had sensed that his son despised and rejected him.

When the son began to demonstrate love for him — to assure him that he cared for him, whether he drank or did not drink — it prompted the father to commit his life to Christ and to trust Him to help him overcome the problem which had plagued him most of his life.

Through this new relationship with the Lord, my friend's father became a new creature and was able to gain victory over the addiction to alcohol several years before he died, a dramatic example of the power of love.

Bible Reading: Romans 5:9-15

ACTION POINT: Knowing Christ's great love for me, I will claim His supernatural love for others today.

He Wonderfully Comforts

"What a wonderful God we have — He is the Father of our Lord Jesus Christ, the source of every mercy, and the one who so wonderfully comforts and strengthens us in our hardships and trials. And why does He do this? So that when others are troubled, needing our sympathy and encouragement, we can pass on to them this same help and comfort God has given us" (2 Corinthians 1:3,4).

Whatever God does for you and me is without merit on our part and by pure grace on His part, and it is done for a purpose. Here the apostle Paul tells the Corinthian believers why God so wonderfully comforts and strengthens them, and us, in our hardships and trials.

This scriptural principle is a good one to remember: God never gives to or benefits His children solely for their own selfish ends. We are not comforted and strengthened in our hardships and trials just so that we will feel better.

Eleven out of the 13 Pauline epistles begin with exclamations of joy, praise and thanksgiving. Second Corinthians, obviously, is one of those. Though Paul had been afflicted and persecuted, he had also been favored with God's comfort and consolation.

Paul delighted in tracing all his comforts back to God. He found no other real source of happiness. The apostle does not say that God's comfort and strength is given solely for the benefit of others, but he does say that this is an important purpose. We are not to hoard God's blessings.

Bible Reading: Hebrews 13:15-19

ACTION POINT: As I live in the supernatural strength of the Lord God, I will make an effort, with His help, to share that strength (and other blessings) with others.

Like a Sweet Perfume

"But thanks be to God! For through what Christ has done, He has triumphed over us so that now wherever we go He uses us to tell others about the Lord and to spread the Gospel like a sweet perfume" (2 Corinthians 2:14).

We can certainly learn a lesson from the apostle Paul. He frequently begins a chapter or a verse with a note of praise. To say that he had a thankful spirit would be understating the case. That perhaps is the key to victory in every area of our lives, to begin with thanksgiving.

It is God who leads us to triumph over principalities and powers. And in leading us to triumph, He is then able to use us to tell others of His love and forgiveness through the Lord Jesus. As we rest in His victory and in His command, with its promise of "Lo, I am with you always," we spread the gospel like a sweet perfume.

In your own home and in your own neighborhood, perhaps, are those who need the sweet perfume of the gospel, that heavenly aroma that comes first from God, then through us as His servants, and finally in the message itself: the good news of sins forgiven and a heavenly home assured.

Around the world, literally, I personally have seen multitudes of men and women, old and young, become new creatures in Christ. The aroma indeed is one of sweet perfume, for tangled lives have become untangled to the glory of God, and joy abounds in hearts and lives where only sadness and despair had been known.

Bible Reading: 2 Corinthians 2:14-17

ACTION POINT: "Dear Lord, help me to bear a heavenly aroma as I share the sweet perfume of the gospel with others."

God Uses Sorrow

"For God sometimes uses sorrow in our lives to help us turn away from sin and seek eternal life. We should never regret His sending it. But the sorrow of the man who is not a Christian is not the sorrow of true repentance and does not prevent eternal death" (2 Corinthians 7:10).

Frank, one of the leading business-men in his community, often referred to himself proudly as a self-made man. He bragged that in his youth he had been so poor that he didn't have two nickels to rub together. But now his real estate holdings and various business enterprises were worth tens of millions of dollars. He was a pillar in the community, able to give generously to various civic and philanthropic causes. He had done it all himself. Nobody helped him. His philosophy was that there was no God, and every man had to make it on his own. He laughed at the weaklings who needed the crutch of their church.

Then, when it seemed as though everything was going his way, his world began to fall apart. First, his only son was sent to prison for pushing drugs. Then his daughter had an unfortunate automobile accident that left her partially paralyzed for life; and his wife, who had been largely ignored for some years, announced that she was in love with someone else and demanded a divorce. In the meantime, because he had become lax in his business dealings, one of his partners embezzled several million dollars from him.

By this time, he was devastated and, therefore, open to spiritual counsel. After the Holy Spirit showed him his sin of pride and selfishness, he opened his heart to Christ and the miracle took place. Now, he frequently quotes this passage: "God sometimes uses sorrow in our lives to help us turn away from sin and seek eternal life."

Though his son is still in prison and his daughter still paralyzed, he and his wife are in the process of working toward a reconciliation, and his heart is filled with joy, praise and thanksgiving to God. He is no longer a proud, selfish, "successful" businessman, but a humble child of God, a servant who discovered the hard way that every man needs God.

Of course, for every Frank there are hundreds of others who are experiencing heartache, tragedy, and all kinds of difficulties, and who, unlike Frank, have not repented. Yet, God offers to all men the priceless gift of abundant and supernatural life.

Bible Reading: Proverbs 28: 12-14

ACTION POINT: I shall seek to live the full, abundant, supernatural life, walking in faith and obedience, so that God will not find it necessary to discipline me in order to bless me.

Able to Keep Promises

"He was completely sure that God was well able to do anything He promised" (Romans 4:21).

Occasionally, I hear people say, "Bill Bright is a man of great faith."

The statement is made because our ministry is involved with millions of Christians from many thousands of churches of all denominations and other Christian organizations in gargantuan undertakings — massive worldwide programs of evangelism and discipleship in which we have, by faith, trusted God for the salvation of at least one billion additional souls for Christ and His kingdom.

As a new Christian, I trusted God for one soul, then six, then ten souls; then hundreds, thousands, millions. And now, after more than 35 years of witnessing His mighty, miraculous power and blessing in response to faith, I am praying and believing God for a billion souls for Christ by the year 2000.

These goals are not built on careless presumptions or figures plucked out of the air in some kind of a mystical, emotional, spiritual experience, but they are based upon my confidence in the sovereignty, holiness, love, wisdom, power and grace of the omnipotent God whom I serve and upon His gracious blessings on past efforts that have been undertaken for His glory and praise. No credit should be given to me or to the ministry of which I am a part, but only to the One in whom I place my faith.

Faith must have an object, and the object of my faith is God and His inspired Word. The right view of God generates faith. Faith is like a muscle; it grows with exercise. The more we see God accomplish in and through our lives, the more we can be assured that He will accomplish as we trust and obey Him more.

Bible Reading: Romans 4:13-20

ACTION POINT: I will place my faith in God alone — not in myself or in other men's efforts or abilities — and I will encourage others to trust God, too.

Mighty Weapons

"I use God's mighty weapons, not those made by men, to knock down the devil's strongholds. These weapons can break down every proud argument against God and every wall that can be built to keep men from finding Him. With these weapons I can capture rebels and bring them back to God, and change them into men whose hearts' desire is obedience to Christ" (2 Corinthians 10:4,5).

Joe came to share with me how his leader in a particular Christian organization had been most unfair to him. He was being relieved of his responsibilities and replaced by another who, in his opinion, was not nearly as well qualified. As we talked it became apparent that Satan easily could sabotage the ministry.

After listening to Joe's grievances for some time, seeking to know the truth of the matter, I inquired as to his walk with God. "Is there any sin in your life? Do you know for sure that you're filled with the Holy Spirit?" Then I brought the other party into private conference and inquired as to his relationship with God. "Is there any sin in your life? Do you know for sure that you're filled with the Holy Spirit?" Both assured me that they were filled with the Spirit and that they genuinely desired to know and do the will of God. I was convinced that they were both sincere.

How then could two men without sin in their lives and who claimed to be filled with the Holy Spirit be at such odds? I sought further truth. In the meantime, we brought to bear the weapons of prayer and the Word of God. God says that when brothers are at odds we should claim in prayer the release of His supernatural wisdom to resolve the matter, and, finally, claim by faith that Satan will be routed, that all of his influence will be overcome.

The counseling required several hours. I talked to one individual, then the other, then both of them together. Finally, we were on our knees praising God and then embracing each other, and the men genuinely felt that their relationship with each other and with the Lord was fully restored. Satan had lost another battle. Another miracle had happened. Another tragedy had been averted and the Body of Christ had been spared another scandal.

What are those weapons? A holy life, the Holy Spirit, prayer, the Word of God, faith, truth — these are the weapons of God for supernatural warfare. Learn how to use them for His glory.

Bible Reading: Ephesians 6:10-17

ACTION POINT: Whenever Satan attacks me, or I observe conflicts in the Body of Christ due to his influence, I will seek to defeat him by using God's mighty weapons and will teach other Christians how to apply them in times of spiritual battle.

Filled With Good Things

"He fills my life with good things! My youth is renewed like the eagle's!" (Psalm 103:5).

One day a poor woman greatly desired and sought a bunch of grapes from the king's conservatory for her sick child.

Taking half a crown, she approached the king's gardener and tried to purchase the grapes. Rudely repulsed, she made a second effort — with more money. Again she was refused.

Finally, the king's daughter heard the crying of the woman and the angry words of the gardener. When she inquired into the matter, the woman told her story.

"My dear woman," said the princess, "you are mistaken. My father is not a merchant, but a king. His business is not to sell, but to give."

Plucking a bunch of grapes from the vine, she gently dropped it into the woman's apron.

What a picture of the goodness and bounty of our wonderful Lord! He fills our lives with good things, and even as we approach and reach old age, He renews our strength and vigor so that in effect we become young again.

This truth was impressed upon me anew when I reached my 60th birthday in late 1981. Age really did not seem to matter at all; God continues to give liberally — not only all good things that are needful, but also a renewal of strength and vigor for each day and for each task. I seem to have as much strength and energy at 60 as when I was 30 — with far more experience and wisdom.

Bible Reading: Psalm 103:1-8

ACTION POINT: I will dare to believe God is filling my life with good things. Even when a particular thing may not seem good at the moment, I will still praise and thank Him as an expression of my love, gratitude and faith.

Everything Belongs to Us

"Now we are no longer slaves, but God's own sons. And since we are His sons, everything He has belongs to us, for that is the way God planned" (Galatians 4:7).

In the sense of being under the servitude of sin, you and I are no longer servants or slaves. We are sons, children of God, adopted into His family, and are to be treated as sons.

What a glorious privilege is ours in Christ!

In our exalted position as sons, of course we are to be treated as sons. We are to share God's favors, His blessings. And as sons, it follows that we have responsibilities — not only to our heavenly Father, but also to other sons (and daughters) in Christ.

All that God has, Paul is saying, belongs to us as well for we are His sons. But there is another side to our exalted position — obedience to the Lord. And His calling is sure: "Follow Me and I will make you fishers of men."

If we are following our Lord, we are becoming fishers of men — soul-winners. We are regularly and naturally, as a part of our daily routine, sharing the good news of the gospel with those whose lives we touch.

That does not necessarily mean buttonholing people and making a nuisance of ourselves; it does mean being available for God's Holy Spirit to speak through us in every conversation as He chooses. It also means being "prayed up," with no unconfessed sin in our lives.

Bible Reading: Revelation 8:14-17

ACTION POINT: With the Power of the Holy Spirit available to me by faith, I will behave like a child of the King — a son of the Most High. I will live a supernatural life for the Glory of God.

God's Protection

"Now you don't need to be afraid of the dark any more, nor fear the dangers of the day; nor dread the plagues of darkness, nor disasters in the morning" (Psalm 91:5,6).

On what basis can we believe that promise? We can believe it because, as we read in the first four verses of that great chapter, "We live within the shadow of the Almighty, sheltered by the God who is above all gods. This I declare, that He alone is my refuge, my place of safety; He is my God and I am trusting Him. For He rescues you from every trap, and protects you from the fatal plague." I would encourage you to memorize this great promise.

During the past few years there has been an alarming growth in the number of cases of various types of venereal disease in the United States as well as in other countries of the world. One particular venereal disease which recently has come into increased prominence is AIDS, or Acquired Immune Deficiency Syndrome.

The reason for this is explained in Romans 1:18-32. "But God shows His anger from heaven against all sinful, evil men who push away the truth from them" (verse 18). Because they chose not to believe in God and not to obey His commands, "God let them go ahead into every sort of sex sin, and do whatever they wanted to — yes, vile and sinful things with each other's bodies. Instead of believing what they knew was the truth about God, they deliberately chose to believe lies.... That is why God let go of them and let them do all these evil things, so that even their women turned against God's natural plan for them and indulged in sex sin with each other. And the men, instead of having a normal sex relationship with women, burned with lust for each other, men doing shameful things with other men and, as a result, getting paid within their own souls with the penalty they so richly deserved.... They were fully aware of God's death penalty for these crimes, yet they went right ahead and did them anyway, and encouraged others to do them, too" (verses 24-27, 32).

What a contrast between those who obey God and live within the sheltering shadow of the Almighty and those who refuse to have any God over them and, as a result, pay the penalty of their disobedience.

Bible Reading: Psalm 91:8-16

ACTION POINT: With God's help, I will live within the shadow of the Almighty, sheltered by the God, who is above all gods, knowing that He will protect me and that I need not be afraid of any danger. This is because I have chosen to live a holy life depending upon God to guide me and protect me.

Calm in the Storm

"Immediately after this, Jesus told His disciples to get into their boat and cross to the other side of the lake while He stayed to get the people started home. Then afterwards He went up into the hills to pray. Night fell, and out on the lake the disciples were in trouble. For the wind had risen and they were fighting heavy seas. About four o'clock in the morning Jesus came to them, walking on the water! They screamed in terror, for they thought He was a ghost. But Jesus immediately spoke to them, reassuring them. 'Don't be afraid!' He said" (Matthew 14:22-27).

I had flown at least a couple of million miles in the last thirty years, but this was the most violent storm I had ever encountered. Vonette and I were on our way from New York City to Washington, when suddenly the airplane began to buck like a wild mustang with its first rider. It felt as though no one was in control. The lightning was constant and for nearly fifteen minutes we seemed to be surrounded by a ball of fire. We had good reason to believe that the plane would soon plummet to earth.

The disciples had shouted to the Lord, "Save us, we're sinking!" In the same manner, Vonette and I began to pray.

Then, as we called upon God, our petitions turned to praise and thanksgiving. We were reminded of the biblical storm and we prayed, "Oh Lord, You have not lost Your power over nature. We ask You to still the storm and to save us, though we're ready to meet with You if need be. If You have something yet for us to do in this life, we ask You not to allow the enemy to destroy us and all these other passengers."

Almost immediately the turbulence stopped. The plane was righted, and we continued on our course, though we discovered later that the plane had been severely damaged.

One of the greatest blessings to come from this experience was the indescribable peace that enveloped us as we considered that at any moment we could plummet to earth and our lives could be snuffed out. I asked the Lord why the disciples were so fearful during the storm while Vonette and I had such peace and confidence that He was in control. The answer was that the fruit of the Spirit is love, joy, peace, etc., and the disciples had not yet been filled with the Spirit at the time of their Galilean storm experience. Later they went to their martyrs' deaths with the same peace that God gives to all who place their faith and trust in Him.

Bible Reading: John 6:16-21

ACTION POINT: The mighty power which Jesus demonstrated when He walked this earth centuries ago still abides in Him, and He abides in me. Therefore, I shall claim supernatural miraculous power whenever the occasion demands.

Saved From Trouble

"Yes, the Lord hears the good man when he calls to Him for help, and saves him out of all his troubles" (Psalm 34:17).

You and I have one of the greatest privileges ever known to mankind — that of calling on God with the assurance that He will hear and answer us.

No trouble we face today will be too great for us to bring to God, who has promised to save us out of all our troubles.

True, He suggests certain conditions that must be met for such praying to be effective, but these conditions are not grievous. They are attainable by "whosoever will."

One of these conditions is referred to by the psalmist, "If I regard iniquity in my heart, the Lord will not hear me" (Psalm 66:18, KJV). According to God's Word, that means I must not even allow wrong feelings and critical attitudes against others to fester in my heart and mind, but rather I must confess them the moment they arise and then trust God for the forgiveness He promises.

Another condition is suggested in that well-known verse on revival: "If my people. . . will *humble* themselves, and pray. . ." (2 Chronicles 7:14, KJV). Even before that time of intercession with the Lord, I must be sure to humble myself, to recognize God as my Lord and Master, and His Holy Spirit as one who sits and rules and reigns on the throne of my life.

As a result, God will produce in my life those qualities of the supernatural life.

Bible Reading: Psalm 35:1-9

ACTION POINT: Confession and humbling will precede prayer in my life this day, so that I may be sure God hears and will answer.

He Does the Work

"And I am sure the God who began the good work within you will keep right on helping you grow in His grace until His task within you is finally finished on that day when Jesus Christ returns" (Philippians 1:6).

Howard was adamant in his conviction. "I would never lead anyone to Christ that I could not personally follow up to be sure he matures and grows and becomes all that God wants him to be."

"Since when did you assume the responsibility of the Holy Spirit?" I asked.

Obviously, we are to do everything we can to help a new believer grow to maturity in Christ — by teaching him to trust God, study His Word, pray, live a holy life, and share his faith with others. But no matter how much we do, it is the Holy Spirit who helps the new believer come to Christ, and who illumines his heart with the Word. The Holy Spirit teaches us how to pray and empowers us to witness. In fact, there would be no supernatural life apart from the Holy Spirit.

Paradoxically, you and I can be confident, yet humble, when we think of all that we are, and all that we have in Christ, and realize that we are not responsible for any of it, but it is something which God has given us according to His grace. My only boast is in God, His Son Jesus Christ and His indwelling Holy Spirit. How can I boast of my abilities and achievements, when it is the Giver alone who is worthy of all honor and praise? The apostle Paul had the strong conviction that the work God had begun in the believer would be permanent. All events that transpire in our lives, all influences, heartaches, testings and sorrows, as well as all of the blessings, are designed to conform us to the image of Christ.

Bible Reading: 1 Corinthians 1:4-9

ACTION POINT: God, who saved me, continues to work in my life, conforming me to the image of Christ. Therefore, I will continue to trust and obey Him, as I draw upon His supernatural resources.

Just As He Promised

"God, who called you to become His child, will do all this for you, just as He promised" (1 Thessalonians 5:24).

Have you ever substituted your own name in a promise like that? I have, and the result is staggering, overwhelming. "God, who called Bill Bright to become His child, will do all this for me, just as He promised."

Include your name in the verse, and the effect will be the same for you. It is incredible that before the very foundation of the world God chose and called you and me to become His children. His foreknowledge makes possible many of the mysteries we puzzle over today.

Your sanctification (setting apart) — and mine — depends upon God, and since He has begun a good work in us, He will see it through to completion. God requires holiness (another word for sanctification) and He is the resource upon whom we may call for accomplishment of that requirement.

While it is true we will never be completely and totally holy in this life, it is equally true that provision is made for us to be holy. Every moment that you and I are under the control of God's Holy Spirit, is a moment that we are holy! Looked at in that light, the task of acquiring holiness does not seem so impossible to attain.

The principle is clear: God never gives a command without the enablement to obey it.

Bible Reading: 2 Thessalonians 3:3-5

ACTION POINT: I will see myself as a child of God, the beneficiary of His multitudinous blessings, capable of living a supernatural life and bearing fruit for His glory through His enablement.

PROMISES — DAY 334

Peace and Joy

"Always be full of joy in the Lord; I say it again, rejoice! Let everyone see that you are unselfish and considerate in all you do. Remember that the Lord is coming soon. Don't worry about anything; instead, pray about everything; tell God your needs and don't forget to thank Him for His answers. If you do this you will experience God's peace, which is far more wonderful than the human mind can understand. His peace will keep your thoughts and your hearts quiet and at rest as you trust in Christ Jesus" (Philippians 4:4-7).

Don and Ann wanted with all their hearts to please the Lord and worked at being victorious Christians. They diligently kept their quiet time and memorized Scripture, and they were faithful in church attendance. They did everything right. But as they said, "Even though we've claimed the fullness of the Holy Spirit by faith and tried to understand and apply identification truths [in which they sought to identify themselves with Christ, his crucifixion, burial and resurrection], we just don't seem to be enjoying the Christian life. There's something missing."

"In Philippians 4," I told them, "you will find a surefire spiritual formula for victory in the Christian life. Just allow the Holy Spirit to make this passage a reality to you and apply the following as He enables you:

1. As an act of your will, decide that you're going to be full of the joy of the Lord. You are the one who decides whether you're going to rejoice or be discouraged and sad.
2. Demonstrate before all men an unselfish, considerate attitude.
3. Remember that the Lord can come at any moment, and be prepared.
4. Do not worry about anything.
5. Pray about everything.
6. Thank Him in faith for His answers."

The result of practicing these steps is the most priceless and wonderful experience one can know, the supernatural peace of God that cannot be purchased or acquired in any other way. In order to succeed in this formula for supernatural living, of course, you must already be studying the Word of God, applying its truths to your life daily, living in the power of the Holy Spirit and sharing your faith in Christ with others.

Bible Reading: Isaiah 12:1-5

ACTION POINT: Today, as an act of my will, I shall claim the supernatural resources of God by faith and continue to experience and share the abundant life which is the heritage of all who trust and obey Him.

Strength and Peace

"He will give His people strength. He will bless them with peace" (Psalm 29:11).

Scott, a professing atheist with the morals of an alley cat, insisted that he had peace in his heart. Though rare, it is possible for people to so harden their hearts that God ceases to draw them to Himself, and they experience a counterfeit peace.

The psalmist, of course, is talking about a different kind of peace. Ocean voyagers in the storm are at peace because they know the ship is sound and the pilot is skillful. In the same way, we as believers are at peace because we serve God who gives His people strength and blesses them with peace.

"His people," of course, refers to those who have placed their trust and faith in His Son, Jesus Christ, as Lord and Savior. None other may claim such a wonderful promise.

Significantly, "strength" comes before "peace." This is God's strength: "Who giveth power to the faint." We would certainly fail without it. Then this very same strength results in peace, God's peace "that passes all understanding."

God's strength enables us to contend with the powers of darkness, with the world and with our own natural depravity.

Peace, the great blessing of the gospel is two-fold: (1) peace with God through Christ and (2) peace of mind.

Strength and peace to live the abundant, supernatural life is available to all His people. You may claim your share today by faith.

Bible Reading: Psalm 71:9-16

ACTION POINT: Those two great blessings, strength and peace, will be mine today in direct proportion to my faith and trust in Him, who is my peace.

He Gives Richly

"Tell those who are rich not to be proud and not to trust in their money, which will soon be gone, but their pride and trust should be in the living God who always richly gives us all we need for our enjoyment" (1 Timothy 6:17).

Arthur S. DeMoss was a gifted and godly businessman. He had built one of the most successful businesses of its kind in America and in the process had amassed a huge fortune of an estimated half a billion dollars. Then suddenly an economic recession began and stock in his company plummeted. He lost $360 million in a period of only four months — an average of $3 million a day — more than anybody had ever before lost in such a short time. One would have thought he would have been devastated. Instead, in order to avoid decreasing his Christian giving, he (personally) borrowed funds, at an incredibly high rate of interest, to enable him to *increase* his giving. As we talked together during that period, he was rejoicing in the Lord.

"The Lord gave me everything I have," he said. "It all belongs to Him and if He wants to take it away that's His business. I don't lose any sleep. I still have a wonderful family and my life-style remains unchanged. I am prepared to do anything that God wants me to do. If He takes away everything I own and wants me to go to the mission field, I'm ready to do it. All He needs to do is tell me."

Art had his trust completely in the Lord and not in his vast fortune. God honored his faith and obedience and ultimately restored all that he had lost and much more. Art has gone to be with the Lord, but his fortune is still being used for the glory of God.

Paul's answer to the believers of his day is just as appropriate to the believers of our time. No person should be unduly impressed with his wealth and look down with pride and arrogance on those whom he considers to be inferior. Riches are uncertain because they can be very quickly taken away from us. In the personal emergencies of life one cannot depend upon material possessions for strength and comfort. In times of tragedy — the loss of a loved one, a financial reversal, or some other disappointment — material possessions do not insure peace. Our trust must be in the living God who is able to supply all of our needs and do for us what riches cannot do.

Bible Reading: 1 Timothy 6:6-16

ACTION POINT: I will not take the blessings of God for granted and will not place my trust in any earthly possession. My confidence will be in Him who is the source of the supernatural life.

Recipe for Growth

"As newborn babes, desire the sincere milk of the word, that ye may grow thereby" (1 Peter 2:2, KJV).

S am was very impatient with himself. Though he was a new Christian, he could not understand why he was not as spiritual as some of the other students who had walked with the Lord for several years.

I explained to him that Christian life, like physical life, involves a process of growth. A person begins as a baby and goes through the various stages of childhood, adolescence and young adulthood to reach Christian maturity. Very few, if any, Christians, I explained to him, become spiritually mature overnight.

Lane Adams, a beloved colleague, gifted teacher, preacher and author, said, "I shrink inside when I think of the times I have mounted the pulpit, recited the conversion experience of the apostle Paul, and then indicated that he went out and turned the world upside down for Jesus Christ immediately."

He continued, "This simply was not the case. There is a difference of opinion among scholars concerning New Testament dating, but it seems rather plain that many years went by before the Holy Spirit laid the dramatic burden on Paul as a missionary of the cross."

If you strongly desire to serve the Lord in some particular way, such as teaching, ask the Holy Spirit in faith to empower you to become an effective teacher. Now, it may be that the Holy Spirit will see fit to make you a great teacher overnight, but this is most unlikely. So if it does not happen, do not be discouraged. Have faith!

Continue to ask and believe that the Holy Spirit will make you an effective teacher of the Word of God and be willing to *work hard* and long to develop your natural ability. The Bible reminds us that "faith without works is useless."

If we are unique members of the Body of Christ, and we are, if we possess special tasks to accomplish, and we do, then the Holy Spirit will empower us to carry out those tasks. God does indeed have a plan for each of our lives. And He gives us the direction and power of His Holy Spirit to accomplish that plan as we continue to trust and obey Him.

Bible Reading: 2 Peter 3:14-18

ACTION POINT: Recognizing that I am in the process of maturing spiritually, I shall seek to accelerate my spiritual growth by hiding the Word of God in my heart, spending time in prayer, walking in the Spirit and sharing my faith in Christ with others as a way of life.

He Cannot Disown Us

"Even when we are too weak to have any faith left, He remains faithful to us and will help us, for He cannot disown us who are part of Himself, and He will always carry out His promises to us" (2 Timothy 2:13).

Have you ever run out of faith? I have — in times of great testing and trial, especially in earlier years as a young Christian. But as I have learned more and more about the many attributes of God, I have come to understand why the apostle Paul was so convinced of the faithfulness of God — that He still remains faithful to us and will help us, even when we are our weakest.

The meaning seems clear, though perhaps controversial to some: If we have truly been born again by the Spirit of God, and thus have become "part of Himself," Paul asserts that He cannot disown us. We need not argue or discuss the point of eternal security, for God's Holy Spirit, that great Teacher of spiritual truths, will reveal true meanings to each one of us individually.

We can be more certain of unanimous agreement on the latter part of the verse: "He will always carry out His promises to us." At least we all believe that theoretically, if not experientially.

Have you, for example, laid hold of one of God's promises, and not yet having seen the answer, begun to wonder and even doubt if He is indeed carrying out His promise? It might help each one of us to remind ourselves constantly that God has His own time-table; He need not be bound by ours.

Someone has well said, "God's timing is always perfect." Let us not try to improve on that perfection.

Bible Reading: Romans 3:3,4; Numbers 23:19

ACTION POINT: "Dear Lord, because You are always faithful despite my faithlessness at times, I will depend on You to fulfill your promises."

Fishers of Men

"And He saith unto them, Follow Me, and I will make you fishers of men" (Matthew 4:19, KJV).

Each morning I kneel to acknowledge Christ's lordship of my life and ask Him to have complete, unhindered control of my life for that day, to walk around in my body, to think with my mind, to love with my heart, to speak with my lips and to continue seeking and saving the lost through me.

Sometime ago I was at a conference in a midwestern city, anticipating an early adjournment so that I could catch a plane to Los Angeles and rejoin my waiting family.

When I arrived at the airport, I discovered that flight after flight had been cancelled because of poor weather conditions. Rushing from one airline ticket counter to another, I hoped to find one that was still flying its planes. Finally, to my disappointment, I discovered that all the airlines had cancelled their flights.

On one hand I was discouraged, but on the other I was encouraged by the promise of the Bible, "And we know that all that happens to us is working for our good if we love God and are fitting into His plans" (Romans 8:28, LB).

Back at the hotel for the night, in the lobby I met a businessman who was hungry for God. As I shared Christ with him, I learned that he and his wife had been visiting a different church every Sunday for the past couple of years. They were looking for God but had not been able to find Him.

I explained to my new friend how to receive Christ. Together, we knelt and prayed, and he received Christ into his life as his personal Lord and Savior.

With great joy and enthusiasm my new brother in Christ announced, "I want to take these things you have shared with me to my wife because she too is eager to receive Christ." It is our responsibility to follow Christ. It is His responsibility to make us fishers of men.

Bible Reading: Matthew 4:18-22

ACTION POINT: As I follow Christ today, I will recognize that even the delays, hindrances and closed doors may well be opportunities for me to share my faith in Jesus Christ. I shall remember, with God's help, to share Him with others at every opportunity.

The Way to Wisdom

"For the Lord giveth wisdom: out of His mouth cometh knowledge and understanding. He layeth up sound wisdom for the righteous: He is a buckler for them that walk uprightly" (Proverbs 2:6,7, KJV).

One of my brothers and a sister and I recently stood at the bedside of our 93-year-old mother. The doctor and nurses had just left the room after informing her that she needed a pacemaker for her heart.

After the doctor left, she called us around her. "Now I want you to join with me in prayer," she said. She began to pray, her countenance radiant from the joyful assurance that God was listening and would answer:

"Father in heaven, I need Your help. I do not know if I need a pacemaker, but You do. Tell me what to do, because You know what is best for me."

"Mother," I asked, when she had finished praying, "how will you know when God answers you?"

She replied, "God will tell me what to do as He always does." Later in the day she informed the doctor that she would not need a pacemaker. The doctor was disappointed, and he encouraged her to reconsider.

After he left, I inquired, "Mother, how do you know that you're not to have a pacemaker?"

"Well," she replied, "before I prayed I had an impression that this was the right thing to do because the doctor and nurses felt so strongly, but as I prayed God seemed to take away the desire. Months later we all agreed that she had made the right decision as her health was greatly improved.

For more than 75 years this beloved saint has known the faithfulness of this promise for wisdom. "He layeth up sound wisdom for the righteous. He is a buckler for them that walk uprightly."

Is Christ real? Does He give answers to practical problems of life? Inquire of one who has walked with Him for more than three-quarters of a century and you will have no doubts. To achieve this wisdom, you must seek it with all you heart. The world's wisdom, great as it may be, cannot begin to measure up to the divine wisdom available to one who faithfully reads, studies, and meditates upon God's Word and who has a close intimate relationship with Him in prayer.

Bible Reading: Proverbs 2:1-5

ACTION POINT: I will seek God's supernatural wisdom by diligently studying God's Word, through prayer and through fellowship with others who walk with God.

Entirely by Faith

"And this is the confidence that we have in Him, that, if we ask anything according to His will, He heareth us: And if we know that He hear us, whatsoever we ask, we know that we have the petitions that we desired of Him" (1 John 5:14,15, KJV).

A friend who had participated in one of our lay institutes a few years ago shared with me his experience when he first realized the practical benefits of the biblical concept which I like to call "spiritual breathing" — exhale by confession and inhale by claiming the fullness of the Holy Spirit by faith in accordance with the promise of 1 John 5:14,15.

This friend had agreed to teach a Sunday school class of young students. But there was one problem: he was apprehensive about the assignment because he had never taught students of that age.

My friend planned to arrive at church early in order to make proper preparation for the arrival of his new class. He had asked his family to be ready to leave the house early on that Sunday morning.

As sometimes happens, the family was late in getting ready and, as he sat in the car in the hot sun, he began to resent his family's tardiness. He began to fume and fuss while waiting for them. The longer he waited, the more tense and irritated he became.

Finally, his family loaded into the car — and he was ready to explode with anger. Before he went very far, the Holy Spirit reminded him that his attitude and actions were not honoring to the Lord.

Furthermore, he knew that he would be sharing with the children in Sunday school about God's love, forgiveness and patience. Applying the principle of "spiritual breathing," he exhaled by confessing his sin and inhaled by appropriating the fullness of the Holy Spirit by faith. Filled with the Holy Spirit and overflowing with God's love, he introduced several young men to Christ that morning.

Bible Reading: Romans 1:8-16

ACTION POINT: Whenever the need arises, I will practice "spiritual breathing" to help me experience spiritual victory and live a supernatural life. I will tell other Christians about the concept of "spiritual breathing."

He Will Preserve Me

"And the Lord shall deliver me from every evil work, and will preserve me unto His heavenly kingdom; to whom be glory for ever and ever. Amen" (2 Timothy 4:18, KJV).

Do you and I have that same kind of confidence in God?

Note that the apostle Paul did not mention the word *death* here, for earlier verses in this chapter reveal that he expected to die — and he was ready. But he was assured that God would keep him from shrinking from death when the hour approached. God would keep Paul from apostasy, and from displaying an improper spirit at the time of his death.

In the same way, we can ask the Lord today, in faith believing, for that inner peace we need to face up to all that He allows to happen in our lives. His perfect peace is sufficient for every testing and trial and trouble and temptation.

By keeping us from every evil work, He likewise enables us to reach His heavenly kingdom.

An appropriate time for praise to God is when a person knows he is about to be brought to heaven, and Paul introduces such a doxology here: "to whom be glory for ever and ever."

The truth is clear: we are protected on every side, and even at death we can sing the doxology, for we are about to meet the altogether lovely One in His heavenly home. To remain in constant fellowship with our heavenly Father will maintain a spirit of joy, love and peace in our lives that nothing can shake.

Bible Reading: Psalm 3:1-6

ACTION POINT: Like the apostle Paul, I will confidently expect God to protect me from every evil work and enable me to live the supernatural life for His glory.

Another Comforter

"If ye love Me, keep My commandments. And I will pray the Father, and He shall give you another Comforter, that He may abide with you forever" (John 14:15,16, KJV).

Some time ago, a young business-man came to see me. He was very eager to be a man of God. He wanted to know the fullness of the Holy Spirit in his life, but he said that every time he got on his knees to pray, all he could see was the merchandise he had stolen from his employer.

"God doesn't hear my prayers," he lamented. "I feel miserable and don't know what to do."

I suggested he confess his sin to his employer and make restitution.

"I don't have the money to pay for the merchandise I have stolen," he said. "What should I do? I'm afraid to tell my employer what I have done. I'm sure he will fire me, and he could send me to jail."

"The Holy Spirit is convicting you," I told him. "You can never experience the fullness of God's Spirit and you'll never be a man of God or have your prayers answered until you deal with this sin. You must trust the Lord to help you make restitution."

So the next day he went to his employer, confessed he had stolen the merchandise and offered to make restitution. The employer received him warmly and with understanding. He suggested that my friend pay a certain amount each month out of his salary until the debt was paid, which he was more than happy to do. He came immediately to tell me what had happened.

"Now God is hearing my prayers," he said. "Now I know I am filled with the Holy Spirit. My heart is filled with joy and praise to God."

Bible Reading: John 14:22-26

ACTION POINT: I will remain sensitive and alert for any unconfessed sin that might grieve or quench the indwelling Holy Spirit and hinder His working in and through me, robbing me of the supernatural life which God has commanded and enabled me to live, if only I will trust and obey Him.

The Same Father

"We who have been made holy by Jesus, now have the same Father He has. That is why Jesus is not ashamed to call us His brothers." (Hebrews 2:11).

Though you and I have been made holy by Jesus, we need to ask ourselves a question: Have we really been set apart, consecrated, devoted to God experientially?

A practical definition of the word *consecration* would carry the idea that you and I are willing to do anything the Lord asks us to do. Is that really the case? Are we listening closely enough to His still small voice even to know what He really wants us to do?

Once a popular TV commercial asked, "How do you spell *relief?*" We might well ask ourselves, "How do you spell *commitment?*" Too many of us, I'm afraid, spell it C-O-N-V-E-N-I-E-N-C-E. If it is convenient for us to share the good news of the gospel, we will do it; if it is convenient for us to go to Sunday school, church or prayer meeting, we will do it.

True commitment is a rare commodity these days — even among Bible-believing, evangelical Christians. Otherwise, our churches would be full; our witnessing would be a normal daily routine; our lives would be more Christlike.

We have already been made holy, but we need to reckon on that fact — and through the enabling of the Holy Spirit, live like holy people. Meditate on this fact: We have the same Father as Jesus, and Jesus calls us His brothers. What a great honor and privilege is ours!

Bible Reading: Hebrews 10:5-14

ACTION POINT: I will count on the holiness of Christ within me to make me all that He wants and intends me to be. As a member of God's supernatural family I shall claim God's power to live supernaturally.

Teach You Much

"But when the Father sends the Comforter instead of Me — and by the Comforter I mean the Holy Spirit — He will teach you much, as well as remind you of everything I myself have told you" (John 14:26).

Some years ago, at one of our week-long Lay Institutes for Evangelism, attended by more than 4,000 trainees, I gave a message on how to be filled with the Holy Spirit.

Afterward, a missionary who had just retired after 20 years of service in Africa came to see me. He was very excited as he came to share how, during that meeting, he had finally found what he had sought throughout his entire Christian life.

"Today, as you spoke," he said, "I was filled with the Spirit. For 20 years I have tried to serve God on the mission field, but I have served Him in the energy of the flesh and have had very little results. Now, though I have retired and returned to America, I want to go back to Africa.

"This time, I want to concentrate on working just with missionaries, because I know from experience that many of them are still searching for what I have sought all these years. The most important message I can take to them is how they can be filled with the Holy Spirit by faith.

"I want to teach them what you taught me so that they, in turn, will be able to teach the Africans how they too can be filled with the Holy Spirit."

Dr. J. Edwin Orr, a leading authority on spiritual revival, describes the Holy Spirit as "the Commander-in-Chief of the Army of Christ. He is the Lord of the harvest, supreme in revival, evangelism and missionary endeavor.

"Without His consent, plans are bound to fail. It behooves us as Christians to fit our tactical operations into the plan of His strategy, which is the reviving of the church and the evangelization of the world."

Bible Reading: John 14:13-17

ACTION POINT: I will look to God's indwelling Holy Spirit for the spiritual lessons I need to learn today and claim His power to serve the Lord Jesus Christ supernaturally.

A Place of Rest

"So there is a full complete rest still waiting for the people of God. Christ has already entered there. He is resting from His work, just as God did after the creation. Let us do our best to go into that place of rest, too, being careful not to disobey God as the children of Israel did, thus failing to get in" (Hebrews 4:9-11).

A Christian leader was asked: "How do you handle the incredible pressure of your schedule — speaking, writing, giving leadership to a great movement that touches the lives of millions of people around the world? How do you do it? You must carry a tremendous load!"

The inquirer was surprised at the response. "No, quite honestly I don't carry the load. I'm not under any pressure. I made a great discovery, probably the greatest discovery that a Christian can make. In the Christian life there is a place of rest which one enters by faith and obedience. No matter how great the pressure, or how terrible the testing, the supernatural resources of God sustain, empower, bless and encourage us and our Lord carries the load and fights for us."

Though few Christians ever enter into this rest, it is available to all believers. When the Israelites were on their way to the promised land, God had already prepared the hearts of the inhabitants, filling them with fear. There is reason to believe that they would have capitulated readily. But when the twelve spies returned after forty days of checking out the land, ten of them reported, "There are giants in the land, and we felt like grasshoppers in their sight." Only Joshua and Caleb said, "Let's go in and take the land. God has withdrawn His blessing from the people and He will fight for us."

But three million Israelites agreed with the majority report, and as a result, wandered in the wilderness for forty years. Why did it take so long for them to enter the land God had already given them? Because, as recorded in verse 2, they failed to mix the promises of God with faith.

Why does the average Christian not enter into a place of rest with God — that supernatural life which produces an abundance of fruit? Because he fails to mix the promises of God with faith. That is what this book, *Promises,* is all about — to remind us daily of our heritage as children of God and to show us how we can draw upon the mighty, inexhaustible resources of deity to live the supernatural life. Are you experiencing the life of the Spirit? Have you entered into God's rest? If not, you can begin to do so now.

Bible Reading: 2 Thessalonians 1:3-12

ACTION POINT: As an act of faith and obedience, I will enter that place of rest and I will encourage every believer with whom I have contact today to join me in the adventure.

At Least As Much

"And if even sinful persons like yourselves give children what they need, don't you realize that your heavenly Father will do at least as much, and give the Holy Spirit to those who ask for Him?" (Luke 11:13).

A Christian leader approached me after one of my messages on the person and ministry of the Holy Spirit.

"I want to be a Spirit-filled person," he said, "but I don't know what to do. I have read many books about the Holy Spirit and have sincerely sought His fullness, but to no avail. I am seriously considering giving up the Christian ministry and returning to a business career. Please help me."

With great delight I shared with this earnest seeker the truths about the Holy Spirit. To be filled with the Holy Spirit is to be controlled and empowered by the Holy Spirit. We cannot have two masters.

There is a throne, a control center, in every life and either self or Christ is on that throne. This concept of Christ being on the throne is so simple that even a child can understand it.

It is such a simple truth, and yet, in its distilled essence, that is what the supernatural, Spirit-controlled life is all about — *just keeping Christ on the throne.* We do this when we understand how to walk in the control and power of the Holy Spirit, for the Spirit came for the express purpose of glorifying Christ by enabling the believer to live a holy life and to be a productive witness for the Savior.

The key to supernatural living is a life centered in the Holy Spirit of Jesus Christ. This supernatural life is often called the Spirit-filled life or the Christ-centered life. The spirit-filled Christian is one who, according to Romans 6:11, has considered himself to be dead to sin but alive to God in Christ Jesus. Christ is now at the center of his life; He is Lord.

Bible Reading: Romans 8:9-14

ACTION POINT: I will not allow self to usurp the rightful place of Jesus Christ — in the person of His Holy Spirit — at the control center, the throne, of my life.

Quick and Powerful

"For the word of God is quick, and powerful, and sharper than any two-edged sword, piercing even to the dividing asunder of soul and spirit, and of the joints and marrow, and is a discerner of the thoughts and intents of the heart" (Hebrews 4:12, KJV).

Often, what you and I have to say may seem weak and insipid. But when we use the Word of God, we have the clear promise that it really will accomplish something, for it has several characteristics that guarantee such results.

First, the holy inspired Word of God is impregnated with the power of the Holy Spirit and is *quick* — living. It is energetic and active — not dead, inert or powerless.

Second, the Word is *powerful.* Its mighty power awakens the conscience, reveals our fears, bares the secret feelings of the heart and causes the sinner to tremble at the threat of impending judgment.

Third, the Word is *sharp* — sharper than a two-edged sword. The Word has power to penetrate. It reaches the heart, laying open our motives and feelings.

Fourth, the Word *pierces* — penetrates.

Fifth, the Word *discerns* — shows what our thoughts and intentions are. Men see their real character in the mirror of God's Word.

Those are some of the reasons for choosing to use the Word of God in every possible situation, allowing it to be its own best defense. God's Word will never return unto Him void.

Bible Reading: Psalm 1

ACTION POINT: I will make more use of the sword, the Word of God, as I draw upon God's power to life supernaturally.

Learn to Be Patient

"We can rejoice, too, when we run into problems and trials for we know that they are good for us — they help us learn to be patient" (Romans 5:3).

A Christian family was struggling with the trials of being parents (they had four young children — two of them in diapers). One day the wife, who was frustrated to her wits' end, came to me for spiritual counsel. As she phrased it, she was at the point of losing her sanity.

How could she cope with rearing her children? She told how angry she got with the children when they disobeyed her. In fact, she indicated there were times when she feared she might physically harm her children, though she loved them dearly.

How could she cope with rearing her children? She needed the fruit of the Spirit, patience and love. The only way she could obtain such patience was by faith, confessing her sins and appropriating the fullness of the Holy Spirit. This she began to do, continually. Today, she is a woman of godly patience, and being a parent has become a joyful privilege for her.

All of us need Christ's patience, regardless of who we are or in what circumstances we find ourselves. Patience is granted to us by the grace of God through the Holy Spirit. It is produced by faith as a fruit of the Spirit, and it is granted in times of great crises (Luke 21:15-19); in dealing with church situations (2 Corinthians 12:12); in opposing evil (Revelation 2:2), for soundness of faith (Titus 2:2) and in waiting for the return of Jesus Christ (James 5:7,8).

Bible Reading: Romans 5:1-8

ACTION POINT: I will look on trials and problems as a forerunner of great patience in my life, while claiming the supernatural power of the Holy Spirit to strengthen me.

Trusting an Unchanging God

"God also bound Himself with an oath, so that those He promised to help would be perfectly sure and never need to wonder whether He might change His plans" (Hebrews 6:17).

If there is one characteristic that might describe us all, more than any other trait, it would have to be that we are changeable and unpredictable. We are not dependable. How wonderful then to know and serve someone who never changes — who is the same yesterday, today and forever. We can know what to expect from Him in any given situation without fear of a sudden change in behavior, thought or purpose.

A scientist knows there are laws governing the universe and that those laws are inviolate. Thus, when President John F. Kennedy challenged industry to put a man on the moon, a mobilized army of scientists and engineers was able to accomplish the feat within nine years from the drawing board stage. When the assignment was given, no one knew what to do, and yet there were basic laws — dependable, trustworthy laws of the universe — on which they could build. Through much creative planning and thinking, the miracle occurred.

Today, it is commonplace to send men into space. God of the universe, who established the laws that govern all life, never changes. Our moods and our attitudes and actions vacillate, but God never changes. That is the reason we can absolutely, without question, believe His promises, and in so doing, release His mighty supernatural resources in terms of money, manpower and technology to envelop the entire world of almost five billion people with the most joyful news ever announced.

We are reminded in Hebrews 11:6 that without faith it is impossible to please God. Have you learned how to claim the promises of God by faith? When you do, you will learn how to live supernaturally.

Bible Reading: Psalms 102:24-28

ACTION POINT: Realizing that God has bound Himself with an oath to keep His promise, I shall trust and obey Him no matter what happens, for this is the way to supernatural living. This is the way to maximize myself for the glory of God.

He Rewards All Who Look for Him

*"You can never please God without faith, without depending on Him.
Anyone who wants to come to God must believe that there is a God
and that He rewards those who sincerely look for Him"* (Hebrews 11:6).

A friend of mine, one of the most dedicated men I have ever known, lived by a little black book. In this book he kept a careful record of all his activities, past, present and future.

In it he recorded the time he was to get up every morning, how long to have his devotions, how many verses of Scripture he should memorize that day, and to how many people he should witness. I was impressed; I wanted to be like him.

One day he had a mental breakdown, however. After he was released from the hospital, he said to me, "I was unable to live the Christian life. I tried to be a man of God by imposing upon myself certain rigid spiritual disciplines.

"Before they took me to the hospital, my last conscious act was to throw that little black book, which had become my god, into the corner. I never wanted to see it again."

This man had to discover what I discovered with great relief some years ago: I will never be able to live the Christian life through my own self-efforts.

My only hope for victory, power and fruitfulness is to trust Christ to live His resurrection life in and through me. He and He alone can enable me to live the Christian life. It is faith, not effort, that pleases Him, though we should never forget that faith without works is dead. Genuine faith always produces action — good works that please and glorify Him.

Bible Reading: Hebrews 7:17-22

ACTION POINT: Today by faith I will claim Christ's resurrection life, and since He alone is holy I will claim His power to live a supernatural life. Since He came to seek and to save the lost, I will claim by faith His ability to seek and to save the lost.

He Is Faithful

"Let us hold fast the profession of our faith without wavering; (for He is faithful that promised)" (Hebrews 10:23, KJV).

When we share our faith with others — hopefully a natural part of our daily walk, though we need not "preach a sermon" to share — we can remain stedfast in that profession of our faith, not wavering as we consider all He has done for us.

Why is that possible?

Simply this: *He is faithful that promised.*

The writer of Hebrews, presumably the apostle Paul, knew that the believers had been suffering persecution and there might be a tendency or temptation to become weak in their faith. Even serious doubts might have crept in. So Paul is seeking to guard against any kind of apostasy.

He wants to be sure the people are not shaken by their trials or by the arguments of their enemies. So he exhorts them in unmistakable terms.

Paul's reasoning to the people about faithfulness was this: Since God is so faithful to us, His children, we ought to be faithful to Him. Further, the fact that He is faithful should be an encouragement to us. We are dependent upon Him for grace to hold fast the profession of our faith.

All that God has promised, He will perform. He is faithful.

Bible Reading: 1 Corinthians 1:4-9

ACTION POINT: I will state in positive, confident terms what God has done for me, knowing that He is the faithful One who will do all He has promised. With this assurance, I can draw open His faithfulness to live supernaturally.

God's Gift of Himself

"Wherefore, come out from among them, and be ye separate, saith the Lord, and touch not the unclean thing; and I will receive you, and will be a Father unto you, and ye shall be My sons and daughters, saith the Lord Almighty" (2 Corinthians 6:17,18, KJV).

Near the Church of St. Mark's in Venice are three 17th century churches often admired for their highly ornate sculpture. On closer inspection, Ruskin points out, they are found to be "entirely destitute of every religious symbol, sculpture or inscription."

They are really monuments to the glory of three Venetian families who provided the funds for their construction. "Impious buildings, manifestations of insolent atheism," they were called by John Ruskin, English writer, art critic and sociologist.

Many Christians are like these buildings. Their association with God is more of a facade, formal and ritualistic. They do not know God as a caring Father with whom they experience a delightful, loving relationship.

As we meet God's conditions, He becomes our Father, and we become His sons and daughters. His gift of Himself is illustrated in the life of a successful young attorney.

"The greatest gift I ever received," he said, "was a Christmas gift from my dad. Inside a small box was a note saying, 'Son, I will give you an hour every day after dinner — 365 days. It's all yours. We'll talk about what you want to talk about, we'll go where you want to go, we'll play what you want to play. It will be your hour.'

"He not only kept his promise, but every year he renewed it — and it was the greatest gift I ever had in my life. I had so much of his time."

Bible Reading: 2 Corinthians 6:11-16

ACTION POINT: I will count myself richly blessed for having so much of my Father's time and will seek diligently to be worthy of His love and availability to me.

Practicing Patience

"You need to keep on patiently doing God's will if you want Him to do for you all that He has promised" (Hebrews 10:36).

During a Bible study on this passage, Ted made this contribution: "Spiritually," he said, "I'm a sprinter, not a long distance runner."

Numerous Christians would identify with that for there is little patience, persistence, and tenacity among believers. When adversity comes, many of us are prone to give up and lose our wind. That is the reason James says in his first chapter, verses 2-4, "Dear brothers, is your life full of difficulties and temptations? Then be happy, for when the way is rough, your patience has a chance to grow. So let it grow, and don't try to squirm out of your problems. For when your patience is finally in full bloom, then you will be ready for anything, strong in character, full and complete."

You will note the emphasis on patience. All of us are faced with problems, testings, temptations, adversities and trials in varying degrees. We can determine, by our attitudes and actions, whether or not our tragedies will turn to triumph. Our heartache and sorrow can become joy and rejoicing simply by our patience, which is the ability to relax in the confidence that God rules in the affairs of men and nations. Everything is under His control. And as we walk in faith and obedience, we will be a part of His wonderful and perfect plan.

But the question may be asked, how can we increase this rare trait or gift of patience that unlocks the door to supernatural living? The answer is simple. It is found in Galatians 5:22-23 in the listing of the fruit of the Spirit, for one of the nine characteristics mentioned is patience or longsuffering.

Are you patient with your husband, wife, parents, children, neighbors and those with whom you work in the office? Or do you find yourself critical and complaining — more prone to judge than to bless?

As we more and more yield ourselves to God's indwelling Holy Spirit, the fruit of patience is increased, along with all the other fruit.

Bible Reading: Hebrews 6:12-15

ACTION POINT: I will invite the Holy Spirit to control and empower my life moment by moment, day by day, knowing that the fruit of the Spirit, including patience, will increase and mature in my life.

The Holy Spirit Promised

"But when the Holy Spirit has come upon you, you will receive power to testify about Me with great effect, to the people in Jerusalem, throughout Judea, in Samaria, and to the ends of the earth, about my death and resurrection" (Acts 1:8).

Evangelists were gathered in Amsterdam, Holland, from more than 130 countries around the world to attend the International Conference for Itinerant Evangelists sponsored by the Billy Graham Evangelistic Association. On the third night of this historic event I was asked to bring the address on "How to be Filled With the Holy Spirit." Just before I was to speak, a note from Billy Graham was handed to me. It said, "I consider this one of the most important addresses of the entire conference."

According to the hundreds of thousands of surveys which our ministry has taken all over the world, 95 percent of the professing believers do not understand the ministry of the Holy Spirit. This includes a majority of the pastors, evangelists and missionaries. In fact, if I had only one message to give to the Christian world, it would be how to be filled with the Holy Spirit and how to walk moment by moment in the fullness of His power. Indeed if I had to choose between introducing a non-believer to Christ or helping a defeated, fruitless, impotent Christian to understand the ministry of the Holy Spirit and share his faith in Christ with others, I would choose the latter

because inevitably the end result would be far greater in terms of the number of people who would be introduced to Christ. The one great need of the Body of Christ today that transcends all other needs is to be awakened to the person and ministry of the Holy Spirit, to be empowered and controlled by Him, to allow Him to exalt and honor our Lord Jesus Christ in and through us, for that is the purpose of His coming. "He (the Holy Spirit) shall praise Me and bring Me great honor by showing you My glory" (John 16:14).

On hundreds of occasions throughout the world I have spoken on this subject and always, when the invitation is given, a good percentage indicate their desire to be filled with the Spirit. The Scripture promises, "Blessed are they that hunger and thirst after righteousness for they shall be filled." Do you hunger and thirst after righteousness? If so, you are a candidate for the fullness of God's Spirit. You can by faith appropriate His fullness right now by claiming His promise that God will release His power through you in order that you may be an effective witness for the Lord Jesus Christ.

Bible Reading: Romans 15: 15-21

ACTION POINT: Today I will claim by faith the fullness of God's Spirit in order to live the supernatural life and to be a more fruitful witness for the Lord Jesus Christ. I know that it is the Holy Spirit who will enable me to live that exciting, supernatural life.

Proof of His Love

"For when He punishes you, it proves that He loves you. When He whips you it proves you are really His child" (Hebrews 12:6).

Most of us prefer more pleasant ways of having others prove their love for us. Children, for example, never particularly relish the idea of having the "board of education" applied to the "seat of learning," but sometimes the disciplinary spanking is necessary.

We do that to our children because we love them. How much more important that our heavenly Father discipline us to keep us in line with His perfect plan and will for our lives. Sometimes that discipline is tough and painful.

This does not mean, of course, that God sends chastisement which is not deserved, or that He sends it for the mere purpose of inflicting pain. But it does mean that He is showing His paternal, loving care for us as His children when He punishes us.

As a child, a practical illustration helped me with this concept, so much so that it still sticks with me. When I allow my life to be flexible, like putty or soft clay, God can take it and mold it as He chooses. When I decide to be stubborn and resistant — hard like concrete — He sometimes has to smooth off the rough edges, and that always hurts.

We sing a chorus about the Spirit of God falling afresh on us. "Melt me, *mold* me, fill me, use me." When you and I are like putty in His hands, yielded and committed to Him, He can indeed mold us in His image.

Bible Reading: Revelation 3:19-22

ACTION POINT: I will surrender to God's disciplinary action in my life realizing that as a kind, loving heavenly Father He must take such action for my own good and benefit, when I am in need of correction.

Power Over Discouragement

"And let us not get tired of doing what is right, for after a while we will reap a harvest of blessing if we don't get discouraged and give up" (Galatians 6:9).

"Yes, I do get tired *in* the work, but I never get tired *of* the work."

I have heard many missionaries, ministers and other Christian leaders make such a statement. I echo their sentiments.

The first half of this wonderful verse is the sower's imperative; the second half is the sower's reward. The first half is my responsibility; the second is God's — which of course means that I should concern myself only with the first half, since our faithful God always keeps His promises.

One of the enemy's greatest weapons is discouragement. Years ago that great saint and prophet, A. W. Tozer, preached a sermon on this subject in which he recognized discouragement solely as a tool of the devil, hence one he would refuse to accept in his own life.

It is because of Satan's wiles in this regard — in causing us to be discouraged and give up — that one of God's greatest gifts to His children is the gift of exhortation and encouragement, with emphasis on the latter. How many believers have been strengthened to carry on because of the helpful, encouraging word of a friend! And how important that you and I become that kind of a friend. Yet, God's promise of encouragement is far more important.

To "keep on keeping on" is easier when we know that God is faithful.

Bible Reading: Galatians 6:1-8

ACTION POINT: With power from the Holy Spirit who lives within me, I will refuse to allow Satan's trick of discouragement to hinder my work, my walk and my witness for the Lord.

The Way Up Is Down

"But among you it is quite different. Anyone wanting to be a leader among you must be your servant. And if you want to be right at the top, you must serve like a slave. Your attitude must be like My own, for I, the Messiah, did not come to be served, but to serve, and to give My life as a ransom for many" (Matthew 20:26-28).

This is another one of those remarkable paradoxes of the Christian life. If you want to live, you must die. If you want to receive, you must give. If you want to lead, you must serve — contrary to the secular emphasis in the area of business, education, government and media. There the law of the jungle, the survival of the fittest, prevails. Do not worry about the mangled, mutilated bodies on which you tread as you climb the ladder of success. The important thing is to reach the top.

Not so with Jesus or for those who truly follow Him. The way up in the spiritual realm is down. To command is to humble yourself, then God will exalt you. Take the low seat and be invited to a higher place of honor, because there is strength in weakness and power in serving.

Much emphasis is placed on the importance of building leaders even in the Christian world. However, if we are going to follow the example of our Lord and obey the biblical concepts of leadership, by our attitudes and actions we must become servants. One of the byproducts of serving others is the law of sowing and reaping. The more you serve others, the more God blesses you. If you have a problem with feelings of inadequacy, poor self-image, undue introspection, or depression and frustration, one of the best remedies is to begin to serve others. Give someone else your time, your talent and your treasure. Inevitably, your life will be blessed and enriched and you will become more fruitful as a result of such service.

Bible Reading: Philippians 2:3-11

ACTION POINT: I will resolve with God's help to be more of a servant to those around me, following the example of my Lord as one of the keys to supernatural living.

He Is My Helper

"That is why we can say without any doubt or fear, 'The Lord is my Helper and I am not afraid of anything that mere man can do to me'" (Hebrews 13:6).

Do you and I really exercise perfect confidence that God will help us in our times of need?

The writer to the Hebrews borrows a clause, an expression, used by the psalmist. "The Lord taketh my part with them that *help* me: therefore shall I see my desire upon them that hate me" (Psalm 118:7, KJV).

With the Lord as our helper, mere man can do nothing to us or against us except that which God permits (Acts 4:28). Whatever trials we face, the fact remains that God will be our protector and friend in and through them all.

One effective tool of the enemy is to bring up "exception clauses" time and time again. "My God is able to do *anything*, but...I'm not quite sure of His interest and/or power in this particular situation." "I know He can help me, but it may not be His will at this particular time or in this particular case."

In the face of God's power, mere man begins to look pretty small, and that is just the way God intends it to be. He wants to give us confidence that He is able for every need we have: large, small or medium. None is too large, none too small for Him.

Bible Reading: Psalm 118:5-9

ACTION POINT: "Dear Lord, thank You that You are indeed my Helper. I will depend upon You as never before in living the supernatural life which will bring the greatest possible glory to You."

Resist the Devil

"Submit yourselves therefore to God. Resist the devil, and he will flee from you" (James 4:7, KJV).

I received a call for help one day from the wife of an alcoholic. He is a wonderful person when he is sober, but a demon when he is drinking. Why does he keep drinking?

Another day I talked with a young man who was on drugs. He is deathly afraid that someone will find him out and he will be caught, end up in jail and have a police record. Still, something about drugs woos him to go on another trip, to smoke another joint.

While it is true that addiction plays an important part in such enslavement, it is also true that Satan is chortling behind the scenes — and he needs to be resisted.

Satan manifests himself in various ways. At times he presents himself as one who has world authority. Another time he comes as an angel of light, or as a roaring lion. Satan's demons can have direct influence in your life or mine.

We wrestle against supernatural power. Satan is not just a man. He possesses supernatural powers. He is a very real enemy. True, he has no authority over us except that which is given to him of God, but we dare not become careless about our Christian walk and yield to temptations which he engineers through "the world, the flesh and the devil."

And that's the reason I shudder when I think of individuals who are careless in their use of alcohol and drugs, and who become involved in unscriptural sex relationships. The drug culture has spawned a Satan-worship cult, and men are committed to Satan just as you and I are committed to Jesus Christ. In the words of James, we need to resist the devil, knowing he then will flee from us.

Bible Reading: 1 Peter 5:8-11

ACTION POINT: Upon every entrance of satanic influence into my life, I will submit myself to the Lord and resist the devil, and I will claim by faith the power of the Holy Spirit to live victoriously and supernaturally.

Mighty Things Through Faith

"And so [Jesus] did only a few great miracles there, because of their unbelief" (Matthew 13:58).

It was my first visit to Nazareth, and through a series of fortuitous circumstances, I found myself enjoying lunch with one of the city's prominent leaders. As we talked together in the crowded dining room our conversation turned to Jesus Christ, and ultimately this gentleman bowed his head and began to pray aloud, inviting Christ to be his Savior and Lord.

The change seemed to be immediate and dramatic, and follow-up has proven that God did meet him and change his life. During the course of our conversation, he indicated that what I had shared with him was a new truth. Though he was religious and active in his church, he never had been told that he should receive Christ.

Upon further exploration, I found that, in the entire community of Nazareth, there were but a few in those days who understood the truth of the living Christ indwelling the believer. I was amazed!

Nazareth was the town in which our Lord had spent approximately thirty years of His life. The son of a carpenter, He had walked those winding streets, living, loving and laughing with other young children as they were growing up. He left the town when He entered His public ministry, and went on to perform mighty miracles, die on the cross for our sins and be raised from the dead — and He changed the whole course of history. But 2,000 years have passed since then, and there is still little evidence of the influence of Jesus in the lives of the people of Nazareth.

Then I remembered that it was said of our Lord, He could do no mighty things in Nazareth because of their unbelief. That seems to be true in more than just that city today. Even though there are a billion and a half professing followers of Christ throughout the world, the majority seem to be practical atheists.

And so, our Lord cannot do mighty things in Nazareth, or throughout the world, because of unbelief. The key to releasing His power to accomplish revolutionary, supernatural things in the world — and in individual lives — is faith.

"According to your faith be it unto you" (Matthew 9:29, KJV). "Whatsoever is not of faith is sin" (Romans 14:23, KJV). "The just shall live by faith" (Romans 1:17, KJV).

Bible Reading: Mark 6:1-5

ACTION POINT: Remembering that Jesus Christ lives within me in all of His supernatural power, waiting to accomplish great and mighty things through me, I will trust and obey Him for a life that is characterized by the supernatural, and I will encourage others to do the same.

Praying for Results

"Ask and you will be given what you ask for. Seek, and you will find. Knock and the door will be opened. For everyone who asks, receives. Anyone who seeks, finds. If only you will knock, the door will open" (Matthew 7:7,8).

W e were conducting a Bible study on the subject of prayer when Amy, a professing Christian most of her life, said, "God never answers my prayers. In fact, I cannot recall a single prayer of mine that God has answered specifically."

Several others in the group chimed in and said, "Neither can I." So we turned to this passage and discussed it together. Would God lie to us? Is His Word trustworthy? Or is prayer an exercise in futility? Are we simply talking to ourselves and each other, or is there a God who hears and answers? If so, why have these not had their prayers answered?

First of all, we had to review the qualifications for prayer. Jesus said, "If you abide in Me and My Word abides in you, ask what you will and it shall be done unto you." The Scripture also says, "If I regard iniquity in my heart, the Lord will not hear me." So if we expect to have our prayers answered, Jesus Christ must be the Lord of our lives. There must be no unconfessed sin in our lives and we must be filled with the Holy Spirit.

Further, 1 John 5:14,15 reminds us: "If we ask anything according to God's will, He hears us and answers," so we must be sure that we are praying according to the Word of God. As we pray, the Spirit of God impresses upon us certain things for which to pray specifically, such as the salvation of a friend, the healing of a body or a financial need. If the prayer is offered with a pure motive and according to God's will, we can expect an answer to it.

And we cannot pray just casually. We must enter into an expectant spirit of prayer, knowing that, when we meet His conditions, God will hear and answer us.

Within a matter of weeks everyone in that Bible study, especially Amy, was inspired by the exciting challenge of prayer. God had truly heard, and again and again, they were able to point to specific answers.

Bible Reading: Luke 11:5-13

ACTION POINT: I shall review my spiritual walk to be sure I am meeting God's conditions: (1) Christ is Lord of my life. (2) I am filled with the Holy Spirit. (3) There is no unconfessed sin in my life (4) I am praying according to God's Word. And (5) I am praying specifically. As a result, I expect my prayers to be answered because God promises they will be.

Tempted Like We Are

"For we have not an high priest which cannot be touched with the feeling of our infirmities; but was in all points tempted like as we are, yet without sin" (Hebrews 4:15, KJV).

"In your opinion, who is the greatest person who ever lived, and who has done more good for mankind than anyone else who ever lived?" I asked a student who was both an atheist and a card-carrying Communist.

There was an awkward silence. Then finally came this reluctant reply, "I guess I would have to say Jesus of Nazareth."

How could an atheist and a Communist, who had been reared in another religion, give such an answer?

Jesus has done more good for mankind than anyone else who has ever lived. He is the greatest person of the centuries, because it is a fact. Compare Jesus, even as a man, with any other person — Muhammad, Buddha, Confucius, Socrates, Plato, Aristotle, anyone else in any country at any time in history — and it would be like comparing a giant with a midget.

Though he lived 2,000 years ago and changed the course of history, though He was the greatest leader, the greatest teacher, the greatest example the world has ever known, He is infinitely more than these. He is God.

The omnipotent Creator God visited this little planet earth and became a man, the God-man, Jesus of Nazareth. He was perfect God and perfect man, and as perfect man He understands our weaknesses, since He had the same temptations we do — though He never once gave way to them and sinned.

Do you believe that Jesus ever had the temptation to lie, to lust, to steal or to be immoral? Make a list of your temptations, all your weaknesses, all your failures, and then, as suggested in the verse following our reference, "Let us come boldly to the very throne of God and stay there to receive His mercy and to find grace to help us in our times of need" (Hebrews 4:16).

Bible Reading: Hebrews 2:14-18

ACTION POINT: Since Jesus is my high priest and knows everything about me, having been tempted as I am and yet without sin, I will come boldly into His presence today and every day. I will come to receive His mercy and grace to live a supernatural life, which will enable me to live victoriously and to be fruitful for the glory and praise of His matchless name.

God Is a Loving God

"If a child asks his father for a loaf of bread, will he be given a stone instead? If he asks for fish, will he be given a poisonous snake? Of course not! And if you hardhearted, sinful men know how to give good gifts to your children, won't your Father in heaven even more certainly give good gifts to those who ask Him for them?" (Matthew 7:9).

Roger interrupted our Bible study on this passage of Scripture to say, "I guess I have trouble believing God is a good God because my earthly father was a tyrant. He hated me, and I hated him. I do not recall a single experience in my life where he encouraged me. I want to believe that God is good, but I have difficulty. Please help me."

Unfortunately, there are multitudes of men and women who are relatively new Christians and who have come from similar backgrounds where there was no love, no compassion, no concern, and their view of God is therefore distorted. They somehow equate the loving, forgiving God with their own tyrannical fathers. When such is the case, only the Holy Spirit can heal these deep wounds and remove these scars.

So, I assigned Roger a special project. I asked him to make a list of all the attributes and qualities of God recorded from Genesis to Revelation. The project lasted several months, but in the process a transformation took place in Roger's life.

The day came when he exclaimed with great joy, "The Holy Spirit has illumined my mind and taught me that God is truly a loving God, worthy of my trust. Now I can believe Him for anything. I know that even if my father on earth was the best father ever, God's love, compassion and care for me transcends anything that he could do for me. Therefore, I can ask Him for good gifts, knowing that He will hear and answer me. I want to live only for His glory for the rest of my life."

Are you having difficulty trusting God because of an unfortunate early relationship with your father or mother? If so, I encourage you to do what Roger did. Saturate your mind with the attributes of God — His love, sovereignty, wisdom, grace, compassion, power and holiness. As you do, the Holy Spirit will use the Word of God to cleanse your mind of all the memories that weigh you down, and you will be able to say with Roger, "I can trust God for anything, because I know He is a loving God who cares for me."

Bible Reading: 1 John 3:1-3

ACTION POINT: I will continue to meditate upon the attributes of God, knowing that the more I trust Him, the more sure I can be of His faithfulness to enable me to live a supernatural life for His glory.

A Solid Foundation

"All who listen to My instructions and follow them are wise, like a man who builds his house on solid rock. Though the rain comes in torrents, and the floods rise and the storm winds beat against his house, it won't collapse, for it is built on rock. But those who hear My instructions and ignore them are foolish, like a man who builds his house on sand. For when the rains and floods come, and storm winds beat against his house, it will fall with a mighty crash" (Matthew 7:24-27).

What a wonderful promise for supernatural living to know that no matter what happens — the greatest tragedies, adversities or losses — your house will stand. You will not only survive, but mature, grow and become more like Jesus.

As you listen to and follow His instructions, you will observe that He has been speaking to the multitudes in what is frequently referred to as the Sermon on the Mount. Review chapters 5, 6 and 7 of Matthew. List all the things that He commands us to do, and then by faith claim those instructions in your life. For there is nothing that God ever commands that He will not enable us to do if we seek His help.

Remember, too, His promise recorded in Matthew 22:37-40, that all of the commandments in the Sermon on the Mount are fulfilled when we love God with all of our heart, soul, mind and strength, and when we love our neighbor as ourselves. So the instructions that He is giving are not difficult,

for He who gives the command will enable us to build on a sure foundation of solid rock.

Note, however, the admonishment for those who ignore His instructions. For those foolish people who build their houses on sand, collapse of those houses is the certain consequence. One need only look around to see evidence of the fulfillment of God's warning in the lives of numerous loved ones, neighbors and friends. God loves us, and He wants to bless us, but He cannot if we ignore Him.

Are you following the instructions of the Lord Jesus Christ? If not, I encourage you to begin today, with the assurance that He will bless you, your family and all who are dear to you.

Bible Reading: 1 John 2:3-9

ACTION POINT: I will meditate upon our Lord's instructions as contained in the Sermon on the Mount, as well as the Ten Commandments and the Golden Rule. I will meditate upon 1 Corinthians 13 and other commandments of our Lord on love. Through the enabling of the Holy Spirit, I will obey His instructions for supernatural living.